Regulatory Freedom and Indirect Expropriation in Investment Arbitration

Regulatory Freedom and Indirect Expropriation in Investment Arbitration

Aniruddha Rajput

Published by:
Kluwer Law International B.V.
PO Box 316
2400 AH Alphen aan den Rijn
The Netherlands
E-mail: international-sales@wolterskluwer.com
Website: lrus.wolterskluwer.com

Sold and distributed in North, Central and South America by:
Wolters Kluwer Legal & Regulatory U.S.
7201 McKinney Circle
Frederick, MD 21704
United States of America
Email: customer.service@wolterskluwer.com

Sold and distributed in all other countries by:
Air Business Subscriptions
Rockwood House
Haywards Heath
West Sussex
RH16 3DH
United Kingdom
Email: international-customerservice@wolterskluwer.com

Printed on acid-free paper.

ISBN 978-94-035-0624-1

e-Book: ISBN 978-94-035-0625-8
web-PDF: ISBN 978-94-035-0630-2

Printed in the United Kingdom.

Acknowledgements

This book is a revised version of the PhD thesis presented at the National University of Singapore. The acknowledgements in the thesis continue and I remain in the debt of persons and institutions mentioned there.

I could undertake the revision of the thesis to convert it into a book during my stay in Berlin from September to December 2017 at the KFG International Rule of Law -Rise or Decline? This stay was an outcome of a generous invitation of Professors Georg Nolte, Heike Krieger and Andreas Zimmermann. I thank them all, as well as other participants of the research group, with whom I had fruitful and stimulating discussions. The research assistants were particularly helpful in procuring necessary material.

I received immense assistance from Vikhyat Oberoi, Aarushi Nargas, Somabha Bandopadhay, Mreganka Kukreja, Tulika Gupta, Aditya Gupta, Kriti Misra, Manya Oberoi and Vrinda Aggarwal, with the editing of the manuscript. Tanishtha Vaid and Bhavesh Seth were particularly prompt and helpful in the final stages of editing the manuscript. I am grateful to them. My sincere thanks to all others who were involved directly and or indirectly in this work and I could not mention them all. Needless to say, the responsibility of the views and the errors are entirely mine.

This is my second book with Kluwer and it has been a smooth experience, like last time. My sincere thanks to Eleanor Taylor and the publishing team. They have been exceptionally prompt and efficient in the preparation the book.

Last but not the least, I thank my parents for their unfailing faith and confidence in me. It is this source of inspiration that has motivated me to achieve, all of which was unthinkable!

Table of Contents

Acknowledgements v

CHAPTER 1
Introduction 1

CHAPTER 2
The Concept of 'Regulatory Measure' and 'Expropriatory Measure' 7
§2.01 Meaning of 'Measure' 8
§2.02 The Concept of a 'Regulatory Measure' or the 'Police Powers Doctrine' 9
§2.03 The Concept of an 'Expropriatory Measure' 11
§2.04 Distinguishing Features Between a 'Regulatory Measure' and 'Expropriatory Measure' 13
§2.05 Municipal Law vis-à-vis International Law 16
§2.06 Conclusions 18

CHAPTER 3
Types of Expropriatory Measures in Treaty Practice and Arbitral Jurisprudence 21
§3.01 Types of Expropriatory Measures 21
[A] Direct Expropriation 22
[B] Indirect Expropriation 23
[C] 'Equivalent to Expropriation', 'Tantamount to Expropriation' or 'Creeping Expropriation' 24
§3.02 Textual Interpretation of the Types of Expropriatory Measures 28
§3.03 Trends in Recent Treaty Practice 30
§3.04 Arbitral Jurisprudence 32
[A] No Right to Regulate 33
[B] The Sole Effects Doctrine 34
[C] Regulatory Freedom Exists 39
§3.05 Conclusions 44

CHAPTER 4
The 'Sole Effects Doctrine' and the 'Nature of the Measure' 47
§4.01 Genesis of the Sole Effects Doctrine 47
[A] Christie's Claim of the Sole Effects Doctrine 47
[B] The Iran-US Claims Tribunal and the Sole Effects Doctrine 55
[1] Emergence of the Sole Effects Doctrine 57
[2] Procedural and Other Problems with the Origin and Application of the Sole Effects Doctrine 59
[3] Influence of 'Other Measures Affecting Property Rights' 61
§4.02 The 'Nature of the Measure' in the Decision of International Courts and Tribunals 66

CHAPTER 5
Theoretical Approaches 73
§5.01 Case-by-Case Method 73
§5.02 Theoretical Justifications for the Sole Effects Doctrine 79
[A] Prior to the BITs 79
[B] Post BITs 82
[C] Problems with the Sole Effects Doctrine and Its Impact on Regulatory Freedom 86
§5.03 Regulatory Freedom and the Right to Property 92
§5.04 Global Administrative Law 98

CHAPTER 6
Regulatory Freedom as Customary International Law 103
§6.01 Regulatory Freedom as an Attribute of State Sovereignty 103
§6.02 Regulatory Freedom as a Permissible Rule 111
§6.03 Regulatory Freedom and the Requirements of Custom 121
[A] Statements in Diplomatic Correspondences Between States 124
[B] Restatement of the Law Third, the Foreign Relations Law of the United States 125
[C] Pleadings of States Before International Courts and Tribunals 127
[D] Domestic Laws of States and Decisions of International and National Courts and Tribunals 130

CHAPTER 7
Regulatory Freedom (Customary Norm) and Indirect Expropriation (Treaty Norm): Interaction of Norms 133
§7.01 Whether Indirect Expropriation (as a Treaty Norm) Is Hierarchically Superior to Regulatory Freedom (as a Customary Norms)? 133
§7.02 The Relationship Between a Customary Norm and Treaty Norm in International Law 136
[A] Systematic Integration 136

[B] No Implied Exclusion of a Customary Norm 142
[C] Concurrent Operation of Custom and Treaty 144
§7.03 Whether There is a Conflict Between Regulatory Freedom and Indirect Expropriation? 148
[A] What is a Conflict? 149
[B] The Role of Conflict of Norms in Resolving a Conflict Between Regulatory Freedom and Indirect Expropriation 152
[C] Co-existence of Regulatory Freedom and Indirect Expropriation 155
§7.04 The Scope of Regulatory Freedom in Light of Treaty Provisions in the Jurisprudence of International Courts and Tribunals 156

CHAPTER 8
Elements of Regulatory Freedom and Standard of Review 165
§8.01 Bona Fide 165
[A] Intention to Injure 173
[B] Fictitious Exercise Aimed at Defeating Treaty Provisions 173
[C] Colourable Exercise 173
[D] Regulations Adopted Solely for a Malicious Purpose 174
[E] Arbitrary or Unreasonable Actions 174
§8.02 Non-discrimination 174
§8.03 Public Interest 177
§8.04 Standard of Review 183
[A] Meaning of Standard of Review 183
[B] Proportionality Analysis and Necessity Test 184
[C] Reasonableness or Good Faith Review 191

CHAPTER 9
Conclusions 195

Bibliography 199

Table of Cases 219

Table of Treaties 229

Index 231

CHAPTER 1

Introduction

States are organs of collective governance and exercise of regulatory function is their primary responsibility. The role of regulations in the administration of State and their ability to influence private actors has transformed over centuries as per the needs of the society. The scope and nature of regulatory functions have transformed from a 'laissez-fair State', to a 'welfare State', and finally, to a 'regulatory State'.[1] In the laissez-faire system, the role of State was minimal and therefore, confined mostly to internal and external security and foreign relations.[2] With time, the functions of the State diversified and multiplied. States started engaging into various socio-economic activities and ceased to be a mere bystander.[3] The participation of State in micro-economic activities expanded and government entered key industries, public utility services and natural resources based industries, some of which related to gas, electricity, water, telecommunications and the railways.[4] With passage of time and waning of socialist tendencies, the State started withdrawing from its engagement at micro-economic level, such as manufacturing and strategic industries, and started taking up the role of a regulator. Through 'hollowing of functions', State shifted from the role of 'rowing to steering',[5] thereby creating the present regulatory State.[6] In a welfare State, State is an active participant in various sectors of the economy, whereas in the case of a regulatory State, the State is an impersonal actor stationed in its role of

1. *See* Robert Baldwin, Martin Cave & Martin Lodge (eds), *The Oxford Handbook of Regulation* (New York: Oxford University Press, 2010).
2. Sidney Fine, *Laissez Faire and the General-Welfare State; A Study of Conflict in American Thought, 1865-1901* (USA: University of Michigan, 1956).
3. *See* Martin Loughlin & Colin Scott, 'The Regulatory State' in Patrick Dunleavy, Andrew Gamble, Ian Holliday & Gillian Peele (eds) *Developments in British Politics* (Basingstoke: Macmillan Press, 1997); John Braithwaite, 'The New Regulatory State and the Transformation of Criminology' *British Journal of Criminology* 40 (2007): 222–238.
4. Karen Yeung, 'Regulatory State' in above note 1 (Baldwin, Cave & Lodge: Oxford Handbook, 2010), 65–66.
5. *See* David Osborne & Ted Gaebler, *Reinventing Government: How the Entrepreneurial Spirit is Transforming the Public Sector* (USA: Addision Wesley, 1992), 25.
6. Above note 5 (Yeung), 66–67.

setting rules and overseeing its compliance. The models of governance that exist in the world today possess features of a 'welfare State' and a 'regulatory State'. But in both the models, and its variations, role of regulations is central. To that extent, despite internal differences, the modern State at a meta level is a 'regulatory State'. [7]

Regulations have expanded into several social systems, State organizations and government strategies.[8] Regulations are necessary for protection of public interest because there is no assurance that markets would always take account of public interest.[9] In genuine regulatory actions, non-economic factors play a prominent role.[10] That goal to be achieved through the regulation would depend upon the public interest that is at stake. For example, regulations of economy are prominent as well as necessary. It is treated as a right emanating from State sovereignty. The global recession of 2008 has busted the myth of rational markets and the conscientious nature of the 'invisible hand'.[11] State is to think beyond 'reward of merit principle' and strive for goals of distributive justice and fairness.[12] States need to often adopt regulations of a problem-solving character or innovating regulations. In whichever manner they are exercised, they are a long-term phenomenon and would continue.[13] The arena of activity of the modern State has expanded to respond to domestic as well as international challenges. Climate change is an important problem and States are adopting different regulations for protection of the environment. Likewise, human and animal health is prioritized. There are constant demands – and rightly so – for improvement of labour standards. These are only few examples. It is difficult to conceive which other and more complex issues will demand the attention of the State, thereby expanding the sphere of regulatory functions of the State. [14]

More often than not, while performing these functions, the actions of the State result into harm to private parties. If one takes a laissez-faire approach, then the State would have stop interfering and regulating completely – which does not seem to be a possibility in the near future. If it is demanded of the State that the State should

7. *See* Giandomenico Majone, 'The Rise of the Regulatory State in Europe' *West European Politics* 17 (1994): 77–101; Giandomenico Majone, 'From the Positive to the Regulatory State: Causes and Consequences of Changes in the Modern Governance' *Journal of Public Policy* 17(2) (1997): 139–168; Micheal Moran, 'Understanding the Regulatory State' *British Journal of Political Science* 32(2) (2002): 391–413; Micheal Moran, *The British Regulatory State: High Modernism and Hyper Innovation* (Oxford: Oxford University Press, 2003).
8. Robert Baldwin, Martin Cave & Martin Lodge, 'Introduction: Regulation – The Field and the Developing Agenda' in above note 1 (Baldwin, Cave & Lodge: Oxford Handbook, 2010), 6–8.
9. Cento Veljanovski, 'Economic Approaches to Regulation' in above note 1 (Baldwin, Cave & Lodge: Oxford Handbook, 2010), 21; Mike Feintuck, 'Regulatory Rationales Beyond the Economic: In Search of the Public Interest' in above note 1 (Baldwin, Cave & Lodge: Oxford Handbook, 2010), 42–51.
10. John Jackson, *The World Trading System: Law and Policy of International Economic Relations* (2nd ed., MIT Press, 1997), 23.
11. *See* Justin Fox, *The Myth of Rational Markets: A History of Risk, Reward, and Delusion on Wall Street* (Harper Business/Harper Collins Publishers, 2011).
12. *Ibid.*, at 23.
13. Robert Baldwin, Martin Cave & Martin Lodge 'The Future of Regulation' in above note 1 (Baldwin, Cave & Lodge, Oxford Handbook, 2010), 614–617.
14. Antonios Estache & Liam Wren-Lewis, 'On the Theory and Evidence on Regulation of Network Industries in Developing Countries' in above note 1 (Baldwin, Cave & Lodge: Oxford Handbook, 2010), 373–382, 392–394.

compensate for every private loss that is a consequence of a State action, the function of governance would become impossible. Even with economies that run on a surplus (which are in any case very few) would be unable to sustain and survive. There has to be a possibility of protecting legitimate regulatory measures - situations where the State can harm private parties without having to pay compensation. States have to often make difficult and controversial decisions which may turn out to be improper and dysfunctional, but this is 'inherent to the dilemmas of governance'.[15] Traditionally, a State was never considered responsible for losses caused to the property of aliens as a consequence of legitimate regulations because adoption of regulations is seen as an indispensable function of a State. As encapsulated in the Latin maxim *salus populi suprema lex esto*: a State is responsible for protection and promotion of public interest.

This challenge has become particularly acute with the rapid developments in the field of international investment law. The peculiarity of this field is that there is a dense network of more than 3,000 treaties to which most of the States are parties. These treaties - most of which are bilateral and therefore called Bilateral Investment Treaties (BITs) - impose an obligation to protect foreign investments in the State.

The subject matter of the challenge is the regulatory actions of the States. The international investment tribunals adjudicate regulatory disputes arising out of investment treaties to the exclusion of other disputes such as disputes arising out of contractual or commercial transactions.[16] Investment treaty arbitration is characterized as regulatory adjudication.[17] Investment tribunals perform review of sovereign actions. Sovereign actions include multitude of State actions ranging from rules, regulations, legislations, administrative actions and judicial decisions. Investment treaty arbitration judges the governmental discretion, therefore the 'regulatory context' of arbitration proceedings is important.[18] To that extent, theoretically, investment arbitration mirrors domestic administrative law at the international law.

The challenge really is, if the freedom to regulate is too broad, it could be turned into abusive exercise by the State and if the freedom is too narrow, then regulatory function would become impossible. A balance has to be drawn based on the test of 'legitimate regulations'. This book is about the balance that is to be drawn between competing interests to protect 'legitimate regulations' in the context of the standard of indirect expropriation in investment treaty arbitration.

The extent of protection to be given to the foreign investors depends on the treatment standards in investment treaties. These treaties contain a mandatory dispute

15. Gus Van Hartern, *Investment Treaty Arbitration and Public Law* (New York: Oxford University Press, 2007), 89.
16. Article 1(2) of the International Convention for Settlement of Investment Disputes, 1965 (hereinafter referred as ICSID Convention) limits the application of Convention to '.....investment disputes between Contracting States and nationals of other Contracting States'. Tribunals have declined to entertain pure commercial disputes from time to time. *El Paso Energy International Company v The Argentine Republic*, Award, ICSID Case No. ARB/03/15, 27 April 2006, Decision on Jurisdiction, paras 74, 76; *SGS Société Générale de Surveillance S.A. v Islamic Republic of Pakistan*, Decision of the Tribunal on Objections to Jurisdiction, ICSID Case No. ARB/01/13, 6 August 2003, para. 173; *ibid.*, at 45, 47, 49 50.
17. Above note 15 (Harten) at 58.
18. Above note 15 (Hartern) at 121.

resolution clause, forcing the host State to participate in arbitration proceedings. Most of the treatment standards are open-ended and are prone to expansive interpretation by investment tribunals.[19] This book focuses on the impact of the standard of 'indirect expropriation' on regulatory freedom.

Expropriation is the oldest standard for treatment of foreign investors.[20] Expropriation clause was a regular phenomenon in Friendship Commence and Navigation (FCN) Treaties, which preceded the present investment treaties.[21] Expropriation clauses are omnipresent in investment treaties.[22] The threat of expropriation was a principal motivating factor in the origin of investor protection through investment treaties.[23] With rising protectionist tendencies, expropriations are bound to remain relevant. There are widespread regulations and greater possibility of States resorting to expropriation. The complex relation between regulatory freedom and expropriation will continue to unfold. This work is intended to guide practitioners, adjudicators and policy makers about the different aspects of the relationship between regulatory freedom and indirect expropriation and the manner in which they exist and interact.

The natural starting point for a discussion on the relationship between regulatory freedom and expropriation – and precisely indirect expropriation – is a survey of investment treaty texts and arbitral jurisprudence. Chapter 2 explores the conceptual foundations of a regulatory measure and an expropriatory measure would be discussed. A regulatory measure would be a valid exercise of regulatory freedom and covered by the police power doctrine: developed and regularly applied in municipal law. An indirect expropriation belongs to the category of an expropriatory measure, also known and applied in domestic law as 'eminent domain'. The independent existence and evolution of both these concepts in municipal (domestic) and international law is elaborated based on the jurisprudence of various international courts and tribunals. This discussion will point to the independent background and understanding of these concepts in the literature and case law.

19. There is immense literature on this topic. For a concise account *see* M Sornarajah, *Resistance and Change in the International Law on Foreign Investment* (Cambridge University Press, 2015).
20. Campbell McLachlan, Laurence Shore & Matthew Weiniger, *International Investment Arbitration: Substantive Principles* (Oxford: Oxford University Press, 2007), 266–267.
21. Article V.2, Treaty of Friendship Commerce and Navigation between Italy and the United States, 2 February 1948. The clause on expropriation was: 'The property of nationals, corporations and associations of either High Contracting Party shall not be taken within the territories of the other High Contracting Party without due process of law and without the prompt payment of just and effective compensation. The recipient of such compensation shall, in conformity with such applicable laws and regulations as are not inconsistent with paragraph 3 of Article XVII of this Treaty, be permitted without interference to withdraw the compensation by obtaining foreign exchange, in the currency of the High Contracting Party of which such recipient is a national, corporation or association, upon the most favourable terms applicable to such currency at the time of the taking of the property, and exempt from any transfer or remittance tax, provided application for such exchange is made within one year after receipt of the compensation to which it relates'; Also *see* Art. V.4, Treaty of Friendship Commerce and Navigation between the United States and Germany, 8 December 1923; Art. XII.
22. Kenneth Vandevelde, *Bilateral Investment Treaties: History, Policy and Interpretation* (New York: Oxford University Press, 2010), 282.
23. *Ibid.*, at 271.

Chapter 3 surveys the treaty practice and arbitral jurisprudence on the relationship between regulatory freedom and indirect expropriation. Treaty practice on indirect expropriation has evolved over time. In past, BITs never defined indirect expropriation or expropriation, which left a lot of discretion with the arbitral tribunals. In recent years, States have revised their BITs and started identifying elements to describe indirect expropriation and ways of distinguishing it from regulatory freedom. The evolution of treaty practice with a focus on recent trends would be discussed in the first part of the Chapter. The second part would focus upon jurisprudence of investment tribunals on indirect expropriation and regulatory freedom. The ways in which tribunals have described these concepts and distinguished them will be discussed. Broadly, the cases fall into three categories. First, that take a position that regulatory freedom does not exist once States have entered into BITs. Very few arbitral tribunals that have taken this position. Second, States can exercise regulatory freedom, but whether the measure would amount to indirect expropriation has to be determined solely on the basis of the effect of the measure on the property of the foreign investor – called the 'sole effects doctrine'. Majority of investment tribunals follow this doctrine. Third, some tribunals have recognized regulatory freedom as a customary international law norm that is unaffected by indirect expropriation provisions, as long as the measure in question is bona fide, non-discriminatory and in public interest.

Chapter 4 takes stock of the sole effects doctrine, which is frequently applied by investment tribunals to distinguish between regulatory freedom and indirect expropriation. The Chapter would first elaborate the meaning and content of the sole effects doctrine. This would be followed by the genesis and emergence of the sole effects doctrine, with particular focus on the jurisprudence of the Iran-US Claims Tribunal on indirect expropriation and the sole effects doctrine. Thereafter, the emergence of a competing doctrine 'nature of the measure' would be discussed. According to this doctrine, the effect of the measure is irrelevant and it is only the nature of the measure that is to be assessed to decide whether a measure is a legitimate regulatory measure or indirect expropriation.

Chapter 5 analyses different theoretical approaches that direct and indirectly reflect upon the relationship between regulatory freedom and indirect expropriation. Conceptual foundations for distinguishing regulatory freedom from indirect expropriation are crucial. Some theories in relation to investment treaty arbitration generally, and indirect expropriation in particular, have developed, which would perform a crucial role in distinguishing regulatory freedom from indirect expropriation. The general theoretical paradigm that would impact the relationship and distinction between regulatory freedom and indirect expropriation is global administrative law (GAL) and associated theories and general theoretical framework created as a consequence of BIT practice. There are some specific theoretical arguments in relation to regulatory freedom and indirect expropriation that have been developed within the framework of these general theories on investment treaty arbitration. Theories developed particularly in relation to indirect expropriation and regulatory freedom include the sole effects doctrine and the case-by-case method. This Chapter would analyse all the related theories and how far they assist in understanding the concepts of regulatory freedom and indirect expropriation, their relationship with each other, and the method for distinguishing between them.

Chapter 6 is purely doctrinal. This Chapter argues that regulatory freedom is a customary international law norm. This is based on two arguments. First, regulatory freedom is an attribute of state sovereignty, which by itself is a customary international law norm. Sovereignty is a legal concept and is treated as a bundle of rights. Regulatory freedom is one of the attributes of state sovereignty and exists until it has been specifically given away. BITs do not exclude the operation of regulatory freedom. Second, evidence of state practice is used to establish that regulatory freedom has a customary law status. Statements at diplomatic conferences, pleadings of States before international courts and tribunals making a claim that regulatory freedom is a customary international law norm, and municipal laws of States and judicial decisions of national and international adjudication bodies are relied upon.

Chapter 7 investigates whether there is a conflict between regulatory freedom and indirect expropriation, based upon the relationship between a customary international law norm and a treaty norm. Regulatory freedom is a customary international law norm (this would be shown in Chapter 6) and indirect expropriation is a treaty norm since it exists in BITs. Is there a conflict between these two norms in the field of investment treaty arbitration? If there is a conflict, then which norm will supersede the other or can they co-exist? These and other principles in relation to interpretation and conflict of norms, originating in two different sources: treaty and custom, would be discussed further.

Chapter 8 elaborates the elements of regulatory freedom and looks at the appropriate standard of review that should be applied in cases where regulatory freedom is in question. The elements of regulatory freedom recognised in the jurisprudence are bona fide, non-discriminatory and public interest. Each of these concepts is discussed in detail and how they can be used to identify a regulatory measure and distinguish it from indirect expropriation would be discussed. An associated concept is the standard of review that the judicial body would have to exercise while distinguishing regulatory freedom from indirect expropriation. Some tribunals have been employing the proportionality analysis, be drawing support from the jurisprudence of the Panels and Appellate Body of the WTO under GATT Article XX and the jurisprudence of the European Court of Human Rights. Proportionality analysis has come to prominence in the literature as well. The appropriateness of proportionality analysis in the process of delineating between regulatory freedom and indirect expropriation would also be discussed.

Finally, Chapter 9 – the concluding chapter will bring together all the principal themes and arguments discussed in preceding Chapters.

CHAPTER 2

The Concept of 'Regulatory Measure' and 'Expropriatory Measure'

An appropriate methodology for distinguishing between regulatory freedom and indirect expropriation cannot be identified until the concepts underlying these rules are not fully explored. This Chapter is about the 'concepts' underlying regulatory freedom and indirect expropriation rather than 'rules'. The scope, operation and interplay of the 'rules' is discussed in the following Chapters.

The concept behind the customary law rule of regulatory freedom is referred to as 'police powers' doctrine in international law and domestic constitutional law jurisprudence. The conceptual basis of indirect expropriation is an expropriatory measure, referred to as 'eminent domain' or 'taking'. Police powers doctrine encompasses measures legitimately undertaken for the protection of public interest and could be characterized and analysed as 'regulatory measures'. Eminent domain represents the right of a State to take foreign property after payment of compensation. The activity of 'taking' of private property by a State may take either a direct, or an indirect form. That however, would not change the underlying nature of the action – which continues to remain 'expropriatory'. Therefore, the distinction that has to be made is between the two concepts of a 'regulatory measure' and an 'expropriatory measure'. The distinction between the two concepts is fairly developed and the theoretical basis for that distinction can be identified based on jurisprudence.[1] The following discussion is on the origin of these and underlying differences between the two.

In the case of exercise of police powers, the primary objective of the State is of regulating or achieving some public interest. Police powers is also known as regulatory freedom or right to regulate. The terms 'regulatory freedom', 'right to regulate' and 'police powers' are used interchangeably. Regulatory freedom represents 'legitimate exercise of police powers'. It is a reservoir of innumerable regulatory measures that a State can undertake. Regulatory measure would be the specific instances of exercise of

1. *See* Chapter 5.

regulatory freedom. Whereas, in the case of eminent domain, the objective is to appropriate private property to itself, or to a third party, or simply destroy the property. The specific exercise of 'eminent domain' would be the adoption of an expropriatory measure: which may take the form of a 'direct' or 'indirect expropriation'. It is a fundamental task to distinguish between a regulatory measure from an expropriatory measure. In the case of a regulatory measure, despite the loss suffered by a foreign investor, the host State would not be responsible for payment of compensation, whereas in the case of an 'expropriatory measure', the host State would have to pay compensation. While the rest of the book elaborates on the different nature and the manner of distinction between these two concepts, this chapter is focused on the origin of these two concepts in international law and municipal law.

§2.01 MEANING OF 'MEASURE'

A 'regulatory' or an 'expropriatory' measure is fundamentally a 'measure'. A measure is simply an action undertaken by a State, and a specific instance of exercise of regulatory freedom, or an expropriatory measure. It is the basic unit and object of legal analysis. It is a measure that would have resulted into losses to a foreign investor. It is the nature and characteristics of the measure that would decide whether the measure is 'regulatory' or 'expropriatory'.

The 'measure' – irrespective of its nature of being 'regulatory' or 'expropriatory' may take various forms. A measure would be an action of a State through legislative, executive or judicial branches. A measure encompasses all rules, regulations, legislations, administrative actions and judicial decisions.[2] Some investment treaties contain a definition of the measure.[3] For example, measure is defined in Article 201 of North America Free Trade Agreement (NAFTA) to include 'any law, regulation, procedure, requirement or practice'.[4] Even where it is not defined in a BIT, it is used as a concept to see whether there are actions undertaken by the State, and these actions are interpreted broadly.[5] In *Suez v Argentina*, since measure was not defined in the BIT, the Tribunal referred to the dictionary where measure was defined as an action taken to achieve a particular purpose.[6] Normally, in addition to action, even inaction on the part

2. Article 1, ASEAN Framework Agreement on the Facilitation of Goods in Transit, 1998 https://cil.nus.edu.sg/rp/pdf/1998%20ASEAN%20Framework%20Agreement%20on%20the%20Facilitation%20of%20Goods%20in%20Transit-pdf.pdf, 6 June 2018; Art. 1, Canada Model Foreign Protection and Promotion Agreement, 2004 https://www.italaw.com/documents/Canadian2004-FIPA-model-en.pdf, 6 June 2018; Art. 1, US Model Bilateral Investment Treaty, 2012 https://www.state.gov/documents/organization/188371.pdf, 6 June 2018.
3. German Model Bilateral Investment Treaty, 2008 http://investmentpolicyhub.unctad.org/Download/TreatyFile/2865, 6 June 2018; French Model Bilateral Investment Treaty, 2006 http://italaw.com/documents/ModelTreatyFrance2006.pdf, 6 June 2018.
4. Article 201, North American Free Trade Agreement (adopted 17 December 1992, entered into force 1 January 1994) 32 I.L.M 289 and 605 (1993).
5. United Nations Conference on Trade and Development, *Most Favoured Nation Treatment: UNCTAD Series on Issues in International Investment Agreements II*, (United Nations, 2010), 28.
6. *Suez, Sociedad General de Aguas de Barcelona, S.A. and Vivendi Universal, S.A. v Argentine Republic*, Decision on Liability, ICSID Case No. ARB/03/19, 30 June 2010, para. 131.

of a State could amount to violation of treatment standards. In the case of regulatory freedom, there is always some form of action undertaken by the State.

§2.02 THE CONCEPT OF A 'REGULATORY MEASURE' OR THE 'POLICE POWERS DOCTRINE'

Regulatory freedom is the description of freedom States enjoy for regulatory purposes, whereas 'regulatory measure' represents the conduct of the freedom through actual measures. Both the phrases have been used interchangeably. Most of the discussion on regulatory freedom in classical international law has taken place under the rubric of police powers doctrine. The phrase 'police powers' sounds confusing due to the meaning attached to 'police'. It gives the impression of being limited to the activity of law enforcement or policing – maintaining law and order. Police powers have been used in a wider context to depict the prerogative of the Government to regulate activities within its jurisdiction, and not merely policing functions.[7] Therefore, the meaning of the word 'police' is different from 'police powers' and shall not be conflated.

Black's Law Dictionary has two distinct entries for 'police' and 'police powers'. The entry for 'police' refers to the police department responsible for public order, public safety and prevention and detection of crime.[8] Whereas, 'police power' is defined as:

> The inherent and plenary power of a sovereign to make all laws necessary and proper to preserve the public security, order, health, morality, and justice. It is a fundamental power essential to government, and it cannot be surrendered by the legislature or irrevocably transferred away from government.[9]

'Police' and its cognates, 'policy' and 'polity' originate in the Latin word '*polītīa*'. It has descended from the Greek word '*politeia*' and ultimately from '*polis*'.[10] '*Polītia*' meant administration or government. Since the sixteenth century, 'policy' has been used as a synonym for these word in English.[11] Reflecting on the genesis of the word 'police powers', Worcestor's Academic Dictionary defines 'police' to stand 'for "policy" condition of a State'.[12] From early eighteenth century, it started denoting regulation, discipline, control of community, civil administration and public order.[13]

7. Santiago Legarre, 'The Historical Background of the Police Power' *Journal of Constitutional Law* 9(3) (2007): 745, 761–762 (citing *Chambers Dictionary of Etymology*, ed. Robert K Barnhart, (1988), 812–813).
8. Bryan Garner, *Black's Law Dictionary* (10th ed., United States of America: Thomson Reuters, 2014), 1344.
9. *Ibid.*, at 1345.
10. *See* Walter Skeat, *Etymological Dictionary of the English Language* (Oxford, Clarendon Press, 1935), 461–462.
11. Above note 7 (Legarre, Historical Background of Police Power), 812–813.
12. Joseph Worcester, *Worcester's Academic Dictionary: A New Etymological Dictionary of the English Language* (Philadelphia: J.B. Lippincott Company, 1910), 421.
13. Above note 7 (Legarre, Historical Background of Police Powers), 749, 750 citing *Oxford English Dictionary*, (2nd ed., Oxford: Oxford University Press, 1989), 22.

Blackstone discussed police powers as a broader phrase encompassing economic regulations and domestic polity.[14] Different domestic statues have used police powers as power of State to make different laws, including regulation of economic activity.[15] Adam Smith has referred to the word police powers to mean civil administration[16] and 'the theory of the general principles of law and government'.[17] He further elaborated that all regulations of a country in relation to trade, commerce, agriculture and manufacturing belong to the regulatory power of the State.[18] Vattel also defined police power in equally broad words:

> It must also be observed, that individuals are not free in the economy or government of their affairs as not to be subject to the *regulations of polity,* made by the sovereign. For instance, if vines are greatly multiplied in a country, which is in want of corn, the sovereign may forbid the planting of the vine in fields proper for tillage, for here the public welfare and the safety of the state are concerned. When a reason of such importance requires it, the sovereign, or the magistrate, may oblige an individual to sell all the provisions that are more than sufficient for the subsistence of his family, and fix the price. The public authority may and ought to hinder monopolies, and suppress all practices tending to raise the price of provisions ....[19]

'Police powers' have been long understood as the power of a State to cause harm for protection of public interest. Grotius saw the concept of police powers as a legitimate method for a State to cause harm to private persons. He viewed the price control by the States that would cause losses to private persons, including foreigners as legitimate regulations for which the State would not be responsible.[20] Vattel also supported this position.[21] Imposing limitation on the use of property is seen as an important component of the power of regulation for public interest and achievement of non-economic objectives such as morals, good manners, controlling gambling, etc. which would be covered under police powers.[22]

The freedom of States to cause harm to foreigners for protection of public interest does not extend to causing deliberate harm. While emphasizing the non-responsibility of States for legitimate regulatory exercises, the early writers of international law understood the need for controlling arbitrary deprivations of private property of foreigners. This position was aptly summarized by Sax in the following words:

---

14. George Sharswood (ed.), *Sir William Blackstone, Commentaries on the Laws of England in Four Books*, vol. 1 (Philadelphia: J.B. Lippincott Company, 1893), 274.
15. Above note 7 (Legarre, Historical Background of Police Powers), 750–752.
16. R.L. Meek, D.D. Raphael & Peter Stein (eds.), *Lectures on Jurisprudence by Adam Smith* (Oxford: Clarendon Press, 1978), 586.
17. *Ibid.*, at 398.
18. *Ibid.*, at 5.
19. Above note 7 (Legarre, Historical Background of Police Powers), 749, 754–755 citing Emerich de Vattel, *Le Droit Des Gens, Ou Principles De La Naturelle, Appliques a La Conduit Et Aux Affaires Des Nations Et Des Souvrains,* Book I (London, Newbery et al. 1759–1760), 104; also citing Chitty's edition of 1834 states: 'It must also be observed, that individuals are not so perfectly free in the economy or government of their affairs, as not to be subject to the laws and regulations of police made by the sovereign.'
20. Hugo Grotius, Chapter II, *De Jure Belli Et Pacis*, Book II, (1625), para. XIX.
21. Emer de Vattel, Chapter VIII, *The Law of Nations* Book I, (1758), para. 88.
22. Above note 7 (Legarre, Historical Background of Police Powers), 745, 763.

> What seemed to concern the early writers was not the fact of loss but the imposition of loss by unjust means. It was the exercise of arbitrary or tyrannical powers that were sought to be controlled. As Pufendorf put it, the fear was that 'ill Princes,' unless constrained, 'may sometimes abuse [their powers] to the damage and ruin of their subjects.' The examples they gave suggest a principal fear of ill-considered, hasty, or even discriminatory impositions created by the pressing necessity of the state to get a job done, and of a possible animus against those citizens who were not, as Pufendorf put it, 'kind or public spirited enough to offer their money [or property] voluntarily'.
>
> Certainly, the foregoing evidence is at least sufficient to suggest that we must look to some principle other than value maintenance *per se* if we are to find a historically accurate as well as currently workable theory for the taking cases. Scanty though it is, there is at least some basis in the early writers for finding that their real concern was a protection of values only as against government conduct which raised the dangers of arbitrary or tyrannical treatment.[23]

§2.03 THE CONCEPT OF AN 'EXPROPRIATORY MEASURE'

An expropriatory measure is a measure aimed at inflicting 'harm' of certain kind and not all harms to property. The precise contents of the standard of expropriation would depend upon the language employed in the BIT. The concept of expropriatory measure provides the normative foundation for the treaty rules on expropriation. This is important since BITs do not define 'expropriation'. Expropriation involves deliberate severing the relationship of ownership. A precise definition of expropriation was given in *Olguin v Paraguay*, observing:

> For an expropriation to occur, there must be actions that can be considered reasonably appropriate for producing the effect of depriving the affected party of the property it owns, in such a way that whoever performs those actions will acquire, directly or indirectly, control, or at least the fruits of the expropriated property. Expropriation therefore requires teleologically driven action for it to occur; omissions, however egregious they may be, are not sufficient for it to take place.[24]

The cessation of relationship may take various forms. If the cessation of ownership is direct, then it is direct expropriation, but if it is achieved through covert means, such as denying the freedom to go to the court to challenge expropriatory actions, it will be indirect expropriation. Wortley highlights this nuance in the following words:

> When, by the action of State E, O, an owner, is expropriated, the legal bond between O and the thing claimed by him is severed by the law of State E, and, *by that law*, O is no longer regarded as having an enforceable claim to the thing

23. Joseph Sax, 'Takings and the Police Power' *Yale Law Journal* (1964): 36, 57.
24. *Eudoro Armando Olguín v Republic of Paraguay*, Award, ICSID Case No. ARB/98/5, 26 January 2001, para. 84; Brownlie also describes expropriation as a process where, 'deprivation may be followed by transfer to the territorial State or to the third parties, as in systems of land distribution as a means of agrarian reform'. Ian Brownlie, *Principles of Public International Law* (7th ed., Oxford: Oxford University Press, 2008), 532 (footnotes omitted).

> expropriated; State E thenceforward accords to itself, or to its nominee, the protection of an owner in respect of the thing taken. This may be done either by State E's recognizing itself, or some other person, as the new owner; or merely be State E's withdrawing the protection of its Courts from O, the owner expropriated, and tacitly allowing a *defacto* possessor to remain in possession of the things seized, as did the Roman praetor in allowing *longi temporis praescriptio*.[25]

The object of the action or the measure of the State is to deprive a private entity of the property in such a way that the State or anybody else acquires the property or control of the property or the fruits of the property. In cases of expropriation, there is an element of gaining something of value for public benefit. The property and the benefits from the property are transferred from the owner of the party to the State or its organs or some third party. There is an element of unjust enrichment.[26] For example, if a State makes a regulation, ultimately aimed at interfering with the markets in such a fashion that a public corporation benefits from the regulation, as opposed to its competitors. This would be unjust enrichment and an instance of an expropriatory measure.

The character of an expropriatory measure is aptly represented in the term 'takings' – used for exercises under eminent domain. As the name 'taking' connotes, there has to be taking away of property – either directly or indirectly.

Although all deprivations of property caused due to the measure of a State cannot be termed expropriatory, severing of relationship with property could take various other indirect forms. A situation may be created where the owner is left with no option but to sell or the sale occurred under duress. Such situations would amount to indirect severance of ownership and will be considered an expropriatory measure.[27] A State would not have gained any direct economic benefit.[28] The sovereign power may be used surreptitiously to destroy the property of foreign investor. This occurs in indirect expropriation cases. In *Antonie Biloune v Ghana Investments Centre*, the foreign investor was involved in the construction of a hotel in Ghana. The Government issued summons for arrest, followed by detention and deportation without possibility of re-entry of the foreign investor, making him lose the control of his investment in a company called MDCL.[29] These measures ensured that the investment was destroyed and thus were characterized as expropriatory by the Tribunal. The Tribunal held:

25. B.A. Wortley, *Expropriation in International Law* (Cambridge: Cambridge University Press, 1959), 1.
26. *S.D. Myers, Inc. v Government of Canada*, UNCITRAL, 12 November 2000, Separate Opinion by Dr Bryan Schwartz (on the Partial Award), para. 212; Christoph Schreuer, 'Unjustified Enrichment in International Law' *American Journal of Comparative Law* 22 (1974): 281; Christina Binder & Christoph Schreuer, 'Unjust Enrichment' in Rüdiger Wolfrum (ed.) *Max Planck Encyclopedia of Public International Law* (New York: Oxford University Press, 2008).
27. Above note 25 (Wortley, Expropriation) at 1.
28. International Law Commission, International Responsibility, Fourth Report by F.V. García Amador, Special Rapporteur: Responsibility of the State for Injuries Caused in its Territory to the Person or Property of Aliens – Measures Affecting Acquired Rights Document (26 February 1959) UN Doc A/CN.4/119, (1959) II Yearbook of the International Law Commission 1, para. 46.
29. *Antoine Biloune, Marine Drive Complex Ltd. v Ghana Investments Centre*, the Government of Ghana, Awards, 27 October 1989, (1994) XIX Yearbook Commercial Arbitration 11, 12–13.

> What is clear is that the conjunction of the stop work order, the demolition, the summons, the arrest, the detention, the requirement of filing assets declaration forms, and the deportation of Mr Biloune without possibility of re-entry had the effect of causing the irreparable cessation of work on the project. Given the central role of Mr Biloune in promoting, financing and managing MDCL, his expulsion from the country effectively prevented MDCL from further pursuing the project. In the view of the Tribunal, such prevention of MDCL from pursuing its approved project would constitute constructive expropriation of MDCL's contractual rights in the project and, accordingly, the expropriation of the value of Mr Biloune's interest in MDCL, unless the respondents can establish by persuasive evidence sufficient for these events.[30]

An expropriatory measure would include situations of 'legal' as well as 'illegal' expropriation. In both the situations, the underlying measure is expropriatory in nature. These situations are different from a regulatory measure where the underlying measure is regulatory in nature and not expropriatory. Therefore, the distinction between 'legal' and 'illegal' measure applies only in case of expropriatory measure and not a regulatory measure. This principle was recognized in *Kardassopoulos v Georgia*.[31]

Thus, the focus of an expropriatory measure is on severance of the relationship between the owner and the property, which may be achieved through an expropriatory measure: 'unjust enrichment' or 'intended deprivation'.

§2.04 DISTINGUISHING FEATURES BETWEEN A 'REGULATORY MEASURE' AND 'EXPROPRIATORY MEASURE'

Both, a regulatory and an expropriatory measure impact the property or the value of the property. If the impact on property is used as the only basis for analysing the character of a measure, then simply the outcome is looked at and the objective behind the measure is ignored. The objective behind a regulatory measure is different from an expropriatory measure.

A regulatory measure is conceptually different from an expropriatory measure. A regulatory measure is a legitimate exercise of sovereign power for protection of public interest. An expropriatory measures is undertaken for taking over the property of private person – either directly or indirectly. In the case of regulatory measure, the losses are an unintended consequence of the regulation, whereas in the case of an expropriatory measure, losses are an intended consequence. In the case of regulations, the State may be aware that its measures would result into losses, but the reason for adoption of regulations is not to cause losses. Losses are only the 'consequence' rather than the 'objective'. The objective would be of conserving and promoting public interest while performing the multitude of functions that the State has to perform. The economic injury caused due to the exercise of regulatory measure is incidental or indirect. On the contrary, in cases of expropriatory measures, the impact on private property is targeted and intended. According to Wortley:

30. *Ibid.*, at 19–20.
31. *Ioannis Kardassopoulos v The Republic of Georgia*, ICSID Case Nos ARB/05/18 and ARB/07/15, Award, 3 March 2010, para. 387.

> The distinction between indirect loss resulting from reasonable and general restrictions imposed in the social interest, and an indirect loss amounting to a mere smoke-screen for the taking of an asset, is a real one.[32] Therefore, incidental losses arising from town planning etc. do not amount to expropriation.[33]

As a principle of law, a State is not responsible for incidental losses arising from lawful exercise of police powers.[34] Explaining the role of distinction between regulatory and expropriatory measure based on the indirect loss of property, Brownlie had said:

> State measures, prima facie a lawful exercise of powers of government, may affect foreign interests considerably without amounting to expropriation. Thus foreign assets and their use may be subjected to taxation, trade restrictions involving licenses and quotas, or measures of devaluation. While special facts may alter cases, in principle such measures are not unlawful and do not constitute expropriation. If the state gives a public enterprise special advantages, for example by direction that it charges nominal rates of freight, the resulting *de facto* or quasi monopoly is not an expropriation of the competitors driven out of business: it might be otherwise if this were the primary of sole object of a monopoly regime. Taxation which has the precise object and effect of confiscation is unlawful.[35]

This could be best explained with the example of asbestos industry. The adverse health effects of asbestos are scientifically established. If a State makes a regulation banning the asbestos industry, the measure is a legitimate regulatory measure since it is for the protection of human life, health and environment. The losses suffered by the asbestos manufacturer are incidental. The objective of the regulation is health protection. Such a measure for health protection cannot be treated as expropriatory, there is no taking of property by the State. The State does not intend to take over the asbestos industry. Rather, since the idea behind banning asbestos industry is to stop its use there is no use to the State by taking over those assets.

However, if the State decides to take over all the private banks then by severing the bond of ownership of the private investor with its property, the State takes the properties for itself or transfers it to somebody else. The intention of the State is to take over the banks for which compensation would be payable. Although public interest may be involved in such a measure, the ultimate idea is to take over the property. Thus, falling into the category of an expropriatory measure. The indirect nature of losses is aptly elucidated by Sax:

> If the government wants to convert a private house into a post office, or run a new highway through a farm, or build a dam which will flood nearby land, it is going to have to compensate the losses sustained as a result of these activities. In such cases courts uniformly hold that property has been taken by the government, thus bringing into operation the constitutional mandate that private property may not be taken for public use without just compensation. But if government prohibits the continuance of a business which has been established for a long time, or outlaws

32. Above note 25 (Wortley, expropriation), 51.
33. *Ibid.*, at 50–53.
34. Above note 23 (Sax, Taking and Police Powers).
35. Above note 24 (Brownlie, Principles of Public International Law), 532.

> certain businesses altogether, or prohibits the use of land for any of the purposes which give it substantial economic value, it may not have to pay a penny. In cases of this type, where the government is engaged in zoning, nuisance abatement, conservation, business regulation, or a host of other functions, courts will usually decide that the economic loss suffered by the private citizen was a *mere incident of the lawful exercise of the 'police power'*, and thus not compensable.[36] (emphasis added)

In the American case of *Mugler v Kansas*, a regulation forbidding manufacture of intoxicating liquor was held to fall under the police powers doctrine and not eminent domain. The State was therefore not responsible to pay compensation for losses caused.[37] These are two distinct situations because police powers, i.e., regulation does not involve appropriation of property for public benefit by the State but merely a limitation on its use for certain purposes, declared as injuries to general public.[38]

The role of State while adopting a regulatory measure is different from that while adopting an expropriatory measure. While exercising expropriatory regulation, the State takes away the property and is therefore seen as an 'enterprise' involved in the markets and participating actively to deprive competitors of their rights. In the case of regulatory measures, the State acts as an arbitrator or mediator, where the limitations on other actions are not imposed to gain some benefit in the market place. But the limitations so imposed, are a result of performing their functions as an arbiter.[39] In a separate opinion in *SD Myres v Canada*, the arbitrator explained the distinction in the following words:

> Expropriations tend to deprive the owner and to enrich – by a corresponding amount – the public authority that the property, or the third party to whom the property is given. There is both unfair deprivation and unjust enrichment when an expropriation is carried out with compensation. By contrast, regulatory action tends to prevent an owner from using property in a way that unjustly enriches the owner. For example, an unregulated manufacturing operation might make more money by not bothering to reduce the amount of pollution it sends into the wider community. The government that imposes the regulation does not necessarily profit from its intervention; indeed, it may be expensive to both enact and administer regulations.[40]

It is possible to discern the objectives behind adoption of either of the two measures. The methodology for this determination is discussed in greater detail in the following chapters.

36. Above note 23 (Sax, Taking and Police Powers) at 36.
37. *Mugler v Kansas* 123 US 623 (1887) at 668.
38. *Ibid.*, at 669.
39. Frank Michelman, 'Property, Utility, and Fairness: Comments on the Ethical Foundations of the "Just Compensation" Law' *Harvard Law Review* 80 (1967): 1165, 1200–1201; above note 23 (Sax, Taking and Police Powers) at 60.
40. Above note 26 (S.D. Myers, Inc. Separate Opinion by Dr Bryan Schwartz) at para. 212.

§2.05 MUNICIPAL LAW VIS-À-VIS INTERNATIONAL LAW

The principle of police powers and eminent domain or regulatory freedom and expropriation exists in municipal law as well. However, the genesis and the nature of these concepts have developed differently in international law and municipal law. Under municipal law, the classical legal thought has been that the crown is the owner of all lands. Therefore, it was the prerogative of the State to take whichever property they wished to take away. It was only with the progress of constitutional law that the right of private property versus the right of State to interfere with that property was recognized.

In international law, the trajectory of development of these principles has been very different. The principles arose in the context of treatment of foreigners by the host State. The hypothesis that the crown is the owner of all lands would not operate. Violation of rights of a foreigner would amount to violation of the rights of the home State. The dynamics of development of the law at the international law is very different. This does not mean that these principles at the national and international level do not influence each other. They do form appropriate analogies and provide theoretical underpinnings for understanding and distinguishing the two principles.

The doctrine of 'police powers' has been used extensively in American constitutional law. It was introduced in American constitutional law in 1827 in the case of *Brown v Maryland*.[41] American courts have used this doctrine to protect legislations passed for securing public health, safety and morals.[42] It shall not be assumed that the role of police powers is limited to these specific instances. Police powers stand for 'unexplained head of power'.[43] In American constitutional law, it is often used to defend residual legislative powers of the constituent States of the United States of America. It connotes the whole range of legislative power retained by the States (provinces) and not delegated to the federal government. These are innumerable and cannot be itemized. Hence, they are residual and not expressly stipulated in the Constitution.[44]

Therefore, a likely assumption that may arise is that regulatory freedom belongs exclusively to the domain of municipal law. This assumption is understandable, since the use of 'police powers' has been mostly in American constitutional law. The analogy between the scope of police powers in international law and domestic law[45] is simplistic and ignores the actual purport of regulatory freedom under international law. In Roman law, police powers were considered to be a part of 'law of nations' – *jus genitum*. The law applied by the Roman *praetor peregrinus* to relations involving

41. *Brown v Maryland* 25 US (12 Wheat) 419, 442–443 (1827). Although, *Brown v Maryland* was the first case where the word was expressly used, some argue that it is such a natural phrase that it is difficult to conceive that it was not used before. *See* William Crosskey, *Politics and the Constitution in the History of the United States* (Chicago: University of Chicago Press, 1953), 1305.
42. *Barnes v Glen Theatre* 501 US 560, 569 (1991).
43. Above note 7 (Legarre, Historical Background of Police Power) at 745, 747–778.
44. *United States v Lopez* 514 US 549, 566–568 (1995).
45. *See* generally, Stephan Schill (ed.), *Investment Treaty Arbitration and Comparative Public Law* (Oxford: New York; Oxford University Press, 2010).

persons other than Roman citizens.[46] In addition to the classical authors discussed above, Vattel's discussion on regulatory freedom is also exclusively in the context of international law.[47]

During the seventeenth and eighteenth century, the use of police powers in municipal law was extensive. This may have been the case for the application of sovereign powers to own citizens. However, when it came to infraction of private property of aliens, the discussion veered around regulatory freedom.[48] The understanding of sovereign power in municipal law was that '[e]verything actually in the territory of the State, considered in itself and independently of the persons to whom it belongs, must be deemed subject to the right of imperium of the territorial sovereign'.[49] A sovereign in domestic law was free to affect the properties in any manner it liked since it was owner of all the lands within its territories. On the contrary, a sovereign in international law could never exercise such plenary powers because sovereignty under international law is not equal to ownership of all territories.[50] As a consequence, in international law, police powers requires an element of reasonableness in its exercise.[51] According to Wortley:

> [i]t is important, however, to consider the instances where a confiscation, or similar operation, by the *lex situs* is generally held to be permissible by States forming part of the international community, since, in those cases, no remedy by public or private international law will be available to the owners for securing compensation for their loss unless they can show some abuse of the normal rights of the territorial State, or some unjustified enrichment at the expense of the owners.[52]

The scope, nature and foundational thinking of police powers in international and municipal law are distinguishable. The vital distinction between the two is their source. In municipal law, the constitutional law or other municipal statutes of the State govern the scope of police powers. In international law, customary international law governs regulatory freedom and stipulates a uniform standard. *See* Chapter 6 for detailed arguments on the point that regulatory freedom is customary international law. The discussion in international law has been purely in relation to the application of regulations on aliens and losses incurred by them, rather than a general discussion on plenary sovereign power of State over its own citizens.

---

46. Seidl-Hohenveldren, 'The Social Functions of Property and Property Protection in Present-day International Law' in Frits Kalshoven Pleter Jan Kuyper & Johan G. Lammers (eds) *Essays on the Development of the International Leal Order: In Memory of Haro F Van Panhuys* (USA: Sijthoff & Noordhoff, 1980), 78.
47. *See* Emer de Vattel, *The Law of Nations: Or, Principles of the Law of Nature, Applied to the Conduct and Affairs of Nations and Sovereigns, with Three Early Essays on the Origin and Nature of Natural Law and on Luxury*, edited and with an Introduction by Béla Kapossy and Richard Whatmore (United States of America: Liberty Fund, 2008).
48. Above note 23 (Sax, Taking and Police Powers) at 36, 54–55.
49. Pasquale Fiore, *International Law Codified and Its Legal Sanction: Or, the Legal Organisation of the Society of States* (New York: Baker, 1918), 18.
50. Above note 25 (Wortley, Expropriation) at 12.
51. Francisco Vicñia, 'Carlos Calvo: Honorary NAFTA Citizen', *New York University Environmental Law Journal* 11 (2002–2003): 19, 27.
52. Above note 25 (Wortley, Expropriation) at 39.

§2.06 CONCLUSIONS

Confusion looms between regulatory freedom and indirect expropriation because they both result into loss to property of a foreigner. The similarity of outcome has led scholars and tribunals to find the simplistic solution of looking at the losses caused and hold the host State to pay compensation. This approach makes the distinction between these two concepts redundant. If a host State is directed to pay compensation for all financial losses, then the existence of these two independent rights becomes an unnecessary formality. After initial skepticism, tribunals have recognized the importance and relevance of regulatory freedom as an independent concept. But, the criteria for distinguishing them are not yet accepted in investment treaty arbitration, although they are available in international law. By failing to recognize those criteria and distinguish between regulatory freedom and indirect expropriation, they have made the legal requirement of regulatory freedom inconsequential. The next chapter will present the attitude of investment tribunals and investment treaty practice on regulatory freedom and indirect expropriation. This will assist in assessing the present position of regulatory freedom in investment arbitral jurisprudence.

The methodological course to be adopted in the cases where indirect expropriation measure is adopted should start with the analysis of the nature of the measure: whether that measure falls within the limits of a legitimate regulatory exercise. Whatever may be the form of activity that affects the proprietary right, the appropriate approach is to investigate the substance of the activity of the State.

It is not suggested that every exercise by the State can be protected once claimed to be a part of exercise of police powers. Even classical scholars contemplated limitations on the right of sovereign to regulate. They articulated the limitations as 'prudential considerations'[53] and devised formulae for identifying it. In contemporary international investment law, the limitations on this otherwise broad or plenary power are stipulated in investment treaties.

The factors which legitimize and identify a regulatory measure, operate as limitations on the freedom of the State to exercise regulatory or police powers. These factors can be categorized into preliminary factors and determinative factors. Preliminary would be taking, unjust enrichment and neutralization. The existence of preliminary factors would be necessary before the nature of the measure is investigated. Once these are satisfied, then it is necessary to examine the nature of the measure. Within the nature of the measure, the determinative factors are: bona fide, non-discriminatory and public interest.

These three constitutive elements of regulatory freedom emerge from state practice. They are customary in nature. These elements have been provided for in the Third American Restatement and also presented by States in their pleadings before International Court and tribunals. The way in which these elements have emerged has been discussed in chapter six and each of these elements are discussed in detail in chapter eight.

53. Above note 7 (Legarre, Historical Background of Police Power) at 812–813.

Although in most of the cases, identifying indirect expropriation is fact-specific and best 'rationalized on a case-by-case basis', scholarly attempts to identify these elements and factors shall not cease.[54]

54. August Reinisch, 'Expropriation' in Peter Muchlinski, Frederico Ortino & Christoph Schreuer (eds) *The Oxford Handbook of International Investment Law* (Oxford: Oxford University Press, 2008), 426.

CHAPTER 3

Types of Expropriatory Measures in Treaty Practice and Arbitral Jurisprudence

The relationship between regulatory freedom and indirect expropriation would primarily depend on the scope of expropriation provisions in the BITs[1] and their interpretation by arbitral tribunals. The types of measures declared as expropriatory in the treaty practice cannot be treated as regulatory measures. Therefore, the wider the scope of expropriation provisions and their interpretation, narrower would be the scope for regulatory freedom. This Chapter traces the types of measures declared as expropriatory in treaty practice and the interpretation of those provisions in the arbitral jurisprudence.

§3.01 TYPES OF EXPROPRIATORY MEASURES

The treaty practice on expropriation has been mostly consistent with minor textual divergences. Therefore, it is possible to draw general conclusions based on the treaty texts. Article 1110 (1) of NAFTA can form a basis of the general discussion because it represents the most common formulation of expropriation clauses:

> Article 1110: Expropriation and Compensation:
> 1. No Party may directly or indirectly nationalize or expropriate an investment of an investor of another Party in its territory or take a measure tantamount to nationalization or expropriation of such an investment ('expropriation'), except:
>   (a) for a public purpose;
>   (b) on a non-discriminatory basis;
>   (c) in accordance with due process of law and Article 1105(1); and

1. BIT is used as a generic reference to Bilateral Investment Treaties (BITs) as well as Free Trade Agreements (FTAs).

(d) on payment of compensation in accordance with paragraphs 2 through 6.[2]

The elements of legal expropriation contained in clauses (a) to (d) differ from treaty to treaty, but the provisions on the nature of the expropriatory measure contained in paragraph (1) of Article 1110 are mostly the same across different treaties. These treaties do not contain any explicit reference to regulatory freedom. The treaty practice (as contained in NAFTA Article 1110 (1)) shows that expropriation clauses cover three types of expropriatory measures: direct, indirect and equivalent to, tantamount to, having effect equivalent to or creeping expropriation (referred collectively for convenience as the 'third category'). BITs do not define any of these terms hence their meaning would be informed by the discussion in Chapter 2 on the notion of an expropriatory measure.

[A] Direct Expropriation

Direct expropriation takes place where the State takes over the title of the property for its own use or transfers it to a third party. Direct expropriation may be in the form of 'expropriation' or 'nationalization'.

The Institute de Droit International defines nationalization in the following words:

> La nationalization est le transferet à l'Etat, par measure législative et dans un intérèt public, de biens ou droits privés d'une certaine catégorie, en vue de leur exploitation ou controle par l'Etat, ou d'une nouvelle destination qui leur serat donnée par celui-ci.[3]

Nationalization is a targeted legislative measure aimed at directing the property to new destinations. Wortley explains, '"Nationalization" is not a term of art, but it usually signifies expropriation in pursuance of some national political programme intended to create out of existing enterprises, or to strengthen, a nationally controlled industry. Nationalization differs in its scope and extent rather than in its juridical nature from other types of expropriation.'[4]

Expropriation is thus a wider concept and subsumes nationalization. Sornarajah defines nationalization as 'a situation in which a State embarks on a wholesale taking of the property of foreigners to end their economic domination of the whole economy or of sectors of the economy' and expropriation as 'a specific term that could be used

2. North America Free Trade Agreement between Canada, Mexico and the United States (adopted 17 December 1992, entered into force 1 January 1994) 32 ILM 289, 605 (1993); Canada Model BIT, 2004 art 13(1); US Model BIT, 2012 Art. 6(1); UK Model BIT (2008) Art. 5; Canada-China BIT (signed on 9 September 2012, entered into force 1 October 2014) Art. 10; Canada-Argentina BIT (signed on 5 November 1991, entered into force 29 April 1993) Art. VII; UK-Chile BIT (signed 8 January 1996, entered into force 21 April 1997) Art. 4; UK-Kenya BIT (signed 13 September 1999, entered into force 13 September 1999) Art. 5; US-Sri Lanka (signed 20 September 1991, entered into force 1 May 1993) Art. III; US-Ukraine BIT (signed 4 March 1994, entered into force 16 November 1996) Art. III.
3. 44 Annuaire de l'Institut de Droit International (II) 279 et seq. (1952), 238.
4. B.A. Wortley, *Expropriation in International Law* (Cambridge: Cambridge University Press, 1959), 36.

to describe the targeting of individual businesses for interference for specific economic or other reasons'.[5] Nationalization may involve either the taking away of the private property by the State or taking over of an activity such as banking, insurance, etc.[6] The objective of nationalization is to confer or transfer the title to: (a) certain activities or certain branches of the economy; (b) certain undertakings of paramount importance to the national economy; or (c) economic activity as a whole.[7]

Another difference between expropriation and nationalization lies in the duration of the measure and the process of transfer. Once an expropriation law is enacted, it typically authorizes the transfer of property anytime during the continuation of the law. It is a compulsory acquisition law, which gives a prospective authorization to the State to acquire property in future, during the existence of the authorizing law. Whereas nationalization involves transfer of assets to State or to State controlled bodies which has to be carried out upon the enactment of the law and does not contemplate future transfers to be carried out in an indefinite period of time. Thus, while a nationalization measure sets into motion a process with a foreseeable end, an expropriation measure occurs under an ongoing process founded on and controlled by the authorizing statute.[8]

Despite such differences, the nature of the underlying measure under both expropriation and nationalization remains the same and can be collectively referred to as an expropriatory measure. Older treaties limited their application to incidences of direct expropriation and nationalization,[9] since insulating foreign investments from expropriation was the fundamental driving factor for entering into bilateral investment treaties. In the case of such treaties, the question of responsibility of States for losses caused to foreign investors as a consequence of a general regulatory measure would not arise because it is easier to identify direct expropriation. The challenge is of identifying indirect expropriation, which exists in all BITs of the present time.

[B] Indirect Expropriation

Unlike direct expropriation, determination of indirect expropriation is complex. In the present world scenario, although not impossible, the instances of direct expropriation are comparatively rare. A lot of measures of States may result in indirect expropriation.

---

5. M. Sornarajah, *The International Law on Foreign Investment* (3rd ed., Cambridge: Cambridge University Press, 2010), 365–366; A similar definition is proposed by Sacerdoti: 'By expropriation is meant the coercive appropriation by the State of private property, usually by means of individual administrative measures. Nationalizations do not differ in substance from expropriation except that they are directly statutorily based and have a wide coverage.' *See* G Sacerdoti, 'Bilateral Treaties and Multilateral Instruments on Investment Protection' *Recueil des Cours* 269 (1997): 261, 379; Also *see* Ian Brownlie, *Principles of Public International Law* (7th ed., Oxford: Oxford University Press, 2008), 537.
6. Konstantin Katzarov, *The Theory of Nationalisation* (The Hague: Martinus Nijhoff, 1964), 141–142.
7. *Ibid.*, 138.
8. Gillian White, *Nationalization of Foreign Property* (London: Stevens & Sons Limited, 1961), 43.
9. Treaty for the Promotion and Protection of Investments, with Protocol and Exchange Notes (Germany-Pakistan) (signed 25 November 1959, entered into force 28 April 1962) Art. 3(2).

A measure may be short of directly taking over of the property, but it may still destroy the value of the property. In such cases, it is difficult to determine if the losses caused are a result of a regulatory measure or an expropriatory measure. Investment treaties do not define indirect expropriation and do no more than simply stating that the expropriation may be direct or indirect.[10]

Indirect expropriation 'involves total or near-total deprivation of an investment but without a formal transfer of title or outright seizure'.[11] Indirect expropriation represents situations where the objective of taking property is achieved through indirect means. In these situations, expropriation is not visible de jure but it exists de facto. The goal of indirect expropriation is the surreptitious infraction of property rights. The host State achieves the objective of expropriation, without resorting to a formal expropriation measure. In *Techmed v Mexico*, the Tribunal observed:

> Although formally an expropriation means a forcible taking by the Government of tangible or intangible property owned by private persons by means of administrative or legislative action to that effect, the term also covers a number of situations defined as *de facto* expropriation, where such actions or laws transfer the assets to third parties different from the expropriating State or where such laws or actions deprive persons of their ownership over such assets without allocating such assets to third parties.[12]

The Tribunal in *Suez v Argentina* declared that indirect expropriation exists when 'host states invoke their legislative and regulatory powers to enact measures that reduce the benefits investors derive from their investments without actually changing or cancelling investor's title to their assets or diminishing their control over them'.[13]

[C] 'Equivalent to Expropriation', 'Tantamount to Expropriation' or 'Creeping Expropriation'

In investment treaties, indirect expropriation is normally followed by the third category of expropriatory measures. They are in one or more of the following formulations:

10. US-Egypt BIT (signed 11 March 1986, entered into force 27 June 1992) Art. III; US-Jordan (signed 2 July 1997) Art. III; France-Mexico BIT (signed 12 November 1998, entered into force 12 October 2000) Art. 5; China-Germany BIT (signed 1 December 2003, entered into force 11 November 2005) Art. 4; Germany-Libya BIT (signed 15 October 2004, entered into force 14 July 2010) Art. 4; US-Ukraine BIT (signed 4 March 1994, entered into force 16 November 1996) Art. III; India- Qatar BIT (signed 7 April 1999) Art. 5.
11. UNCTAD, *Expropriation: UNCTAD Series on Issues in International Investment Agreements II*, (New York: United Nations, 2012), 7; August Reinisch, 'Expropriation' in Peter Muchlinski, Frederico Ortino and Christoph Schreuer (eds.) *The Oxford Handbook of International Investment Law* (Oxford: Oxford University Press, 2008), 421–423 (footnotes excluded); Christoph Schreuer, 'The Concept of Expropriation under the ECT and Other Investment Protection Treaties' in Clarisse Ribeiro (ed.) *Investment Arbitration and the Energy Charter Treaty* (Juris Publishing, 2006), 126–133.
12. *Medioambientales Techmed S.A. v The United Mexican States*, Award, ICSID Case No. ARB (AF)/00/2, 29 May 2003, para. 113 (footnote omitted).
13. *Suez, Sociedad General de Aguas de Barcelona S.A. and Vivendi Universal S.A. v The Argentine Republic*, Award, ICSID Case No. ARB/03/19, 30 July 2010, para. 132.

'equivalent to expropriation'[14] or 'tantamount to expropriation'[15] or 'effect equivalent to expropriation'[16] (for convenience they are collectively referred to as the 'third type'). The third type of expropriatory measures describes expropriation in terms of its effect. Through the third category, treaties extend the concept of expropriation to measures whose effect will be equivalent to that caused by direct expropriation or nationalization.[17] Some treaties do not contain indirect expropriation but only the first category (expropriation) and third category.[18]

An independent reference to these sub-categories in the expropriation clause may generate an impression that they expand the scope of direct and indirect expropriation. Relying on the generality of the third category and the meaning of 'tantamount', Salacuse suggests that the broad category 'allows expropriation treaty provisions to capture the multiplicity of host State acts that might have an expropriatory effect on foreign investment'.[19] From the third type of expropriatory measures, creeping expropriation stands out. Its content has been elaborated essentially in academic writings and arbitral jurisprudence. According to creeping expropriation, expropriation may take place through a series of actions, which individually may not constitute expropriation. But in sum they result in deprivation of property.[20] Creeping expropriation would happen when actions of a State diminished the value of property without affecting the ownership of property. In *Generation Ukraine v Ukraine*, the Tribunal defined creeping expropriation as follows:

---

14. Mexico-UK BIT (signed 12 May 2006, entered into force 25 July 2007) Art. 7; Canada-Slovakia (signed 20 July 2010, entered into force 14 March 2012) Art. VI.1; Netherlands-Oman BIT (signed 17 January 2009) Art. 4; Japan-Cambodia BIT (signed 14 June 2007, entered into force 31 July 2008) Art. 12(1); US-Uruguay BIT (signed 4 November 2005, entered into force 31 October 2006) Art. 6; Russia-Egypt BIT (signed 23 September 1997) Art. VI.
15. Egypt-Germany BIT (signed 16 June 2005, entered into force 22 November 2009) Art. 4; Japan-Lao People's Democratic Republic BIT (signed 16 January 2008, entered into force 3 August 2008) Art. 12; Egypt-Japan BIT (signed 28 January 1977, entered into force 14 January 1978) Art. 5; Japan-Vietnam BIT (signed 14 November 2003, entered into force 19 December 2004) Art. 9; Japan Turkey BIT (signed 12 February 1992, entered into force 12 March 1993) Art. 5(2); Japan-Egypt BIT (signed 28 January 1977, entered into force 14 January 1978) Art. 5(2); US-Congo BIT (signed 12 February 1990, entered into force 13 August 1994) Art. III; US-Honduras BIT (signed 1 July 1995, entered into force 11 July 2001) Art. III; US-Turkey BIT (signed 3 December 1985, entered into force 18 May 1990) Art. III.
16. These treaties only use the language, 'effect equivalent to', without any reference to the measure 'tantamount' or 'equivalent to'. UK-Sierra Leone BIT (signed 13 January 2000, entered into force 20 November 2001) Art. 5. These provisions expressly incorporate neutralization requirement, which is implicit in the second category; Energy Charter Treaty (signed 17 December 1994, entered into force 30 September 1999) Art. 13(1); Agreement for the Promotion and Reciprocal Protection of Investments (Canada-Ecuador) (signed on 29 April 1996, entered into force 6 June 1997) Art. VIII. 1; Agreement for the Promotion and Protection of Investments (Argentina-United Kingdom) (11 December 1990) Art. 5(1); Mexico-UK BIT, 2006 (signed on 12 May 2006, entered into force 25 July 2007) Art. 7; Canada-Slovakia BIT (signed on 20 July 2010, entered into force 14 March 2012) Art. VI.1; Netherlands-Oman BIT (signed on 17 January 2009) Art. 4.
17. Jeswald W Salacuse, *The Law of Investment Treaties* (New York: Oxford University Press, 2010), 294.
18. Energy Charter Treaty (signed 17 December 1994, entered into force 30 September 1999) 2080 UNTS 95 Art. 13(1).
19. Above note 17 (Salacuse), 293.
20. Above note 11 (Reinisch), 426–427 (footnotes excluded).

> Creeping expropriation is a form of indirect expropriation with a distinctive temporal quality in the sense that it encapsulates the situation whereby a series of acts attributable to the State over a period of time culminate in the expropriatory taking of such property.[21]

Sornarajah describes that the process 'could be a slow, insidious erosion of such rights and interests set in motion by an initial act and spreading over a period of time'.[22] According to Dolzer, '" Creeping expropriation" suggests a deliberate strategy on the part of the State, which may imply a negative moral judgment.'[23] Further, Reisman and Sloane have stated that 'A creeping expropriation therefore denotes, in the paradigmatic case, an expropriation accomplished by a cumulative series of regulatory acts or omissions over a prolonged period of time, none of which can necessarily be identified as the decisive event that deprived the foreign national of the value of its investment.'[24] They have further argued that creeping expropriation is a separate category capable of covering all losses of property. In their view, it creates a standard higher than customary law standard of expropriation.[25] Dolzer and Stevens argue that the third category is the broadest in scope and concerned only with the effect. Creeping expropriation allows relying solely on impairment of economic value, and thus conceptually is broader than expropriation as provided in international law or under liberal systems of domestic law.[26]

The view of the creation of a higher standard through the third type of expropriatory measures was taken in *Waste Management v Mexico*.[27] The Tribunal, however, clarified that the broad interpretation was an outcome of context rather than the text.[28] It defended its interpretation on the basis that the treaty language in NAFTA may be interpreted broadly considering its peculiar context, and further acknowledged that this may not be the case with other treaties.[29] The Tribunal was careful to clarify that the broad interpretation does not apply in relation to the exercise of regulatory takings (regulatory freedom).[30]

---

21. *Generation Ukraine, Inc. v Ukraine*, Award, ICSID Case No. ARB/00/9, 16 September 2003, para. 20.22.
22. Above note 5 (Sornarajah), 369.
23. Rudolph Dolzer, 'Indirect Expropriation of Alien Property' *ICSID Review-FILJ* 1 (1988): 41, 44.
24. W. Michael Reisman & Robert D. Sloane, 'Indirect Expropriation and Its Valuation in the BIT Generation' *BYIL* 74 (2003): 115, 128.
25. *Ibid.*
26. Rudolf Dolzer & Margarete Stevens, *Bilateral Investment Treaties* (Hague: Martinus Nijhoff Publishers, 1995), 102.
27. *Waste Management Inc. v United Mexican States*, Award, ICSID Case No. ARB(AF)/00/3, 30 April 2004, paras 143–145.
28. *Ibid.*
29. Article 1110 (8) of NAFTA stipulates that 'a measure of general application shall not be considered a measure tantamount to an expropriation of a debt security or loan covered by this Chapter solely on the ground that the measure imposes costs on the debtor that cause it to default on the debt'. The Tribunal read this clause in light of the expropriation clause in Art. 1110(1), containing the broad category of 'tantamount to expropriation' and held that the measures relating to debt security and loan only are excluded, thus other measures could be covered under the broad category since through para. (8), 'drafters entertained a broad view of what might be "tantamount to an expropriation"'; *ibid.*, para. 144.
30. *Ibid.*, para. 155.

In some cases under NAFTA, claimants argued that since there is a separate third category included it represents an additional ground separate from indirect expropriation, which is an easier standard to meet. However, the tribunals have rejected this argument observing that no additional grounds are created through the measures tantamount to expropriation.[31] For example, the Claimants in *Pope & Talbot v Canada* tried to expand the scope of 'tantamount to expropriation' by contending that this clause aimed at expanding the customary international law scope of expropriation and therefore to include any interference with property as was done by the Iran-United States Claims Tribunal.[32] The Tribunal rejected this argument and it did not broaden the scope of expropriation as laid down in customary international law.[33] Various versions stated in the third category are covered within indirect expropriation, since they restate the same principle. They do not extend the scope of expropriation to cover all losses of property.[34] Agreeing with the interpretation of *Pope & Talbot* that 'tantamount' does not expand the scope of expropriation, the Tribunal in *SD Myres v Canada* held that 'tantamount' embraces 'creeping' expropriation and does not expand the scope of expropriation as a concept and of 'tantamount' any further beyond the accepted position of international law.[35] The broad interpretation in *Metaclad v Mexico* was criticized by the Supreme Court of British Columbia when the enforcement of the award was challenged (although the finding was not set aside due to the limitations of review jurisdiction).[36] Rejecting the argument of expanding the meaning of expropriation through the broad interpretation of these categories, the Tribunal in *Marvin Feldman v Mexico* declared that all these categories are 'functionally equivalent'.[37] Furthermore, States have issued clarifications appended to BITs that different categories in expropriation clause do not create a standard of treatment higher than that in customary international law.[38]

31. Gary H Sampliner, 'Arbitration of Expropriation Cases under US Investment Treaties A Threat to Democracy or the Dog That Didn't Bark?' *ICSID Review-FILJ* 18 (2003): 1, 6; *Telenor Mobile Communications S.A. v The Republic of Hungary*, Award, ICSID Case No. ARB/04/15, 13 September 2006, para. 63.
32. *Pope & Talbot Inc. v The Government of Canada*, Interim Award, UNCITRAL, 26 June 2000, paras 83–84.
33. *Ibid.*, para. 92.
34. Above note 12 (*Techmed v Mexico*), para. 114.
35. *S.D. Myres, Inc. v Government of Canada*, Partial Award, 13 November 2000, para. 286.
36. *The United Mexican States v Metaclad Corporation* Reasons for the Judgment of the Honourable Mr Justice Tysoe, The Supreme Court of British Columbia, (2001) BCSC 664, para. 99. According to Tyose J: 'The Tribunal gave an extremely broad definition of expropriation for the purposes of Article 1110. In addition to the more conventional notion of expropriation involving a taking of property, the Tribunal held that expropriation under the NAFTA includes covert or incidental interference with the use of property which has the effect of depriving the owner, in whole or in significant part, of the use or reasonably-to-be-expected economic benefit of property. This definition is sufficiently broad to include a legitimate rezoning of property by a municipality or other zoning authority. However, the definition of expropriation is a question of law with which this Court is not entitled to interfere under the International CAA.'
37. *Marvin Feldman v Mexico*, Award, ICSID Case No. ARB (AF)/99/1, 16 December 2002, para. 100; Also *see Petrobart Limited v The Kyrgyz Republic*, Arbitration Institute of the Stockholm Chamber of Commerce, Award, 29 March 2005, p. 77.
38. Treaty Concerning the Encouragement and Reciprocal Protection of Investment (Bolivia-United States) (signed 17 April 1988, entered into force 6 June 2001) Art. III.1; Treaty Concerning the

Furthermore, as per the *ejusdem generis* rule of treaty interpretation, if a general or residual clause is preceded by special words then the general or residual clause is circumscribed by the genus.[39] Therefore, the third category shall be interpreted in light of the first category – nationalization and expropriation. For example, the German BITs after using the expression 'tantamount' further clarify that the measures tantamount shall be 'comparable' to the preceding categories of measures.[40]

The treaty language does not support an expansive interpretation whereby creeping expropriation and other kinds of expropriation included in the third category would include every deprivation of property. The differences in the various formulations in the third category are primarily textual.[41] Most of the tribunals have been careful not to expand the scope of the third type of expropriatory measures beyond indirect expropriation.[42] Further, expansionary interpretation of the third category is of little relevance in practice because there has not been a case where the measure was alleged to be tantamount to expropriation but not indirect expropriation.[43] It is also inconceivable that such a claim can arise.

Therefore, the third category does not expand the scope of expropriation provisions to include all losses of property, particularly when caused by measures undertaken as a part of regulatory freedom. The paradigm that continues to influence the scope of regulatory freedom is indirect expropriation since it represents the broadest categorization of expropriatory measures.

§3.02 TEXTUAL INTERPRETATION OF THE TYPES OF EXPROPRIATORY MEASURES

In addition to expressing the types of expropriatory measures, the text of NAFTA Article 1110 (1) comprises of two components: 'directly or indirectly nationalize or expropriate' and 'measure tantamount to nationalization or expropriation of such an investment ("expropriation")'. Both the components that encapsulate all the types of expropriatory measure focus on the characterization of the measure, i.e., the nature of

---

Encouragement and Reciprocal Protection of Investment (United States-Jordan) (signed 2 July 1997, entered into force 13 June 2003) Art. XII; Campbell McLachlan, Laurence Shore & Matthew Weiniger, *International Investment Arbitration: Substantive Principles* (Oxford: Oxford University Press, 2007), 276–280.

39. Robert Jennings & Arthur Watts, *Oppenheim's International Law*, vol. I (9th ed., Oxford: Oxford University Press, 2008), 1279–1280; Also *see* note 20 at 1280; Richard Gardiner, *Treaty Interpretation* (Oxford: Oxford University Press, 2010), 311–312; *Fourth report on the most-favoured-nation clause, by Mr Endre Ustor, Special Rapporteur Draft articles with commentaries*, UN Doc A/CN.4/266, 1973 (2) Yearbook of International Law Commission 98, 102–108.
40. Treaty Concerning the Reciprocal Encouragement and Protection of Investments (Germany-Jamaica) (signed 24 September 1992, entered into force 29 May 1996) Art. 4(2).
41. *S.D. Myers, Inc. v Government of Canada*, First Partial Award, UNCITRAL/NAFTA, 13 November 2000, para. 285. According to the Tribunal: 'The primary meaning of the word "tantamount" given by the Oxford English Dictionary is "equivalent". Both words require a tribunal to look at the substance of what has occurred and not only the form.'
42. Above note 31 (Sampliner), 6; Above note 32 (*Pope & Talbot v Canada*), paras 103–104; Above note 41 (S.D. Myers), paras 285–286.
43. Above note 17 (Salacuse), 300.

the measure. In either of the formulations, there is no reference to 'effect'. Thus, if one resorts to textual interpretation, an inquiry into allegations of indirect expropriation or measure tantamount to expropriation quintessentially has to be based on the analysis of the measure rather than the effect.

It would be appropriate to consider another example of Energy Charter Treaty (ECT). Article 13 (1) states that:

> Investments of Investors of a Contracting Party...shall not be nationalized, expropriated or subjected to a measure or measures having effect equivalent to nationalization or expropriation (hereinafter referred to as 'Expropriation').

Applying the two stage analysis used to describe the NAFTA expropriation clause, the first part remains the same: 'nationalized or expropriated'. Thus, the focus in the first part is in the nature of the measure. The second part however is slightly different because it adds an element of 'effect'. It states: 'measures or measure having effect equivalent to nationalization or expropriation'. Unlike the second part in NAFTA expropriation clause ECT expects that the effect of the measure shall be equivalent to that of nationalization or expropriation. This second part is open for two interpretations. First, since the effect of nationalization is loss of property, all losses or property shall amount to expropriation. Second, since the text states that the effect shall not only be loss but losses caused as a consequence of an expropriatory measure, an analysis of nature of measure is indispensable.[44] In other words, mere loss is insufficient to invoke the second part. Instead, loss has to be occasioned by a measure which is akin to expropriation – i.e., an expropriatory measure.

The express mention of 'expropriation' at the end of the description of the second part, in brackets, hints that the effect caused has to be caused by an expropriatory measure rather than any general effect on the property. The architecture of the text suggests that the distinction between losses caused due to expropriatory measures should be distinguished from the losses caused due to regulatory measures. This distinction of losses is important because compensation would be payable if losses are caused by an expropriatory measure and not payable if caused due to a regulatory measure. This practice is represented in the treaty practice of several States.[45]

Additionally, there is no indication in the text to the meaning of direct or indirect. Since they appear next to 'expropriate' and 'nationalize', the measure has to be

44. *See* Chapters 4 and 5 to see the role and consequences of effects on distinguishing regulatory freedom from indirect expropriation.
45. For example the BIT between the UK and Sierra Leone states: 'Investments of nationals or companies of either Contracting Party shall not be nationalized, expropriated or subject to measures having effect equivalent to nationalization or expropriation (hereinafter referred as "expropriation")....' Agreement for the Promotion and Protection of Investments (UK-Sierra Leone) (signed 13 January 2000, entered into force 20 November 2001) Art. 5. For exactly same or similar provisions *see* Agreement for the Promotion and Protection of the Investments (Canada-Costa Rica) (signed 18 March 1998, entered into force 29 September 1999) Art. VI; Agreement on the Promotion and Protection of Investments (Australia-Egypt) (5 September 2002) Art. 7; Agreement on the Promotion and Protection of Investments (Australia-Vietnam) (11 September 1991) Art. 7; Agreement for the Promotion and Protection of Investments (Singapore-Mongolia) (signed 24 July 1994, entered into force 14 January 1996) Art. 6; Agreement for the Promotion and Protection of Investments (Singapore-Vietnam) (signed 29

understood in connection with these verbs.[46] Therefore, direct and indirect have to be interpreted in light of meaning of expropriation and nationalization, cumulatively described as expropriatory measure. Hence, indirect and other categories of expropriation have to be an outcome of an expropriatory measure which requires an analysis of the nature of measure.

In situations where States intend expropriation to cover all losses of property, they have specifically said so. The BIT between Netherlands and Bosnia and Herzegovina, the emphasis is on any measure that deprives the foreigners of their property. The expropriation standard of the BIT states:

> Neither Contracting Party shall take any measures depriving nationals of the other Contracting Party of their investments or any measures having effect equivalent to nationalisation or expropriation...

This clause includes responsibility for two kinds of property deprivations: property deprivation caused due to 'any measure' and property deprivation due to expropriatory measure.[47]

Therefore, unless otherwise stated, whatever may be the comprehension of the expropriation clause the measure has to be expropriatory in nature. Effect by itself is insufficient to arrive at the conclusion of whether a measure amounts to expropriation.

§3.03 TRENDS IN RECENT TREATY PRACTICE

In the past, BITs rarely contained provisions on regulatory freedom. Few BITs contained specific mention of regulatory measures as exceptions from responsibility, such as tax measures,[48] measures for essential security and public order,[49] protection of health and natural resources,[50] cultural exceptions,[51] prudential measures for regulating financial services[52] and regulations controlling monopoly.[53] In some recent BITs regulatory freedom is visibly present within or alongside expropriation provisions

---

October 1992) Art. 6; Agreement for the Promotion and Protection of Investments (Czech Republic-Moldova) (signed 12 May 1999, entered into force 21 June 2000) Art. 110(1); Art. 5, Above note 2 (NAFTA).

46. Above note 38 (McLachlan, Shore and Weiniger), 271.
47. Agreement on Encouragement and Reciprocal Protection of Investments (Netherlands-Bosnia and Herzegovina) (signed 13 May 1998, entered into force 1 January 2002) Art. 6; Agreement for the Reciprocal Promotion and Protection of Investments) (France-Mexico) (signed 12 November 1998, entered into force 12 October 2000) Art. 5(1).
48. Treaty Concerning the Encouragement and Reciprocal Protection of Investment (Bolivia-United States) (signed 17 April 1988, entered into force 6 June 2001) Art. XII; Treaty Concerning the Encouragement and Reciprocal Protection of Investment (United States-Jordan) (signed 2 July 1997, entered into force 13 June 2003) Art. XII; UNCTAD, *Bilateral Investment Treaties 1995-2006: Trends in Investment Rule Making* (New York and Geneva: United Nations, 2007), 81–83.
49. *Ibid.*, (UNCTAD), 83–87.
50. *Ibid.*, 87–89.
51. *Ibid.*, 89–90.
52. *Ibid.*, 90–91. For a discussion on arbitral award, *see Fireman's Fund Insurance Company v The United Mexican States*, Award, ICSID Case No. ARB(AF)/02/01, 17 July 2006, paras 156–168.
53. Canada Model BIT, 2004 Art. 8.

and methods for distinguishing regulatory freedom and indirect expropriation have been set out. The prominent is the United State Model BIT of 2012, and its relevant portion is as under:

> The Parties confirm their shared understanding that:
>
> 1. Article 6 [Expropriation and Compensation] (1) is intended to reflect customary international law concerning the obligation of States with respect to expropriation.
> 2. An action or a series of actions by a Party cannot constitute an expropriation unless it interferes with a tangible or intangible property right or property interest in an investment.
> 3. Article 6 [Expropriation and Compensation] (1) addresses two situations. The first is direct expropriation, where an investment is nationalized or otherwise directly expropriated through formal transfer of title or outright seizure.
> 4. The second situation addressed by Article 6 [Expropriation and Compensation] (1) is indirect expropriation, where an action or series of actions by a Party has an effect equivalent to direct expropriation without formal transfer of title or outright seizure.
>   (a) The determination of whether an action or series of actions by a Party, in a specific fact situation, constitutes an indirect expropriation, requires a case-by- case, fact-based inquiry that considers, among other factors:
>   (i) the economic impact of the government action, although the fact that an action or series of actions by a Party has an adverse effect on the economic value of an investment, standing alone, does not establish that an indirect expropriation has occurred;
>   (ii) the extent to which the government action interferes with distinct, reasonable investment-backed expectations; and
>   (iii) the character of the government action.
>   (b) Except in rare circumstances, non-discriminatory regulatory actions by a Party that are designed and applied to protect legitimate public welfare objectives, such as public health, safety, and the environment, do not constitute indirect expropriations.[54]

Treaties entered into by United States thereafter have mostly followed this pattern.[55]

These treaties exclude liability for exercise of regulatory freedom and further lay down the criteria based on which such a determination is expected to be made by the arbitral tribunal. The grant of freedom to regulate without attracting responsibility is tailored by States in different languages. A slightly different pattern than the US Model BIT has been adopted by the Indian Model BIT of 2015. It is as follows:

> 5.3 The Parties confirm their shared understanding that: a) Expropriation may be direct or indirect:

54. US Model BIT, 2012, para. 2 Annex B. These criteria are based on the decision of the US Supreme Court *Penn Central Transportation Company v New York City*, (1978) 438 US 104; Kenneth Vandevelde, *Bilateral Investment Treaties: History, Policy and Interpretation* (New York: Oxford University Press, 2010), 280; Canada Model BIT, 2004, Annex B.13.
55. US-Australia FTA (signed 18 May 2004, entered into force 1 January 2005) Art. 11.7; US-Chile FTA (signed 6 June 2003, entered into force 1 January 2004) Annexure 10-A; Letter Annexed to the US-Singapore FTA, signed 6 May 2003, entered into force 1 January 2004; Canada-Peru FTA (signed on 29 May 2008, came into force on 1 August 2009) Annexure 812.1.

(i) direct expropriation occurs when an investment is nationalized or otherwise directly expropriated through formal transfer of title or outright seizure; and
(ii) indirect expropriation occurs if a measure or series of measures of a Party has an effect equivalent to direct expropriation, in that it substantially or permanently deprives the investor of the fundamental attributes of property in its investment, including the right to use, enjoy and dispose of its investment, without formal transfer of title or outright seizure.

b) The determination of whether a measure or a series of measures have an effect equivalent to expropriation requires a case-by-case, fact-based inquiry, that takes into consideration:

(i) the economic impact of the measure or series of measures, although the sole fact that a measure or series of measures of a Party has an adverse effect on the economic value of an investment does not establish that an indirect expropriation has occurred;
(ii) the duration of the measure or series of measures of a Party;
(iii) the character of the measure or series of measures, notably their object, context and intent; and
(iv) whether a measure by a Party breaches the Party's prior binding written commitment to the investor whether by contract, licence or other legal document.

5.4 For the avoidance of doubt, the Parties agree that an action taken by a Party in its commercial capacity shall not constitute expropriation or any other measure having similar effect.

5.5 Non-discriminatory regulatory measures by a Party or measures or awards by judicial bodies of a Party that are designed and applied to protect legitimate public interest or public purpose objectives such as public health, safety and the environment shall not constitute expropriation under this Article.

5.6 In considering an alleged breach of this Article, a Tribunal shall take account of whether the investor or, as appropriate, the locally-established enterprise, pursued action for remedies before domestic courts or tribunals prior to initiating a claim under this Treaty.

Some BITs create exceptions in favour of regulatory freedom through carve out provisions such as GATT Article XX.[56] It is not clear whether these provisions are declaratory of customary international law or change the purview of customary international law when incorporated in a BIT.[57]

§3.04 ARBITRAL JURISPRUDENCE

The discussion in the preceding section has shown that indirect expropriation sufficiently capture the broadest formulation of an expropriatory measure. Since direct expropriations are manifest and clear they do not conflict with a regulatory measure.

56. Indian Model BIT, 2015, Art. 5.5; India-Slovenia BIT (signed 14 June 2011) Protocol; India-Malaysia FTA (signed 18 February 2011) Annex 10; China-India BIT (signed 21 November 2006) Protocol; Canada-Slovakia BIT (signed 20 July 2010) Annex A.
57. For further discussion *see* Chapters 6 and 7.

Thus, any direct taking of property does not and cannot be characterized as an exercise of regulatory freedom. The second and the third types of expropriatory measures collectively represent indirect expropriation. It is tricky to distinguish between indirect expropriation and regulatory freedom. It would be appropriate to keep the focus of the discussion on the relationship between indirect expropriation and regulatory freedom in arbitral jurisprudence, which is discussed in this section.

[A] No Right to Regulate

There have been few instances of outright rejection of regulatory freedom by investment tribunals, but they nevertheless exist. In *Pope & Talbot v Canada,* the Tribunal opined that, 'a blanket exception for regulatory measures would create a gaping hole in international protection against expropriation.'[58] The Tribunal considered that the expropriation clause in NAFTA is peculiar and thus interpreted it broadly. The Tribunal also observed that the scope of the expropriation clause in NAFTA is broad enough to cover 'non-discriminatory regulation that might be said to fall within an exercise of a state's so-called police powers'.[59]

The often-quoted award by investment tribunals[60] to reject regulatory freedom or to treat it subsidiary to expropriation is from *Santa Elena v Costa Rica,* wherein the Tribunal observed:

> Expropriatory environmental measures—no matter how laudable and beneficial to society as a whole—are, in this respect, similar to any other expropriatory measures that a State may take in order to implement its policies: where property is expropriated, even for environmental purposes, whether domestic or international, the State's obligation to pay compensation remains.[61]

This paragraph has to be understood in its context. These observations were made in relation to the responsibility of a State to pay for compensation and not generally on regulatory freedom. This was a case of direct expropriation and the Tribunal was deciding on the responsibility of the host State to pay compensation for expropriation. It was an admitted fact that property was taken by the government and is reflected in the following paragraph from the award:

> While an expropriation or taking for environmental reasons may be classified as a taking for a public purpose, and thus may be legitimate, the fact that the Property was taken for this reason does not affect either the nature or the measure of the compensation to be paid for the taking. That is, the purpose of protecting the environment for which the Property was taken does not alter the legal character of

58. Above note 32 (*Pope & Talbot v Canada*), para. 99. The Tribunal based these observations on the Third American Restatement on Foreign Relations Law in footnote 72, where it wrongly stated that the Third American Restatement considered the effect of the measure to be the sole criteria.
59. *Ibid.*, para. 96.
60. Tribunals relying on this award: Above note 12 (*Techmed v Mexico*), para. 121; *Compañiá de Aguas del Aconquija S.A. and Vivendi Universal S.A. v Argentine Republic*, Award, ICSID Case No. ARB/97/3, para. 7.5.15.
61. *Compañía del Desarrollo de Santa Elena, S.A. v The Republic of Costa Rica*, Award, ICSID Case No. ARB/96/1, 17 February 2000, para. 72.

> the taking for which adequate compensation must be paid. The international source of the obligation to protect the environment makes no difference.[62]

The Tribunal never had occasion to comment on regulatory freedom because it was 'a case of expropriation in which the only issue before the Tribunal [was] the amount of compensation' payable for direct expropriation.[63] The Tribunal was conscious that it only had to decide the amount of compensation for an 'expropriatory measure' and the Tribunal specifically used the words 'expropriatory measure'.[64]

Therefore, there are two awards where regulatory freedom was rejected. The first is clear, whereas the second has been misunderstood to have rejected regulatory freedom. In majority of cases, investment tribunals have acknowledged the presence of regulatory freedom but then subjected it to the sole effects doctrine. The following discussion is focused on this stream of decisions.

[B] The Sole Effects Doctrine

In the awards in this this group, the tribunals have applied the 'sole effects doctrine' to see whether the standard of expropriation was breached.[65] The sole effects doctrine has been used to distinguish a regulatory freedom (regulatory measure) from indirect expropriation (expropriatory measure). In some cases in this group, tribunals have declined to recognize regulatory freedom, like the cases in the first category.

According to the tribunals relying on the sole effects doctrine, a regulatory measure, whether justified under international law or not, becomes indirect expropriation depending on the degree of interference with the property rights of the investor.[66] The degree of interference with the right of property is the only criterion for determining if indirect expropriation has taken place. Except for the impact on the property, no other factor is relevant for determining indirect expropriation. The nature of the measure and the circumstances in which the Government adopted a measure or the intention for the measure are irrelevant. Since 'effect' on the investment is the sole criterion, the doctrine is called the 'sole effects doctrine'.[67]

The first Tribunal to apply the sole effects doctrine was *Metaclad v Mexico* wherein it stated that a State is responsible for expropriation for 'covert or incidental interference with the use of property which has the effect of depriving the owner, in whole or in significant part, of the use or reasonably-to-be-expected economic benefit

62. *Ibid.*, para. 71.
63. *Ibid.*, para. 54.
64. *Ibid.*, paras 17, 19, 20, 23, 54, 67, 73, 74. It is therefore that in para. 72 the Tribunal refers to the measure, the consequences of which it had to decide, as 'expropriatory measures'.
65. *See* Chapter 4 for a detailed discussion on the sole effects doctrine.
66. *Nykomb Synergetics Technology Holding AB, Stockholm v The Republic of Latvia*, Award, The Arbitration Institute of Stockholm Chamber of Commerce, 16 December 2003, para. 4.3.1; Above note 70 (*BG Group case*), para. 268.
67. Rudolph Dolzer & Christoph Schreuer, *Principles of International Investment Law* (2nd ed., Oxford: Oxford University Press, 2012), 112–115.

of property even if not necessarily to the obvious benefit of the host State'.[68] The Tribunal even addressed a question hypothetically (even when it was not involved in the dispute) and declared that even a regulation for environment protection would be invalid.[69] These observations of the Tribunal were later found by the court enforcing the award (by the Supreme Court of British Columbia) to be 'extremely broad'.[70]

The Tribunal in *Techmed v Mexico* adopted the sole effects doctrine by taking the view that while deciding cases of indirect expropriation a tribunal has to find if the investor was 'radically deprived of the economical use and enjoyment of its investments'. According to the Tribunal, this question is important since depending on this single criterion, a regulatory measure can be distinguished from an expropriatory measure.[71] The Tribunal based its observations on three grounds: customary international law, principles of treaty interpretation and proportionality analysis developed by the European Court of Human Rights.

First, regarding customary international law, the Tribunal, based on the decisions of the Iran-United States Claims Tribunal and European Court of Human Rights declared that the determination of the existence of indirect expropriation and its delineation from regulatory freedom is done only on the basis of the sole effects doctrine. According to the Tribunal, the decisions have advanced customary international law and are a source of international law under Article 38 of the ICJ Statute.[72] No other tribunal has gone to the extent of claiming that the sole effects doctrine has become customary international law. Even scholars, who have traditionally supported the sole effects doctrine have not supported such a claim.[73]

Second, based on the principles of treaty interpretation under Article 31 (1) of the VCLT, the Tribunal claimed that the language of the expropriation clause does not exempt a regulatory measure covered under the police powers doctrine from responsibility. In the words of Tribunal: 'we find no principle stating that regulatory administrative actions are *per se* excluded from the scope of the Agreement, even if

68. *Metaclad Corporation v The United Mexican States*, Award, ICSID Case No. ARB(AF)/97/1, 30 August 2000, para. 103. Also *see* paras 104–107. The Tribunal only incidentally relied on *Biloune v Ghana Investment Centre* to draw an analogy that a stop work order amounts to indirect expropriation in para. 108. The analogy is superficial and unsustainable. In *Biloune* the facts were serious, the foreign investor was taken into arrest and detained without following due process and deported. The investor was denied access to his investments as well and the Government ensured that the investment is destroyed. The Government played an active role in destruction of foreign investor's property. *Antoine Biloune, Marine Drive Complex Ltd. v Ghana Investments Centre, the Government of Ghana*, Awards, 27 October 1989, (1994) XIX Yearbook Commercial Arbitration 11, 19–20. Unlike in *Methanex*, where the question related to denial of permission for construction of an environmentally hazardous landfill and a regulation made to that effect.
69. *Ibid*., (*Metaclad v Mexico*), para. 109.
70. Above note 36 (*Mexico v Metaclad*), para. 99.
71. Above note 12 (*Techmed v Mexico*), para. 115; Also above note 66 (*Nykonb Synergetics v Latvia*), para. 4.3.2.
72. *Ibid*., 12 (*Techmed v Mexico*), para. 116.
73. Dolzer states sole effects doctrine to be 'dominant thinking' in arbitral awards, but adds a caveat that there is a line of awards which emphasizes on the context and purpose of the measure in question. Rudolph Dolzer, 'Indirect Expropriations: New Developments?' *NYU Environmental Law Journal* 11 (2002): 64, 90–92.

they are beneficial to society as a whole – such as environment protection – particularly if the negative economic impact' is caused to the foreign investor.[74] In other words, if the treaty intended to protect regulatory measures, it would have specifically stated so. These findings are supported with a reference to the paragraph from *Santa Elena v Costa Rica* discussed above and a mere reference to Article 31 (1) of VCLT. There is no discussion as to which tool of interpretation was relevant and used to arrive at the conclusion.

The Tribunal rejected existence of doctrine of police powers in international law. According to the Tribunal, such a right exists only in domestic law and protection of police powers doctrine can be decided only under domestic law before courts of the concerned State.[75] Rejecting the relevance of police powers before an international tribunal, the Tribunal stated that, 'their impact cannot be assessed by an international tribunal making a decision based on international law and determinations based on municipal cannot be a justification for non-compliance with obligations under international law'.[76] The Tribunal relegated the police powers doctrine from the level of international law[77] to domestic law and rejected its relevance for international law altogether.

Third, although the Tribunal rejected the role of regulatory freedom in international law, it relied on proportionality analysis based on the decisions of the European Court of Human Rights (ECtHR). According to the Tribunal, since regulatory exercises are not excluded from the scope of expropriation clause, whether they amount to expropriation or not shall be decided based on proportionality analysis. It further observed that the question whether the measure is proportional for protection of public interest is to be decided based on the significance of the impact on the foreign investor.[78] The consequence of the proportionality analysis was looking at the impact on the property of the foreign investor – a variation of the sole effects doctrine. According to the Tribunal, there shall be reasonable relationship of proportionality between the burden on the foreign investor and the public interest sought to be achieved through the expropriatory measure.[79] The Tribunal never reflected upon the reasons for using proportionality analysis from the jurisprudence of the ECtHR despite differences in the treaty – particularly expropriation and the different context of the European Convention of Human Rights.[80] In sum, according to the Tribunal the intention of the government is less important than the effect of the measure on the investors.[81]

74. Above note 12 (*Techmed v Mexico*), para. 121.
75. *Ibid.*, para. 119.
76. *Ibid.*, para. 120. Further the Tribunal through footnotes 137–138 in the award relied on principles of State responsibility to support the position that municipal law is no defence for non-compliance with international obligations.
77. *See* Chapters 2 and 6 for the position of regulatory freedom (police powers) at the level of international law.
78. *Ibid.*, para. 122. (footnotes omitted).
79. *Ibid.*
80. The problems with proportionality analysis are discussed in detail in Chapter 8.
81. Above note 12 (*Techmed v Mexico*), para. 116 (footnotes omitted).

In *El Passo v Argentina*, the Tribunal exhaustively discussed the jurisprudence on regulatory freedom and the impact of indirect expropriation. The Tribunal firstly stated its position that regulatory freedom does not have any place in view of indirect expropriation and subscribed to the view in *Techmed v Mexico*.[82] It even agreed with the view of *Pope & Talbot v Canada* that recognizing regulatory freedom will create a gaping hole in the protection of foreign investors.[83] It then discussed the awards recognizing regulatory freedom, whereby the States may affect property but yet not be responsible for the losses caused.[84] Then, after alluding to customary international law, it concluded that a State has a right to regulate, in the following words:

> In sum, a general regulation is a lawful act rather than an expropriation if it is non-discriminatory, made for a public purpose and taken in conformity with due process. In other words, *in principle, general non-discriminatory regulatory measures, adopted in accordance with the rules of good faith and due process, do not entail a duty of compensation*.[85]

After agreeing that regulatory freedom exists, the Tribunal further stated that regulatory exercises have to be reasonable. It invoked proportionality to decide reasonableness of the measure.[86] The Tribunal adopted the proportionality test from *Techmed v Mexico* to distinguish a regulatory measure from an expropriatory measure and described a disproportionate regulation to mean 'a regulation in which the interference with the private rights of the investors is disproportionate to the public interest'.[87] According to the Tribunal, the real criterion to distinguish between a regulatory measure and indirect expropriation is neutralization – whereby, essential component of property right must have disappeared.[88] Neutralization falls within the sole effects doctrine and the Tribunal never undertook a review of the measure to see if it was a genuine regulatory measure but only looked at the extent of interference the measure caused to find responsibility.[89]

The Tribunal in *Telenor v Hungary* recognized the right of States to regulate and declared that regulatory powers by themselves do not constitute expropriation. An investor must always be aware that there are risks involved while investing in a foreign country and an investor shall be willing to bear losses.[90] While deciding the test to be applied by the Tribunal, it relied on the sole effects doctrine, as applied in the cases

82. *El Paso Energy International Company v The Argentine Republic*, Award, ICSID Case No. ARB/03/15, 31 October 2011, para. 234. The Tribunal said: 'No absolute position can be taken in such delicate matters, where contradictory interests have to be reconciled. In this sense, the Tribunal subscribes to the decisions which have refused to hold that a general regulation issued by a State and interfering with the rights of foreign investors can never be considered expropriatory because it should be analysed as an exercise of the State's sovereign power or of its police powers.' It said that an absolute position to this situation cannot be taken, in a way ushering the path of proportionality, adhered in later paragraphs.
83. *Ibid.*, para. 235.
84. *Ibid.*, paras 237–239.
85. *Ibid.*, para. 240.
86. *Ibid.*, para. 241.
87. *Ibid.*, para. 243.
88. *Ibid.*, paras 244–256.
89. *Ibid.*, paras 265–280.
90. Above note 31 (*Telenor v Hungary*), para. 64.

decided by the Iran-United States Claims Tribunal, whereby the 'magnitude of the interference with the investor's property or economic rights' is the determinative factor for determining if expropriation exists.[91] The Tribunal noted that there exists a controversy as to whether the objective of the government in introducing the measure is to be given consideration or the sole-effects doctrine to be applied. But it did not comment on the appropriateness of either of the views on the ground that deprivation was in any way not serious and thus the Tribunal need not enter the controversy.[92] What seems to weigh with the Tribunal is that neutralization of investment is a threshold requirement and the question of the nature of measure may or may not be entertained. Therefore, the sole effects doctrine is the dominant point of view in the current arbitral jurisprudence.[93] In investment arbitration jurisprudence, the analysis of the nature of the measure is under-developed, since the tribunals that base the findings on the rejection of the right to regulate or the sole-effects doctrine do not venture into this discussion.

The Tribunal in *Pope & Talbot v Canada* interpreted expropriation in light of state practice, treaties and judicial interpretation in international law to carry 'the connotation of "taking" by a government-type authority of a person's "property" with a view to transfer ownership of that property to another person, that exercised its *de jure or de facto* power to do the "taking".'[94] It recognized the right of State to regulate but then conscribed its analysis to the sole effects doctrine. The Tribunal used a rather mechanical formula – interference to a lesser degree is regulation and interference to a greater degree is expropriation.[95] The formula is simple but does not account for the nuances of the relationship and distinction between regulatory freedom and indirect expropriation. Based on these awards, scholars claim that the sole effects doctrine is the dominant thinking in arbitral jurisprudence.[96]

91. *Ibid.*, paras 65–66, 69–70.
92. *Ibid.*, para. 70.
93. *Sempra Energy International v The Argentine Republic*, Award, ICSID Case No. ARB/02/16, 28 September 2007, para. 286. The Tribunal held that: 'A finding of indirect expropriation would require more than adverse effects. It would require that the investor no longer be in control of its business operations, or that the value of the business have been virtually annihilated. This is not the case in the present dispute.'; Above note 66 (*Nykonb Synergetics v Latvia*), para. 4.3.1; Above note 52 (*Fireman's Fund v Mexico*), para. 176 (f); Above note 60 (*Vivendi v Argentina*), paras 7.5.12–7.5.17.
94. Above note 35 (*S.D. Myres v Canada*), para. 280.
95. *Ibid.*, paras 282–283. The Separate Opinion of Dr Bryan Schwartz accepts this position in para. 211, however, later it is stated that some measures would not be covered within this realm for determining responsibility in para. 207: 'There may be some cases where a measure that is presented as a regulation must, in law and justice, be treated as a nationalization or expropriation for the purposes of Article 1110. That said, I can also state that in the vast run of cases, regulatory conduct by public authorities is not remotely the subject of legitimate complaints under Article 1110.'
96. Above note 73 (Dolzer), 90–92; Anne K Hoffmann, 'Indirect Expropriation' in August Reinisch (ed.) *Standards of Investment Protection* (Oxford: Oxford University Press, 2008), 158-159.

[C] Regulatory Freedom Exists

The third group of awards recognizes regulatory freedom as a customary international law right and a State is not responsible, irrespective of the economic effect on the investor and the investment. Despite the recognition of regulatory freedom the reasoning of arbitral tribunals and the consequential relationship with indirect expropriation differs.

In *Marvin Feldman v Mexico*, the foreign investor challenged the tax measure which declined tax rebate granted to cigarette exported by the foreign investor.[97] The Tribunal rejected the claim of creeping and indirect expropriation by analysing the nature of the measure since the crucial task is to distinguish between a governmental action constituting an expropriation or nationalization on the one hand and a valid governmental activity on the other. If the measure is not expropriatory, then the criteria of valid expropriation: public purpose, non-discriminatory, compensation and due process are not of any assistance.[98] Therefore, the justifiability of a measure would depend on the nature of the measure and conditions for valid expropriation are irrelevant. The Tribunal referred to the Third American Restatement and concluded that for resolving the dichotomy of expropriation and regulation, it shall be seen whether the measure is discriminatory or arbitrary.[99] The Tribunal acknowledged that measures may be adopted by States to deprive foreign investors of their property, but legitimate regulatory measures in public interest shall not be so categorized. In the words of the Tribunal:

> The Tribunal notes that the ways in which governmental authorities may force a company out of business, or significantly reduce the economic benefits of its business, are many. In the past, confiscatory taxation, denial of access to infrastructure or necessary raw materials, imposition of unreasonable regulatory regimes, among others, have been considered to be expropriatory actions. At the same time, governments must be free to act in the broader public interest through protection of the environment, new or modified tax regimes, the granting or withdrawal of government subsidies, reductions or increases in tariff levels, imposition of zoning restrictions and the like. Reasonable governmental regulation of this type cannot be achieved if any business that is adversely affected may seek compensation, and it is safe to say that customary international law recognizes this.[100]

Based on the American Restatement, the Tribunal concluded that a State would not attract responsibility for loss of property or other economic disadvantages resulting from bona fide general regulation since such actions are exempted under the police powers of the State.[101] In customary international law, the police powers doctrine gives a broad leeway to States for changing the policy and regulations (tax regulation in that case), 'even if their effect is to make it impractical for certain business activities to

97. Above note 37 (*Marvin Feldman v Mexico*), para. 1.
98. *Ibid.*, para. 98.
99. *Ibid.*, para. 99.
100. *Ibid.*, para. 103.
101. *Ibid.*, paras 105–106.

continue'.[102] The Tribunal looked exclusively at the nature of the measure and the contents of the measure and thereafter concluded that the measures were legitimate regulatory exercise since police powers is unaffected by expropriation clause in an investment treaty.[103] Besides, the Tribunal disregarded the exclusive influence of loss of property for a finding of expropriation.[104]

The Tribunal in *Saluka v Czech Republic* was mindful of absence of a specific protection of regulatory power in the expropriation clause and the BIT generally, but it was still relevant due to its nature as customary international law.[105] It thus stood incorporated into the expropriation clause.[106] Commenting on the presence of regulatory freedom in contemporary international law, the Tribunal held that:

> It is now established in international law that States are not liable to pay compensation to a foreign investor when, in the normal exercise of their regulatory powers, they adopt in a non-discriminatory manner bona fide regulations that are aimed at the general welfare.[107]

Applying these principles to the facts of the case, the Tribunal concluded that the State is not responsible even if 'the measure had the effect of eviscerating' the investment[108]- a positive rejection of the sole-effects doctrine. However, the Tribunal was concerned that 'a bright and distinguishable line' between non-compensable regulations and indirect expropriation measures which are compensable are yet to be drawn.[109]

Likewise, in *Link-Trading v Moldova*, the Claimant challenged the revocation of exemption from import duties and value added taxes on imported products into certain areas.[110] The ground of challenge was that the government made a promise through tax regulations, not to change the legal regime for ten years and did not adhere to that promise.[111] The Tribunal succinctly stated that a fiscal measure might become expropriatory if it is an 'abusive taking'. It elaborated that an '[a]buse arises where it is demonstrated that the State has acted unfairly or inequitably towards the investment, where it has adopted measures that are arbitrary or discriminatory in character or in their manner of implementation, or where the measure taken violate an obligation undertaken by the State in regard to the investment'.[112] The Tribunal focused on the nature of the measure and stated that it was necessary to establish that the measure is

102. *Ibid.*, para. 116; Similar conclusion was arrived at by the Permanent Court of International Justice in the Oscar Chinn Case. Discussed in detail in Chapter 4.
103. *Ibid.*, paras 128–130.
104. *Ibid.*, paras 109–117.
105. *Saluka Investments BV (The Netherlands) v The Czech Republic*, Partial Award, Permanent Court of Arbitration, 17 March 2006, paras 256–261.
106. *Ibid.*, para. 262, citing *Methanex* with approval. The Tribunal however did not elaborate the reasons for this conclusion, possibility with judicial economy in mind.
107. *Ibid.*, para. 255.
108. *Ibid.*, para. 276.
109. *Ibid.*, para. 263.
110. *Link-Trading Joint Stock Company v Department for Customs Control of Moldova*, Final Award, 18 April 2002, para. 3.
111. *Ibid.*, paras 30, 33, 38.
112. *Ibid.*, para. 64.

abusive. The Tribunal found that the measure was uniformly applied to everyone without discrimination.[113] Therefore, regulation under challenge is covered by the right of State to regulate under customary law.[114] The change in tax regulations is an ordinary event occurring in every State and it is a measure of 'general application' and not directed specifically against the investor.[115]

A measure may become expropriatory, even if it is not arbitrary or discriminatory if a State has undertaken specific obligation towards a particular investor or a class of investors.[116] Addressing the question of an undertaking not to alter the regulatory regime, the Tribunal held that the so-called undertaking, if at all it existed, was based on a regulation which drew its powers from the budget law. There was nothing in the budget law that would show a promise not to change exemption clauses and the exemption was 'subject to legislative review and possible modification each year in the context of the annual budget'.[117]

In *Methanex v USA*, the measure in question was investigated under the general clause of tantamount to expropriation and whether a regulatory measure imposing a ban on the sale and use of the gasoline additive called 'MTBE' by the State of California was a valid exercise of regulatory powers.[118] In its analysis, the Tribunal did refer to the impact of the measure on the investor but instead accepted the investor's argument that an intentionally discriminatory regulation amounts to expropriation. It further added that 'as a matter of general international law, a non-discriminatory regulation for public purpose, which is enacted in accordance with due process and, which affects, *inter alia*, a foreign investor or investment is not deemed expropriatory and compensable unless specific commitments have been given by the regulating government to the then putative foreign investor contemplating investment that the government would refrain from such regulation'.[119] The State of California had not made any specific commitments to that effect, and while entering the market and actively participating in it, the investor was aware of the regulatory structure and process.[120] The criteria on which the regulation was declared as genuine and justifiable were public purpose, non-discriminatory, accompanied with due process.[121]

In *EnCana Corporation v Ecuador*, the alleged expropriatory measure was a tax measure which allowed refund in certain situations.[122] As a matter of general principle, like other activities, investments are subject to taxation which result into certain degree of reduction in economic benefits and in the 'absence of any specific commitment from the host State, the foreign investor has neither the right nor any legitimate expectation

113. *Ibid.*, para. 71.
114. *Ibid.*, para. 68.
115. *Ibid.*, paras 69, 72.
116. *Ibid.*, para. 73.
117. *Ibid.*, para. 83.
118. *Methanex Corporation v United States of America*, Final Award of the Tribunal on Jurisdiction and Merits, 3 August 2005, Part IV-Chapter D, para. 6.
119. *Ibid.*, para. 7.
120. *Ibid.*, para. 10.
121. *Ibid.*, para. 15.
122. *EnCana Corporation v Republic of Ecuador*, Award, UNCITRAL Rules, 3 February 2006, para. 23.

that the tax regime will not change, perhaps to its disadvantage, during the period of investment'.[123]

The Tribunal distinguished observations in *Metaclad v Mexico* that even incidental interference with reasonable-to-be expected benefits would amount to indirect expropriation, on the ground that the current case involved a taxation measure.[124] Basing its conclusions on the nature of the measure, the Tribunal observed that the taxation law in itself cannot constitute taking of property, because '[f]rom the perspective of expropriation taxation is in a special category. In principle a tax law creates a new legal liability on a class of persons to pay money to the State in respect of some defined class of transactions, the money to be used for public purpose'.[125] A State could attract responsibility for a tax measure, '[o]nly if a tax law is extraordinary, punitive in amount or arbitrary'.[126] The Tribunal distinguished between responsibility of a State for non-payment under contractual clauses versus non-payment under a statute, and tax refund in particular, because only States can enter into a conduct of later category. Therefore, the substance of the governmental action is to be seen, rather than the form.[127] Emphasizing the regulatory freedom of States, the Tribunal made an important statement of law:

> In terms of the BIT the executive is entitled to take a position in relation to claims put forward by individuals, even if that position may turn out to be wrong in law, provided it does so in good faith and stands ready to defend its position before the courts. Like private parties, governments do not repudiate obligations merely by contesting their existence. An executive agency does not expropriate the value represented by a statutory obligation to make a payment or refund by mere refusal to pay, provided at least that (a) the refusal is not merely willful, (b) the courts are open to the aggrieved private party, (c) the courts' decisions are not themselves overridden or repudiated by the State.[128]

Not only the tax authorities, but the executive in general have the complete discretion in deciding suitable policy and it is not reviewable under the BIT, unless it effectively repudiates legal rights.[129]

While upholding a general regulatory measure, the tribunals in *Chemutra v Canada* and *Suez v t*he tribunals firstly inquired whether there was neutralization, as a threshold test satisfying indirect expropriation. Thereafter they looked at the nature of the measure to see if it was a legitimate regulatory exercise. Other tribunals adhering to the sole effects doctrine stopped at the stage of neutralization, whereas these tribunals went further to look at the nature of the measure. In both the cases, the measures were found to be genuine regulatory measure having general application and the host States were not found responsible for their adoption. In *Chemtura v Canada*, the Tribunal firstly assessed whether the degree of interference caused by the alleged

123. *Ibid.*, para. 173. (footnote omitted).
124. *Ibid.*, para. 177.
125. *Ibid.*
126. *Ibid.*
127. *Ibid.*, para. 193.
128. *Ibid.*, para. 194.
129. *Ibid.*, para. 195.

measure was of a substantial degree to satisfy the threshold requirement of neutralization for expropriation to exist.[130] Thereafter, it held that the measure was justified, including for the consequences of contractual deprivation since the measure was a valid exercise of police powers. The measure in question was non-discriminatory, 'motivated by the increasing awareness of the dangers presented....for human health and environment'.[131] It can be deducted from the Tribunal's reasoning, in spite of alleged contractual commitments to the contrary, a State would not be responsible for expropriation as long as the measure is a regulatory exercise. But the Tribunal did not elaborate on the elements of regulatory freedom (police powers) or its existence unaffected by expropriation provisions in the BIT.

In *Suez v Argentina,* the Tribunal separated the impugned regulatory measure of general application from other alleged breaches of investment treaty and upheld the regulatory exercise by the State. Indeed, effect on the investor is an important ingredient for establishing expropriation.[132] The alleged governmental measure should have resulted in a substantial degree of deprivation, without formal transfer of title, effectively resulting into neutralization.[133] But, the 'fact that the effect of such measures may have diminished the value of an investment does not in and of itself constitute an indirect expropriation'.[134] In claims of expropriation, 'it is important to recognize a State's legitimate right to regulate and to exercise its police power in the interests of public welfare and not to confuse measures of that nature with expropriation'.[135] Applying these principles to the facts of the case, the Tribunal found that the general regulatory measures adopted by the host State were with the intention of tackling the financial crisis and the actions of the State were perfectly justifiable within its regulatory powers, for which no responsibility can be imposed for the breach of expropriation standard.[136]

In the recent case of *Philip Morris v Uruguay,* the Tribunal explicitly recognized regulatory freedom as a right extant and unaffected by indirect expropriation standard contained in the BIT. The Tribunal upheld two laws of tobacco control, the fist limiting to single cigarette in a single brand and 80% health warning on the cigarette packets. The Tribunal noted that the first stage in determination of existence of indirect expropriation is whether there is substantial deprivation of the investment.[137] It noted

---

130. *Chemtura Corporation v Government of Canada*, Award, UNCITRAL Rules, 2 August 2010, paras 259-265.
131. *Ibid.*, para. 266. This approach differs greatly from the approach of the tribunals using the test of neutralization to determine existence of expropriation, as a part of the sole effects doctrine. Those tribunals have would stop at the stage of neutralization. Once neutralization is found, indirect expropriation would be implicitly present. But the Tribunal in *Chemtura v Canada*, first saw whether there was neutralization and then saw if the measure was justified as an exercise of police powers.
132. Above note 13 (*Suez Sociedad v Argentine Republic*), para. 133.
133. *Ibid.*, para. 134.
134. *Ibid.*, para. 137.
135. *Ibid.*, para. 139.
136. *Ibid.*, para. 140.
137. *Philip Morris Brands Sàrl, Philip Morris Products S.A. and Abal Hermanos S.A. v Oriental Republic of Uruguay (formerly FTR Holding SA, Philip Morris Products S.A. and Abal Hermanos S.A. v Oriental Republic of Uruguay)*, Award, ICSID Case No. ARB/10/7, 8 July 2016, para. 192.

that since substantial deprivation was not proved, indirect expropriation was not established.[138] The Tribunal viewed that in addition to the fact that the losses had not reached the threshold of indirect expropriation, the measures could be justified as regulatory measure.[139] This was a point where the Tribunal in *Telenor v Hungary* stopped and declined to comment on the character of the regulatory measure. Also, the Tribunal in *Cemtura v Canada* stopped at making a mere reference to regulatory freedom. But the Tribunal in *Philip Morris v Uruguay* went a step further and commented on the scope of regulatory freedom. It found that regulatory freedom continues to exist as a customary law norm and has to be taken into account as per the requirements of systematic interpretation contained in Article 31 (3) (c).[140] After tracing the background material that constitutes it as a customary law norm, the Tribunal concluded that the measures under challenge were regulatory for which no compensation was payable.[141]

§3.05 CONCLUSIONS

Some tribunals in the second category (the sole effects doctrine) and the third category (regulatory freedom exists) have recognized regulatory freedom. However, there is a fundamental difference in their approach, which impacts on the scope and operation of regulatory freedom. The third category has focused on the nature of the measure, whereas the second category has focused exclusively on the effect of the measure and disregarded the role of the nature of the measure. The effect of which is that once it is established that the investor has suffered loss that meets a certain threshold, the State is responsible to pay compensation. The nature or circumstances for adoption of the measure become irrelevant. Even in arbitration awards where a State has not been found responsible for indirect expropriation, the basis of the decision has been that the extent of interference does not meet the threshold necessary for indirect expropriation.[142] It would be in the realm of speculation, whether the tribunals would have looked at the nature of the measure if the interference had risen to the level of complete destruction of property. The tribunals taking this approach ignored the means that have caused the loss - i.e., whether the loss was caused by a regulatory measure or an expropriatory measure and instead focused exclusively on the outcome, i.e., the loss of property. In theory, the tribunals following the sole effects doctrine have acknowledged regulatory freedom, but by applying the sole effects doctrine, they have made

138. *Ibid.*, paras 283-284.
139. *Ibid.*, para. 287.
140. *Ibid.*, para. 290.
141. *Ibid.*, paras 292-307.
142. *See Occidental Exploration and Production Company v The Republic of Ecuador*, Final Award, UNCITRAL Arbitration Rules (London Court of International Arbitration Administered Case No. UN 3467), 1 July 2004, paras 85-92; *LG & E Energy Corp., LG & E Capital Corp., LG & E International Inc. v The Argentine Republic*, Decision on Liability, ICSID Case No. ARB/02/1, 3 October 2006, para. 188; *CMS Gas Transmission Company v The Argentine Republic*, Award, ICSID Case No. ARB/01/8, 12 May 2005, paras 262-264.

regulatory freedom redundant in practice. Therefore, the awards in the second category functionally fall in the first category of the rejection of regulatory freedom.

The foregoing discussion represents that the third category of awards has upheld regulatory freedom of States and granted it distinct treatment. The timeline of the awards suggests that tribunals in recent times are more concerned towards conserving regulatory space, unlike prior awards, which were disposed to narrow the scope of regulatory freedom.[143] In a regime where *stare decisis* is inapplicable, general conclusions are difficult to make, the preponderance in reasoning of later tribunals may be tending towards protection of regulatory freedom. Although the second category, at times conceding and at times denying such a right, have stressed the preponderance of the sole effects doctrine.

143. It is certainly implausible to suggest that the subsequent tribunals will follow the modern trend of investment tribunals in accommodating regulatory freedom due to absence of formal precedent and non-application of *stare decisis*. However, their role cannot be ignored. *See* generally Gabrielle Kauffman-Kohler, 'Arbitral Precedent: Dream, Necessity or Excuse?: The 2006 Freshfields Lecture' *Arbitration International* 23(3) (2007): 357. Tribunals in future may decline to accommodate the right to regulate, but that will be an aberration to the emerging trend.

CHAPTER 4
The 'Sole Effects Doctrine' and the 'Nature of the Measure'

The discussion in the previous chapter has shown that the sole effects doctrine is the prominent method employed in distinguishing indirect expropriation and regulatory freedom. Few tribunals have applied the competing doctrine, the nature of the measure to see whether a measure is expropriatory or regulatory. This chapter focuses on the genesis of the two competing doctrines: sole effects and the nature of the measure, with particular attention on the jurisprudence of international courts and tribunals prior to investment arbitration jurisprudence.

§4.01 GENESIS OF THE SOLE EFFECTS DOCTRINE

Investment tribunals cite the decisions of the Iran-US Claims Tribunal as an authority for the sole effects doctrine. The Iran-US Claims Tribunal was the first judicial body to use the sole effects doctrine extensively in its jurisprudence. The sole effects doctrine was expounded in its early cases based on a famous article by Christie called 'What Constitutes a Taking of Property under International Law' published in the *British Yearbook of International Law* in 1962. Christie was the first person to propound the sole effects doctrine based on his interpretation of two important cases: the *Norwegian Shipowner's* case and the *Certain German Interests in Polish Upper Silesia* case.

[A] Christie's Claim of the Sole Effects Doctrine

Based on the *Norwegian Shipowner's* case and the *Certain German Interests in Polish Upper Silesia* cases, Christie made two claims: first, the effect of the measure is the only criterion for determining the expropriatory nature of a measure. In other words, once there is a loss of property then the inevitable conclusion is that the property has been expropriated. Second, the nature of the measure, i.e., the intention or the reasons for the adoption of the measure are irrelevant. It has no role in the determination of expropriation. Both these propositions are expressed in the following extract from Christie's article (often cited in the literature in the field of international investment law with approval):[1]

> The *Norwegian Claims* and the *German Interests in Polish Upper Silesia* cases show that a State may expropriate property, where it interferes with it, even though the State expressly disclaims any such intention. More important, the two cases taken together illustrate that even though a State may not purport to interfere with rights to property, it may, by its actions, render those rights so useless that it will be deemed to have expropriated them.[2]

Some scholars have cemented the position of the sole effects doctrine by claiming that: '[s]cholars, finally, almost without exception, concur' with these observations.[3]

Since the foundations of Christie's argument are two cases, it would be appropriate to look at the cases closely to see whether they support Christie's conclusions. In the *Norwegian Shipowners* case, the arbitration proceeding were brought by Norway against the United States for the 'quantification' of compensation payable by the United States to Norway for requisitioning (expropriation) of ships constructed in the United States for Norwegian subjects.[4] During the Second World War, there was a shortage of ships in Europe. United States had not yet joined the war hence Norwegian subjects started shipbuilding in the United States for fulfilling their contractual obligations. Also, the outsourcing of ship building in the United States was profitable. However, once the United States joined the war, to satisfy the demands of ships, a statutory framework was created to regulate the shipbuilding sector. The President of the United States was given wide powers, *inter alia*, placing order for ships and war material on any person deemed appropriate and to 'modify, suspend, cancel, or requisition any existing or future contract for the building, or purchase of ships or material'. These orders were to have precedence over all other contracts and orders placed on ship builders. The legislative framework for requisition provided that all requisition orders were subject to payment of just compensation.[5] Exercising these powers, a requisitioning order was issued to all shipyards. The order did not specify the details of shipyards

1. Rudolph Dolzer & Christoph Schreuer, *Principles of International Investment Law* (2nd ed., Oxford: Oxford University Press, 2012), 112–115; Rudolph Dolzer, 'Indirect Expropriations: New Developments?' *New York University Environmental Law Journal* 11 (2002): 64, 66; Rosalyn Higgins, 'The Taking of Property by the State: Recent Developments in International Law' *Recueil des Cours de l'Académie de Droit International* III (1982): 267, 322–324; Martin Domle, 'Foreign Nationalizations: Some Aspects of Contemporary International Law' *AJIL* 55(1961): 585, 588–589; W. Michael Reisman & Robert D. Sloane, 'Indirect Expropriation and Its Valuation in the BIT Generation' *British Yearbook International Law* 74 (2003): 115, 119; Reinisch refers to these observations but also expresses implicit – if not patent skepticism – by starting with the caveat 'arguable'; *See* August Reinisch, 'Expropriation' in Peter Muchlinski, Frederico Ortino & Christoph Schreuer (eds.) *The Oxford Handbook of International Investment Law* (Oxford: Oxford University Press, 2008), 444–445.
2. G.C. Christie, 'What Constitutes a Taking of Property under International Law' *British Yearbook International Law* 38 (1962): 307, 311.
3. Above note 1 (Reisman & Sloane), 115, 121.
4. *Norwegian Shipowner's Claims (Norway v USA)* (1922) 1 RIAA 307, 309, 314.
5. *Ibid.*, 316–317.

and contracts which were covered by the order, since it was a uniformly applicable general order.[6] The shipbuilding business of Norwegian nationals, including their contracts was requisitioned and the United States and Norway entered into a *compromis* to refer the dispute for arbitration.

The Tribunal had to decide two principal issues. First, the scope of the requisitioning order: whether 'in fact' the requisitioning order was extended to contractual rights? Second, if the requisitioning order was extended to contractual rights, then, whether the United States had paid compensation for the requisitioning of the contractual rights. The Tribunal was not called upon to decide the nature of the measure: whether it was expropriatory or not. The parties had already agreed that it was expropriatory.

The Tribunal observed that: 'whatever the intentions may have been, the United States took, both in fact and in law, the contracts under which the ships in question were being or were to be constructed'.[7] Christie relied on this sentence to claim: 'contract rights were held to have been expropriated by the action of States which disclaimed any intention to expropriate such rights'.[8] After analysing the award, he further observed that: 'it has been recognized that property rights may be *so interfered* with that it may be said that to all intents and purposes those property rights have been expropriated even though the State in question has not purported to expropriate.'[9] (emphasis added) Thus proposing that the *Norwegian Shipowners* case supports the propositions that the intention behind adopted of the measure is irrelevant in cases of expropriation and only the effect of the measures matters.

The elementary point is that this was not a case of indirect expropriation, rather of direct expropriation. The reference to intention in the award was not with regard to the issuance of requisition order. The question of intention for the requisition order was neither left to the Tribunal and nor did the Tribunal decide on that issue or made any *obiter* observations. The jurisdiction of the Tribunal extended only to the scope of property rights that were affected by the measure and disputed by the parties.[10] The reference to intention in the award was with regard to whether the United States had the intention to pay compensation for requisitioned contractual property rights[11] and

6. *Ibid.*, 318.
7. Above note 4 (*Norwegian Shipowner's Claims*), 325.
8. Above note 2 (Christie), 316.
9. *Ibid.*, 311.
10. Appending a note of caution while deriving legal principles from decisions based on *compromis*, Friedman has preceded the discussion on the *Norwegian Shipowner's Claims* case with a strong tone of doubt:

> It is similarly necessary to deny any measure of authority to a second group of cases, frequently quoted by writers, ... the *compromise* or international agreement forming the basis of such a decision had already settled the question of law. As the function of the arbitral tribunal set up was limited, as far as legal questions were concerned, to the application of principles already laid down in the *compromis*, these decisions cannot be regarded as making any legal contribution towards the solution of the problem under consideration. S. Friedman, *Expropriation in International Law* (London: Stevens & Sons Ltd, 1953), 69.

11. This is clear from the paragraph immediately preceding the conclusions, where the Tribunal said: 'The Corporation may have intended, up to October 6th. 1917, to settle accounts with

not whether intention is an irrelevant factor in expropriation cases as presented by Christie. Christie ignored that the question decided by the tribunal was of the scope of the requisitioning order in fact, rather than in law. Whether the scope of the measure in fact extended to intangible property. The tribunal was not laying down any legal principle but only making a decision based on facts. The United States argued that the order was implemented only against physical properties, whereas Norway claimed that 'in fact' the order was applied to all rights including contractual rights.[12] On the analysis of the evidence, the Tribunal found that there was 'abundant evidence' to establish that tangible as well as intangible properties were expropriated.[13] Furthermore, after taking over the contractual rights under the requisitioning order, they were performed and the amounts received were appropriated by the United States – without paying them to the Norwegian nationals whose contracts were taken away.[14] The evidence proved that the United States had taken over the contractual rights along with physical property.[15] The United States had paid compensation for requisition of physical property, but according to the Tribunal, 'seemed to have forgotten that it had assumed certain contractual obligations', for which payment of compensation was ordered.[16] The United States was not held responsible to pay compensation for losses to the intangible properties although it did not have the intention to expropriate them, as proposed by Christie.

While the Tribunal found the United States responsible for payment of compensation for requisitioning of the contractual rights of the Norwegian nationals, the Tribunal never arrived at that conclusion on the basis of extent interference with property rights. The literature that followed immediately after the case underscored that the case was of direct expropriation.[17] Even Dolzer – a strong supporter of the sole effects doctrine – concedes that the real issue in the case revolved around the definition

regard to these claims, namely so long as it was expected that the property of the claimants would be restored at the end of the war' but it 'seemed to have forgotten....' Above note 4 (*Norwegian Shipowner's Claims*), 324.

12. *Ibid.*, 318.
13. *Ibid.*, 323.
14. *Ibid.*
15. Above note 4 (*Norwegian Shipowner's Claims*), 318–323. The Tribunal found following evidence supporting the conclusion that the order in fact covered contractual rights as well. First, requisitioning order expressly contained 'not only the ships and the material, but also the contracts, the plans, detailed specifications and payments made, and it even commandeered the yards (depriving them of their right to accept any further contracts)' (at 318). Second, the Claims Committee constituted by the United States of America for going into the claims found that the Norwegian claimants were entitled to these amounts and United States failed to establish before the Tribunal that it had made these payments. (at 319). Third, the correspondence between the public corporation responsible for requisition and the owners of shipyards states that compensation was payable for the contractual rights taken over under the requisitioning order. (at 320–323). Fourthly, the evidence established that the contract of the Norwegian Shipbuilders were not cancelled by the United States and were performed. The property was not destroyed and the American public corporation 'took over the legal rights and duties of the shipowners towards the shipbuilders. The necessary consequence is that the Corporation took over the rights and duties of the shipbuilders towards the shipowners' (at 323).
16. Above note 4 (*Norwegian Shipowner's Claims*), 324–325.
17. James W. Garner, 'An Arbitration Case Between Norway and the United States' *British Yearbook International Law* 4 (1923–1924): 159, 160; Above note 1 (Reinisch), 411–412.

of property for the purposes of international law and the question of indirect taking was inconsequential.[18]

The question of whether the measure was expropriatory was neither referred nor decided by the Tribunal. The legislation under which the President had authorized requisition of shipbuilding businesses itself contemplated payment of 'just compensation'[19] and right from the inception and throughout the proceedings, United States always maintained that it was an expropriatory action and consistently 'declared its willingness and desire to make just compensation'.[20] Even commentators, writing immediately after the award came out saw amount of compensation based on the scope of the measure to be the as the only real issues.[21] It was noted in the award that: 'in fact the claimants were fully and forever deprived of their property and that this amounts to a requisitioning by the exercise of the power of eminent domain within the meaning of American municipal law'.[22] It was eminent domain because the public corporation had appropriated the physical assets and contractual rights and transposed itself into the place of shipbuilding contractor. It took over the main contractual obligation of the construction and delivery of the ships to the owners of contracts and received payments under those contracts.[23] There was no occasion or reason to decide the nature of the measure. The issue was limited to the scope of the expropriatory measure and whether compensation was paid for expropriation properties. Thus, it cannot form the basis for distinction between an expropriatory measure and a regulatory measure.

Additionally, the relevance of this decision as an authoritative statement of the law has been doubted in academic literature (prior to investment arbitration) and contradicted by state practice. According to Schwarzenberger, the decision was not based on 'strict law' but 'in accordance with the principles of law and equity'.[24] The constitutional law of United States, particularly the Fifth Amendment, played a major role in the conclusions of the Tribunal.[25] The award evoked strong protest on the part of United States which was expressed through a diplomatic note. United States paid compensation as per the award with a clarification that it was doing so only to show its commitment towards pacific settlement. But the Secretary of State clarified the position

18. Rudolph Dolzer, 'Indirect Expropriation of Alien Property' *ICSID Rev.-FILJ* 1 (1988): 41, 45.
19. Above note 4 (*Norwegian Shipowner's Claims*), 307, 316, 317.
20. *Ibid.*, 307, 313.
21. Above note 17 (Garner).
22. *Ibid.*, 325; Christie makes a general argument that '[t]here are several well-known international cases in which it has been recognized that property rights may be so interfered with that it may be said that to all intents and purposes those property rights have been expropriated'. *See* above note 2 (Christie), 310. He does not refer to any specific paragraph but only makes a general reference to *Norwegian Shipowners* case and *Certain German interests in Polish Upper Silesia* cases. There is no reference in any of these decisions to the principle that a state is responsible for expropriation depending on the degree of interference and intention of the state is irrelevant. The only reference to any language suggestive of such a principle is in the second conclusion. Seen as a whole, the conclusion is in the specific factual context where the Tribunal was giving a factual finding and not giving legal analysis or laying down legal principles.
23. *Ibid.*, 324.
24. George Schwarzenberger, *International Law: As Applied by International Courts and Tribunals: I*, vol. I (3rd ed., London: Stevens & Sons Limited, 1957), 203–204. Article I of the *compromis* provided the applicable law. *Norwegian Shipowner's Claims* (n 4) 310.
25. Friedman (n 10), 72–73. Also *see Norwegian Shipowner's Claims* (n 4), 330–332.

of the United States that '[t]he award cannot be deemed... to possess an authoritative character of precedent'.[26] According to Scott, in view of the influence of state practice on the formulation of law, by objecting to the reasoning, the United States has deprived the observations in the case of any legal value.[27]

The second case that formed the basis of Christie's claim is the *Certain German Interests in Polish Upper Silesia* – a case brought by Germany against Poland before the Permanent Court of International Justice (PCIJ).[28] This case involved a serious of complex cases arising out of measures in the nature of direct expropriation undertaken by Poland against various properties owned by the German Government in Polish Upper Silesia. The prominent one being taking over of the nitrate factory owned by the German Government at Chorzów. The allegation of the German Government was that while taking the possession and control of working of the factory, Poland also took over intangible rights such as patents, licenses, contractual rights, etc.[29] The defence of Poland was that it was entitled to take over the properties under the Treaty of Versailles and the Geneva Convention, as compensation for losses suffered during the war. The Court rejected this argument because the right to expropriate was given only to a few States under these treaties and Poland was not one of them.[30]

Christie analysed the case to conclude the following:

> The Permanent Court of International Justice ruled that, by seizing the factory and its machinery, the Polish Government also expropriated the patents and contract rights of the management company, even though the Polish Government did not purport to expropriate these particular items of property.[31]

Christie has claimed that in this case there were certain properties that the Polish Government did not 'purport' to expropriate, but those properties lost their value nevertheless. Therefore, loss of intangible properties that were not covered by the measure also amounts to expropriation. The intention of the State to expropriate is irrelevant. Additionally, Christie's conclusion is based on the assumption that the tangible and intangible properties can be clinically isolated and the same measure applied to different set of properties, simultaneously, could be treated to result into direct expropriation in the case of tangible properties and indirect expropriation in the case of intangible properties. The Court never held that expropriation of intangible assets was illegal and that of tangible was legal. The observation of the Court were in

26. Letter of the Secretary of State to the Norwegian Minister at Washington, 26 February 1923, reproduced in James Brown Scott, 'United States-Norway Arbitration Award' *AJIL* 17 (1923): 287, 289. These observations are important in view of consensual nature of public international law. A judicial decision is declared as a subsidiary source for finding a legal principle under Art. 38 (1) (d) of the ICJ Statute, and a state by a custom only if it is a 'general practice accepted as law'. Furthermore, a claim that indirect expropriation is a general principle is doubtful and would be denied any status in cases of express repudiation by a State.
27. *Ibid.*, 289–290.
28. *Case Concerning Certain German Interests in Polish Upper Silesia (Germany v Poland)* (1925) PCIJ Rep Series A No. 6, 5.
29. *Ibid.*, 9.
30. *Ibid.*, 27-31.
31. Above note 2 (Christie), 311.

relation to the measure that was uniformly applied to tangible as well as intangible properties.

The paragraph on which Christie relies to draw this conclusion from the case, does not say so. The paragraph relied upon by Christie was as under:

> The question is whether, by taking possession of the Chorzow factory on July 3rd, 1922, and, by operating it, making use of the experiments, patents and licences, etc. of the Bayerische, Poland has unlawfully expropriated the contractual rights of that Company. In regard to this point, the Court does not think that any importance attaches to the fact that, according to the contract of November 9th, 1920, the management of the exploitation was undertaken by the Management Committee of the Oberschlesische. In actual fact, it was the members of the Management Committee of the Bayerische, appointed for this purpose, who had the management of the exploitation. Moreover, it is clear that the rights of the Bayerische to the exploitation of the factory and to the remuneration fixed by the contract for the management of the exploitation and for the use of its patents, licences, experiments, etc., have been directly prejudiced by the taking over of the factory by Poland. As these rights related to the Chorzow factory and were, so to speak, concentrated in that factory, the prohibition contained in the last sentence of Article 6 of the Geneva Convention applies in respect of them. Poland should have respected the rights held by the Bayerische under its contracts with the Oberschlesische and the Treuhand; and the attitude of Poland in regard to the Bayerische has therefore, like its attitude in regard to the Oberschlesische, been contrary to Article 6 and the following articles of the Geneva Convention.[32]

This section, relied upon by Christie, is actually dealing with the question of scope of the property right - whether contractual rights were covered under the scope of property rights.[33] Like the *Norwegian Shipowners* case, it was undisputed that the measure in question was an expropriatory measure and Poland had always maintained so. The point of dispute was whether the expropriatory measure was justified under the treaties through which the action was taken or was it a case of unauthorized liquidation.[34] The observations made by the Court were not a reflection on the position of general international law, rather merely the effect of the treaties in question. Germany had restricted itself only to the interpretation of the treaties in question. No attempt was made to argue that a distinction between direct and indirect expropriation exists depending on the nature of properties. Friedman emphasized this point after studying the pleadings of Germany in the following words:

> In particular, the German applications did not at any time invoke either the general principles of law within the meaning of Article 38 of the Statute of the Court, or a particular legal principle protecting property against the encroachments of a foreign government.[35]

Even Polish argument was not based on any other foundation, they too were arguing on the same provision of the two treaties, albeit, proposing an alternate

32. *Ibid.*, 44.
33. Above note 1 (Reinisch), 413–14.
34. Above note 28 (*German Interests in Polish Upper Silesia*), 19–22.
35. Above note 10 (Friedman), 78. For arguments by Germany *see* above note 28 (*German Interests in Polish Upper Silesia*), 20–24.

interpretation. As per their argument, the property expropriated was actually the property of German Reich – fraudulently entered in the register in favour of the claimants.[36] Moreover, the Court gave judgment with reference to a particular legal situation of state succession, it is therefore not appropriate to go further and maintain that there was a general principle relating to expropriation.[37]

The Court never looked at the impact of the measure to draw a legal conclusion that there was expropriation. The conclusion of the Court that there was an expropriatory measure was based on the analyses of the nature of the measure.[38] Impact was never taken into account.

Friedman has exposed the problems arising from out of context interpretation of the decision of the Court in the following words:

> Nevertheless, in view of the perfectly clear judgment of the Court, limiting itself to a consideration of a specific measure solely be reference to the conventional law of the parties, and of numerous statements in the pleadings placing the problem exclusively on this footing, to look for the hidden intentions of the Court by interpretation of some of its reasoning is to push legal analysis to a point where, departing from provisions sufficiently clear in themselves, it substitutes daring legal constructions which a regard for strict interpretation would not warrant.[39]

Taken together, the *Norwegian Shipowners* case and the *Certain German Interests in Polish Upper Silesia* cases, that form the basis of the sole effects doctrine, were cases of direct expropriation and had nothing to do with indirect expropriation in fact or in law. None of them laid down that indirect expropriation could be determined only based on the effect of the measures and the intention was irrelevant. In these cases, the *compromis* defined the dispute narrowly and the jurisdiction of the judicial bodies was conscribed to the limited question of properties covered under the measure, rather than the nature of the measure. The outcome in these cases was dictated by the limited flexibility offered by the *compromis* and principles, which neither party disputed.[40] The Respondent State had agreed beforehand about the nature of the measure, i.e. they were expropriatory in nature. The question of nature of the measure was never left for the judicial bodies. They cannot form the basis of support for indirect expropriation. Brierly called these decisions 'inconclusive'.[41]

Although in contemporary scholarship and practice these cases and Christie's conclusions are uncontested, Friedman had lamented the reliance on these decisions in 1953 in the following words:

36. *Ibid.*, 79. For arguments of Poland *see* above note 28 (*German Interests in Polish Upper Silesia*), 25.
37. *Ibid.*, 94.
38. *Ibid.*, 21–25, 33.
39. Above note 10 (Friedman), 81.
40. *Ibid.*, 69. Friedman even doubts the value of these decisions as precedent since extremely limited scope was left for the Tribunal to decide (at 73).
41. *Ibid.*, 86, 109–110 citing Georges Scelle, 'Regles generals du Droit de la Paix', (1936) 58 Hague Recueil, 170.

> In spite of the abundance of published material, perhaps even because of it, the question has remained obscure. Frequently invoked in the heat of legal controversy, the precedents selected have not always been analysed with cold objectivity of the scientific method. Frequently it has been sought to prove too much, and precedents whose value is not considerable have been put forward as unquestionable authorities.[42]

[B] The Iran-US Claims Tribunal and the Sole Effects Doctrine

Christie's analysis of these two cases was applied and cemented through the decisions of the Iran-United States (Iran-US) Claims Tribunal, thus bringing the sole effects doctrine to prominence.[43,44] The reliance on the jurisprudence of the Iran-US Claims Tribunal on indirect expropriation in the scholarship of international investment law is sizeable, recurring and mostly positive. It can be grouped into three. The first group has relied on the decisions without questioning their probative value.[45] Scholarship in the second group mentions the peculiarities of the jurisprudence: the specific and broad language of the expropriation clause - making the jurisprudence *lex specialis*; but continues to rely upon it.[46] The insistence of these two groups on the relevance of the decisions appears to be rooted less in the conviction of its appropriateness and more in its frequent appearance in the decisions of investment tribunals. The third group engages with the criticism and defends its relevance.[47] Before understanding the reasons and the manner of adoption of the sole effects doctrine by the Iran-US Claims Tribunal, it will be pertinent to briefly state the circumstances for the creation of the Tribunal which will help in understanding the context in which the decisions were taken.

---

42. *Ibid.*, 67.
43. Some of the ideas expressed here are drawn from the prior work of the author. *See* Aniruddha Rajput, 'Problems with the Jurisprudence of the Iran-US Claims Tribunal on Indirect Expropriation' *ICSID Review- FILJ* 30 (2015): 589.
44. Above note 1 (Reinisch), 444-445.
45. *Ibid.*, 424-425, 428, 444-446; Above note 1 (Dolzer), 86-90; Christoph Schreuer, 'Rapport: The Concept of Expropriation under the ECT and other Investment Protection Treaties' in Clarisse Ribeiro (ed.) *Investment Arbitration and the Energy Charter Treaty* (New York: Jurisnet, 2006), 117-118, 131, 149-150, 156-158; Hassan Sedigh, 'What Level of Host State Interference Amounts to a Taking under Contemporary International Law' *J.W.T.* 2 (2001): 631, 647-681; Campbell McLachlan, Laurence Shore & Matthew Weiniger, *International Investment Arbitration: Substantive Principles* (Oxford: Oxford University Press, 2007), 291, 297, 301; R. Doak Bishop, James Crawford & W. Michael Reisman, *Foreign Investment Disputes: Cases, Materials and Commentary* (The Hague: Kluwer Law International, 2005); Above note 1 (Reisman & Sloane), 119-120, 122-149; Above note 1 (Dolzer & Schreuer), 102-103.
46. Andrew Newcomb & Lulis Paradell, *Law and Practice of Investment Treaties* (The Netherlands: Kluwer Law International, 2009), 367-368, footnote 26.
47. Veijo Heiskanen, 'The Doctrine of Indirect Expropriation in Light of the Practice of the Iran-United States Claims Tribunal' *JWIT* 8 (2007): 215; Maurizio Brunetti, 'The Iran-United States Claims Tribunal, NAFTA Chapter 11, and the Doctrine of Indirect Expropriation' *CJIL* 2 (2001): 203; Romesh Weeramantry, 'The Law of Indirect Expropriation and the Iran-United States Claims Tribunal's Role in its Development' in Leon E. Trakman and Nicola W. Raneri (ed.) *Regionalism in International Investment Law* (Oxford: Oxford University Press, 2013), 314-343.

The Iran-US Claims Tribunal was setup in the aftermath of the Iranian revolution. The Iranian revolution overthrew the regime of the Shah, which had permitted control of economically vital and strategic industries in the hands of Americans. The peak of the revolution involved the hostage crisis that went on for 444 days (4 November 1979–20 January 1981). The American embassy in Tehran was seized and Americans inside were taken hostages. After the downfall of Shah's regime, the new government sought to withdraw its assets and holdings lying in various American banks. In response, the United States froze all Iranian assets. The crisis was diffused with the good offices offered by the Government of Algeria.[48] On 19 January 1981, the Government of Algeria recorded the commitments of the Governments of Iran and the United States to resolve the outstanding disputes amicably and release the hostages. It resulted in the Algiers Accord, 1975. The Accord consisted of the General Declaration[49] and the Claims Settlement Declaration.[50] The General Declaration recorded that within the framework of the declarations, United States and Iran were to 'terminate all litigation between the government of each party and the nationals of the other, and to bring about the settlement and termination of all such claims through binding arbitration'.[51] Thus, came into being the Iran-US Claims Tribunal.

The Iran-US Claims Tribunal did not have the occasion to pay sufficient attention to the nature of the measure, which was a consequence of the peculiar circumstances in which these awards were delivered. The social, economic and political background in which the Tribunal operated was unique and ruled out the possibility or necessity of determining the nature and circumstances of the governmental measure. The properties lost, which formed the basis of claims, had a common fact pattern and it occurred in two ways: i) 'property lost during the height of the civil turbulence during the revolution; and ii) property over which the Government of the Islamic Republic of Iran assumed control or ownership after that time'.[52] The civil disruption caused by strikes, riots and other strife created a condition of force majeure: running business was impossible and the governmental authorities and agencies were not able to perform certain contractual obligations.[53] In other words, in all the claims brought against the Government of Iran, intention to expropriate, coupled with an expropriatory measure was presumed.

48. For a detailed description of events *see* Charles N. Brower & Jason D. Brueschke, *The Iran-United States Claims Tribunal* (The Hague: Martinus Nijhoff Publishers, 1998), 1–25; George Aldrich, *The Jurisprudence of the Iran-United States Claims Tribunal* (New York: Clarendon Press Oxford, 1996), 2–9; Allahyar Mouri, *The International Law of Expropriation as Reflected in the Work of the Iran-U.S. Claims Tribunal* (The Netherlands: Martinus Nijhoff Publishers, 1994), 1–6.
49. Declaration of the Government of the Democratic and Popular Republic of Algeria (General Declaration), 19 January 1981, (1981–1982) 1 Iran-US CTR 3.
50. Declaration of the Government of the Democratic and Popular Republic of Algeria Concerning the Settlement of Claims by the Government of the United States of America and the Government of the Islamic Republic of Iran (Claims Settlement Declaration), 19 January 1981, (1981–1982) 1 Iran-US CTR 9.
51. *Ibid.*, General Principles B.
52. Above note 49 (Brower & Brueschke), 369–370; George Aldrich, 'What Constitutes Compensable Taking of Property? The Decisions of the Iran-United States Claims Tribunal' AJIL 88 (1994): 587–589.
53. *Sylvania Technical Systems Inc. v Iran*, (1985) 8 Iran-USCTR 298, 308.

The background fact of the Iranian revolution weighed in most of the indirect expropriation cases decided by the Iran-US Claims Tribunal. In almost all the cases, intention on the part of the Iranian Government to expropriate was presumed and the nature of the measure was rarely taken into account. [54] In all the cases:

> Tribunal effectively appears to have presumed that a loss of property in the circumstances prevailing in Iran in 1978-81, if attributable to the Government, was a result of irregular measures that failed to comply with international law and therefore could not be characterized as a materialization of a political risk.[55]

This presumption may be correct in cases of mass claims arising in an environment of animosity between the home State of the investor and the host State. In ordinary cases, for establishing that a State is responsible for expropriation, the State must have acquired something of value. However, this was not considered desirable by the Iran-US Claims Tribunals. [56]

[1] Emergence of the Sole Effects Doctrine

The cases on expropriation arose in two contexts. The first were cases of direct expropriation by the Iranian Government, where companies under American ownership were nationalized. These cases were simple, relatively few and happened only in two situations: nationalization of insurance companies and banks.[57] The cases of indirect or de facto expropriation were complex. In majority of the cases, due to the environment created by the Iranian Revolution, Americans left the companies owned by them and returned to the United States. The Iranian Government appointed 'provisional' or 'temporary' managers on the boards of these companies. In many cases these appointments were made through Iranian laws.[58] Later these appointments resulted in permanent assumption of control since the original American owners and managers never returned.[59] Additionally, there were various other cases involving loss of property as a direct or indirect consequence of the revolution. In order to decide whether these cases amounted to indirect or de facto expropriation, the Iran-US Claims Tribunal applied the sole effects doctrine.

According to Dolzer and Schreuer, the 'authority for the sole effects doctrine comes from the decisions of the Iran-US Claims Tribunal'.[60] The decisions of the Iran-US Claims Tribunal do not use the phrase the 'sole effects doctrine', but authors commenting on this principle coined it.[61] According to the Tribunal,

> property may be taken under international law through interference by a State in the use of that property or with the enjoyment of its benefits, even where legal title

54. Above note 48 (Aldrich, Jurisprudence of Iran-US CT), 178.
55. Above note 47 (Heiskanen), 227–228.
56. *Ibid.*, 228.
57. Above note 52 (Aldrich, What Constitutes Compensable Taking of Property?), 585, 587–588.
58. *Ibid.*, 585, 588–589.
59. Above note 48 (Aldrich, Jurisprudence of Iran-US CT), 174–175.
60. Above note 1 (Dolzer & Schreuer), 114–115.
61. Above note 18 (Dolzer, Indirect Expropriation).

> to the property is not affected.....while assumption of control over property by a government does not automatically and immediately justify a conclusion that the property has been taken by the government, thus requiring compensation under international law, such a conclusion is warranted whenever events demonstrate that the owner was deprived of fundamental rights of ownership and it appears that this deprivation is not merely ephemeral.[62]

The crux of the sole effects doctrine is that the 'intention of the government is less important than the effects of the measure on the owner, and the form of the measure of control or interference is less important than the reality of their impact'.[63] If an impact on the investments exists then, according to sole effects doctrine, the measure under challenge, by default, is indirect expropriation and it does not matter whether the measure was a legitimate exercise of sovereign authority.[64] The State must pay compensation for all losses in such a case. The 'nature' of the measure and the 'intention' for the adoption of the measure is irrelevant, except may be, at the time of quantification of compensation. Since the 'effect' on the investor is the sole criterion to decide whether the measure is indirect or de facto expropriation, this principle is called the 'sole effects' doctrine.[65]

Further, the extent of impact on the property shall be such that it deprives the owner of 'fundamental rights of ownership, use enjoyment or management of the business'.[66] The chambers of the Tribunal have applied different standards on the degree of interference necessary to constitute expropriation. They range from 'unreasonable interference'[67] to an interference which is of such a degree that the property "must be deemed to have been expropriated"[68] or interference with the effective use of

---

62. *ITT Industries Inc. v Iran* (1983) 2 Iran-USCTR 348, 351–352 (Separate Opinion of Judge Aldrich).
63. *Tippets, Abbett McCarthy, Stratton v TAMS-AFFA Consulting Engineers of Iran* (1984) 6 Iran-USCTR 219, 225–226. *See also Phillips Petroleum Co. Iran v Islamic Republic of Iran* (1989) 21 Iran-USCTR 79, 115; A similar phraseology was adopted in another often cited award in *Starret Housing Corporation*:

    > 'it is recognized in international law that measures taken by State can interfere with property rights to such an extent that these rights are rendered so useless that they must be deemed to have been expropriated, even though the State does not purport to have expropriated them and the legal title to the property formally remains with the original owner.' *Starrett Housing Corp. v Iran* (1983) 4 Iran-US CTR 122, 162 (Concurring Opinion of Holtzman).

64. Losses caused to investors due to legitimate exercise of sovereign authority do not amount to expropriation. These actions are categorized as police powers for which a State does not attract responsibility. Jorge E. Viñuales, 'Sovereignty in Foreign Investment Law' in Zachary Douglas, Joost Pauwelyn & Jorge E. Viñuales, *The Foundations of International Investment Law: Bringing Theory into Practice* (Oxford: Oxford University Press, 2014), 327–337. Also *see* below 20–21.
65. Above note 18 (Dolzer, Indirect Expropriation), 79–80.
66. Above note 62 (*ITT Industries* case), 351–352 (Separate Opinion of Judge Aldrich).
67. *Harza Engineering Co. v Iran* (1982-3) 2 Iran-USCTR 499, 504; *Ataollah Golpira v Iran*, (1983) 2 Iran-USCTR 171, 177; *International Technical Products Corporation v Iran* (1985) 9 Iran-US CTR 206, 238–239.
68. Above note 63 (*Starrett Housing* case), 154; *Foremost Tehran Inc v Iran* (1987) 10 Iran-USCTR 228, 244; Above note 63 (*Tippets* case), 225–226; *Phelps Dodge Corpn. v Iran* (1987) 10 Iran-USCTR 121, 130.

the property.[69] The State may have interfered with the enjoyment of the incidents of ownership, such as control of the property, income and other economic benefits to satisfy the standard of the sole effects doctrine.[70]

[2] Procedural and Other Problems with the Origin and Application of the Sole Effects Doctrine

The first systematic articulation[71] of the sole effects doctrine was in *ITT Industries v Islamic Republic of Iran* through a separate opinion. The award was delivered by the majority, based on agreed terms of settlement between the parties.[72] In a highly unusual manner, a separate opinion was appended discussing the merits of the case and espousing the sole effects doctrine. According to the Judge, the reasons for adopting this course, were:

> Settlements are always to be encouraged and are difficult to resist, so I join in incorporating the settlement in this case into an award on agreed terms. Nevertheless, I cannot in good conscience refrain from setting forth my views on the international law questions of expropriation raised by the claim. I do not believe that the settlement should deprive parties or the public of these views on important questions of international law, particularly as *I believe the settlement may well have been inspired, at least in part, by the Respondent's desire to prevent these views from appearing in the Award.* (emphasis added)[73]

The Judge then discussed the facts and his version of the state of the law.[74] Even the amount of compensation that should have been paid if the case was decided on merits was quantified.[75] The views were based on the subjective belief that one of the parties was keen on avoiding a decision on merits. The Judge never gave reasons for forming the basis for these conclusions. The observations may not even properly be described as *obiter*. In international law, there is a procedure and circumstances in which dissenting opinion could be expressed. A judge is not to give 'abstract opinions on troublesome questions or points of law'.[76] Two requirements are associated with dissenting opinions. First, when can a dissenting opinion be issued and second, in response to what can a dissenting opinion be issued. Dissenting opinions in international law are delivered in response to a judgment or a 'dispositive'. The Statute of the

69. *Constantine A. Gianoplus v Iran* (1986) 11 Iran-US CTR 217, 222.
70. *Amco International Finance Corporation v Iran* (1987)15 Iran-USCTR 189, 220–221.
71. *Harza Engineering v Iran* was the first occasion for the Tribunal to comment on the sole effects doctrine. It simply accepted the assertion of the Claims that 'taking of property may occur under international law, even in the absence of a formal nationalization or expropriation, if a government has interfered unreasonably with the use of property', however on facts it held that expropriation did not exist since the interference was sufficiently serious. Above note 67 (*Harza Engineering* case), 504. (footnotes excluded).
72. Above note 62 (*ITT Industries* case), 348–349.
73. *Ibid.*, 349.
74. *Ibid.*, 349–350.
75. *Ibid.*, 355.
76. Edward Dumbauld, 'Dissenting Opinions in International Adjudication' *U. Pa. Law Review* 90 (1942): 929, 932.

International Court of Justice (ICJ Statute) allows a judge to express a dissenting opinion 'if the judgment does not represent in whole or in part the unanimous opinion of the judges'.[77] The pre-requisite for a separate opinion is existence of a 'judgment' – encompassing application of the judicial mind to the contentions of parties.[78] The dissenting opinion is expected to be a reasoned statement expressing the inability of the judge to agree with the 'operative part' of the judgment.[79] A resolution of the PCIJ on the practice of dissenting opinions states that: 'dissenting opinions are designed solely to set forth the reasons for which judges do not feel able to accept the opinion of the Court'.[80]

An agreed settlement between the parties cannot be called a judgment since there is no decision as such (nothing adversarial in the proceedings). There has to be a 'live' dispute. A legal dispute in international law is the one where the parties claim rights based on a system of law conceived as existing, 'whether or not they are so claiming such rights can only be decided by examining the contentions which at its own arbitrary discretion each State chooses to advance'.[81] The jurisdiction of an international tribunal is strictly limited to the jurisdiction granted to a tribunal. If any decision is rendered beyond the scope of competence, the decision is null and void.[82] Settlement on agreed terms was allowed under Article 34 (1) of the Rules of the Tribunal. As per this rule, the proceedings ought to be terminated if the settlement is 'requested by both parties and accepted by the tribunal'.[83] The Tribunal is to 'record the settlement in the form of an arbitral award on agreed terms'.[84] The majority of the Tribunal had recognized and endorsed the settlement. The Tribunal or its members ought not to have proceeded beyond recording settlement any observation transgressing the judicial function.

Moreover, the materials cited in support of the view are subsidiary means and – inconclusive opinions of scholars and draft conventions. Two judicial decisions are also cited in the dissenting opinion which formed the basis of the sole effects doctrine: *Norwegian Ship Owner's* case and *Certain German Interests in Polish Upper Silesia*

77. Article 57, Statute of the International Court of Justice http://www.icj-cij.org/documents/?p1=4&p2=2 accessed 15 January 2015.
78. For a role of dissents, *see* R. P. Anand, 'The Role of Individual and Dissenting Opinions in International Adjudication' International and Comparative Law Quarterly 14 (1965): 788, 803, 806–807.
79. Rainer Hofmann & Tilmann Laubner (eds.), 'Article 57' in Andreas Zimmerman, Christian Tomuschat & Karin Oellers-Frahm (eds.) *The Statute of the International Court of Justice: A Commentary* (New York: Oxford University Press, 2006), 1203.
80. Resolution of the Permanent Court of International Justice dated 17 February 1928, reproduced in the Fourth Report PCIJ, 291, http://www.icj-cij.org/pcij/serie_E/English/E_04_en.pdf accessed 15 January 2015.
81. John Fischer Williams, 'Justiciable and Other Disputes' *AJIL* 26 (1932): 31, 36.
82. W. Michael Reisman, 'Has the International Court Exceeded Its Jurisdiction?' *AJIL* 80 (1986): 128, 128 citing *Case of the Mavrommatis Palestine Concessions (Greece v GB)* (1924) PCIJ, ser. A No. 2, at 42 (dissenting opinion of Lord Finlay, J); at 60 (dissenting opinion of Judge Moore); ILC, Commentary on the Draft Convention on Arbitral Procedure Adopted by the International Law Commission at its Fifth Session, UN Doc. A/CN.4/92, at 105–110 (1955).
83. Article 34 (1), Tribunal Rules of Procedure, 3 May 1983, http://www.iusct.net/General%20Documents/5-TRIBUNAL%20RULES%20OF%20PROCEDURE.pdf accessed 15 January 2015.
84. *Ibid.*

cases. The peculiarities of these cases and their inapplicability for indirect expropriation has been discussed above.

There are further questions of neutrality in dissents by party appointed arbitrators in the Iran-US Claims Tribunal. Mouri complains that State appointed judges often wrote separate and dissenting opinions to alter the scope of the award. These opinions normally supported the position convenient to the appointing State. It was the judge of the third nationality whose decision would influence the outcome.[85] Hence the influence of such separate opinions on future judicial decisions was expected to be minimal.[86]

Some of the separate and dissenting opinions, particularly on expropriation were often referred as precedents subsequently. Investment tribunals frequently rely on separate opinions of the Iran-US Claims Tribunal for indirect expropriation cases.[87] They ignore that a dissenting opinion[88] may be followed only if it provides precise 'solution based upon the ascertainment of what international law ordains'.[89]

[3] Influence of 'Other Measures Affecting Property Rights'

The sole effects doctrine could be developed and applied by the Iran-US Claims Tribunal because the jurisdictional clause of the Claims Settlement Declaration was broad and could accommodate it. Article II of the Claims Settlement Declaration authorized the Tribunal to decided disputes 'arising out of debts, contracts (including transactions which are the subject of letters of credit or bank guarantees), expropriation or other measures affecting property rights'.[90] This clause granted jurisdiction to the Tribunal over two categories of property deprivation: 'expropriation' and 'other measures affecting property rights'. The clause does not contain a third category of indirect expropriation or measures tantamount to expropriation.

Arguably, expropriation could be interpreted widely to include instances of direct and indirect expropriation.[91] But for this interpretation to be accepted, a clear indication on the part of State Parties to the Declaration is necessary. Indirect expropriation is broader in its scope than expropriation. Obligations beyond those expressly agreed

85. Mouri (n 48) at 16–18.
86. Albert Jan van den Berg, 'Dissenting Opinions by Party-Appointed Arbitrators in Investment Arbitration' in Mahnoush Arsanjani et al (eds) *Looking to the future: Essays on International Law in Honor of W. Michael Reisman* (The Netherlands: Martinus Nijhof Publishers, 2011), 825, 828–831.
87. *Compañiá de Aguas del Aconquija S.A. and Vivendi Universal S.A. v Argentine Republic*, Award, ICSID Case No. ARB/97/3, 20 August 2007, para. 7.5.16; *Telenor Mobile Communications S.A. v The Republic of Hungary*, Award, ICSID Case No. ARB/04/15, 13 September 2006, paras 65–66, 69–70; *BG Group Plc. v The Republic of Argentina*, Final Award, UNCITRAL Arbitration Rules, 24 December 2007, para. 261.
88. According to Dumbauld, as a principle the decisions of majority shall be preferred, unless it is a thin majority opposed by the dissent of the 'ablest and most learned judges.' Dumbauld (n 76), 937.
89. *Ibid.*, 934–935.
90. Article II.1, Claims Settlement Declaration (n 50).
91. Sebastian Escarcena, *Indirect Expropriation in International Law* (Cheltenham, UK: Edward Elgar Publishing, 2014), 83.

by the States cannot be presumed. They have to be specifically incorporated.[92] A text of a treaty cannot be enlarged to add additional obligations than those stipulated in the text which represents the consent of State Parties.[93] Since indirect expropriation introduces a more onerous obligation than direct expropriation, absence of reference to indirect expropriation cannot be interpreted as inclusionary and shall be rather treated as exclusionary.[94]

However, the other clause 'other measures affecting property rights' was broad to cover all property deprivations, including indirect expropriation. But, the clause does not distinguish between all deprivations and deprivations arising out of indirect expropriation. The cases of direct expropriation decided by the Tribunal were clearly marked out and the rest – purportedly decided under indirect or de facto expropriation – appropriately fell under 'other measures affecting property rights'. Therefore, the suggestion that the cases are not *lex specialis* because few cases were decided under the residual clause and the majority under indirect expropriation[95] does not hold ground.

The Tribunal treated the language of the jurisdictional clause to be a permission to interpret 'expropriation' and 'other measures affecting property rights' broadly. [96] In this quest, the Tribunal did not bother whether or not the actions strictly fell within the contours of expropriation. An example of this approach is the *American International Group v Islamic Republic of Iran* case. The lack of attention of the Tribunal to distinguish between expropriation and 'other means affecting property rights' is evident from the following:

> The Tribunal finds that its jurisdiction over 'expropriations' by virtue of Article II, paragraph 1, of the Claims Settlement Declaration applies equally to 'nationalizations' and other forms of takings. In any event, the Tribunal's jurisdiction through residual clause – 'other measures affecting property rights' is, by itself sufficiently broad to encompass the subject matter of the claim in this case.[97]

The cases purportedly decided under the category of indirect expropriation (which did not exist as an independent standard under the Claims Settlement Declaration) were influenced by the residual clause: 'other measures affecting property rights'. Giving an insight into the mind of the judges, Judge Aldrich summarizes the impact of the residual clause in the following words:

> The Declaration explicitly gave the Tribunal jurisdiction over claims that arose out of both 'expropriations' and 'other measures affecting property rights', thereby

92. *The Case of The S.S. "Lotus" (France v Turkey)* (1927) PCIJ Series A, No. 10, p. 18.
93. *Access to, or Anchorage in, the port of Danzig, of Polish War Vessels* (Advisory Opinion) (1931) PCIJ Series A/B No 43, 128, 144.
94. Richard Gardiner, *Treaty Interpretation* (Oxford: Oxford University Press, 2008), 144–147.
95. Brunetti states that from approximately sixty awards rendered on the subject, only few were based on any other measures affecting property and the bulk of awards are on indirect expropriation. While deciding cases on indirect expropriation, the Tribunals 'have almost always applied customary international law'. Above note 47 (Brunetti), 205; Above note 47 (Heiskanen), 218–219.
96. *Kenneth P. Yeager v Iran* (1987) 17 Iran-US CTR 92, 99.
97. *American International Group Inc. v Iran* (1983) 4 Iran-US CTR 96, 101.

> suggesting clearly that neither the terminology nor the intent of actions attributable to either Government would affect the Tribunal's jurisdiction to award compensation if the actions had adversely affected a claimant's property rights.[98]

The effect of the clause 'other measures affecting property rights' was that the Tribunal never maintained the distinction between 'taking' (expropriation) and 'wealth deprivation' (to mean general loss of property). [99] Traditionally in international law, expropriation always has a connotation of a State taking the property and appropriating it.[100] Whereas, 'deprivation' may be any deprivation caused as an unintended consequence of governmental action. Expropriation is conceptually different from general wealth deprivation. The clause 'other measures affecting property rights' certainly encompasses all forms of wealth deprivation, including 'taking' or 'expropriation'. But expropriation, including indirect expropriation, would not include all forms of property deprivation. On one occasion, the Tribunal acknowledged that for 'expropriation' to exist the government would have to obtain something of value.[101] But while applying this principle to cases, the Tribunal treated expropriation to mean general wealth deprivation and thus falling under 'other measures affecting property rights'.[102] The failure of the Tribunal to 'distinguish' between 'expropriation' and 'wealth deprivation' is evident from the following paragraph from *Tippets v Iran*:

> The Tribunal prefers the term 'deprivation' to the term 'taking' although they are largely synonymous, because the latter may be understood to imply that the Government has acquired something of value, which is not required. A deprivation or taking of property may occur under international law through interference by a State in the use of that property or with the enjoyment of its benefits, even where legal title to the property is not affected.[103]

The hypothesis that 'expropriation' could be equated with 'wealth deprivation' was developed based on an article by Wetson. Wetson's claim was that the easiest way to find expropriation was to see whether there is 'wealth deprivation'. [104] He was careful to clarify that this interpretation of expropriation would be inapplicable in cases of regulatory freedom since a legitimate regulatory measure cannot be said to result into 'wealth deprivation'. [105] The distinction between 'deprivation' and 'taking' is indispensable because 'wealth deprivation' is excessively broad and would hold State

98. Above note 48 (Aldrich, Jurisprudence of Iran-US CT), 173.
99. *Ibid.*, 188.
100. Konstantin Katzarov, *The Theory of Nationalization* (The Hague: Martinus Nijhoff Publishers, 1964), 138–147; *S.D. Myers, Inc. v Government of Canada*, Partial Award, NAFTA, 13 November 2000, para. 280.
101. *Motorola Inc. v Iranian National Airlines Corporation* (1988) 19 Iran-US CTR 73, 95-96 (Dissenting Opinion of Judge Brower).
102. Above note 63 (*Tippets* case), 225–226.
103. *Ibid.*, 225–226.
104. Burns H. Weston, '"Constructive Takings" under International Law: A Modest Foray into the Problem of "Creeping Expropriation"' *Virginia Journal International Law* 16 (1975): 103, 111–113.
105. *Ibid.*, 121.

responsible for every loss that investor may suffer, even arising out of any measure like regular tax measures.[106]

Normally expropriation connotes some benefit being obtained by the State, but in view of the nature of the residual clause this requirement was sidelined.[107] For example, in *Tippetts v Iran* – an award often relied upon by investment tribunals[108]– the entire discussion was under the heading of 'deprivation of property'. The alleged measure was analysed from that perspective without any allusion to expropriation.[109]

The practical reason for laxity in distinguishing expropriation and wealth deprivation was that the awards were 'immediately and automatically satisfied from the Security Account, regardless of the theoretical basis of the award'.[110] In *Eastman Kodak v Iran*, Judge Brower in a separate opinion took the view that a rigorous determination of indirect expropriation is unnecessary since the objective of creating the security account was to provide compensation in all situations of interference with property by Iran.[111]

The Tribunal concluded that de facto expropriation had taken place once the seizure of properties was attributable to the Iranian Government.[112] The bulk of cases that seem to be indirect expropriation, appropriately fall in the category of direct expropriation, particularly those involving appointment of temporary managers. The Iranian Government had obtained benefit through the taking over of the American owned companies.[113] In a sense, majority of the takings in question were direct expropriations – involving taking over of the assets by the Iranian Government or its agents. In the cases of appointments of temporary managers, the Tribunal did not insist on severity of the measure to find expropriation.[114] According to the judges of the Tribunal (writing in private capacity) the factual background of Iranian revolution always weighed heavily on the minds of the judges.[115] In a normal situation, according to Aldrich, a tribunal would have refrained from awarding compensation for temporary appointment of the managers under its laws by the Iranian Government as a legitimate regulatory exercise. But the temporary appointment of managers was presumed to be

106. Above note 1 (Dolzer), 44.
107. Above note 52 (Aldrich, What Constitutes Compensable Taking of Property?), 593.
108. 17 Tribunals under ICSID have referred to this award. Christopher Gibson & Christopher Drahozal, 'Iran-United States Claims Tribunal Precedent in Investor-State Arbitration' Journal International Arbitration 23(6) (2006): 521, 543.
109. Above note 63 (*Tippets* case), 224–226.
110. Above note 48 (Brower & Brueschke), 379–381.
111. *Eastman Kodak Company v Iran* (1987) 17 Iran-USCTR 153, 173–174 (Concurring and Dissenting Opinion of Judge Brower). There are various other instances where the Tribunal was lax due to the availability of the Security Account. *See* Above note 62 (*ITT Industries*), 349–352; Above note 63 (*Tippets* case), 225–226; *Thomas Earl Payne v Iran* (1986) 12 Iran-USCTR 3,10–11; *Alfred L W Short v Iran* (1987) 16 Iran-USCTR 76, 78–79; *Arthur Young & Company Short v Iran* (1987) 17 Iran-USCTR 245, 256; Above note 101 (*Motorola case*) 85; Above note 63 (*Phillips Petroleum Company*), 115. All these are leading cases on indirect expropriation wherein the 'sole effects' doctrine was enunciated.
112. Above note 48 (Brower & Brueschke), 384 citing *Sedco Inc. v National Iranian Oil Company* (1985) 9 Iran-USCTR 248, 275.
113. Above note 47 (Heiskanen), 227.
114. Above note 48 (Brower & Brueschke), 395–410.
115. Above note 48 (Aldrich, Jurisprudence of Iran-US CT), 171–172.

permanent due to the impossibility of return of Americans to their businesses after the revolution.[116] The Tribunal felt that the foreign managers were forcefully driven out and the management was taken over. The circumstances were such that the foreign managers were afraid of returning.[117] In addition to the background, the judges doubted if they had the mandate to 'ascertain the intent of the Iranian Government, if indeed any clear intention existed'. The laws, in accordance with which the appointments of temporary directors were made, did not impose any positive obligations that would ensure proper and profitable running of the companies taken over. The Government never assured that the losses suffered due to bad business judgments by the temporary directors would be compensated.[118]

Despite these problems, the relevance of the 'other measures affecting property rights' has been sought to be sustained in international investment law. It is argued that the catch-all phrase could help tribunals to adopt a broader definition of expropriation, as was done in *Metaclad v Mexico*.[119] Thus, in effect, proposing an interpretation that would expand the scope of BIT expropriation clauses beyond their language. The Court of British Columbia, while deciding the challenge to the *Metaclad* award warned about wide interpretations, beyond the language of the clause in the treaty.[120] The expropriation clauses in international investment agreements are limited to measures: direct, indirect, tantamount or equivalent to expropriation.[121] A similar effort to expand the scope of expropriation clause in investment treaties, based on the residual clause 'other measures affecting property rights' was rejected in *Pope and Talbot v Canada*. The claimant argued that the expropriation clause in Article 1110 of NAFTA included 'measures tantamount to expropriation'. The measure under challenge was the export control regime imposing restrictions on cross-border export of softwood lumber, which affected the business of the foreign investor. The claimant investor conceded that since there was no appropriation, the impugned measure did not amount to expropriation as per customary international law. However, the claimant rested the case upon the 'tantamount to expropriation' part of the expropriation clause and relied on the awards of the Iran-US Claims Tribunal to contend that Article 1110 of NAFTA expanded the scope of expropriation to include 'measures affecting property rights', on which

116. Above note 52 (Aldrich, What Constitutes Compensable Taking of Property?), 590.
117. Above note 48 (Brower & Brueschke), 370–372.
118. *Ibid.*, 178.
119. Above note 47 (Weeramantry), 340.
120. *The United Mexican States v Metaclad Corporation* Reasons for the Judgment of the Honourable Mr Justice Tysoe, The Supreme Court of British Columbia, (2001) BCSC 664, para. 99.
121. Article 1110: No Party may directly or indirectly nationalize or expropriate an investment of an investor of another Party in its territory or take a measure tantamount to nationalization or expropriation of such an investment, North American Free Trade Agreement (adopted 17 December 1992, entered into force 1 January 1994) 32 I.L.M 289 and 605 (1993); Mexico-UK BIT (signed 12 May 2006, entered into force 25 July 2007) Art. 7; Canada-Slovakia BIT (signed 20 July 2010, entered into force 14 March 2012) Art. VI.1; Netherlands-Oman BIT (signed 17 January 2009) Art. 4; Egypt-Germany BIT (signed 16 June 2005, entered into force 22 November 2009) Art. 4; Japan-Lao People's Democratic Republic BIT (signed 16 January 2008, entered into force 3 August 2008) Art. 12.

awards were delivered by the Iran-US Claims Tribunal.[122] In response, the Tribunal held that 'tantamount' is nothing more than equivalent and it does not encompass every deprivation of property. The clause giving power to the Iran-US Claims Tribunal was wide to include every interference with property rights, which was not the case with the investment treaty in question and thus the jurisprudence of the Iran-US Claims Tribunal was not relevant.[123]

The above discussion shows that the jurisprudence of the Iran-US Claims Tribunal is *lex specialis*. It cannot be easily transposed into another treaty regime, particularly one that does not contain a general wealth deprivation clause. Investment treaties do not contain such a clause, except few French BITs.

§4.02 THE 'NATURE OF THE MEASURE' IN THE DECISION OF INTERNATIONAL COURTS AND TRIBUNALS

With the ignorance of inherent failings that coalesce the sole effects doctrine, it has come to prominence as a dominant principle for distinguishing regulatory measure from indirect expropriation in international investment law. As was discussed in the last chapter, some tribunals have noticed that another approach for distinguishing a regulatory measure from indirect expropriation is nature of the measure. According to this principle, the determination of whether a measure in question is a legitimate regulatory measure or an expropriatory measure requires the analysis of the 'measure' and not the 'effect'.

There have been some cases, prior to investment arbitration where international courts and tribunals have looked at the nature of the measure to determine whether there was expropriation. Although, in principle, in all cases before the Iran-US Claims Tribunal, intention to expropriate was implicit, hence the analysis of the nature of the measure was never deemed necessary. Yet, there were a few cases, where the Iran-US Claims Tribunal did adopt the nature of the measure principle.

In *Emanuel Too v Greater Modesto Insurance Associate*, a claim was brought against an American Insurance company and the Government of the United States by an Iranian claimant. The claim sought to recover the insurance claimed for the destruction of commercial property caused by fire. Also, compensation was sought from the Government of the United States for cancellation of claimant's visa, failure to protect property, expropriation of a property by sale of a van by municipal authorities and sales by the tax authorities of claimant's hotel business, liquor permit and home and lien over the bank accounts.[124] In relation to the actions of the Government taken towards fulfilment of tax dues, the Tribunal held that:

> a State is not responsible for loss of property or for other economic disadvantage resulting from bona fide general taxation or any other action that is commonly accepted as within the police power of States, provided it is not discriminatory and

122. *Pope & Talbot Inc. v The Government of Canada*, Interim Award, UNCITRAL, 26 June 2000, para. 94.
123. *Ibid.*, para. 104.
124. *Emanuel Too v Greater Modesto Insurance Associates* (1989) 23 Iran-USCTR 378, 378–379.

is not designed to cause the alien to abandon the property to the State or to sell it at distressed price.[125]

The Tribunal found that the State did not deliberately 'intend to cause harm'.[126] Thereby, the Tribunal recognized the relevance and importance of 'intention' in determination of indirect expropriation. So also, the regulation under which the abandoned van of the claimant was auctioned was a genuine regulation, which did not discriminate between abandoned vehicles. Therefore, the State was not responsible for payment of compensation.[127] On the allegations of failure to provide adequate protection, the Tribunal held that the 'State cannot guarantee the safety of an alien or of alien property', unless the 'police protection falls below a minimum standard of reasonableness'.[128]

In *Sea-Land Service, Inc. v Iran*, a claim was brought against the Ports and Shipping Organization (PSO) of Iran – a government instrumentality responsible for administration and control of Iranian ports and the Government of Iran, claiming that it was deprived of the use of certain facilities constructed and operated at the port. The allegation was that the claimant was allowed to proceed with construction and operation of port facilities in the allotted area. After the claimant incurred considerable expense in constructing the facilities, the usage of the facilities was disallowed. The claimant argued that the resultant deprivation of property was expropriatory in nature. The Tribunal took the view that the losses suffered by the claimant were an outcome of deterioration of the management of PSO. However, the claimant alleged 'no specific, overt or discriminatory acts'.[129] The disruption of ordinary management was caused due to the revolutionary upheaval in Iran and there was no suggestion that 'PSO had embarked upon a policy of deliberate disruption or non-cooperation directed' at the claimant.[130] The Tribunal then affirmed that for expropriation to exist, there must be a deliberate governmental interference'.[131] This is also a reference to the role of intention.

The Tribunal also applied the principle of unjust enrichment to distinguish between a normal regulatory measure and an expropriatory measure. For an expropriation to exist, there has to be a substantial loss suffered by the claimant and the other party should have received some benefit thereby. Since the State or the public corporation was not unjustly enriched in the process, no compensation was payable.[132]

---

125. *Ibid.*, 387.
126. *Ibid.*
127. *Ibid.*, 388–389.
128. *Ibid.*, 386.
129. *Sea-Land Service Inc. v Iran* (1986) 6 Iran-USCTR 149, 164–165.
130. *Ibid.*, 165.
131. *Ibid.*, 166. A dissenting opinion on this point was rendered by Judge Holtzmann. In his view intention of the State was irrelevant and he relied on the decisions discussed above. *See* Opinion of Howard M. Holtzmann Dissenting as to Award on Claims and Concurring as to Dismissal of Counter claims, at 206–207.
132. *Ibid.*, 168–169. There was a dissent registered on this point as well, based on a factual finding that there was unjust enrichment on the part of Respondents. *See* Opinion of Howard M. Holtzmann Dissenting as to Award on Claims and Concurring as to Dismissal of Counterclaims, at 177–178.

In spite of the focus on intention for expropriation, a commentator has suggested that intention was a relevant criterion only because loses were occasioned by omission to act. Therefore, the principle laid down in this case that intention is relevant cannot be applied to cases of expropriation.[133] It is difficult to see how intention would be relevant only in cases of omission and irrelevant in cases of actions. An omission as well as an action would be preceded by an intention. The Tribunal did not limit the observations to situations of omission. The dissent opinion in the case has also considered that the assessment of the majority is generally applicable to expropriation cases and not limited to instances of omissions to act.[134]

Again in *Sedco v National Iraninan Oil Company*, the Tribunal noted the relevance of intention of the State in adoption of regulations, and whenever injury was caused to the alien was due to a bona fide 'regulation', no compensation was payable. The Tribunal considered losses caused due to regulations as 'incidental economic injury' for which a State is not responsible.[135]

In *Dames Moore v Iran*, the Tribunal held that in order to establish expropriation, there should be 'taking of property'. In that case, two sets of properties of the claimant were allegedly taken over by the Government.[136] Regarding the first group of properties, the Tribunal found that the Government had taken property and thus was responsible to compensate.[137] However, regarding the second group, there was no evidence that the Government had requisitioned the properties, hence no compensation was payable.[138] The conclusion in both set of properties was based on the analysis of the nature of the measure.

These decisions are in consonance with decision of the PCIJ in the *Oscar Chinn* case. In this case, the PCIJ held that the real factor that would play a role in distinguishing a regulatory measure from an expropriatory measure is the 'nature of the measure' and not the 'effect' of the measure.

United Kingdom brought a case on behalf of its national Mr Oscan Chinn before the PCIJ against Belgium, alleging that the measures undertaken by the Belgium Government resulted into loss and damage to the business of Mr Chinn. The measures in question were applied to fluvial transport on the river Congo, which fell within the territories of a Belgian colony.[139] The Government of Belgium operated in the fluvial transport business through an entity called 'Unatra'. Unatra was in competition with other private operators. Owing to its character as a government corporation, it was under an obligation to keep a permanent fleet in operation to meet the present and future needs of the colony. Its rates had to be approved by the Government and the colony had the right to insist that the services were continually operational even if it was running into losses. There was also an obligation to keep expanding the fleet from time to time. As a result of these conditions of operation, the expenses kept rising and

133. Above note 1 (Reinisch), 446.
134. *Sea-Land Service v Iran* (n 129), Separate and Dissenting Opinion of Judge Holtzman.
135. *Sedco Inc. v National Iranian Oil Company* (n 112), 275 (footnotes excluded).
136. *Dames and Moore v Iran* (1983) 4 Iran-US CTR 212, 221–222.
137. *Ibid.*, 222–223.
138. *Ibid.*, 223.
139. *The Oscar Chinn* case *(Belgium v UK)* (1934) PCIJ Series A/B 65, 66.

income remained the same for Unatra. To keep the business going, Unatra urged the Government to allow it to 'charge special rates to regular and important customers' and enter into 'fidelity contracts enabling to grant a rebate on tariff charges'.[140] The Government acceded to the request subject to the condition of acting in a non-discriminatory manner. The Government had ordered that 'all shippers of the same category must be treated on the same footing, adding that the slightest complaint might entail, if justified, the withdrawal of this authorization'.[141] In the meanwhile, Mr Chinn, a British subject, established a river transport, shipbuilding and repairing business in areas of operation of Unatra.[142]

During 1930–1931, due to severe commercial depression in the world, the trade in Congo was seriously affected. The Chamber of Commerce of the area requested the Belgian Government to intervene and lend assistance by reducing cost of all transport. To tackle the situation of economic distress, the Belgium Government issued directions to transport services whose tariffs it could control. The tariffs were substantially reduced and the Government undertook to make good the losses, provided that a separate account for the duration was maintained and the annual statement of account or quarterly balance sheet showed a deficit.[143] These measures were issued in public interest and the rigours in the measures ensured transparency.[144] As a consequence of the measure, Mr Chinn being a private operator, without the price support of the Government, was driven out of business entirely. He had to suspend his transportation, shipbuilding and repairing business. Six other private operators, including Mr Chinn, affected by the measure approached the domestic court alleging that there was an effort to create virtual monopoly in favour of Unatra – the State corporation. But the action, as well as the appeal filed thereafter failed.[145] In the meanwhile, the duration of the measure was extended to encompass private operators as well. The Government promised to support them if they provided the requisite guarantees to refund the losses after they make profit again.[146]

Espousing Mr Chinn's claim before the PCIJ, United Kingdom alleged that the measure adopted by the Belgium Government created a de facto monopoly.[147] Therefore, it amounted to an indirect expropriation (although the term indirect expropriation was not used). The Court utilized a three prong methodology to decide whether Belgium was responsible: 'nature of the measure', 'circumstances of the case' and the alleged 'international obligations' breached.[148] Commenting on the nature of the measure, the Court held that the measure did not apply only to Government controlled company Unatra, but to all operating businesses. The reimbursement was allowed to all on compliance with certain conditions.[149] As regards the circumstances of the case,

140. *Ibid.*, 70–71.
141. *Ibid.*, 71.
142. *Ibid.*
143. *Ibid.*, 71–74.
144. *Ibid.*, 74.
145. *Ibid.*, 75–76.
146. *Ibid.*
147. *Ibid.*, 69.
148. *Ibid.*, 77.
149. *Ibid.*, 77–78.

the Court held that Belgium Government was the sole judge of the circumstances and the necessity of the measure. Unatra was under an obligation to keep the transportation service running and at the same time the critical financial situation required the Government to intervene. The measures had to be taken because the entire Colony was subject to the threat of a disaster.[150] Lastly, the United Kingdom alleged that the measures contravened the Convention of Saint Germain and general principles of international law. United Kingdom argued that the *effect* of the measure was creation of a de facto monopoly in favour of Unatra and making the business of Mr Chinn commercially unviable. The Court did not find favour with the sole effects doctrine argument because a treaty promising freedom of trade and perfect equality is not a guarantee of success by the Government of each individual concern.[151] Even under general principles of international law and vested rights in particular, there can be no vested right to profit. The Court recognized the fact that Mr Chinn lost his business entirely but the Court did not find that to be a sufficient ground to hold Belgian Government responsible. The Court was mindful of the exigencies and fluctuations of a business enterprise and summarized it as follows:

> No enterprise-least of all a commercial or transport enterprise, the success of which is dependent on the fluctuating level of prices and rates-can escape from the chances and hazards resulting from general economic conditions. Some industries may be able to make large profits during a period of general prosperity, or else by taking advantage of a treaty of commerce or of an alteration in customs duties; but they are also exposed to the danger of ruin or extinction if circumstances change. Where this is the case, no vested rights are violated by the State.[152]

The measure resulted into concentration of business in the hands of Unatra, but according to the Court, this was not the 'motive and aim of the action of the Belgian Government'.[153] The Court also held that Unatra and Mr Chinn could not be compared because former being a public corporation has to operate in public interest despite suffering losses. Therefore, it took up greater burden.[154] The emphasis of the Court in the reasoning is on the nature of the measure and not on the effect of the measure.

In order to undermine the strength of this point, a commentator has sought to project that the Court disregarded the effect because Mr Chinn's business collapsed as a consequence of the economic downturn and Court's reference to effect was not in connection to the measure.[155] The Court very clearly rejected the argument of United Kingdom that since Chinn had lost the investment entirely, attention shall be paid only to the effect of the measure and Chinn must be compensated. The Court noted that it was aware of the economic consequences on Chinn but held that was not adequate to find international responsibility. According to the Court, the treaty obligation was not insulation from losses[156] and in every business risk of loss is unavoidable.[157] More

150. *Ibid.*, 78–79.
151. *Ibid.*, 85.
152. *Ibid.*, 88.
153. *Ibid.*, 86.
154. *Ibid.*, 87.
155. Above note 1 (Dolzer), 46.
156. *Oscar Chinn* case (n 139), 85.

importantly, none of the dissenting judges expressed any view on the question whether the measures were contrary to general international law.[158] It is also incorrect to suggest that the Court assumed that the destruction of Chinn's business was solely due to the economic situation. A proper reading of the decision shows that the intention of the host State in adopting a measure is important and the host State is not responsible for losses caused to the investor as a consequence of a regulatory measure.

The second criticism of the decision is that from a doctrinal point of view, the Court has not given any special reasons for its analysis.[159] The narration of the analysis of the Court in the preceding paragraphs shows that through the three-prong test, nature of the measure, circumstances of the case and the international obligation on the host State, the Court conducted a detailed doctrinal analysis.

The emphasis on intention of the State to take over the assets is highlighted in Christie's comment on this case. In his view, in the *Oscar Chinn* case, there was absence of intention of the part of the host State to drive the foreign investor out of business, unlike *Norwegian Shipowners* case and *Certain German Interests in Polish Upper Silesia* cases.[160] The disregard of intention in the earlier cases and its prominence in *Oscar Chinn* case was precisely because the measures in question were admittedly expropriatory, whereas in *Oscar Chinn* case this question was left for the Court to decide. Situations of regulatory exercise, as opposed to direct expropriation cases, will require determination of intention of the State in adopting the measure as a weighing factor to distinguish between regulatory power and indirect expropriation.

Another important point to note is that the treatment standards contained in the treaty in that case were much higher than those contained in the present day BITs. It contemplated 'perfect commercial equality'.[161] In any case, Freedom of Commerce and Navigation treaties were distinct from the modern day BITs on the degree of freedom of trade they contemplated and wide range of rights investors enjoyed under them.[162] The interpretation of a regulatory measure in *Oscar Chinn* is in view of much stronger

157. *Ibid.*, 88.
158. Alexander P. Fachiri, 'The Oscar Chinn Case' *British Yearbook International Law* 16 (1935): 189, 198. For a criticism of the minority view *see* generally 'The Chinn Case' *British Yearbook International Law* 16 (1935): 162. Some commentators have tried to downplay the relevance of this case by pointing to the number of dissents. Todd Weiler, 'Saving Oscar Chin: Non-Discrimination in International Investment Law' in N. Horn & S. Kroll (eds.) *Arbitrating Foreign Investment Disputes: Procedural and Substantive Legal Aspects* (Kluwer Law International, 2004), 159. But his criticism is highly superficial in complete ignorance of the substance of dissenting views. The dissents were not on the point of the methodology and the intention behind the measure but on the ground that commercial equality was not maintained because Chinn was not given financial assistance as was given to the company under government's control. *See* Alexander P Fachiri, 'The Oscar Chinn Case' *British Yearbook International Law* 16 (1935): 189, 198. Also the commentator has completely ignored the reasoning of the Court that treaties for protection of rights of investor are not guarantees against financial losses.
159. Above note 1 (Dolzer), 46.
160. Above note 2 (Christie), 322.
161. Above note 139 (*Oscar Chinn* case), 80.
162. R Dolzer & M Stevens, *Bilateral Investment Treaties* (Hague: Martinus Nijhoff Publishers, 1995), 10–11. Dolzer and Stevens lament the retrogression of the treatment standards by saying, 'Furthermore, key features of traditional FCNs (such as the unrestricted right to entry and the unqualified right of national treatment) were thought to be incompatible with the new political realities.' (footnote omitted).

treatment standard restricting the regulatory freedom of States to a much greater extent.

Some investment tribunals also have pointed to the inadequacy of merely looking at the effects and the need to look at the nature of the measure as well.[163] As succinctly put by Sax, '[t]he question never turns upon an examination of the economic consequences of the government's action; these theories postulate a qualitative difference between the police power and a taking, not a mere difference of degree'.[164] The nature of the measure doctrine plays an important role in the case of exercise of regulatory freedom because, '[i]n these cases, in so far as the State touches the property of foreigners, it not be able to justify its action by pleading that no loss has occurred, but it will rather have to be prepared to justify its action by showing its adherence to the normal standards current in the international community'.[165]

In sum, there are two competing doctrines that emerge in the jurisprudence, extant prior to investment arbitrations. The sole effects doctrine, which is currently the dominant principle emanates from doubtful origins, which has been recognized and extensively applied, without realizing its inherent flaws. The nature of the measure doctrine is a principle applied by relatively few tribunals but has an uncontroversial footing in the jurisprudence prior to investment arbitration.

163. *LG & E Energy Corp, LG & E Capital Corp., LG & E International Inc v Argentine Republic,* ICSID Case No. ARB/02/1, Decision on Liability, paras 194–195; SD Myres is a notable exception that looked at the nature of the measure and the purpose and effect of the governmental measure. It however ultimately leaned in favour of the sole effects doctrine. (paras 280–283).
164. Joseph L Sax, 'Takings and the Police Power' *Yale Law Journal* 74 (1964): 36, 39.
165. B.A. Wortley, *Expropriation in International Law* (Cambridge: Cambridge University Press, 1959), 38.

CHAPTER 5

Theoretical Approaches

Theoretical analysis of a legal principle not only provides a descriptive framework of the phenomenon under consideration, but also elucidates the philosophy underpinning the legal principle. At the theoretical level, this contributes towards the understanding of occurrences in a field, and at a practical level, guide the decision-making process. This process becomes acutely important in situations where there are two competing legal principles and a distinction has to be made to identify their domain of operation. Therefore, in this Chapter, the tension between regulatory freedom and indirect expropriation is analysed through a theoretical prism. There are three levels of this theoretical analysis. The first is focused specifically about the relationship between regulatory freedom and indirect expropriation, where the methodology for delineating regulatory freedom and indirect expropriation is specifically debated. This includes the case-by-case method and the sole effects doctrine. The second is about the relationship between regulatory freedom and a right to property in international law. The third is a general theoretical discourse in international investment law and other branches of international law, such as the Global Administrative Law (GAL) in relation to regulatory freedom and indirect expropriation.

§5.01 CASE-BY-CASE METHOD

The case-by-case method is primarily a practice-oriented approach, employed primarily for delineating regulatory freedom and indirect expropriation. Although limited in application, it has been used in some investment cases and is popular amongst some practitioners.[1] These practitioners and commentators take a practice-oriented approach and insist that the distinguishing line between indirect expropriation and

1. Jan Paulsson & Zachary Douglas, 'Indirect Expropriation in Investment Treaty Arbitration' in Norbert Horn & Stephan Kroll (eds) *Arbitrating Foreign Investment Disputes: Procedural and Substantive Legal Aspects* (The Hague: Kluwer Law International, 2004); Jan Paulsson, 'Indirect Expropriation: Is the Right to Regulate at Risk?' Paper presented on 12 December 2005 in Paris at

justifiable regulation shall be left to the discretion of the arbitrators. The requirement of a case-by-case approach is said to arise from the impossibility of drawing a clear dividing line between regulatory freedom and indirect expropriation. The difficulty in drawing the dividing line between regulatory freedom and indirect expropriation was highlighted in *Saluka v Czech Republic* in following words:

> international law has yet to identify in a comprehensive and definitive fashion precisely what regulations are considered 'permissible' and 'commonly accepted' as falling within the police or regulatory power of State and, thus, non-compensable. In other words, it has yet to draw a bright and easy distinguishable line between non-compensable regulations on the one hand and, on the other, measures that have the effect of depriving foreign investors of their investment and are thus unlawful and compensable in international law.[2]

The case-by-case method is seen as a convenient formula that permits the arbitral tribunal to exercise the desired discretion to draw this dividing line. The relevance and utility of the case-by-case method was discussed in *Generation Ukraine v Ukraine*. The Tribunal expressed sympathy over the need to provide a clear distinction but leaned in favour of the case-by-case method as the only practical way forward. According to the Tribunal, '...there is no checklist, no mechanical test to achieve that purpose. The decisive considerations vary from case to case, depending not only on the specific facts of a grievance but also on the way the evidence is presented, and the legal bases pleaded. The outcome is a judgment, i.e. the product of discernment, and not the printout of a computer programme'.[3]

The case-by-case method is preferred because it is convenience. Christie also argued that a common law method of deciding on a case-by-case basis is the best way to determine if the loss of property has resulted into taking.[4] According to one leading arbitrator, case-by-case method is appropriate because:

> Much has been written on how to draw this line and dozens of decisions have attempted to strike the fair and just balance. The fact remains that an abstract definition is probably unworkable. It all depends on the specific facts and circumstances of the case, particularly the gravity and length of the interference, the rights of the parties under a contract or general legislation, and even cultural elements that define shared expectations. However, just keeping in mind the thought of a necessary balance might be helpful to achieve a reasonable result. This is the challenge for judges, arbitrators and international lawyers.[5]

---

a symposium on 'Making the Most of International Investment Agreements' organized by ICSID, OECD and UNCTAD, available at http://www.oecd.org/investment/internationalinvestment agreements/36055332.pdf; L Yves Fortier & Stephen L Drymer, 'Indirect Expropriation in the Law of International Investment: I Know It When I See It, or *Caveat Investor*' *ICSID Review-FILJ* 19 (2004): 293.

2. *Saluka v Czech Republic*, Partial Award, UNCITRAL, 17 March 2006, para. 263.
3. *Generation Ukraine Incorporation v Ukraine*, Award, ICSID Case No. ARB/00/9, 16 September 2003, para. 20.29; Above note 1 (Paulsson, Is the Right to Regulate at Risk?).
4. G C Christie, 'What Constitutes A Taking of Property under International Law' *BYIL* 38 (1962): 307, 338.
5. Francisco Vicñia, 'Carlos Calvo: Honorary NAFTA Citizen' *NYU Environmental Law Journal* 11 (2002–2003): 19, 28.

He further adds that the nature of expropriation disputes is such that they can be decided only with reference to the specific treaty and the scope of the standards contained therein.[6] According to the case-by-case method, there are two variables that influence the outcome of a dispute involving indirect expropriation: treaty text and facts. Since both these factors change from case to case, fixed legal standards cannot be applied. Therefore, the standards shall also be flexible and the hands of arbitrators shall not be tied.

While one strives to achieve certainty and clarity of standards, especially for indirect expropriation, the votaries of the case-by-case method propose that:

> There is no magical formula, susceptible to mechanical application that will guarantee that the same case will be decided in the same way irrespective of how it is presented and irrespective of who decides it. Nor is it possible to guarantee that a particular analysis will endure over time; the law evolves, and so do patterns of economic activity and public regulation.[7]

A 'mechanical formula' cannot be framed but a 'workable formula' based on state practice and precedent can be drawn.[8] Each treaty is an outcome of individual bargain and would result into different outcomes through the process of interpretation. However, this principle is of little impact in cases of regulatory freedom because regulatory freedom, as discussed in the next Chapter, emanates from customary international law and remains uniform despite difference in the language of treaties. Most of the treaties do not even mention regulatory freedom, thus leaving the position in customary law untouched. In the treaties where regulatory freedom has been modified the contents of regulatory freedom as a customary norm would change accordingly.

The mere fact that the treaty texts differ is no basis to discard the role of legal principles, particularly those originating in general international law. Lauterpacht has discussed this phenomenon in relation to the decisions of the ICJ and the PCIJ. He views that although the Court was deciding cases under specific treaties, the Court has developed certain general principles during the interpretative process. These principles emanate from customary law and general principles of law.[9] Therefore, even if cases are decided in relation to a treaty, the guiding principles for adjudication cannot be oblivious to legal principles. They continue to guide the dispute resolution process, especially when the norm in question is of customary nature.

Facts certainly play an important and influential role in shaping the dispute and the outcome. But legal disputes cannot be decided purely on factual basis, unless so agreed by the parties. Once a tribunal had determined the facts of the case, they have to be subjected to the rigours of legal principles. The determination of facts and the

6. *Ibid.*, 19, 29.
7. Above note 1 (Paulsson, Is the Right to Regulate at Risk?), 1.
8. *See* Chapters 7 and 8.
9. Hersch Lauterpacht, *The Development of International Law by the International Court* (Cambridge; Grotius Publications Ltd., 1982), 26–28.

weight to be attached to them is dictated by the legal principles.[10] The presence and discussion on legal standards applied to the findings of facts ensures fairness in the judicial process. Therefore, the legal principles have to remain constant and unaffected by changing facts, unless the legal principles have themselves transformed over time.

The Tribunal in *Feldman v Mexico* acknowledged the influence of facts on the outcome of indirect expropriation cases. The Tribunal did not take the view that factual determinations will replace the role of legal principles. Legal principles will continue and factual conclusions will have to be then tested based on those legal principles.[11] Unlike the Tribunal in *Generation Ukraine v Ukraine*, which based its conclusions solely on the case-by-case method.[12] The tension has to be resolved based on firm and certain legal principles. The legal principles that constitute regulatory freedom and can form the basis to delineate regulatory freedom from indirect expropriation are extant and embedded in public international law and there are no reasons to ignore them. The deeper concern is regarding the tension between objective criteria and subjective preferences of arbitrators. The dilemma is whether regulatory freedom and indirect expropriation are to be distinguished based on the subjective understanding of the arbitrators or on objective criteria, formulated in the so-called abstract terms.

Influence of factual considerations on the outcome of a dispute has to be distinguished from a decision purely based on the discretion of arbitrators. If arbitrators are deciding cases in the absence of legal principles and based simply on facts and their conscience, then they would be deciding cases based on equity (*ex aequo et bono*).[13] *Ex aequo et bono* gives authority to an arbitral tribunal to decide cases based on equity, without applying legal principles. Equity certainly forms a part of the overall adjudication process in the form of a general principle[14] but it cannot be the exclusive basis to decide disputes.[15] Equity or *ex aequo et bono* can be employed by an international tribunal to decide disputes only where parties have specifically agreed to it.[16] Even

10. *Ibid.*, 35–36. Citing *Corfu Channel (United Kingdom of Great Britain and Northern Ireland v Albania)* (Merits) [1949] ICJ Rep 4; *Legal Status of Eastern Greenland (Norway v Denmark)*, PCIJ Series A/B, No. 53, p. 22; *Minquiers and Ecrehos (France/United Kingdom)* [1953] ICJ Rep 47.
11. *Marvin Feldman v Mexico*, Award, ICSID Case No. ARB (AF)/99/1, 16 December 2002, para. 102. This view is different from the exclusive case-by-case basis approach advocated by some scholars, which argue that no legal principles are of any assistance in making the distinction.
12. Above note 3 (*Generation Ukraine Incorporation v Ukraine*).
13. For a similar argument in the context of fair and equitable treatment *see* Paparinskis, *The International Minimum Standard and Fair and Equitable Treatment* (Oxford: Oxford University Press, 2013), 117–120.
14. *Continental Shelf (Tunisia v Libya)* (Merits) [1982] ICJ Rep 18, para. 71.
15. *North Sea Continental Shelf Cases (Germany v Denmark; Germany v Netherlands)* (Merits) [1969] ICJ Rep 3, para. 85.
16. Article 38 (2) of the ICJ Statute provides that: 'This provision shall not prejudice the power of the Court to decide a case *ex aequo et bono*, if the parties agree thereto.' Available at http://legal.un.org/avl/pdf/ha/sicj/icj_statute_e.pdf; last visited: 10 October 2015; *North Sea Continental Shelf Cases* (n 15) para. 88; *Continental Shelf (Tunisia/Libya)* (n 14) para. 71; *Delimitation of the Maritime Boundary in the Gulf of Maine Area (Canada v US)* [1984] ICJ Rep 246, para. 59; *Continental Shelf (Libya v Malta)* [1985] ICJ Rep 13, paras 45–48.

    Antonio Parra, 'Applicable Law in Investor-State Arbitration' in Arthur Rovine (ed.) *Contemporary Issues in International Arbitration and Mediation: The Fordham Papers 2007* (The Netherlands, Martinus Nijhoff, 2013) available at http://www.arbitration-icca.org/articles.html?author=Antonio_Parra&sort=author, last visited: 10 October 2015; Hege Elisabeth Kjos,

equity does not authorize the adjudicator to decide cases on subjective preferences, rules of equity continue to play a role. As stated above, Christie perceived that the judicial body would adopt the common law methodology, implying the use of equity to distinguish regulation from indirect expropriation. A judicial body, including an institution tribunal, cannot decide cases based purely on equity unless parties have agreed to it in clear terms.[17] In the ICSID system too, an arbitral tribunal cannot decide cases based on equity unless so accepted by the parties.[18]

If legal principles are ignored and arbitrators claim freedom to decide disputes as per their subjective preferences, it will result into an uncertain outcome. Uncertainty of outcome is already a troublesome feature in investment arbitrations.[19] There have been instances where tribunals have reached diametrically opposite conclusions on the same facts[20] and two tribunals have come to diametrically opposite conclusion on same issue where they shared common arbitrators.[21] Presence of legal principles is necessary to instil certainty in judicial decisions. Certainty of regulating legal principles is necessary for both litigating parties: foreign investor as well as the State. The outcome may not be assured, but the parties shall be certain about the legal principles that would be applied by the arbitral tribunal. The influence of the manner of presentation and of the personality of the adjudicator is an inescapable evil of every adversarial system - whether domestic or international. This cannot form the basis to leave the discretion with the adjudicator in entirety; rather it is a reason not to leave too much discretion with the adjudicators. Legal principles also ensure that there is transparency and fairness in the decision-making process. They set a standard benchmark that each adjudicator has to follow and tame the influence of subjective preferences of the decision maker. Specially to achieve fairness in the judicial process - 'justice shall not only be done but shall be manifest to be done.'[22] The legal principles have to remain certain and constant.

Applicable Law in Investor-State Arbitration: The Interplay Between National and International Law (Oxford, Oxford University Press, 2013), 295–302; Yas Banifatemi, 'The Law Applicable in Investment Treaty Arbitration', in Katia Yannaca-Small (ed.) *Arbitration under International Investment Agreements: A Guide to the Key Issues* (New York: Oxford University Press, 2010), 196 citing *Autopista Concesionada de Venezuela C.A. (Aucoven) v Bolivarian Republic of Venezuela*, Award, ICSID Case No. ARB/00/5, 23 September 2003, para. 94; *Atlantic Triton v Guinea*, Award, 21 April 1986 (1995) 3 ICSID Reports 17, 23.

17. *Ibid.*
18. Article 42 (3) ICSID Convention. It says: 'The provisions of paragraphs (1) and (2) shall not prejudice the power of the Tribunal to decide a dispute *ex aequo et bono* if the parties so agree.' Available at https://icsid.worldbank.org/ICSID/StaticFiles/basicdoc/partA.htm; last visited: 10 October 2015.
19. *See* M Sornarajah, 'A Coming Crisis: Expansionary Trends in Investment Treaty Arbitration' in Karl P Sauvant (ed.) *Appeals Mechanism in International Investment Disputes* (New York: Oxford University Press, 2008); Andres Rigo Sureda, *Investment Treaty Arbitration: Judging under Uncertainty* (Cambridge: New York: Cambridge University Press, 2012).
20. Compare *Ronald S. Lauder v The Czech Republic*, UNCITRAL, Final Award, 3 September 2001 and *CME Czech Republic B.V. v The Czech Republic*, Partial Award, UNCITRAL, 13 September 2001.
21. *Compare LG&E Energy Corp., LG&E Capital Corp., and LG&E International, Inc. v Argentine Republic*, Decision on Liability, 3 October 2006 and *Enron Corporation and Ponderosa Assets, L.P. v Argentine Republic*, Award, ICSID Case No. ARB/01/3, 22 May 2007.
22. *R v Sussex Justices*, Ex parte McCarthy [1923] All ER Rep 233.

Another argument proposed to exercise arbitral discretion on a case-by-case basis is that the measures through which a State can potentially impact the rights of foreign investors cannot 'fit into a neat formula'. Therefore, the test for indirect expropriation shall be flexible enough to keep pace with the realities of investments and rising regulatory functions.[23] Some scholars have referred to the famous statement by Justice Potter Stuart of the United States Supreme Court: 'I know it when I see it.'[24] This statement was made in the context of indirect takings under American municipal law. According to this view, the process of discerning regulatory freedom from indirect expropriation can occur only through a handpicked analysis by the arbitrator.[25] If municipal judges have successfully utilized this doctrine, then there shall be no impediment for investment tribunals to resort to it.[26]

This point of view ignores the vast difference between the circumstances of adjudication in a municipal forum *vis-à-vis* international. A municipal judge possesses special knowledge and expertise of the constitutional provisions, public law principles, cultural sensitivities, social and the political environment of the jurisdiction. An international tribunal is not only geographically separated but also culturally aloof. It cannot be expected to be conscious and well versed with the judicial culture in the country. Further, an arbitrator, in an international tribunal is often under influence of judicial training and jurisprudential preferences of his or her home State. Influence of these factors on the manner of exercise of discretion is obvious. Judicial decision-making process at municipal level is subject to various checks and balances. The system can structurally ensure that the judges of municipal courts acquire special knowledge and capabilities necessary to exercise discretion. Lauterpacht highlighted the reasons for unacceptability of exercise of wide discretion by international tribunal that equates the discretion of international tribunal with that of municipal courts in the following words:

> If government by men, and not by laws, is resented within the State by individuals, any appearance of it is likely to be viewed with even greater suspicion on the part of sovereign States in relation to judges of foreign nationality.[27]

It is difficult to agree that an international tribunal could and should exercise discretion equivalent to a municipal court and particularly a municipal constitutional court. An international court or tribunal cannot transgress beyond the scope of consent based on which it is created. The strength of decisions of international courts and tribunals lies in the depth and persuasiveness of their reasoning. The enforcement machinery of a State backs the judgments of a municipal court, whereas, for an international tribunal, this luxury does not exist. Thus, it is the strength of the

23. Paulsson & Douglas (n 1), 146.
24. L Yves Fortier & Stephen Drymer, 'Indirect Expropriation in the Law of International Investment: I Know It When I See It, or Caveat Investor' *ICSID Review-FILJ* 19 (2004): 293, 326–327.
25. Frank Michelman, 'Property, Utility, and Fairness: Comments on the Ethical Foundations of the "Just Compensation" Law' *Harvard Law Review* 80 (1967): 1165, 1170–1171.
26. Above note 1 (Paulsson, Is the Right to Regulate at Risk?), 2.
27. *Ibid.*, p. 40.

reasoning that adduces credibility and voluntary compliance.[28] Absence or unwillingness to spell out the legal principles forming the basis of the decision makes the decision vulnerable. An international tribunal has to be careful. Its authority does not depend on the finality of its conclusions but persuasiveness of its reasoning and the legal framework that it employs.[29] There must be clear legal principles based on which the decisions are made. The need that justice should not only be done, but it should be manifest that it is done is acutely necessary in the field on international adjudication.[30]

Amongst recently concluded investment treaties, there is some support emerging for case-by-case analysis as one of the ingredients for determination of indirect expropriation. These treaties refer to the case-by-case method as one of the criterion, juxtaposed with other criteria, such as economic impact of the governmental action on investment. But the impact is not sufficient by itself and there are other conditions such as: interference with reasonable investment backed expectations, and the character of the governmental action. All these factors have to be considered together. A further separate category of regulations is carved out and with independent criteria and treated as exception.[31] They do not consider case-by-case method to be the sole determinative factor.

The case-by-case method may result into dispensation of the requirement of elaboration of legal principles forming the basis of judicial reasoning. Without appropriate and adequate reasoning, legal scrutiny of the conclusions is impossible.[32] Lauterpacht emphasized on the need of legal principles in reasoning of judicial bodies. He gave the example of *Anglo-Norwegian Fisheries* case. It was possible to decide the dispute on the basis of historic title of Norway, and formal issues of acquiescence, but the Court gave a detailed reasoning and based it on customary international law. This shows the concern of the Court in presenting more than one reasons for its determination and moreover, embedding them in legal principles.[33]

§5.02 THEORETICAL JUSTIFICATIONS FOR THE SOLE EFFECTS DOCTRINE

[A] Prior to the BITs

Theoretical approaches towards the relationship and distinction between regulatory freedom and indirect expropriation and the role of the sole effects doctrine have risen after the advent of investment treaty arbitration. However, there have been some

28. Christopher Ford, 'Judicial Discretion in International Jurisprudence: Article 38(1)(c) and "General Principles of Law"' *Duke Journal of Comparative and International Law* 5 (1994–1995): 35, 53–56.
29. Lauterpacht (n 9), 38–43.
30. *Ibid.*, 38–39.
31. Article 11.7, US-Australia FTA 43 ILM 1248; US-Chile BIT 42 ILM 1026; US-Morocco BIT 44 ILM 544 (signed 22 July 1985, entered into force 29 May 1991); US-Singapore FTA; US-Uruguay BIT (signed 4 November 2005, entered into force 31 October 2006); Canada-Peru BIT (signed 14 November 2006, entered into force 20 June 2007).
32. Lauterpacht (n 9), 39–40.
33. *Ibid.*, 45–46.

efforts at theorizing on these issues did take place prior to the BITs. Scholars grappled with these issues based on the decisions of claims commissions, state contracts and other instances of nationalizations.[34] The role of Christie in relation to the sole effects doctrine has been already discussed in extensively in the last Chapter and to some degree above. In this section, argument by Higgins, supporting the sole effects doctrine to resolve the conflict between regulatory freedom and indirect expropriation as a community interest versus individual interest and Wetson's argument of 'wealth deprivation' are discussed.

Higgins made an important and early contribution to the discourse on the sole effects doctrine.[35] According to Higgins, even in domestic law there were problems with distinguishing between regulatory freedom and indirect expropriation. But whenever States resort to measures that significantly deprive the owner of the use of property, that measure amounts to expropriation even if the owner remains in physical possession of the property and the title remains intact.[36] In all these situations compensation shall be paid.[37] Because, according to her, losses suffered by a foreign investor due to regulations are a confrontation between community or societal interest and individual or private interest. There is no reason why an individual shall suffer losses for the benefit of the community. If community wishes to deprive individuals, especially foreigners of their property rights then it must compensate for those losses.[38]

The conceptualization of regulatory freedom versus indirect expropriation would apply to the situations of exercise of eminent domain or an expropriatory measure, where the property of the foreign investor is in fact taken for community interests. In this process, there is a clear act of taking or 'appropriation' of the private property by the State. In these situations, compensation would be payable. The community does not obtain any benefit at the cost of private party in the case of a regulatory measure since there is no direct or indirect transfer of the property to the community. The losses suffered by the private person are incidental.[39] If a State is asked to pay compensation for all losses arising from its regular governmental actions, the government activity will freeze. It will convert the investor protection treaties into assurances of success and payment of compensation in all cases of losses or stabilization clause like situation (discussed in detail below). Higgin's formula, although simple, ignores that a foreign

34. Amador refers to the argument of responsibility of State to pay compensation in all situations as the orthodox school of thought. International Law Commission, International Responsibility, Fourth Report by F V García Amador, Special Rapporteur: Responsibility of the State for Injuries Caused in its Territory to the Person or Property of Aliens – Measures Affecting Acquired Rights Document A/CN.4/119 (26 February 1959), (1959) II Yearbook of the International Law Commission 1, para. 19, described further in footnote 24.

35. Rosalyn Higgings, 'The Taking of Property by the State: Recent Developments in International Law', (1982) III *Recueil des Cours* 267, 268.

36. *Ibid.*, 267, 324 citing King Case: M White, *Damages in International Law*, 1937 vol. 2, 1387–1391.

37. *Ibid.*, 267, 322–330.

38. *Ibid.*, 267, 277–278; Burns H Weston, '"Constructive Takings" under International Law: A Modest Foray into the Problem of "Creeping Expropriation"' *Virginia Journal of International Law* 16 (1975): 103, 116; Rudolph Dolzer, 'Indirect Expropriations: New Developments?' *NYU Environmental Journal* 11 (2002): 64, 75.

39. *See* the discussion in Chapter 2.

investor may suffer losses due to various reasons, which cannot be fully captured within the paradigm of community interests versus private interests, which fundamentally relates to the eminent domain.[40]

Another version of the argument is that the community shall not draw benefits by depriving individual of its property – the argument of 'wealth deprivation'. Weston introduced the concept that wealth deprivation amounts to expropriation. According to Weston, the distinction between a regulatory measure and an expropriatory measure is superficial. Whatever may be the nomenclature of the action of the State, the 'result' is the same: loss of an individual's property.[41] Wealth deprivation is seen as 'normatively neutral'. It encompasses all deprivations of private property 'at whatever time, by whatever means, with whatever intensity, and for whatever claimed purpose'.[42] The emphasis therefore has to be on the 'factual rather than the legal results'.[43]

This argument discards the sophisticated and long settled distinction between the two legal concepts of expropriation (eminent domain) and regulatory freedom (police powers). Wetson's argument is founded on the assumption that irrespective of different normative contents, the principle of expropriation and police powers both 'describe a result than... define the process by which the result is reached'.[44] The concept of wealth deprivation may have been appropriate for the Iran-US Claims Tribunal since its jurisdiction extended not just to expropriatory measures but to 'other measures affecting property rights'. BITs do not contain such a broad formulation in their expropriation clauses. Weston had proposed his analysis prior to the jurisprudence of investment arbitration, nevertheless it does find a place in discussions in international investment law.

The 'wealth deprivation' argument covers all losses irrespective of their intensity. Even the sole effects doctrine, as understood in the current arbitral practice, does not find indirect expropriation until a high threshold of property deprivation is established – referred to as 'neutralization'.[45] In spite of his position that indirect expropriation be interpreted broadly to cover all instances of property deprivation, Weston was conscious and explicit in stating that police powers continue to be an exception for payment of compensation for losses.[46] The criterion proposed by Weston to save regulations from the liability to pay compensation for losses to property is of 'world public order'.[47] The term 'world public order' is not a legal term. It is undefined and obscure. This problem is sought to be overcome by claiming that it should be based on

40. For a further discussion on the relationship between community and individual interests in relation to regulatory freedom and indirect expropriation see the discussion below in Section C.
41. Above note 38 (Weston), 111–112.
42. *Ibid.*, 103, 112.
43. *Ibid.*, 103, 113.
44. *Ibid.*, 103, 111.
45. In language used by the Tribunal in *Sempra v Argentina* is instructive: 'It would require that the investor no longer be in control of its business operation, or that the value of the business have been virtually annihilated.' *Sempra Energy International v The Argentine Republic*, Award, ICSID Case No. ARB/02/16, 28 September 2007; *El Paso Energy International Company v The Argentine Republic*, Award, ICSID Case No. ARB/03/15, 31 October 2011, paras 244–256.
46. *Ibid.*, 103, 111–113.
47. Above note 38 (Weston), 103, 123.

'a policy which favours a peaceful, productive, and equitable global economy perceived in terms of aggregate well-being'.[48] This description makes the concept more elusive.

[B] Post BITs

Some scholars have developed theoretical arguments by taking the emergence of BITs as the points of departure. According to them, although the specific provisions of BITs differ, they contain certain general features aimed at responding to the demands of globalization and increasing interdependence of national economies. BITs are seen as an important shift from the FCN treaties. FCN relied on very simple theories of economic development, whereas BITs are entered with the intention of creating a normative framework expecting transparency, stability of regulations, administrative efficiency, etc. in a host State which normally is a developing or least a developed State.[49] Thus, investment treaties aim at creating a stable 'normative framework'.[50] Investment treaties are - arguably - to be seen as instruments created by developed countries to create a liberal investment regime in other countries.[51] It is in light of these developments that indirect expropriation has to be interpreted. The public policy underlying broader interpretation of indirect expropriation clauses is the objective of encouragement and protection of investments.[52] Therefore, expropriation clauses - especially indirect expropriation - should be interpreted broadly to force the host State to conduct actions that fit with the aspirations of the normative framework created by the BITs. The argument draws support from the preambles of BITs stating that the investment treaties are entered into for creating favourable conditions for greater investments.[53] The contents and rational of the normative framework is stated in the following words by Reisman and Sloane:

> The 'favourable conditions' established by BITs consist, not merely of natural phenomena such as climate, resources, and access to the sea, nor even of an educated population in the host state receptive to and eager to participate in the benefits of foreign investment; they also contemplate, more significantly and innovatively, an effective normative framework: impartial courts, an efficient and legally restrained bureaucracy, and the measure of transparency in decision that has increasingly been recognized as a control mechanism over governments and

48. *Ibid.*, 103, 123-131.
49. W Michael Reisman & Robert D. Sloane, 'Indirect Expropriation and Its Valuation in the BIT Generation' BYIL 74 (2003): 115, 116-118.
50. *Ibid.*, 115. A slightly different argument is made by Schill that investment treaties have resulted into creation of multilateral framework. *See* Stephan Schill, *Multilateralization of International Investment Law* (Cambridge: Cambridge University Press, 2009).
51. Kenneth Vandevelde, *Bilateral Investment Treaties: History, Policy, and Interpretation* (New York: Oxford University Press, 2010), 108-112.
52. *Ibid.*, 115, 144.
53. For example Preamble, Agreement Between the Government of the United Kingdom of Great Britain and Northern Ireland and the Government of the Republic of Panama for the Promotion and Protection of Investments, 7 October 1983; UNCTAD, *Scope and Definition: UNCTAD Series on Issues in International Investment Agreements II* (New York, Geneva; United Nations, 2011), 120.

> as a vital component of the international standard of governance. Hence, in a BIT regime, the host state must do far more than open its doors to foreign investment and refrain from overt expropriation. It must establish and maintain an appropriate legal, administrative, and regulatory framework, the legal environment that modern investment theory has come to recognize as a condition sine qua non of the success of private enterprise. This is not to say, of course, that every governmental adjustment to this normative framework that adversely affects the conditions for foreign investment will constitute an expropriatory act, but that an appropriately operational governmental framework must be in place.[54]

Likewise, investment treaties are seen as a 'system of self-imposed disciplines on States to counter the natural tendencies of governments to be captured by protectionist and narrow ideological special interest groups with an influence that is stronger in the domestic political process than non-voting and politically and emotionally always easily exploitable "foreign" companies. One can view such international treaties as steps towards a proto-constitutional order of global economy to prevent prosperity and civilization creating machine being damaged by the centrifugal forces for domestic politics.'[55] The regulatory framework is said to be a part of a socio-economic revolution based on privatization.[56]

Scholars claim that States have signed up for external disciplines[57] without any corroborative material reflecting the intention of the States in undertaking such obligations. The argument of concurrent rise of privatization and BITs has created a supervening normative framework, which should influence the interpretation of indirect expropriation clauses in investment treaties appears to be hardly seen in the present day global economy. Investment treaties do not profess economic commitment of liberalization. The governance structures of the economies where major flows of investments are presently happening hardly reflect the adherence of the normative obligations of liberalization and privatization.[58] Public corporations continue to wield influence. They have been the engines of expansion and cross-border capital movement.[59] Even international law does not support such a move because the right to choose appropriate economic philosophy is left with individual States.[60] The suggestions that the objective of investment treaties is to implement the objectives of certain

54. Above note 49 (Reisman and Sloane), 115, 117 (citations excluded).
55. *Ibid.*, 115, 814.
56. *Ibid.*, 115, 117–118.
57. Thomas Waelde & Abba Kolo, 'Environmental Regulation, Investment Protection and "Regulatory Taking" in International Law' *ICLQ* 50 (2001): 811, 822–823.
58. M Sornarajah, 'India, China and Foreign Investment' in M Sornarajah & Jiangyu Wang (ed.) *China, India and the International Economic Order* (Cambridge: Cambridge University Press, 2010), 136–139.
59. *See* M Sornarajah, 'Sovereign Wealth Funds and International Investment Law' *Asian Journal of International Law* 1 (2011): 267; *see* generally Albert Badia, *Piercing the Veil of State Enterprises in International Arbitration* (Alphen aan den Rijn: Kluwer Law International, 2014).
60. Atlantic Charter, 14 August 1941; 2625 (XXV). Declaration on Principles of International Law concerning Friendly Relations and Co-operation among States in accordance with the Charter of the United Nations, 24 October 1970, available at http://www.un-documents.net/a25r2625.htm, last visited 10 October 2015; Declaration on the Inadmissibility of Intervention and Interference in the Domestic Affairs of States (UNGA resolution 2131 (XX) 1965), available at http://www.un.org/documents/ga/res/36/a36r103.htm, last visited 10 October 2015.

capital exporting countries to liberalize and privatize other nations undermines the policy of investment treaties to spread capital and achieve economic progress in different parts of the world, while granting adequate protection to the investors.

A comparison between the FCN treaties and the BITs shows that the FCN treaties were more liberal as compared to the BITs. The rights of investors protected under the FCN treaties went beyond those contemplated under the BITs. To some scholars BITs are a regressive step as compared to the FCN treaties.[61] The FCN treaties were entered mostly between advanced economies and contained absolute standards of treatment, such as 'a special protection to the persons and property'[62] or 'a full and perfect protection for ...persons and property'.[63] These broad protections were understandable in view of the power relations between States. Even where treaties were entered into between capital exporting and capital importing States, the power relationship between them was different at the time of entering into FCN treaties. The weakness of the FCN treaties was the lack of a standing to the foreign investor to initiate dispute resolution without diplomatic protection. The hegemonic powers of the time were insistent on strong protection and the capital importing states were not in a position to resist such absolutist protection standards. The arguments of a strong State imposing obligations on a weaker State could have been sustained in the early BITs. In the recent times, with the traditional distinction between capital importing and capital exporting States blurring and the traditional capital importing States becoming capital exporting States, the argument of external disciplines would be counter intuitive. Also, arguments based on the preamble ignore that the preambles also contain the obligation of mutual development. A partial framework favouring some words in the preamble over others is not a proper and holistic understanding of these provisions. The argument of creation of a normative framework is also strengthened through the language of indirect expropriation. It is argued that 'tantamount' to expropriation clause in BITs extends the scope of indirect expropriation.[64] This view has failed to garner support in investment tribunals and they have preferred narrow interpretation of 'tantamount' to expropriation clause.[65]

The necessity for the States to regulate, especially for protection of environment is represented as a return to protectionism and the NIEO, based on opposition to investment liberalization and stalling the role of global markets.[66] Regulatory exercises, especially for environment protection are said to result into 'unexpected change

61. Rudolf Dolzer & Margarete Stevens, *Bilateral Investment Treaties* (Hague: Martinus Nijhoff Publishers, 1995), 10–13; Kenneth Vandevelde 'A Brief History of International Investment Agreements' *UC – Davis Journal of International Law & Policy* 12 (2005): 157, 162–166; Wolfgang Alschner, 'Americanization of the BIT Universe: The Influence of Friendship, Commerce and Navigation (FCN) Treaties on Modern Investment Treaty Law' *Goettingen Journal of International Law* 5 (2013): 455, 463–468.
62. Article XIII, Treaty for Peace, Friendship, Commerce and Navigation between Bolivia and the USA (1958).
63. Article IX, para. 3, Treaty of Friendship, Commerce and Navigation between Paraguay and the USA (1959).
64. Above note 49 (Reisman & Sloane), 115, 118–119, 128–130.
65. *See* above Chapter 3.
66. Above note 57 (Waelde & Kolo), 811–812.

with an excessive detrimental impact on the foreign investor's prior calculation' to favour domestic competitors.[67] This argument supporting the effects doctrine is based on the presumption that if regulatory freedom is recognized it would allow a State to undertake discriminatory measures. Contrary to this perception, a regulatory measure shall be non-discriminatory. Through a rigorous analysis of the nature of the measure would ensure that discriminatory actions of a State are not treated as a regulatory measure.

A lot of weight is appended to the emergence of BITs to realign the existing international law on foreign investment. The BITs certainly have an effect, manifested through the treatment standards, but they can hardly be said to create a normative structure. The argument of creation of a normative structure are based on policy predilections. They propose suppression of rules by policy. The drawback of reliance on a policy is that the policy cannot operate as a replacement for the rule. If a rule exists then the policy must give way. The effect of using theoretical perspectives to expand the scope of treatment standards would amount to revision of treaty clauses. The adjudicating body is entrusted with interpretation and cannot revise the treaties.[68] For international adjudication, theoretical approaches alien to the text of treaties are unwarranted. This is evident from the decisions of the Supreme Court of British Columbia, partially setting aside the award in *Metaclad v Mexico*, for the reason that the Tribunal founded its reason on principles similar to the normative framework argument. In the view of the Court, the reasoning of the Tribunal that the BITs had created a normative framework of transparency at the international level, with which a host State had to comply, is incorrect. Neither was there such specific terms in the BIT nor could they be imported under the pretext of interpretation.[69] This caution and circumspection towards transparency is echoed in some arbitral decisions as well. In *Feldman v Mexico*, the Tribunal declined to conclude existence of indirect expropriation on the grounds that the conduct of the authorities fell short of the reasonable expected standards.[70] Especially in the context of BITs, in contradistinction to adjudication under a multilateral system with adjudicative body like the Dispute Settlement Body (DSB) in World Trade Organization (WTO) the treaty provisions and the institutional structure of the tribunals is free standing.[71] The general systematic concerns can no doubt, not be ignored, but any external policy implications are inconceivable. The negotiators of investment treaties have specific goals in mind, stated expressly in the treatment standards.[72] The legitimacy of the process of

67. *Ibid.*, 819, 820.
68. *Interpretation of Peace Treaties with Bulgaria, Hungary and Romania (Second Phase)* Advisory Opinion (1950) ICJ Reports 221, 229.
69. *United Mexican States v Metaclad Corporation*, Supreme Court of British Columbia, 2 May 2001, 2001 BCSC 664, paras 66–80, pp. 16–18.
70. *Marvin Feldman v Mexico*, Award, ICSID Case No. ARB (AF)/99/1, 16 December 2002, paras 113, 133.
71. *Glaims Gold Ltd. v United States of America*, Award, NAFTA Chapter 11 Tribunal (UNCITRAL), 8 June 2009, para. 3.
72. W Michael Reisman, '"Case Specific Mandates" Versus "Systematic Implications"': How Should Investment Tribunals Decide?: The Freshfields Arbitration Lecture' *Arbitration International* 29 (2013): 131, 142.

application of legal principles depends on the extent to which the interpreters are 'faithful to the expectations of the parties; in international investment law, those expectations derive principally from a specific treaty and contract'.[73] If investment tribunals rely on extraneous theoretical considerations, they would be overstepping from their judicial mandate and attract challenges of legitimacy. When an adjudicator is faced with a choice between a conflict between a rule and policy, then the rule is to be chosen even if it seems contrary to a major community goal.[74] Excessive reliance on policy considerations would 'render the application of virtually all legal rules highly uncertain'.[75] Taken together, these theoretical approaches propose a framework based on accountability of State for providing a system of governance that meets a particular standard. These requirements could at best be 'accountability' expectations. For the purposes of a treaty breach and consequential State responsibility, there shall be a breach of an obligation. The words 'responsibility' and 'accountability' are distinguishable. The prior is narrower in scope, and the later includes wider forms of answerability like financial, political and administrative.[76]

[C] Problems with the Sole Effects Doctrine and Its Impact on Regulatory Freedom

The task of the sole effects doctrine is to distinguish between two competing touchstones: legitimate regulatory measure versus a measure aimed at expropriation. By focusing on the effect, it completely ignores the role of the other competing principle regulatory freedom. The working of this anomaly is evident in the conclusions of an investment tribunal,[77] which concluded that it is immaterial whether the measure is regulatory or not, as long as the effect of the measure is 'irreversible and permanent'. Investment tribunals that have not applied the decisions of the Iran-US Claims Tribunal have been conscious of this distinction. They have looked at the nature of the measure to decide if the measure is expropriatory.[78]

There are several problems inherent in the sole effects doctrine. What should be the degree of interference that is adequate to constitute indirect expropriation? The Tribunals do not apply a uniform standard. Some tribunals have held that there is a possibility of expropriation if only a portion of property is affected, without the entire

73. *Ibid.*, 131, 150.
74. Oscar Schachter, 'International Law in Theory and Practice: General Course in Public International Law' *Recueil des Cours* V (1982): 21, 50.
75. *Ibid.*, 21, 49. Schachter gives a fitting example form the law of the law. The freedom of seas is a major 'community policy', but that cannot override rules of navigation or unlawful conduct on the high seas.
76. James Crawford, *State Responsibility: The General Part* (Cambridge: Cambridge University Press, 2013), 83–85.
77. *Medioambientales Techmed S.A. v The United Mexican States*, Award, ICSID Case No. ARB (AF)/00/2, 29 May 2003, para. 116 (relying on the decisions of the Iran –US Claims Tribunal).
78. *Saluka Investments BV (The Netherlands) v The Czech Republic*, Partial Award, Permanent Court of Arbitration, 17 March 2006, para. 276; *Methanex Corporation v United States of America*, Final Award of the Tribunal on Jurisdiction and Merits, 3 August 2005, Part IV-Chapter D, para. 15; *Marvin Feldman v Mexico*, Award, ICSID Case No. ARB (AF)/99/1, 16 December 2002, para. 103.

investment being affected.[79] This has led some scholars to argue that the responsibility of the State to pay compensation shall be proportional to the extent of interference, whether or not the interference completely destroys the property of the foreign investor.[80] This argument imposes an absolute obligation to compensate on the part of the host State. Some investment tribunals have tried to find a way out of this problem through the 'neutralisation' of assets test.[81] This test expects that for a measure to become expropriatory, it must have resulted in the complete destruction of the assets of the foreign investor. This interpretation does not account for the nature and circumstances of the adoption of the measure.

The practical effect of the sole effects doctrine is of converting investment treaties into insurance from losses – the State undertakes to compensate for any and every loss of property. Investment tribunals have time and again repeated that investment treaties are not a guarantee against all losses.[82] By providing compensation in all situations of loss of property, the sole effects doctrine creates a 'stabilization clause effect', in the absence of one negotiated.[83] A stabilization clause could cause 'regulatory chill'. These clauses create a freezing effect whereby the law of the host State remains fixed at the date of entering into agreement – restricting the power of the State to change the regulatory framework.[84] It stops the host State from altering the legal regime to ensure that the terms of the contract are not affected in any manner.[85] The sole effects doctrine imposes absolute liability, something the ICJ has decried as follows:

> When a State admits into its territory foreign investments or foreign nationals it is... bound to extend to them the protection of the law. However, it does not thereby become an insurer of that part of another State's wealth which these investments represent. Every investment of this kind carries certain risks.[86]

---

79. *Waste Management Inc. v United Mexican States*, Award, ICSID Case No. ARB(AF)/00/3, 30 April 2004, paras 141, 147; *EnCana Corporation v Republic of Ecuador*, Award, UNCITRAL Rules, 3 February 2006, paras 172–183; *Eureko B.V. v Republic of Poland*, Partial Award, 19 August 2005, paras 239–241.
80. F Orrego Vicuña, 'Carlos Calvo, Honorary NAFTA Citizen' *New York University Environmental Law Journal* 11 (2002–2003): 19, 23–24, 27; Ursula Kriebaum, 'Partial Expropriation' *Journal of World Trade & Investment* 8 (2007): 69, 83–84.
81. *El Paso Energy International Company v The Argentine Republic*, Award, ICSID Case No. ARB/03/15, 31 October 2011, paras 244–256.
82. *Emilio Agustín Maffezini v The Kingdom of Spain*, Award, ICSID Case No. ARB/97/7, 13 November 2000, para. 64; *CMS Gas Transmission Company v The Republic of Argentina*, Award on Jurisdiction, ICSID Case No. ARB/01/8, (2003) 42 ILM 788, 17 July 2003, para. 29; *Robert Azinian, Kenneth Davitian, & Ellen Baca v The United Mexican States*, Award, ICSID Case No. ARB (AF)/97/2, 1 November 1999, para. 83; *Marvin Feldman v Mexico*, Award, ICSID Case No. ARB (AF)/99/1, 16 December 2002, paras 111–113.
83. Sornarajah, *International Law on Foreign Investment* (3rd ed., Cambridge: Cambridge University Press, 2010), 281–284.
84. *Duke Energy International Peru Investments No. 1, Ltd. v Peru*, Award, ICSID Case No. ARB/03/28; 18 August 2008, para. 227.
85. Rudolph Dolzer & Christoph Schreuer, *Principles of International Investment Law* (2nd ed., Oxford: Oxford University Press, 2012), 101, 104, 112–114; Andrew Newcombe & Lluis Paradell, *Law and Practice of Investment Treaties: Standards of Treatment* (The Netherlands: Kluwer Law, 2009), 82–85.
86. *Barcelona Traction, Light and Power Company, Limited (Belgium v Spain) (New Application: 1962)*, Second Phase [1970] ICJ Reports 3, para. 87.

A lot of the discussion on the sole effects doctrine originates from the American constitutional law.[87] The sole effects doctrine has not achieved uniform endorsement in the American jurisprudence.[88] Effects is not the sole basis for determining indirect expropriation.[89] It is rather seen as 'a highly unreal view of the actual working of the compensation rule in American law.'[90]

It is suggested that the sole effects doctrine should be preferred over the police powers doctrine because the scope of the police powers doctrine is uncertain as compared to the sole effects doctrine, which would remove uncertainties in decision-making.[91] The sole effects doctrine creates an anomaly by discriminating between two similarly situated foreign investors merely on the basis of the size of their investment and the assets they possess. The sole effects doctrine looks only at the effect on the assets of the investor in question and the effect has to reach the threshold of neutralization. The severity of the impact on one entity would depend on the scale of production, economic strength and scale of assets of that entity. For example, if a regulation is adopted by a State that causes economic loss to companies in a sector. Company X and Y are operating in the same sector. X is a large company and would be able to absorb the losses caused by regulations. The assets would not be neutralized considering its size and market share. Whereas, Y, a small company in the same sector may suffer losses that would meet the threshold of neutralization. If the test of neutralization is applied, then for company X the measure would not be indirect expropriation, but it would be indirect expropriation for company Y.

The value of property is often affected by various factors in the market. An effect based approach fails to recognize this competition driven understanding of property, where its value is not a fixed phenomenon but a matter subject to constant dictates of surrounding market conditions.[92] It is possible that a company that has suffered losses due to its own mismanagement may claim that the losses are an outcome of regulation and exit the State by claiming compensation for expropriation because it has suffered losses.[93]

Expropriatory actions have a 'redistributive function', where the assets of a private person are taken away and distributed for societal use. Regulatory freedom need not be seen as a confrontation between an individual loss versus societal gain because it does not perform that function. It is a creation of environment for greater

87. Vicki Been & Joel C. Beauvais, 'The Global Fifth Amendment? NAFTA's Investment Protections and the Misguided Quest for an International "Regulatory Takings" Doctrine' *NYU Law Review* 78(1) (2003): 30.
88. For examples of cases *see* Joseph Sax, 'Takings and the Police Power' *Yale Law Journal* 36 (1964): 40–46.
89. *Ibid.*, 36, 37. Commenting harshly on the effects doctrine Sax says: 'The Holmesian approach has equal failings. Its central premise – that the right to compensation depends on the magnitude of loss suffered – is historically unsound, has never in fact been accepted by the Court, and wasn't even followed by Holmes himself.'
90. *Ibid.*, 36, 53.
91. Ben Mostafa, 'The Sole Effects Doctrine, Police Powers and Indirect Expropriation under International Law' *Australian International Law Journal* 15 (2008): 267, 294–296.
92. Above note 88 (Sax, Takings and Police Powers), 36, 61–62.
93. Rudolf Dolzer & Margarete Stevens, *Bilateral Investment Treaties* (Hague: Martinus Nijhoff Publishers, 1995), 99.

societal gain and can be used to introduce efficiency in markets. Competition laws are a good example of such regulatory exercises of States. The instances of regulatory function inevitably involve accidental losses, without redistributive objective. Thus, the argument of fairness, demanding equalization between the gains of the society and losses to an individual would not operate in the later cases of regulatory freedom.[94] It may appear that regulations adopted for correcting markets may have adverse economic effect on some private parties but the overall consequence on the health of the economy is much greater and even the losses suffered by certain private parties may be recovered as the markets adjust to the changes.[95] These regulatory measures overrides conflicts, and helps in ensuring equality amongst competing resource.[96]

A regulation would involve balancing of the exercise of rights by one and its impact on the rights of others, including their rights of enjoyment of their respective properties.[97] Non-compensation for regulatory functions can be explained on the basis of 'private fault and public benefit theory'[98] and the suppression of noxious use of property, whereby, 'one cannot obtain a vested right to injure or endanger public'.[99] Measures taken to limit noxious use of property are not expropriation since property rights do not include the right to use the property against public interest.[100] This theory would apply to regulations undertaken to protect public interest such as health and environment, economic stability and other actions capable of causing public distress and necessary for long-term cure. The regulations may be applied for a short term or

94. *Ibid.*, 1165, 1182–1183.
95. Above note 25 (Michelman), 1165, 1225.
96. *Ibid.*, 149, 161.
97. Above note 88 (Sax, Takings and Police Powers), 149, 152–154. Sax explains this paradigm through incisive examples. The government may decide to regulate strip mining having a certain degree of slope. An owner may completely lose the business if the inclination of his property falls within the banned degree. The effects doctrine will expect compensation to be paid. This ignores the hardship the other property owners on the downward side of the slope would suffer as a consequence of the mining. Further, there would be common amenities such as a lake or a common grazing field. The private activity could contaminate water and result into redundancy of the grazing areas, in addition to greater environmental and health cost which would spread beyond immediate area. The concerns of all stake holders need to be taken into account.
98. *See* Dunham, 'A Legal and Economic Basis for City Planning' *Columbia Law Review* 58 (1958): 650, 663-669 stating, 'The "noxious use" theory, which would validate any "regulation" no matter how thoroughly destructive of value, as long as the use prohibited is harmful to others, was apparently embraced by Justice Brandeis dissenting in *Pennsylvania Coal Co. v Mahon*, 260 U.S. 393, 417 (1922).' But cf. *Nashville, C. & St. L. Ry. v Walters*, 294 U.S. 405 (1935). (The theory may extend by analogy to the point of permitting physical occupation by the public. *See Ayres v City of Los Angeles*, 34 Cal. 2d 31, 207 P.2d 1 (1949).) And the converse idea of Professor Dunham, that regulations which effectively force 'innocent' owners to dedicate their holdings to public purposes are compensable as 'takings,' has gained something of a following in modern decisions. *See National Land & Inv.Co. v Easttown Town- ship Bd. of Adjustment*, 419 Pa. 504, 529, 215 A.2d 597,610-ii (1966); *Roark v City of Caldwell*, 87 Idaho 557, 394 P.2d 641 (1964); *Aronson v Town of Sharon*, 346 Mass. 598, 195 N.E.2d 341 (1964); *Morris County Land Improvement Co. v Township of Parsippany-Troy Hills*, 40 N.J. 539, 555–556,193 A.2d 232, 241–242 (1963).
99. Above note 88 (Sax, Takings and Police Powers), 36, 39.
100. *See Gardner v Michingan*, 199 US 325, 330 (1905).

long term depending on the requirement. A legitimate regulatory exercise quintessentially aims at removal of an existing 'harm' or a potential harm. The contributors to the harm have to suffer the impending losses arising due to the measure since the outcome of avoiding the harm is achievement of benefit for the public. A corollary of the noxious use is the 'creation of harm' theory. If someone uses the property that is harmful to public interest, then the instigator of the harm is the creator of the need for regulations.[101] For example the need to regulate financial markets and sale of debt instruments has arisen due to the severe impact that the impropriety of participants in the markets have caused on the entire world economy.

The non-responsibility to pay compensation for adoption of regulations is justified on the 'no compensation because no-property' theory.[102] According to this theory, if the property is being used in a manner contrary to public interest, it loses its legal recognition. According to Sax: 'Destruction of recognized economic interests, on the ground that there is no property interest, is so widespread and pervasive that the policy of preventing individual economic loss as such, can hardly be said to have been given significant recognition by the courts.'[103] The resultant restriction on property use arising from regulations could be an outcome of active or passive restrictions on the use of property. The active restriction would involve a limitation on the use of property for ensuring that the individual use of property does not have 'spill over' of 'inextricable effects' on the common amenities and enjoyment of the rights associated with property of others. The pool of people aimed to be protected through regulatory exercise involves a large group of people therefore they represent 'public rights'.[104] The 'spill over' effects of use of a private property normally involve three occasions: physical restriction on the use of land by another, effect on the use of common amenities or features over which others have equal rights – for example environment, flora and fauna, and use of property that affects the health and well-being of others. In situations where the right over property is restricted for achievement of public intent, the severity of impact is irrelevant.[105] A regulation could be adopted in advance to avoid potential damage. Such preventive regulations are called passive regulations. A passive regulation would also be protected and the State would not attract responsibility for such a regulation. [106] All efforts made towards the protection of public right against the impending or extant problems arising from the use of private property can be curtailed without attracting the responsibility to pay compensation.[107]

101. Sax, Takings and Police Powers (n 88), 36, 48. The minimum wage legislation had to be introduced as a consequence of exploitative practices of certain manufacturers.
102. *United States v Willow River Power Co.*, 324 US 499, 502 (1945).
103. Above note 88 (Sax, Takings and Police Powers), 36, 53.
104. *Ibid.*, 149, 155. For example, the owner of a forested land is free to cut down the trees. However, it is in a public right to ensure that certain numbers of trees are retained for reseeding and restocking. The restriction on his right of commercial logging of the trees and selling for merchandise, is a legitimate regulation, for which no compensation is payable. *See State v Dexter*, 32 Wash.2d 551, 202 P.2d 906 (1949), 338 U.S. 863 (1949); *Allen v McClellan*, 75 N.M. 400, 405 P.2d 405 (1965) (restriction of hunting on private land).
105. *Ibid.*, 149, 161–162.
106. *Ibid.*, 149, 164.
107. *Ibid.*, 149, 161.

An intricate question is of the losses suffered by a private investor in a genuine competition against a public corporation.[108] If the only benchmark for indirect expropriation is loss of assets or fundamental rights of ownership for the investor, it is arguable that an investor could claim compensation for losses suffered at a market place in an arm's-length activity of a public corporation. This argument defeats the very principles of competition and free markets. Michelman, through some examples (decided cases) highlights this distinction aptly:

> Government, it appears, may not cause military jet aircraft to fly at a low altitude over my land, severely detracting from my enjoyment of the surface, unless it compensates me for my losses;[109] but respectable authority has it that government may cause the same aircraft to fly, on the same mission, in a path which, although it does not invade 'my' sector of sky, causes precisely the same kind of harm to my enjoyment of the surface and need not compensate me.[110] If government builds a dam across a navigable stream, impeding the flow of waters away from my lawfully placed mill and reducing its value, it must compensate me if my mill empties into non navigable waters,[111] but not if my mill empties into navigable waters.[112] If government, renovating a highway, encroaches on a foot or two of my frontage which I do not use or contemplate using, causing me negligible harm, it very likely will have to pay me something called the 'fair market value' of the easement or fee which corresponds with its use;[113] but if, renovating the same highway, it causes a change in the traffic flow which devalues my business site drastically, compensation may not be required.[114] Government may perhaps not, in the interest of my neighbors' safety, forbid me (without compensation) to remove coal from my mine;[115] but it plainly may, in the interest of my neighbors' amenity, forbid me (without compensation) to make productive use of my clay quarry and brickyard.[116,117] (footnotes retained from the original text)

While acting in private business in markets, State is acting in an enterprise-capacity. It has to perform resource-acquiring job like a competitor.[118] It is but natural that due to its presence as competitor and due to the influence of market forces a competitor would suffer financial and other losses. It needs to be kept in mind that a State or a State corporation would be required to participate in markets for various reasons such as ensuring competition, need to participate in certain high cost and low output industries, fields for providing other amenities to protect and promote public

108. Above note 25 (Michelman), 1165, 1167.
109. *See Griggs v Allegheny County*, 369 US. 84 (1962); *United States v Causby*, 328 U.S. 256 (1946).
110. *See Batten v United States*, 306 F.2d 580 (10th Cir. 1962), cert. denied, 371 U.S. 995 (1963); *Leavell v United States*, 234 F. Supp. 734 (E.D.S.C. 1964). But *see City of Jacksonville v Schumann*, 167 So. 2d 95 (Fla. 1964) (semble); *Thornburg v Port of Portland*, 233 Ore. 178, 376 P.2nd 100 (1962).
111. *United States v Cress*, 243 U.S. 316 (1917).
112. *United States v Willow River Power Co.*, 324 U.S. 499 (1945).
113. *See City of Los Angeles v Allen*, Cal. 2d 572, 36 P.2d 61 (1934); *First Nat'l Stores, Inc. v Town Plan & Zoning Comm'n*, 26 Conn. Supp. 302, 222 A.2d 228 (C.P. 1966) (semble).
114. *See*, e.g., *Stipe v United States*, 337 F.2d 818 (10th Cir. 1964); *Brock v State Highway Comm'n*, 195 Kan. 361, 404 P.2d 934 (1965).
115. *See Pennsylvania Coal Co. v Mahon*, 260 U.S. 393 (1922).
116. *Hadacheck v Sebastian*, 239 U.S. 394 (1915).
117. Above note 25 (Michelman), 1165, 1169–1170.
118. Above note 88 (Sax, Takings and Police Powers), 36, 62–63.

interest. In such a situation, where, in spite of perfect market condition and arm's-length competitive behaviour, if an investor losses his property, the effect of the sole effects doctrine would be that the host State would be responsible for losses. This situation would make operation of public sector companies impossible. It is understandable that a State would be responsible for expropriation, if it resorts to unfair competition and abuses its position in the structure in the market. But it is difficult to conceive that responsibility may be imposed on a States in situations where the State has acted fairly and within the contours of existing rules, without tampering the rules to gain unfair advantage.[119] In such situations, effect is an utterly misleading exercise. Therefore, the nature of the measure ought to be seen. Sax sees the role of State in two capacities in relation to private businesses: competitor and arbiter of disputes and the actions of the State would amount to expropriation according to him in the following situation:

> It remains now only to observe how the proposed theory works when applied to the cases. The precise rule to be applied is this: when an individual or limited group in society sustains a detriment to legally acquired existing economic values as a consequence of government activity which enhances the economic value of some governmental enterprise, then the act is a taking, and compensation is constitutionally required; but when the challenged act is an improvement of the public condition through resolution of conflict within the private sector of the society, compensation is not constitutionally required.
>
> To be sure, the acquisition of title or the taking of physical possession will be present in the great majority of taking cases under this theory. But - and this is the important point - the presence or absence of a formal title- acquisition and/or invasion will never be conclusive. These formalities are not necessarily present when the government, as an enterpriser, is acquiring resources for its own account. With that in mind, we may now turn to the specific cases.[120]

The underlying essence of all the theories that defend non-compensation for regulatory measures is that there shall be absence of transfer or redistribution of property or unjust enrichment. It is a myth to assume that States bear responsibility to compensate in all cases of losses caused by regulations.[121] It is apt to analyse the nature of the measure to rather than to look solely at the effects of a measure to decide whether a measure is regulatory or expropriatory.

§5.03 REGULATORY FREEDOM AND THE RIGHT TO PROPERTY

Although the texts of BITs do not grant absolute protection of protection through expropriation clauses, it would be appropriate to look at how far has the right to

---

119. *Ibid.*, 63.
120. *Ibid.*, 67.
121. Sax has pithily put this: 'It has been traditional to treat as obvious that the purpose of the compensation rule was to mandate the substantial maintenance of existing economic value against government diminution. This is one of the abiding myths of American constitutional law.' ibid 54.

property evolved in general international law, especially in the human rights instruments and jurisprudence of other international courts and tribunals. This would also aid in understanding whether these developments desire a higher protection of property thus making the sole effects doctrine a relevant feature.

The extent of property protection in law has changed throughout history and has been treated differently in different jurisdictions. Roman law stipulated absolute right to property, which is not the situation in modern domestic and international law.[122] Police powers is a recognized exception from responsibility for losses caused to the investors because property rights are not absolute.[123] In the modern legal thinking, the social functions of property have immensely risen[124] and the social use of property is practiced by all States.[125]

Modern international law does not treat right to property as an absolute right.[126] The standard of protection granted to property of a foreigner in international law was summarized by Amador in the following words:

> International law imposes on the State the obligation to respect the patrimonial rights of alien private individuals. However, the principle of respect for acquired rights does not imply an absolute or unconditional obligation. The idea of 'respect' in no way corresponds to that of 'inviolability'...In fact, from the point of view of international law, respect for acquired rights is conditional upon the subordinate to the paramount needs and general interests of the State.[127]

If international law had adopted an absolute standard of protection, it would be impossible to protect community interests. Therefore, the right to property is conspicuously absent from the two binding convention on human rights:[128] International Convention on the Civil and Political Rights[129] and the International Convention on

122. Seidl-Hohenveldren, 'The Social Functions of Property and Property Protection in Present-day International Law' in Frits Kalshoven et al. (eds.) *Essays on the Development of the International Leal Order: In Memory of Haro F Van Panhuys* (USA: Sijthoff & Noordhoff, 1980), 79–80.
123. Andrew Newcomb, 'The Boundaries of Regulatory Expropriation in International Law' *ICSID Review – FILJ* 20(1) (2005): 27–28 (footnotes excluded).
124. Hassan Sedigh, 'What Level of Host State Interference Amounts to a Taking under Contemporary International Law?' *Journal of World Investment* 2 (2001): 631, 640–641.
125. Above note 122 (Seidl-Social Function of Property), 80.
126. *See* M Sornarajah, *Resistance and Change in the International Law on Foreign Investment* (Cambridge: Cambridge University Press, 2015), 223–237; Bruce Ackerman, *Economic Foundations of Property* (Boston: Little Brown, 1975), 121.
127. International Law Commission, International Responsibility, Fourth Report by F V García Amador, Special Rapporteur: Responsibility of the State for Injuries Caused in its Territory to the Person or Property of Aliens – Measures Affecting Acquired Rights Document A/CN.4/119 (26 February 1959), (1959) II Yearbook of the International Law Commission 1, para. 15.
128. John Sprankling, *The International Law of Property* (Oxford: Oxford University Press, 2014), 10–11.
129. International Covenant on Civil and Political Rights (adopted 16 December 1966, entered into force 23 March 1976) 999 UNTS 171 (ICCPR).

Economic, Social and Cultural Rights.[130] Despite various proposals during negotiations, right to property was not included in these binding instruments.[131] According to Amador:

> It is also, and indeed primarily, due to the fact that, according to a fundamental legal precept, private interests and rights, regardless of their nature and origin or of the nationality of the persons concerned, must yield before the interests and rights of the community. International law cannot ignore this universal precept.[132]

These observations are important because when this report was prepared, the scope of State responsibility was limited to the question of treatment of aliens.[133] International law respects right to property and protects it through legal instruments, but does not make it an absolute unabrigable right, particularly in relation to exercise of regulatory freedom.[134]

A higher standard of property protection is claimed on the basis of the transformation of the world economies towards market economics, embracing and applying higher protection of private ownership. These changes include the changes in the attitude of the Asian and African States towards foreign investment and their simultaneous transformation to globalized, liberalized and privatized.[135] In positive international law, there does not appear to a shift towards a more liberal investment protection and absolute protection of property rights. The protection of property in international law is no higher than that stipulated in investment treaties. A close look at various international instruments containing protection of property clauses shows that they do not create an absolute standard of protection and insist on the social and communitarian use of property. It supports indirect interference caused to private property due to regulatory freedom. The Universal Declaration of Human Rights – the first international instrument to expressly recognize property rights – states in Article 17 that: 'everyone has the right to own property alone as well as in association with others. No one shall be arbitrarily deprived of his property.'[136] The language of Article 17 underwent a lot of change during negotiations. Traditional capital exporting States such as UK and Sweden were opposed to the inclusion of right to property.[137]

The American Convention on Human Rights guarantees a right to property and '[i]t may only be encroached upon in the interest of public need or in the general

130. International Covenant on Economic, Social and Cultural Rights (adopted 16 December 1966, entered into force 3 January 1976) 993 UNTS 3 (ICESCR).
131. Gudmundur Alfredsson 'Article 17' in Asbjørn Eide & Others (eds.) *The Universal Declaration of Human Rights: A Commentary* (Scandinavian University Press: Norway, 1992), 259.
132. International Law Commission, International Responsibility, Fourth Report by F V García Amador, Special Rapporteur: Responsibility of the State for Injuries Caused in its Territory to the Person or Property of Aliens – Measures Affecting Acquired Rights Document A/CN.4/119 (26 February 1959), (1959) II Yearbook of the International Law Commission 1, para. 15.
133. The scope of the work was expanded subsequently. *See* Crawford discussing the history of drafting of the ILC Articles in the books.
134. *Arbitration between Germany and Portugal* (1919), Award II (1930), United Nations, Reports of International Arbitral Awards, vol. II, p. 1039.
135. Above note 128 (Sprankling, International Law of Property), 8–9, 15–16.
136. Universal Declaration of Human Rights (adopted 10 December 1948 UNGA Res 217 A(III) (UDHR) Art. 17.
137. Above note 35 (Higgins), 358.

interest of the community and in accordance with the provisions of appropriate laws'.[138] The Convention does not contemplate absolute protection – rather exonerates State from responsibility in certain instances – these circumstances squarely relate to the exercise of regulatory power by States.

Article 31 of the Arab Charter on Human Rights states – 'No person shall under any circumstances by divested of all or any part of his property in an arbitrary or unlawful manner.'

While granting a right to own property, the UDHR in Article 29 (2) prescribes limits of the rights of individuals. It says:

> In the exercise of his rights and freedoms, everyone shall be subject only to such limitations as are determined by law solely for the purpose of securing due recognition and respect for the rights and freedoms of others and of meeting the just requirements of morality, public order and the general welfare in a democratic society.[139]

The provision is of general application and would cover right to property under Article 17 as well. Also, in view of its language it cannot be clearly stated that the doctrine of proportionality in incorporated.[140] Article 17 of ASEAN Human Rights Declaration, 2012, states, 'No person shall be arbitrarily deprived of such property.'[141] Article 1, Protocol 1 of the European Convention on Human Rights recognizes the right to property and further clarifies that: 'The preceding provisions shall not, however, in any way impair the right of a State to enforce such laws as it deems necessary to control the use of property in accordance with the general interest or to secure the payment of taxes or other contributions or penalties.'[142]

The core of international human rights law is protection of rights of human beings or natural persons. The preamble to the UDHR stresses the importance of protecting the 'rights of all members of the human family'.[143] 'In this context, the references in the UDHR that recognize rights in "everyone" or provide that "no one" shall be subject to certain conduct are generally understood to apply only to natural persons.'[144] Although it could be argued that Article 17 includes ownership 'in association with others', thus legal persons 'that own property such as partnership, unincorporated associations, and other entities' could be included.[145] The practice of regional human rights conventions differs. The ECHR, for example, protect 'natural or legal' persons.[146] The ACHR does not specify whether it extends to legal persons. The African Commission on Human and People's Rights held in a case that legal persons are

138. American Convention on Human Rights (adopted 22 November 1969, entered into force 18 July 1978) 1144 UNTS 123 Art. 14.
139. Above note 136 (UDHR), Art. 29(2).
140. Above note 128 (Sprankling, International Law of Property), 258.
141. ASEAN Human Rights Declaration, 18 November 2012, (2012) 32 Human Rights LJ 219.
142. European Convention on Human Rights. European Convention for the Protection of Human Rights and Fundamental Freedoms, (adopted 4 November 1950, entered into force 3 September 1953) 213 UNTS 221, Protocol 1, Art. 1 (ECHR).
143. Above note 136 (UDHR), Preamble, para. 1.
144. Above note 128 (Sprankling, International Law of Property), 206.
145. *Ibid.*, 206.
146. Above note 142 (ECHR), Protocol 1, Art. 1.

not protected under ACHR.[147] Under some circumstances, an individual may rely on the ACHR to enforce protected rights "even when they are encompassed in a legal figure or fiction created by the same system of law".[148] Accordingly, the right to property held by a legal person may be enforced indirectly under this convention.[149] The Inter-American Court's jurisprudence only recognizes human rights of individual and not legal entities.[150]

It is further argued that since the right to property is a 'human right' and not merely a 'right' – it is an important right and 'entitled to higher protection' and preference over other rights.[151] It shall be noted that all human rights occupy an equal status under international law. However, this is not true for socio-economic rights such as the right to property, which are relative in nature. There is every temptation to argue that since the human rights rules may contain "functionally analogous rules" to investor protection, it is safe to extrapolate the principles for human rights protection for the protection of investors.[152] This argument would not be viable in light of the difference between the 'context' of investment treaties and human right treaties, context being an important component of treaty interpretation under Article 31 of VCLT. It is evident that the underlying purpose of human rights treaties and investment treaties is different. Furthermore, it is doubtful if the protection of human rights treaties extends to properties of large scale foreign investors.[153]

The human right to property is subject to a substantial degree of regulation under domestic law, as reflected both by the formulations of the right in regional conventions and case law generated by human rights tribunals. The understanding of right to property and the standard of protection in investment law is different from human rights.[154] If not all, many human rights are aimed at the protection of special and

147. *See Mouvement Ivoirien de Droits de l'Homme v Cote d'Ivorie*, Comm no 262/02 (ACHPR, 22 May 2008).

148. *Cantos v Argentina* Series C no 85 (IACtHR, 7 September 2001), para. 27.

149. Above note 128 (Sprankling, International Law of Property), 206.

150. *Perozo v Venezuela*, Inter-American Court of Human Rights Series C No. 195, 28 February 2009, paras 396–403.

151. Above note 128 (Sprankling, International Law of Property). Sparkling gives the example of protection from torture. However, torture and property are not comparable. Human right connotes a pressing situation of peril to life or dignity, one wonders if that could be the case with foreign investors. The rationale of extending liberally interpreted human rights to protect investor rights would be problematic.

152. Martins Paparinskis, *The International Minimum Standard and Fair and Equitable Treatment* (Oxford: Oxford University Press, 2013), 175–176.

153. Above note 128 (Sprankling, International Law of Property), 205–206. He says: 'It is often said that all human rights occupy an equal status under international law. However, this is not true for socio-economic rights such as the right to property, which are relative in nature. The human right to property is subject to a substantial degree of regulation under domestic law, as reflected both by the formulations of the right in regional conventions and case law generated by human rights tribunals. Recognising an absolute right to property in one owner would inevitably conflict with parallel absolute rights of other owners. Therefore, it must be questioned whether characterizing the right to property as a human right elevates its status in relation to other rights.'

154. Ursula Kriebaum & Christoph Schreuer, 'The Concept of Property in Human Rights Law and International Investment Law' in Stephan Breitenmoser ua (eds) *Liber Amicorum Luzius Wildhaber, Human Rights Democracy and the Rule of Law* (Germany: Nomos Verlagsgesellschaft, Baden-Baden, 2007), 19–20.

vulnerable groups like women protection[155] from racial discrimination.[156] If these rights come into conflict with the rights of foreign investors, it could not be simply claimed that the rights of foreign investors are to be granted a higher treatment. Therefore, the characterization of the right to property as a human right may not necessarily elevate it in comparison to other rights which may be of the same character.[157]

The right to property may not be a customary law right, but it does emanate from general principles of law recognized in national jurisdictions. The standard of protection of property in national constitutions differs greatly but is not absolute.[158] Reasonable restrictions on the right to property are recognized. Courts constituted under regional treaties that refer to property rights have upheld interference with property for regulatory purposes without the need to pay compensation.[159] After acknowledging divergences in practice, the Third American Restatement concludes that it 'weighs against the conclusion that a human right to property has become a principle of customary law'.[160]

Additionally, investment treaties do not protect property as such. They protect investments. Investments encompass property, but the property must possess some additional qualities. An example of additional attributes would be those laid down in *Salini v* Morocco – known famously as *Salini test.* The contents of *Salini test* are: substantial contribution, certain duration, an element of risk and significance for the host State's development.[161] Also, the rights over assets affected by the regulation shall be defined under the municipal law.[162] According to the PCIJ: 'In principle, the property rights and the contractual rights of individuals depend in every State on municipal law...'[163]

155. Convention on the Elimination of All Forms of Discrimination Against Women (adopted 18 December 1979, entered into force 3 September 1981) 1249 UNTS 13 Arts 15, 16.
156. International Convention on the Elimination of All Forms of Racial Discrimination (adopted 7 March 1966, entered into force 4 January 1969) 660 UNTS 195, Art. 5.
157. Sprankling, International Law of Property (n 128), 206.
158. *See* AJ van der Walt, *Constitutional Property Clauses: A Comparative Analysis* (Kluwer Law International, 1999).
159. *Handyside v UK* ECtHR, paras 62–63. (App No. 5493/72) (1975) Series B no 22; Also *see Chaparro Álvarez and Lapo Íñiguez v Ecuador* (Judgment) Inter-American Court of Human Rights Series C No 170 (21 November 2007) [183]–[218]; *Abrill Alosilla et al. v Peru* (Judgment) Inter-American Court of Human Rights Series C No 223 (4 March 2011) [77]–[85]; *Ivcher Bronstein v Peru* (Judgment) Inter-American Court of Human Rights Series C No 74 (6 Februar 2001) [119]–[131]; *Salvador Chiriboga v Ecuador* (Judgment) Inter-American Court of Huma Rights Series C No 179 (6 May 2008) [60]–[118]. Cf. *Case of Sporrong and Lönnroth v Swede* Application no. 7151/75; 7152/75, Judgment, 23 September 1982.
160. Restatement of the Law Third, The Foreign Relations Law of the United States, (St. Paul, Min American Law Institute Publishers, 1987), section 702, note k.
161. *Salini Costruttori SpA et Italstrade SpA v Morocco,* Decision on Jurisdiction, 23 July 2001, p 53. Also *see* Aniruddha Rajput, 'Definition of Investment – A Developmental Perspect *Indian Journal of Arbitration Law* 2 (2013): 12.
162. *EnCana Corporation v Ecuador,* Award, UNCITRAL Rules, 3 February 2006, para. 184.
163. *The Panevezys-Saldutiskis Railway* Preliminary Objections, PCIJ Series A / B, No. 76, case

§5.04 GLOBAL ADMINISTRATIVE LAW

Global Administrative Law (GAL) is a prominent theoretical approach of recent origin that studies the rising regulatory activity at the transnational or international level. This increase in regulatory activities at the transnational or international level poses an obvious challenge to the regulatory freedom of States, especially since according to GAL the organizations at the international or transnational level are taking over the regulatory functions of States. Consequently, the regulatory domain of States is rapidly shrinking. The proliferation of judicial bodies with compulsory jurisdiction is seen as erosion of sovereignty and States are either ceding or accidentally losing their regulatory space in favour of international tribunals. A substantial literature is written on GAL[164] and its impact on international law.

According to the proponents of GAL, the present structure of international law is undergoing a change due to globalization and rising global governance. The number of international legal instruments and international organizations, sometimes with strong enforcement mechanisms has increased. These institutions are equipped with treaty making powers.[165] In past, the structure of international interactions was such that domestic and international could be clearly identified. But in the ongoing process, the strict distinction between domestic and international is blurring. Due to the reduction in this clear demarcation, soft law is playing a larger role. In its traditional pattern, international law required domestic ratification and implementation of the international obligations by States. This is not the case anymore. A variety of administrative functions are performed as a complex interplay between officials and institutions at different levels and regulations that are an outcome of such a process are becoming influential. The activities occurring at this newly created space are not binding but the situation of international relations has become such that States habitually treat them as binding. The outcome of this interwovenness and transfusion has resulted into creation of a 'global administrative space'.[166] Various international bodies, such as the WTO dispute settlement, UNHCR, Basil Committee for Banking Supervision, ICANN, etc have occupied the global administrative space and the classical distribution of power between different levels has broken down.[167] These institutions are performing administrative functions, most of which were traditionally performed by the States.

A lot of administrative and regulatory functions are occurring in this space. If the functions performed at the level of this global administrative space were performed

164. Writings and activities in this area are regularly updated on the website of the Global Administrative Law Project, available at http://www.iilj.org/gal/. Most of the articles on this topic are published in the following two volumes: (2006) 17 EJIL and (2004–2005) 68 Law and Contemporary Problems.
165. Nico Krisch & Benedict Kingsbury, 'Introduction: Global Governance and Global Administrative Law in the International Legal Order' *EJIL* 17(1) (2006): 1.
166. *Ibid.*, 1–3. For a detailed discussion on the factors and institutions contributing towards the creation of global administrative space, *see* Benedict Kingsbury, Nico Krisch & Richard Stewart, 'The Emergence of Global Administrative Law' *Law and Contemporary Problems* 68 (2004–2005): 15, 18-27.
167. *Ibid.*, 1, 4.

within the State level, these activities would undoubtedly be characterized as administrative in nature.[168] Administrative law therefore is an appropriate perspective to study the organization and activity occurring at the level of global administrative space. The creators of GAL have summarized their position through the following definition:

> These developments lead us to define global administrative law as comprising the mechanisms, principles, practices, and supporting social understandings that promote or otherwise affect the accountability of global administrative bodies, in particular by ensuring they meet adequate standards of transparency, participation, reasoned decision, and legality, and by providing effective review of the rules and decisions they make. Global administrative bodies include formal intergovernmental regulatory bodies, informal intergovernmental regulatory networks and coordination arrangements, national regulatory bodies operating with reference to an international intergovernmental regime, hybrid public-private regulatory bodies, and some private regulatory bodies exercising transnational governance functions of particular public significance.[169]

In spite of similarities in the character of the activity at the domestic and international level, the supporters of GAL have advised that a great deal of caution needs to be exercised before any specific principles are imported from domestic administrative law to the global administrative law.[170] The distinctiveness of this system at the international level, as against domestic administrative law, is that it is primarily adjudicative in nature.[171] Investment arbitration is an adjudicative regime thus an important example of GAL.

What GAL entails for investment arbitration is important, since some see investment treaties as relinquishment of sovereign 'policy space' in deference to a greater good.[172] The extension of GAL to investment arbitration has received some attention.[173] The first effort in this direction was by Van Harten and Loughlin. They proposed that investment arbitration could potentially be a strong instance of operation of GAL.[174]

In the context of investment treaty arbitration, GAL is not seen as taking over of regulatory power by transnational or international bodies, rather reduction in the

---

168. *Ibid.*, 1, 3 (footnote excluded).
169. Above note 166 (Kingsbury, Krisch & Stewart), 15, 17.
170. *Ibid.*, 15, 28.
171. Above note 165 (Krisch & Kingsbury), 1–3.
172. José Alvarez, 'The Once and Future Foreign Investment Regime' in Mahnoush Arsanjani (ed.) *Looking to the Future: Essays on International Law in Honour of W Michael Reisman* (Boston: Martinus Nijhoff Publishers, 2011), 607, 627.
173. Gus Van Harten & Martin Loughlin, 'Investment Treaty Arbitration as a Species of Global Administrative Law' *EJIL* 17 (2006): 121; Benedict Kingsbury & Stephan Schill, 'Investor-State Arbitration as Governance: Fair and Equitable Treatment, Proportionality and the Emerging Global Administrative Law' NYU School of Law, Public Law Research Paper No. 09-46; available at: http://www.iilj.org/publications/documents/2009-6.KingsburySchill.pdf; last visited: 10 October 2015; Daniel Kalderimis, 'Investment Treaty Arbitration as Global Administrative Law: What this Might Mean in Practice?' in Chester Brown & Katie Miles (eds.) *Evolution in Investment Treaty Law and Arbitration* (Cambridge: Cambridge University Press, 2012).
174. *Ibid.*, 121-122.

sphere of regulatory functions of State. While introducing GAL into investment arbitration, Van Harten and Loughlin were unclear about the exact application and repercussions for investment treaty arbitration. They contended that the emergence of GAL in investment treaty arbitration could be seen from public law perspective,[175] but doubted the desirability of extension of GAL which is primarily concerned with regulatory practices of international organizations.[176]

Despite this scepticism, others have built their theories on the premise of prevalence of GAL in investment arbitration. Montt argues that investment arbitration ought to be seen as a regime of Global Administrative and Constitutional Law. Investment tribunals adopting interpretations that exceed the standard of protection granted to private individuals under advanced municipal law jurisdictions. Hence, they have created a revised Calvo Doctrine, which shall be seen as Global Administrative and Constitutional Law.[177] Kullick makes a slightly different argument that the regime created by international investment law shall be seen as Global Public Interest.[178]

The original study of GAL aimed at not only studying the phenomenon of performance of global regulatory functions, but also the challenges of legitimacy and democratic deficit in the institutions performing these functions.[179] Understood in that sense, the primary concern of GAL should be with problems of taking over and performance of regulatory functions by investment tribunals rather the manner of limiting the regulatory functions of the State without any justification. The GAL theory, as proposed originally, appears to be benign as compared to the manner in which it is applied in the field of investment treaty arbitration. Conceding on the limitations of the scope of application of GAL, the original proposers accepted that GAL would not take over the space occupied by traditional international law, based on interstate relations, or the scope of domestic administrative law. It is only a phenomenon occurring between the two levels: national and international or at some occasions of overlap between the two.[180]

Further, it would be footless to suggest that the entire regulatory space has been taken over by global bodies. The scope of the activity of transnational organizations has to be identified; it would also depend on the sectors of its operation. The actions of States might have been influenced by the decisions of the tribunals, beyond the specific domain of treaties. These limitations have now met with opposition by States. In any event, tolerance by States of activity in excess of powers conferred does not create right against the State in those international organizations.[181] The fact often ignored in the discourse of GAL is that the States can always take back the powers that they conferred

175. *Ibid.*, 121, 149–150.
176. Above note 165 (Krisch & Kingsbury), 1, 8.
177. Santiago Montt, *State Liability in Investment Treaty Arbitration: Global Constitutional and Administrative Law in the BIT Generation* (Oxford: Hart Publishing, 2009), 74–82, 369–374.
178. Andreas Kulick, *Global Public Interest in International Investment Law* (Cambridge: Cambridge University Press, 2012), 77–167.
179. Above note 166 (Kingsbury, Krisch & Stewart), 15, 37–51.
180. *Ibid.*, 15, 26.
181. *Jurisdiction of the European Commission of the Danube*, (1927) PCIJ Series B, No. 4, 6, 36 (8 December 1927).

through treaties on international organizations. Investment treaty regime is an excellent example of this occurrence.[182] The entire effort of recalibration of treaties is aimed towards taking back the sovereign policy space.[183] The fear of overemphasis on GAL and consequential politicization of dispute resolution process has come to fore in the example of investment arbitration, where States have started withdrawing and there is reduction in compliance with the awards.[184]

It is improper to compare the activity of investment tribunals with the Security Council or the WTO. The Security Council and the WTO possess the coercive powers because they are permanent institutions created under the treaty and backed by the treaty. Investment tribunal is not a permanent institution. It is not backed by a uniform treaty structure or other institutional structures that are necessary to create a synergy at the international level to wield necessary coercive powers. There are questions about the manner of enforcement of investment arbitration awards. Even ICSID awards that are treated at par with the highest court of land are difficult to enforce.[185] Unlike some interference within regimes of international law, where there is greater scope for institutions to influence and curb regulatory power of a State, investment arbitration is different. The impact on the regulatory power of States is indirect and raises questions of legitimacy of such exercises.[186]

The problem with global policy making is the concern that global administrators, dictated by the concerns of preserving the specialized field they form a part of, would not be able to take into account the needs, priorities and cultural preferences of local populace. They are neither equipped to formulate policies for the States nor competent to review the policies, except for testing them on set international law standards. They are unsuitable to find alternative approaches to resolve domestic problems. With the backlash towards investment arbitration and international organizations, it would be safe to assume that the GAL movement in relation to investment arbitration is receding.

182. José Alvarez, 'State Sovereignty Is Not Withering Away: A Few Lessons for the Future' in Antonio Cassese (ed.) *Realizing Utopia: The Future of International Law* (Oxford: Oxford University Press, 2012), 26; José Alvarez, 'The Return of the State' *Minnesota Journal of International Law* 20 (2011): 223, 231–241.
183. *Ibid.*, (Return of the State), 254.
184. Above note 182 (Alvarez, Sovereignty is Not Withering), 35.
185. Vincent Nmehielle, 'Enforcing Arbitration Awards under the International Convention for the Settlement of Investment Disputes (ICSID Convention)' *Annual Survey of International and Comparative Law* 7 (2001): 19, 31–38; Freya Baetens, 'Enforcement of Arbitral Awards: "To ICSID or Not to ICSID" is Not the Question' in Todd Weiler, Ian Laird (eds.) *The Future of ICSID* (The Netherlands: Juris Arbitration Series, Martinus Nijhoff Publishers, 2013).
186. GAL proponents, in spite of their enthusiasm towards the project have realized and accentuated the problems of legitimacy from time to time. *See* generally above note 165 (Krisch & Kingsbury), 1.

CHAPTER 6

Regulatory Freedom as Customary International Law

After laying down the conceptual foundations of regulatory freedom, treatment of regulatory freedom in the jurisprudence of international courts and tribunals – particularly investment tribunals and theoretical foundations for upholding regulatory freedom despite the existence of the treatment standard of indirect expropriation, this chapter looks at regulatory freedom from a doctrinal perspective. This chapter argues that regulatory freedom is a customary international law rule. This discussion is extended in the next chapter to look at the interaction between regulatory freedom and indirect expropriation as an interaction between a customary law norm and a treaty norm.

§6.01 REGULATORY FREEDOM AS AN ATTRIBUTE OF STATE SOVEREIGNTY

Most of the tribunals that have recognized regulatory freedom, declared it to be a norm of customary international law and a principle emanating from State sovereignty. However, they have not elaborated this linkage – probably due to the concerns of judicial economy. This section dwells into the link between regulatory freedom and sovereignty.

Regulatory freedom has a basis in positive international law and possesses the character of customary international law because sovereignty, from which it stems itself, is a legal concept. The operation of sovereignty is not excluded by investment treaties. Sovereignty, as an attribute of State, continues to operate because it 'characterizes powers and privileges resting on customary law and independent of the particular consent of another state'.[1] States need not mention it to claim and exercise rights under it. Judge Weiss articulated the principle in a fitting fashion as follows:

> Among the foremost of these rules there is one which is paramount and which does not even require to be embodied in a treaty: that is the rule sanctioning the sovereignty of States. If States were not sovereign, no international law would be possible, since the purpose of this law precisely is to harmonize and reconcile the different sovereignties over which it exercises its sway.[2]

Sovereignty is a personified legal order that collectively represents humans that constitute and grant power to the concerned State. The State thus represents its constituents and it is not an abstract and impersonal entity. Despite severe criticism, international law remains a State-centred system based on sovereignty.[3]

Sovereignty has a prominent role to play in economic activities, within and outside the State. It constitutes the foundation of economic regulations. Markets exist due to the State and they do not take over the State. Sovereignty ensures parity and fairly in markets, because there is an inherent relationship between sovereignty and development, greater the freedom to regulate more are the prospects of implementing developmental policies.[4] Doyle elaborates on this in the following words:

> Rational producers and consumers would also want a national sovereign state. It has long been recognized that the state provides important foundations for economies. It establishes and regulates money. It helps enforce contracts, allowing for the better realization of exchange value. It legislates property rights, so that producers will try to become owners. It creates limited liability, so shareholders will invest. It creates 'entity liability' so that creditors will lend. States can also realize public goods, under normal schemes of administration: street lamps, police, schools, etc (sic). Putting these things all together in conducive to efficiency and growth.[5]

Sovereignty in international law is a juridical concept and its understanding is very different from that in political science or international relations. [6] Therefore, analysis of political science and international relations is of little relevance for analysing sovereignty as a legal principle in international law.[7] The difference in political and legal understanding of sovereignty has been captured in the phrases:

1. Ian Brownlie, *Principles of Public International Law* (7th ed., Oxford: Oxford University Press, 2008), 291.
2. *The Case of the S.S. 'Lotus' (France v Turkey)*, 7 September 1927 (Dissenting Opinion of Judge Weiss), (1927) PCIJ Series A, No. 10, 4, 121.
3. Luzius Wildhaber, 'Sovereignty and International Law' in R. St. J. Macdonald, Douglas M. Johnston (eds), *The Structure and Process of International Law: Essays in Legal Philosophy, Doctrine, and Theory* (The Hague: Kluwer Boston, 1983), 438.
4. Asif Qureshi, 'Sovereignty Issues in the WTO Dispute Settlement – A "Development Sovereignty" Perspective' in Wenhua Shan, Penelope Simons and Dalvinder Singh (eds) *Redefining Sovereignty in International Economic Law* (USA: Hart Publishing, 2008), 162.
5. Remarks by Michael Doyle, 'How Should Sovereignty Be Defended?' available at http://www.law.harvard.edu/faculty/dkennedy/publications/DKennedy_SovereigntyDefended.pdf; last visited 18 October 2018.
6. Marek Korowicz, 'Some Present Aspects of Sovereignty in International Law' *Recueil des Cours* 102 (1961): 5, 14–16.
7. *See* Ian Brownlie, 'The Reality and Efficacy of International Law' *BYIL* 52 (1981): 1.

pouvoir constitué and pouvir constitutant respectively. Elaborating on this distinction, Wildhaber says:

> The legal sovereign would be the final and determining power according to the existing legal order. The political sovereign would be that power the will of which is ultimately effectively obeyed. In the former sense, sovereignty means the highest legislative power and as such the 'constituted' order of the state community. ... Political sovereignty is understood here as unfettered and absolute, therefore, while legal sovereignty is legally bound and in that sense merely relative.[8]

There is some disagreement about the precise character of sovereignty in the legal domain: whether it is *jus cogens* or customary law. Basson suggests that sovereignty is *jus cogens*.[9] Whereas Wildhaber disagrees about its *jus cogens* nature and treats it as a customary principle.[10] Sovereignty is a multifaceted principle and the character of each of its facets or constituents differs. Some are *jus cogens*, such as acquisition of territory of a State against territorial integrity and the right of self-determination.[11] Whereas others are customary international law. Regulatory freedom is custom. States can undertake restrictions on exercise of regulatory freedom through a treaty, but if they give away territorial sovereignty, then they lose their very existence.

Sovereignty is a legal and 'evolutionary concept'.[12] It encompasses the general plenary power to address different circumstances that arise from time to time. These responses are in the form of regulatory exercises. The occurrence of these situations cannot be fixed in time or to specific instances. The responsive nature of regulatory exercises as a sovereign requires desires flexibility. The contents of sovereignty also change from time to time because 'the set of attributes that define a state changes over time and varies with the state in question'.[13]

In its various forms, in different languages, sovereignty is considered to be a concrete concept with doctrinal value; described as 'concretely hierarchical, rather than abstractly dogmatic'.[14] For the modern State, sovereignty expresses certain basic features such as 'supremacy of law'.[15] According to Oakeshott, the main characteristic of sovereign authority of the modern State is 'the authority and the procedures to emancipate itself continuously from its legal past', in the sense that 'there was no law

8. Above note 3 (Wildhaber), 429. Also *see Reservations to the Convention on the Prevention and Punishment of the Crime of Genocide* (Advisory Opinion) (28 May 1951) (1951) ICJ Reports 15, 24.
9. Samantha Besson, 'Sovereignty' in Rüdiger Wolfrum (ed.) *Max Planck Encyclopedia of Public International Law* (New York: Oxford University Press, 2008).
10. Above note 3 (Wildhaber), 442–444.
11. James Crawford, *The Creation of States in International Law* (2nd ed., Oxford: Oxford University Press, 2006), 107.
12. Kal Raustiala, 'Rethinking the Sovereignty Debate in International Economic Law' *Journal of International Economic Law* 6 (2003): 841, 860-862.
13. José Alvarez, 'State Sovereignty Is Not Withering Away: A Few Lessons for the Future' in Antonio Cassese (ed.) *Realizing Utopia: The Future of International Law* (Oxford: Oxford University Press, 2012), 31.
14. Above note 3 (Wildhaber) 425 (footnote excluded).
15. *See* Blandine Kriegel, *The State and the Rule of Law*, Marc A LePain & Jeffrey C Cohen trans (Princeton: Princeton University Press, 1995), 29.

so ancient and so entrenched that it could not be amended or repealed'.[16] In relation to the operation of sovereignty within the territory, following was observed in the *Island of Palmas* case:

> The fact that the functions of a State can be performed by any State within a given zone is on the other hand, precisely the characteristic feature of the legal situation pertaining in those parts of the globe which, like the high seas or lands without a master, cannot or do not yet form the territory of a State.[17]

The reference to sovereignty in international law is not limited to describe legal personality and accompanied independence, but it is a reference to various types of rights. These various types of 'sovereign rights' States possess are in addition to jurisdiction exercised as a part of territorial sovereignty.[18] Sovereignty represents legal competence over a territory. It is 'the legal competence which states have in general, to refer to a particular function of this competence, or to provide a rationale for a particular aspect of the competence'.[19] This competence is not merely a theoretical construct but represented through certain identifiable rights. In theoretical terms sovereignty is in *in abstracto* form and treated as elusive and elastic. Whereas in its application, it is in *in concreto* form containing specific attributes. Positive international law discusses sovereignty in its *in concreto* form. In this form it consists of certain 'attributes'. These attributes of sovereignty are also referred to as 'inherent rights'. Inherent rights comprising sovereignty were recognized in the Declaration of the United Nations General Assembly on Friendly Relations in the following words: 'Each State enjoys the rights inherent in full sovereignty.'[20] This Declaration has been recognized as customary international law on more than one occasion.[21]

An aspect of sovereignty is the choice of appropriate forum for making decisions, which ensures legitimacy. As per the principle of subsidiarity, 'a government closer to the constituents can better reflect the subtleties, necessary complexities, and detail embodied in its decisions in a way that most benefits those constituents'.[22] The fear in remote decision making is that the decision makers are prone to the influence of their own local situations and institutions. This makes the decision distorted and they fail to

16. Michael Oakeshott, 'On the Chartacter of a Modern European State' in Michael Oakeshott (ed.) *On Human Conduct* (Oxford: Clarendon Press, 1975), 182–326.
17. *Island of Palmas* case *(Netherlands, USA)*, 4 April 1928, (1928) 2 RIAA 829, 838.
18. Above note 1 (Brownlie), 107.
19. *Ibid.*, 291.
20. Declaration on Principles of International Law concerning Friendly Relations and Co-operation among States in accordance with the Charter of the United Nations, 2625 (XXV) 24 October 1970, available at http://www.un-documents.net/a25r2625.htm; last visited 18 October 2018.
21. *Military and Paramilitary Activities in and against Nicaragua (Nicaragua v United States of America)*, 27 June 1986, 1986 ICJ Reports 14, para. 187; *Armed Activities on the Territory of the Congo (Democratic Republic of the Congo v Uganda)*, Judgment of 19 December 2005, (2005) ICJ Reports 168, para. 162.
22. *Ibid.*, 14.

accommodate the concerns of the targeted beneficiaries.[23] As it is international institutions lack adequate transparency and control mechanisms.[24]

In substance, sovereignty is a bundle of rights.[25] An analogy with property rights would be apt. The rights over property are also considered as a bundle of rights. Possession is one such right, which may be transferred, but that does not extinguish the title, or other rights such as the right to transfer the property to the third person. Likewise, reducing the discretion of States, or the manner in which they deal with human rights issues does not mean that sovereignty is lost. It would have withered or lost, if it was an exhaustible and constituted of fixed elements. In the *Wimbledon* case, the Court viewed sovereignty as a multifaceted concept. In that case, the facet or attribute in question was the freedom of States to enter into treaties.[26] Through a chain of judicial reasoning, the Court developed a logical conception of various activities conducted by a State as attributes of sovereignty. Therefore, the attributes of sovereignty evolve depending upon the circumstances.

Regulation of internal activity within the enclosure of State territory is a crucial attribute of sovereignty. According to Huber, sovereignty is not merely a negative concept that 'exclude[s] the activities of other States'. It is an enabling power that allows the State to regulate the territories they control, because 'it serves to divide between nations the space upon which human activities are employed, in order to assume them at all points the minimum of protection of which international law is the guardian'.[27] Internal sovereignty occasions various activities, relevant for this discussion are 'the power of a state to determine itself its tasks' and 'the power of a state to determine itself which means are adequate and necessary for the fulfilment of its tasks'.[28] Which, in other words represents regulatory freedom. Therefore, regulatory freedom or 'right to regulate' signifies a positive right of action available to States.

Internal sovereignty is complementary for effectiveness of international law. The enforcement of international obligations (arising from exercise of external sovereignty) is achieved only through exercise of internal sovereignty.[29] Protection of human rights

23. *Ibid.*, 14 citing Thomas O'Neill and Gary Hymel *All Politics Is Local and Other Rules of the Game* (New York: Random House, 1994).
24. *Ibid.*, 15.
25. Remarks by David Kennedy, 'How Should Sovereignty Be Defended?' available at http://www.law.harvard.edu/faculty/dkennedy/publications/DKennedy_SovereigntyDefended.pdf; last visited 10 October 2015.
26. *SS Wimbledon (Britain v Germany)*, Judgment of 17 August 1923, (1923) PCIJ Series A, No. 1, 25.
27. Above note 17 (Island of Palmas case), 839.
28. Wildhaber identifies five activities: 'i) the power of a state to determine itself its tasks; ii) the power of a state to determine itself which means are adequate and necessary for the fulfilment of its tasks; iii) the supreme quality of state power in the sense of a lack of derivation from any other earthly power; iv) the decision which state organ is to be considered supreme within the state in 'normal' times of peace; v) the decision which state organ would be supreme in times of emergency or war'. Above note 3 (Wildhaber), 435–436.
29. Robert Jennings, 'Sovereignty and International Law' in Gerard Kreijen and Others (eds), *State Sovereignty and International Governance* (Oxford: Oxford University Press, 2002), 32. This point could be well explained through the example of environment protection treaty obligations or labour standard obligations. All these are achieved through exercise of internal sovereignty.

is a telling example. It is achieved through two stages: firstly, making and adopting of human rights laws; and secondly, by actual application and enforcement. The international regime relies on municipal courts for enforcement. Implementation of international obligations could be effectively achieved through regulations – an exercise of internal sovereignty.[30] These examples do not limit sovereignty. Rather they strengthen it and highlight the role of regulatory freedom as a tool for enforcement of international obligations. Sovereignty is seen to contradict protection of human rights because the prevalent impression is that sovereignty authorizes or protects despotic power and wrongful exercise of powers of State. A wrongful exercise, being an illegitimate exercise, ought not to be treated as a sovereign exercise. Sovereignty, in its legal form, as opposed to political form does not stipulate 'the idea of absolute, unlimited, arbitrary, totalitarian sovereignty', rather the one 'founded on a constituted legal order of checks and balances'.[31] The attacks on sovereignty are based on the assumption that sovereignty is absolute, where as there is nothing that justifies such an assumption.[32]

A prominent attribute of sovereignty is the exclusive right to regulate domestic life.[33] This is a part of plenary jurisdiction over internal affairs.[34] It is the monopoly of the State over certain exercises of power within the territory of the State – the power to make laws applicable in its territories.[35] At the origin of the concept of sovereignty lays the expectation of maintaining internal order: the power to make regulations and ensure compliance. Commenting on the ideas that contributed to the origin of sovereignty for Bodin (the creator of the concept), Brierly stated that: 'The essential manifestation of sovereignty (*primum ac praecipium caput majestatis*), he thought, is the power to make the laws (*legem universis ac singulis civibus dare posse*)....'[36] The principle of sovereignty, thus, grants sanctity to the power of the States to regulate. Seen another way, it grants as well as possesses the power of States to conduct regulatory exercises in contrast to any other entity. Traditionally, the power to make laws (*legem universis ac singulis civibus dare posse)* is seen as an essential manifestation of sovereignty (*primum ac praecipium caput majestatis)*.[37] According to the ICJ,

30. *Ibid.*, 33, 37–38.
31. Above note 3 (Wildhaber), 436, 438, compare with 429.
32. E N Van Kleffens, 'Sovereignty in International Law', *Recueil des Cours* 82 (1953): 5, 127–128 citing Andrassy, La Souveraineté et la Societé des Nations, *Recueil des Cours* 61 (1937): at 656.
33. Above note 9 (Besson), para. 120.
34. *Ibid.*, para. 121; Above note 21 (Military & Paramilitary Activities against Nicaragua), 133.
35. Martin Laughlin, *The Idea of Public Law* (Oxford: Oxford University Press, 2004), 84.
36. J Brierly, *The Law of Nations* (5th ed., Oxford: Clarendon Press, 1955), 7; Scholars, from time to time associated sovereignty with administration, and treated the history of sovereignty as history of administration. Bertrand de Jouvenel, *De la souveraineté: A la recherche du bien politique* (Paris, Ed. M. Th. Génin, 1960), 226: 'L'histoire de la souuverainerě est liée à l'histoire de l'administration'.
37. *Ibid.*, 7. Brierly cites Bodin. Bodin goes further to say that since the States are sovereign and they make laws they cannot be bound by law. These observations may not hold true anymore with the evolution of international law. The *Wimbledon* case puts it very clearly that it is a consequence of State sovereignty that States can undertake obligations and stand bound by these obligations by virtue of *pacta sunt servanda*.

'legislation is one of the most obvious forms of the exercise of sovereign power....'[38] In the *Tunis-Morocco Nationality Decrees* case, France took the position that right to regulate nationality was within the sovereign power of the State and flowed directly from sovereignty. Thus, unless there is no rule of international law restricting the right, a State is free to adopt the measures it deems appropriate.[39] Therefore, by virtue of sovereignty, in positive international law, State enjoys discretion to determine appropriate regulatory framework. The regulatory powers emanating from sovereignty may be used to regulate various activities, such as fiscal framework.[40] States have the power to regulate property rights within its territory.[41] The right of 'taxation is an act of sovereignty by a State, or State organ, within a territory of that State, whereby property is regularly taken by law for public purposes.'[42] All these examples are instances of exercise of regulatory freedom, which arise from sovereignty. Regulatory freedom is an element of State sovereignty.[43] Therefore, regulatory freedom is treated as an 'inherent right' of State or 'attribute of sovereignty'. Since sovereignty is customary in nature, its individual elements should also constitute custom. Therefore, regulatory freedom foundationally gains its customary character in its capacity as an element of State sovereignty.

Thus, sovereignty includes the right to make, change and remove regulations.

In modern international law, sovereignty is treated as flexible and divisible.[44] Therefore, if a State enters into a treaty with another State and grants some aspects of

38. *Legal Status of Eastern Greenland* (5 April 1933), (1933) PCIJ Series No. 53, 48.
39. *Nationality Decrees Issued in Tunis and Morocco*, Advisory Opinion of 7 February 1923, PCIJ Series B, No. 4, 12. The Court did not address this argument directly. It simply proposed that the sovereign right to regulate would be limited by those obligations undertaken in international law at 24.
40. *United States – Tax Treatment For 'Foreign Sales Corporations'* Panel Report, (WT/DS108/R), para. 7.1222 and Appellate Body Report (WT/DS108AB/R), paras 139 and 148.
41. B.A. Wortley, *Expropriation in International Law* (Cambridge: Cambridge University Press, 1959), 13–14.
42. *Ibid.*, 45.
43. United States – Measures Affecting the Cross Border Supply of Gambling and Betting Services, WT DS 285/R, 10 November 2004, paras 5.16-28, 6.316; paras 3.104; 3.125-9, 3.143, Report of Panel, WT/DS58/ R W).
44. *Ibid.*, 124. The discussion is in the context of splitting of power of control of a territory between different authorities. There is no reason why the divisible nature of territorial sovereignty ought not to be applied to the concept of sovereignty as such. Pufendorf supported the indivisible nature of sovereignty, but was conscious that it is impractical to have this view when it comes to the operation of sovereignty. He supported the divisible view of sovereignty. Samuel Pufendorf, *De Jure Naturae et Gentium Libri Octo* (vol. II, The Translation of the Edition of 1688, CH Oldfather & WA Oldfather, Reprinted in 1964 New York, Oceanic Publications Inc and London, Wildy & Sons Ltd.) Samuel Pufendorf on the Law of Nature and Nations, Book VI pp. 1010-1011. He states: 'It should also be observed that, if any undertake to maintain that the potential parts of sovereignty, as they call them, in one and the same state are entirely vested in several distinct persons and councils, they also admit it to be necessary for him to whom belongs some part of the sovereignty, to be endued with power both to require citizens to observe the decisions and ordinances of that part, and to defend that right of his; and, finally, to be able to ordain, by his own judgment and right, when and how that part of the sovereignty should be exercised. For it is anything else but sovereignty to have only the right to indicate to others what you want done by them, and still to be lacking in power also to compel them, when recalcitrant,

sovereignty in favour of that another State, the granting State does not lose sovereignty entirely or lose other elements of sovereignty.[45] By virtue of its divisible nature, sovereignty may be divided horizontally or vertically. Horizontal division and distribution denotes division of sovereign power and their exercise by various limbs of States through which the State acts. Vertical distribution involves delegation of certain subset of attributes at the international level. For example, some sovereign rights are transferred to international organizations through agreement or certain limitations on the manner of exercise of those sovereign rights.[46] The delegation does not affect the remainder of the pool of sovereign rights.

The discussion of regulatory freedom as an aspect of internal sovereignty needs to be distinguished from *domain réservé*. *Domain réservé* is an exclusionary concept. It is limited to matters 'essentially' or 'solely' within the jurisdiction of the State – such as nationality, etc. Article 2 (7) of the UN Charter states:

> Nothing contained in the present Charter shall authorize the United Nations to intervene in matters which are essentially within the domestic jurisdiction of any state or shall require the Members to submit such matters to settlement under the present Charter; but this principle shall not prejudice the application of enforcement measures under Chapter VII.

Although this language is different from the language employed in the Covenant of the League of Nations, the underlying objective remains the same – exclusion of certain matters of domestic jurisdiction from the purview of international law. Article 15 (8) of the Covenant defined it as:

> If the dispute between the parties is claimed by one of them, and is found by the Council, to arise out of a matter which by international law is solely within the domestic jurisdiction of that party, the Council shall so report, and shall make no recommendation as to its settlement.

Domain réservé excludes the power of international courts and tribunals from commenting on domestic issues. The provision in the UN Charter does not impose such a restriction on international courts and tribunals, but in practice if a matter is found to be within the *domain réservé* of the State, the international tribunal will not proceed to decide that issue. This is evident from the fact that the ICJ in the past has framed issues

to observe what was laid down. And it is but a precarious hold which we have on a thing, when we cannot defend it against another, while he who exercises a right at another's dictation, is only his minister and executor', 1017.

45. For example, after the Second World War, the German territory was in the occupation of the four major Allied Powers. This occupation, without Germany's permission did not amount to extinguishment of German sovereignty. Some aspects of sovereignty were exercised by the Allied Powers, whereas the rest remained with Germany. Above note 1 (Brownlie), 106–107. Also *see* discussion on residual sovereignty at 109–111; *Customs Régime Between German and Austria*, Advisory Opinion, 5 September 1931, PCIJ Series A/B, No. 41, 52; *Light Houses in Crete and Samos (France v Greece)*, Judgment, 8 October 1937, PCIJ Series A/B, No. 71, 103–104.
46. Robert Jennings and Arthur Watts (eds), *Oppenheim's International Law* (vol. 1, 9th ed, Harlow: Longman Group, 1992), 124–125; *See* generally Dan Sarooshi, *International Organizations and Their Exercise of Sovereign Powers* (Oxford: Oxford University Press, 2005).

relating to *domain réservé* as preliminary issues - whether or not it is adduced to the merits.[47]

Domain réservé is narrower in scope than regulatory freedom and fields of their operation are distinct. Scholars view *domain réservé* to be same as internal or domestic sovereignty.[48] This is a highly restrictive view of internal sovereignty. *Domain réservé* has rapidly shrunk as a concept. Internal sovereignty is a dynamic and ever evolving concept. *Domain réservé* is an enumeration of areas where States enjoy exclusive jurisdiction to regulate. It includes topics reserved for municipal administration, such as nationality.[49] These areas are protected from international interference.[50] Regulatory freedom is a much broader concept and operates at the level of international law. It is an expression of internal sovereignty.

§6.02 REGULATORY FREEDOM AS A PERMISSIBLE RULE

Presence of sovereignty in international law has resulted into the 'permissive rule', also known as the 'negative exclusion rule'.[51] A permissive rule grants liberty and discretion to States to act in a particular way in the absence of a specific rule to the contrary. Akehurst calls it 'the presumption in favour of liberty of action'.[52] All attributes of sovereignty continue until there is specific exclusion of any of them. Therefore, in the absence of a specific rule to the contrary, regulatory freedom - an attribute of State sovereignty - continues to operate.

The concept of discretion or a permissive rule is inherent in a 'norm'. Norm originates in the Latin word *nomra*. It normally includes a command or an order as well as an empowerment or permission to derogate.[53] According to Kelsen:

> to have the right to behave in a certain manner may mean to be free to behave in this manner. To be legally free to behave in a certain manner may mean not to be under a legal obligation to behave in another manner. The term 'right', however, may have not a mere negative but a positive significance. The statement that I have

47. *The Losinger & C.* case, Preliminary Objections, 27 June 1936 (1936) PCIJ Series A/B No. 67, 23-25; *Right of Passage case (Portugal v India)*, (1957) ICJ Reports 125, 149–150, *Electricity Company of Sofia and Bulgaria*, Preliminary Objection, 4 April 1939, (1939) PCIJ Series A/B, No. 77, 78, 82–83.
48. Above note 1 (Brownlie), 292–294; Above note 6 (Korowicz), 64–65; Humphery Waldock, 'General Course on Public International Law' *Recueil des Cours* vol. II, 106 (1962): 1, 173–191; Charles Rousseau, 'L'independence de L'Etat Dans L'Ordre International' *Recueil des Cours* vol. II, 73 (1948): 171, 233–249; Hans Kelsen, *Principles of International Law* (1952), 190–202; Antony D'Amato, 'Domestic Jurisdiction' in *Encyclopedia of International Law* (1992), 1090–1096.
49. Above note 1 (Brownlie), 297.
50. *Ibid.*, 292–298. *See* 'Content and Limits of Domain Réservé' in Grigoriĭ Ivanovich Tunkin, Kunihiro Jōjima, Theodor Dams, Rüdiger Wolfrum (eds), *International Law and Municipal Law: Proceedings of the German Soviet Colloquy on International Law*, (Berlin: Dunker & Humblot, 1968).
51. Joost Pauwelyn, *Conflict of Norms in Public International Law: How WTO Law Relates to Other Rules of International Law*, (Cambridge: Cambridge University Press, 2003), 154.
52. Michael Akehurst, 'Custom as a Source of International Law' *BYIL* 47 (1975): 1, 37.
53. Hans Kelsen, *General Theory of Norms*, Michael Hartney trans (Oxford: Clarendon Press, 1991), 1, 97.

> a right to behave in a certain manner may mean that others are obliged not to prevent me from behaving in this manner; and the statement that I have a right to claim that another individual behave in a certain manner may mean that he is obliged to behave in this manner.[54]

The operation and interaction of norms operates in a positive and a negative sense. In a positive sense, the norm itself allows certain activity by virtue of its nature. In the negative sense, an activity is allowed under a norm because there is no other contradicting norm.

In a positive sense, norm signifies 'right' as well as 'discretion'. In its capacity as a right, the norm allows a State to undertake certain actions. In its capacity as a discretion, norm leaves the freedom to a State to decide whether it wants to act or not. If the norm empowers a person to behave in a certain way, then he 'can' do so and when a norm permits a person to behave in a certain way then he 'may' do so.[55] The State may resort to that regulation as a 'right' or a 'discretion' to choose that regulation. Kelsen tellingly concludes that the purview of a norm is broad to include the situations of 'ought', and thus includes all possible normative functions: 'commanding, empowering, permitting and derogating'.[56] This enabling power to act is also an endorsement of legal order to act. One way of looking at it is that if the legal order intended to regulate or limit exercises in a particular field, it would have stipulated commanding obligations. Explaining the freedom of action that emanates from the legal system, Kelsen states:

> This shows that if the people who live under a legal order are free to behave in a certain way, it is *in virtue of the law* that they are free to behave in this way, i.e. to do or refrain from doing some particular act.[57]

The freedom to act falls within the 'virtue of the law'. It becomes a natural right – not in the natural law sense – but as a fundamental right: a right inherent in the authority exercising these rights. If this practical approach is not adopted, the very essence of discretion of activity will be destroyed and will limit the domain of permissible activity to an extremely thin sphere.

Seen negatively, there is absence of a derogatory norm. In this case there are two norms. The first is a 'norm' and the other is a 'derogatory norm'. The derogatory norm restricts or repeals the validity of another norm. If there is no derogatory norm that forbids or commands performance of an activity, then the norm is unaffected. Even if there is a derogatory norm, the norm is limited in its scope, only to the extent of derogation. [58] Simply put – 'what is not forbidden is not forbidden' – any expectation of a positive enactment to reiterate what is permitted is superfluous.[59] This is precisely the situation with regulatory freedom. Regulatory freedom is a norm and in the absence of a derogatory norm that contradicts the norm, the norm continues to exist and

54. *Ibid.*, 8.
55. *Ibid.*, 2–3.
56. *Ibid.*, 2–3.
57. *Ibid.*, 131–132.
58. *Ibid.*, 98.
59. *Ibid.*, 100.

operate. To what extent do treatment standards operate as a derogatory norm in relation to regulatory freedom, is discussed in detail in the next Chapter.

Likewise, if it were argued that States could regulate only if they are so permitted or obliged due to other natural or international obligations, it would introduce artificial and impractical rigidity. Kelsen criticizes insistence on existence of a positive rule for undertaking every action as theoretically imaginable and practically unfeasible.[60] The impracticability of such a principle is evidenced through a pressing question – 'whether it is possible for a legislator to make a rule – that what is not permitted is prohibited?'[61] The clear answer is no because a legislator cannot conceive of all activities that may be required to be undertaken. Especially for States, which have to tackle far more and complex issues in internal administration and external relations.

The principle of permissive rule was recognized by the PCIJ in the *Lotus* case. The discussion on permissive rule was in the context of whether the courts in a State could exercise criminal jurisdiction over persons, property and actions outside their territory. The French argument was that in order to exercise such extra-territorial criminal jurisdiction, 'Turkey must in each case be able to cite a rule of international law authorizing her to exercise jurisdiction....'[62] The Court rejected the French argument and held that: 'in practice, it would therefore in many cases result in paralyzing the action of the courts, owing to the impossibility of citing a universally accepted rule on which to support the exercise of their jurisdiction.'[63] Since there was no specific rule limiting the exercise criminal jurisdiction over persons, property and actions outside their territory, the action of Turkish Courts was found in conformity with international law.[64] The discretion of choosing the rules on jurisdiction was left for States by international law since there is no rule governing that area. The Court explained the rationale behind this in the following words:

> International law governs relations between independent States. The rules of law binding upon States therefore emanate from their own free will as expressed in conventions or by usages generally accepted as expressing principles of law and established in order to regulate the relations between these co-existing independent communities or with a view to the achievement of common aims. Restrictions upon the independence of States cannot therefore be presumed.[65]

The very objective of treaties and other rules of international law is to reduce and regulate this discretion wherever necessary. If it is not removed, the wide range of discretion continues. A State is free to exercise discretion within the contours of the limitations imposed through specific treaties. The Court explained this freedom to exercise discretion as follows:

> It does not, however, follow that international law prohibits a State from exercising jurisdiction in its own territory, in respect of any case which relates to acts which

60. *Ibid.*, 101.
61. *Ibid.*, 101.
62. Above note 2 (*Lotus* case), 19.
63. *Ibid.*, 19–20.
64. *Ibid.*, 22–23.
65. *Ibid.*, 18.

> have taken place abroad, and in which it cannot rely on some permissive rule of international law. Such a view would only be tenable if international law contained a general prohibition to States to extend the application of their laws and the jurisdiction of their courts to persons, property and acts 'outside their territory, and if, as an exception to this general prohibition, it allowed States to do so in certain specific cases. But this is certainly not the case under international law as it stands at present. Far from laying down a general prohibition to the effect that States may not extend the application of their laws and the jurisdiction of their courts to person, property and acts outside their territory, it leaves them in this respect with a wide measure of discretion which is only limited in certain cases by prohibitive rules; as regards other cases, every State remains free to adopt the principles which it regards as best and most suitable.
>
> This discretion left to States by international law explains the great variety of rules which they have been able to adopt without objections or complaints on the part of other States; it is in order to remedy the difficulties resulting from such variety that efforts have been made for many years past, both in Europe and America, to prepare conventions the effect of which would be precisely to limit the discretion at present left to States in this respect by international law, thus making good the existing lacunae in respect of jurisdiction or removing the conflicting jurisdictions arising from the diversity of the principles adopted by the various States.
>
> In these circumstances, all that can be required of a State is that it should not overstep the limits which international law places upon its jurisdiction; within these limits, its title to exercise jurisdiction rests in its sovereignty.[66]

The principle of discretion of States, unless specifically limited by another rule of international law is called the *Lotus principle.*

Another facet of permissive rule is availability of discretion in favour of a State to decide appropriate course of action within the domain of the permissible rule. States enjoy discretion within their territories; if that discretion is intended to be restricted, then the existence of a principle of international law restricting that discretion must be proved.[67] Commenting on the *Oscar Chinn* case, in the context of economic regulations, Lauterpacht points out that the treaties might have been concluded at a time of relative economic liberalism and *laisser faire*, but the conditions of international economic life may have changed for which a regulation would have to be adopted to tackle the situation. Lauterpacht goes to the extent of saying that a State could even adopt discriminatory measures to meet 'economic emergency of some gravity'.[68] States enjoy discretion to regulate internal affairs as a consequence of State sovereignty. This discretion arises from international law and operates within its range.[69] Any derogation from these principles must be clearly established, and 'in case of doubt, the international court or tribunal will decide in favour of freedom of action of States, whether with respect to external or internal affairs'.[70]

66. *Ibid.*, 19.
67. *Ibid.*, 21. The observations were made by the Court in relation to the application of criminal law.
68. Hersch Lauterpacht, *The Development of International Law by the International Court* (Cambridge; Grotius Publications Ltd., 1982), 265.
69. Above note 3 (Wildhaber), 441, citing various authorities footnote 94.
70. James Crawford, 'The Criteria of Statehood in International Law' *BYIL* 48 (1976): 93, 108. (cf footnote 9 at 108).

In the *Lotus* case, Court, referred and emphasized the aspect of discretion. It is evident from the passage:

> Consequently, Turkey, by instituting, in virtue of the discretion which international law leaves to every sovereign State, the criminal proceedings in question, has not, in the absence of such principles, acted in a manner contrary to the principles of international law within the meaning of the special agreement.[71]

Absence of discretion would make administration of States virtually impossible. Even the dissenting judges in the *Lotus* case recognized the freedom of States to adopt a course best suited to respond to the exigencies of the situation. According to Judges Anzilotti and Huber:

> At this point, it must be stated that a State may enter into engagements affecting its freedom of action as regards wars between third States. But engagements of this kind, having regard to the gravity of the consequences which may ensue, can never be assumed; they must always result from provisions expressly contemplating the situations arising out of a war. The right of a State to adopt the course which it considers best suited to the exigencies of its security and to the maintenance of its integrity, is so essential a right that, in case of doubt, treaty stipulations cannot be interpreted as limiting it, even though these stipulations do not conflict with such an interpretation.[72]

Despite a clear statement of law, the *Lotus principle* has come under severe criticism.[73] A potent criticism is that the Court was evenly split in its decision and further, it was based on the casting vote of the President. It is possible that a contrary voting by the President would have had a converse outcome. A close look at the

71. Above note 2 (Lotus case), 31.
72. Dissenting Opinion of Judges Anzilotti and Huber, 17 August 1923, (1923) PCIJ Series A, No. 1, 37.
73. Lauterpacht views these observations as obiter. Above note 68 (Lauterpacht), 361. But Waldock critics this view pithily in the following words: 'However much one may share Lauterpacht's general point of view on the question, it is hardly possible to endorse his way of disposing of the dictum in the *Lotus* case. For the Court there came down expressly in favour of Turkey's thesis, that she was entitled to exercise her territorial jurisdiction unless France could point to a rule restricting its exercise, as against France's thesis, that Turkey must herself be able to point to some title recognised by international law empowering her to exercise jurisdiction over the French vessel. (France claimed that the *Lotus* being a French vessel, and the incident having occurred on the high seas, the right to exercise criminal jurisdiction over the captain with respect to the incident belonged exclusively to France; and she relied on the well-settled customary rule establishing the exclusive jurisdiction if the flag State. On the other hand, she was unable to establish a customary rule forbidding a State to exercise its territorial jurisdiction over a foreign vessel lying in one of its own ports in respect of an occurrence on the high seas. Turkey, for her part, relied essentially in her territorial sovereignty and in the absence of any specific rule of international law preventing her from exercising it over a foreign vessel by reason of the incident having occurred on the high seas. The Court found that no clear rule had been made out covering the particular exercise of jurisdiction, and that in other connections some States had been shown not to conflict the exercise of their territorial jurisdiction to crimes committed actually within their own territory. Starting from the position that no relevant rule had been established restricting Turkey's exercise of jurisdiction over the Lotus in a Turkish port, the Court held that its exercise was not in conflict with international law. Consequently, it is difficult not to see in the decision a clear application of a presumption in favour of territorial sovereignty.' Above note 48 (Waldock), 165-6.

dissenting opinions would show that the fundamental point of divergence was not the permissive rule that allows States to exercise sovereign power. The dissenting opinions were mostly concerned with extraterritorial application of criminal law, especially in cases of collision on high seas rather than limitations on discretion of States. Lord Finlay's opinion did not even refer to the question of sovereign discretion and the need of express limitations on that discretion.[74] Judge Weiss' concern too was extra territorial application of criminal law.[75] He did not object to the negative stipulations for sovereignty principle which found favour with the majority. Same position was of Judge Nyholm.[76] Judge Moore was clearer in restricting his dissent only to the extraterritorial application of criminal law over foreigners, in cases of collision on the high sea.[77] Judge Alamitra also took a similar position.[78]

A study of the separate opinions shows that the dissenting judges too were aware and comfortable with the negative restrictions not to be implied principle; except Judge Loder who specifically objected to the view of the majority: the requirement of a prohibitive rule to limit the exercise of sovereignty. In his words, 'under international law, every door is open unless it is closed by treaty or by established custom...I am unable to concur with the opinion of the Court'.[79] The only reason he raised this objection was that in international community, laws are made by States themselves through a gradual process of agreement, and municipal laws cannot be used to justify non-performance of these obligations.[80] Judge Loder's reservations about the permissible rule spring from the misuse of domestic law as a defence for non-performance of international obligations, rather than the existence of the principle per se.

---

74. Above note 2 (Lotus case), (Dissenting Opinion of Judge Loder), 35; (Dissenting Opinion by Lord Finlay), 51.
75. *Ibid.*, Separate Opinion of Judge Weiss, 42, 44: 'Does international law authorize the application of Turkish law and the intervention of Turkish Courts for the repression of offences or crimes committed by a foreign subject outside Turkey, as is possible under the above-mentioned Article 6?' (42). 'By virtue of sovereignty such as we understand it, every State has jurisdiction to sentence and punish the perpetrators of offences committed within its territory; indeed, this is a question of public security, and of public order, which a State cannot ignore without neglecting its duty as a State, and one which arises whatever the nationality of the delinquent may be.

    But, outside the territory, the frontier having once been traversed, the right of States to exercise police duties and jurisdiction ceases to exist; their sovereignty does not operate, and crimes and offences, even in the case of those inflicting injury upon the States them- selves, fall normally outside the sanctioning force of their courts. *Extra territorium jus dicenti impune non paretur.*' (44).
76. *Ibid.*, Dissenting Opinion of Judge Nyholm, 62–64.
77. *Ibid.*, Dissenting Opinion of Judge Moore, 65.
78. *Ibid.*, 101–102.
79. *Ibid.*, Dissenting Opinion of Judge Loder, 35; 34.
80. According to Judge Loder: 'The Court in its judgment holds that this view is correct, well founded, and in accordance with actual facts. I regret that I am unable to concur with the opinion of the Court. It seems to me that the contention is at variance with the spirit of international law. This law is for the most part unwritten and lacks sanctions; it rests on a general consensus of opinion; on the acceptance by civilized States, members of the great community of nations, of rules, customs and existing conditions which they are bound to respect in their mutual relations, although neither committed to writing nor confirmed by conventions. This body of rules is called international law.

    These rules may be gradually modified, altered or extended, in accordance with the views of a considerable majority (sic) of these States, as this consensus of opinion develops, but is

The principal criticism of the decision was based on the extraterritorial application of municipal criminal law by the State whose flag the ship was carrying in cases of collision of high seas.[81] Article 11 of the High Seas Convention, 1958[82] overrode this conclusion of the Court. The disquiet about the decision being carried by a casting vote, expressed by States was limited only to this point.[83] Except for the principle of exercise of criminal jurisdiction on High Seas, all other principles of the *Lotus* case – particularly the principle of permissive rule – continues to apply with all its vigour. *Lotus principle* has been subsequently followed.[84] Even astute critiques of the *Lotus principle* acknowledge that it continues to form the basis of interpretation of obligations of States.[85]

Although the principle of permissive rule was set out unequivocally in the *Lotus* case, this was not the first reference to this principle. Prior – ironically – in the *Tunis-Morocco Nationality Decrees* case, France argued that the right of a State to legislate on nationality flowed directly from State sovereignty and it would not be limited or controlled by a formal rule of international law that restricts the right.[86] The Court only made a cautious reference to it, in the following words:

> For the purpose of the present opinion, it is enough to observe that it may well happen that, in a matter which, like that of nationality, is not, in principle, regulated by international law, the right of a State to use its discretion is nevertheless restricted by obligations which it may have undertaken towards other

---

seems to me incorrect to say that the municipal law of a minority of States suffices to abrogate or change them'; *ibid.*, 34.

81. *Ibid.*, Dissenting Opinion of Lord Finlay, 52–53.
82. Convention on the High Seas, 29 April 1958, 450 UNTS 11, available at: http://www.gc.noaa.gov/documents/8_1_1958_high_seas.pdf; last visited: 18 October, 2018.
83. (1956) II Yearbook of International Law Commission 253, 281. The Commission said: 'In view of the judgement rendered by the Permanent Court of International Justice on 7 September 1927 in the "Lotus" case, the Commission felt obliged to take a decision on the subject. This judgement, which was carried by the President's casting vote after an equal vote of six to six, was very strongly criticized and caused serious disquiet in international maritime circles. A diplomatic conference held at Brussels in 1952 disagreed with the conclusions of the judgement. The Commission concurred with the decisions of the conference, which were embodied in the International Convention for the Unification of Certain Rules relating to Penal Jurisdiction in matters of Collisions and Other Incidents of Navigation, signed at Brussels on 10 May 1952.'
84. *Asylum* case *(Columbia v Peru)* Judgment of 20 November 1950, (1950) ICJ Reports 266, 274-275; *Free Zones* case, Judgment of 7 June 1932, PCIJ, Series A, No. 24, 11–12; *ibid.*, 275.
85. Judge Simma, while criticizing the majority Judges in the Kosovo opinion, expresses his deep resentment for the Lotus principle and unwillingness of the Court to move forward. His complaining tone in a way establishes that the international law, as it stands today, supports the recognition of sovereign rights of states, unless given up expressly. *Accordance with International Law of the Unilateral Declaration of Independence in Respect of Kosovo* (Advisory Opinion) (22 July 2010) (2010) ICJ Reports 403, 479 (Separate Opinion of Judge Simma).
86. *Nationality Decrees Issued in Tunis and Morocco*, Advisory Opinion, 7 February 1923, (1923) PCIJ Reports, Series B, No. 4, 12. France argued: 'Considérant, le débat ainsi pos.4, qu'il convient d'abord de relever que la question de souveraineté d'une nation pour légiférer en matière de nationalité sur son territoire domine la situation et n'est d'ailleurs pas contestée, et que l'application de ce principe au différend soulevépar le Gouvernement anglais ne peut être contredite ou suspendue que par une règle formelle de droit international applicable a u x faits de la cause ou par une stipulation des traités ou conventions internationaux existant entre les parties.'

> States. In such a case, jurisdiction which, in principle, belongs solely to the State, is limited by rules of international law.[87]

From a theoretical perspective of 'rights obligation' jurisprudence, a critique of the *Lotus principle* is that there can be no right without a corresponding obligation. Freedom of one cannot exist without limiting the freedom of another.[88] International law norms – as argued by some – are to be seen as outcome of interaction between States rather than unilateral actions. For D'Amato, a custom cannot be created without interaction between States.[89] This line of argument has also resulted into confusion about the role of *opinio juris* in formation of custom.[90] However, if customary law norms are seen also as permissive rules, whereby a State possess discretion but is not bound to exercise it each time, then *opinio juris* would play an important role in such circumstances. The corpus of rules of international law comprises of permissive rules as well. Akehurst has emphatically criticized this view and supported the role of permissive rule in international law. He opines that it is often mistakenly assumed that all rules of international law are framed in terms of duties.[91]

Norms cannot always be broken down into a rights-obligation paradigm. Even if States are not interacting with each other, they gain certain rights against another State. Article 48 of the ILC Draft Articles on State Responsibility is based on the foundation that any State other than the injured State is entitled to invoke responsibility of the errant State.[92] This freedom of invoking responsibility in the absence of any specific corresponding right – obligation situation is a consequence of *erga omnes* principle.[93]

---

87. *Ibid.*, 24.
88. Anthony D'Amato, *The Concept of Custom in International Law* (Ithaca, New York: Cornell University Press, 1971), 181.
89. *Ibid.*, 124.
90. Above note 52 (Akehurst), 37.
91. *Ibid.*, 37.
92. Article 48 of the ILC Draft Articles on State Responsibility states:

    'Article 48. Invocation of responsibility by a State other than an injured State
    1. Any State other than an injured State is entitled to invoke the responsibility of another State in accordance with paragraph 2 if:
        (a) the obligation breached is owed to a group of States including that State, and is established for the protection of a collective interest of the group; or
        (b) the obligation breached is owed to the international community as a whole.
    2. Any State entitled to invoke responsibility under paragraph 1 may claim from the responsible State:
        (a) cessation of the internationally wrongful act, and assurances and guarantees of non-repetition in accordance with article 30; and
        (b) performance of the obligation of reparation in accordance with the preceding articles, in the interest of the injured State or of the beneficiaries of the obligation breached.
    3. The requirements for the invocation of responsibility by an injured State under articles 43, 44 and 45 apply to an invocation of responsibility by a State entitled to do so under paragraph 1.'

93. *Case Concerning the Barcelona Traction, Light and Power Company, Limited (Belgium v Spain)*, Second Phase, Judgment, 5 February 1970, (1970) ICJ Reports 3, paras 33–34. The Court has attempted to create the legal fiction that violation of certain obligations results into violation of responsibilities towards the entire international community. The underlying reasoning defends

However, these obligations may not be *erga omnes* all the time and the ILC Draft Articles specifically avoided any reference to *erga omnes*.[94] There have been instances where States have claimed rights in the absence of any corresponding obligation or an injury to that State. For example, Japan challenged the action of Germany in not allowing the voyage of SS Wimbledon through the Kiel Canal, although it never claimed any injury.[95] Limiting recognition of sovereign exercises by States only to actions affecting other States undermines the role of unilateral actions in international law. The ability of unilateral actions to create customary law is acknowledged in present international law.[96]

Another problem with the *Lotus principle*, according to Hulsroj is that it creates race for first exercise of concurrent rights. Any first exercise trumps subsequent exercise by another State even if it enjoys a concurrent right.[97] The competition for first exercise of right may be relevant in cases where States are acting in relation to each other where their actions affect another State externally. However, if the States are acting internally, then the concern of race for early action would not arise. Regulatory freedom is an expression of internal sovereignty. Hulsroj's criticism of the *Lotus principle* was in connection with *non liquet* rather than its role as a negative exclusion rule. In his view, considering actions as legal in the absence of a norm is granting them legal justification and an artificial attempt to evade *non liquet*.[98]

Another version of this argument is that the *Lotus principle* creates disparity between States. If a State succeeds in becoming a respondent, then it is not responsible to establish anything, except stating that no obligations can be implied unless there are specific rules agreed upon and established.[99] A State cannot engineer to be a respondent in a case. Furthermore, as per the rule of burden of proof, the party alleging the

that position that there can be a situation where rights can be claimed by States in the absence of obligations owed by other States.

94. International Law Commission, 'Draft Articles on Responsibility of States for Internationally Wrongful Acts, with Commentaries, 2001', 2001 (II) Yearbook of International Law Commission 31, 127.
95. Above note 26 (SS Wimbledon case), 33.
96. Above note 38 (Legal Status of Eastern Greenland), 70-72; *Nuclear Tests* case *(Australia/ New Zeland v France)*, Judgment, 20 December 1974, (1974) ICJ Reports 253, para. 43; International Law Commission, 'Unilateral Acts of States', Ninth report on unilateral acts of States, by Mr Víctor Rodríguez Cedeño, Special Rapporteur, DOCUMENT A/CN.4/569 and Add.1, 6 April 2006, available at: http://legal.un.org/ilc/documentation/english/a_cn4_569.pdf; last visited: 10 October 2015.
97. Peter Hulsroj, 'Three sources – no river: a hard look at the sources of public international law with particular emphasis on custom and "General Principles of law"' *Australian Journal of Public and International Law* 54(2) (1999), 219, 222-223.
98. *Ibid.*
99. Gerald Fitzmaurice, 'Some Problems Regarding the Formal Sources of International Law' in J H W Verzijl (ed.) *Symbolae Verzijl: présentées au professeur J.H.W. Verzijl à l'occasion de son LXXiéme anniversaire* (The Hague: Martinus Nijhoff; 1958), 157–158. Also republished in Martti Koskenniemi, *Sources of International Law* (England: Ashgate, 2000); Above note 51 (Pauwelyn), 154. Pauwelyn complains that the residual negative principle emanating from the *Lotus* case may not be an appropriate principle, but then states that in the context of WTO cases, this rule ought to apply. His words are: 'It may be relevant in limited contexts such as WTO dispute settlement where only claims under WTO covered agreements can be made so that what is not prohibited by the WTO treaty must, at least for purposes of WTO dispute settlement, be considered as allowed.'

breach has to prove that such a right exists in its favour – *actori incumbit probatio*.[100] These are vagaries of being a claimant in international adjudication which a State chooses. If the obligation of burden of proof is not imposed on the claimant State, then there would be an imbalance in the litigation. For Brownlie, a strict application of the *Lotus principle* may result into inconvenience. Therefore, according to him, the *Lotus principle* may be applied considering the context and the principle in question.[101] The multitude of activities a State may have to undertake for regulatory purposes can never be comprehensively contemplated. Forcing States to look for specific authorization for each exercise will make administration of States impractical. Therefore, regulatory freedom is an appropriate rule even if the *Lotus principle* is applied considering the context. Additionally, Akehurst views that the negative exclusion rule may not have been applied externally but it is certainly applicable in situations of internal administration.[102]

Some principles of international law are considered extremely fundamental and treated as a part of general international law.[103] For example, certain principles of humanitarian law have achieved customary status by virtue of their nature.[104] This led the Court in *Threat or Use of Nuclear Weapons* case to say that some principles are so fundamental that they ought to be treated as customary law.[105] Some principles emanating from sovereignty are indispensable for presence and conduct of activities of State and thus by their very nature, they are implied to exist. It is not uncommon for the ICJ to draw existence of customary international law based on sovereignty. According to Degan:

> In its actual practice the Court has most often deduced rules of conduct from the principle of sovereignty of all States, or from juxtaposed sovereignties in relations of several States. The Court has then simply presumed the existence of *communis opinio juris* in respect to these rules of conduct, without searching for other proofs

100. C. Amerasinghe, *Evidence in International Litigation* (Leiden, Boston: Martinus Nijhoff, 2005), at 139–140, 249. Above note 21 (Military & Paramilitary Activities against Nicaragua), at para. 101; *Case concerning Pulp Mills on the River Uruguay (Argentina v Uruguay)*, Judgment of 20 April 2010, (2010) ICJ Reports 14, para. 162; *Case concerning the Application of the Convention on the Prevention and Punishment of the Crime of Genocide (Bosnia and Herzegovina v Serbia and Montenegro)*, Judgment of 11 July 1996, (2007) ICJ Reports 43, para. 204.
101. Above note 1 (Brownlie), 291.
102. Above note 52 (Akehurst), footnote 10 at 19.
103. Andrew Mitchell, *Legal Principles in WTO Disputes* (Cambridge: Cambridge University Press, 2011), citing, A Cassese, 'The Contribution of ICTY to the Ascertainment of General Principles of Law' in Sienho Yee and Wang Tieya, (eds) *International Law in the Post-Cold War World: Essays in Memory of Li Haopei*, (London: Routledge, 2001) following Certain German Interests in Polish Upper Silesia on responsibility to make reparations.
104. *Corfu Channel Case* (merits) (1949) ICJ Reports 15, p. 22; For a discussion on whether reprisals in international humanitarian law have achieved customary law status *see* David Turns, 'The Law of Armed Conflict (International Humanitarian Law)' in Malcolm Evans (ed.) *International Law* (4th ed., Oxford: Oxford University Press, 2014), 847; *see* generally Daniel Thürer, *International Humanitarian Law: Theory, Practice, Context* (The Netherlands, Martinus Nijhoff, 2011).
105. Above note 8 (Genocide case), para. 79.

> of their existence as customary legal rules. The nature and importance of the norm in question is often a determinative factor in such circumstances.[106]

There is a presumption of existence of certain rights and principles implicit irrespective of a treaty.[107] They enjoy such a leeway because its nature is such that a State would habitually act in a particular way, without making any specific statement to that effect due to the obviousness involved.[108] If a principle forms part of the common legal consciousness of States, then it is capable of being treated as a customary principle.[109] Their character as a custom is not essentially an outcome of their normative value but of their obvious and persistent use in State practice.

Regulatory freedom is of an indispensable character and an activity inherently connected with statehood. States have habitually regulated and would continue to do so even though they may not have specifically asserted the right in overt statements. This is due to the obvious nature of regulatory freedom. The value of the norm is insufficient to create a customary norm. The norm will have to satisfy the rigours that constitute custom. This is discussed in the following section.

§6.03 REGULATORY FREEDOM AND THE REQUIREMENTS OF CUSTOM

Broad principles of law cannot be elevated to custom unless they satisfy the requirements for its formation.[110] In additional to establishing that regulatory freedom is a part of sovereignty, it is argued that regulatory freedom satisfies the requirements of custom and further, that it is a specific rule with precise contents rather than a general principle. Custom is one of the sources of international law stipulated in Article 38 (1) (b) of the ICJ Statute. Article 38 (1) (b) describes custom as: 'international custom, as evidence of a general practice accepted as law.' A custom is a uniform and constant usage practiced by States which they consider binding.[111] Brierly remarks that 'what is sought for is a general recognition among States of a certain practice as obligatory'.[112] Existence of custom can be established through different evidences which include, 'diplomatic correspondence, policy statements, press releases, the opinions of official legal advisers, official manuals on legal questions, for example, manuals of military law, executive decisions and practices, orders to naval forces, etc., comments by

---

106. Karol Wolfake, *Custom in Present International Law* (2nd ed., The Netherlands: Martinus Nijhoff, 1993), 25–29.
107. A J P Tammes, 'Inter-Action of the Sources of International Law' *Netherlands Journal of International Law* 10 (1963): 225, 230-1, citing Lake Lanoux Arbitration (*France v Spain*) Revue ginirale de droit international public 3rd series, X X I X (1958),. 78–119; Above note 104 (Corfu Channel case), 22.
108. *See Legality of Threat or Use of Nuclear Weapons*, Advisory Opinion, 8 July 1996, 1996 ICJ Reports 226, 226.
109. Above note 97 (Hulsroj), 246 (footnotes omitted).
110. *Ibid.*, 229-230.
111. Above note 84 (Asylum case), 276-277.
112. Above note 36 (Brierly), 61; Read J: 'Customary international law is the generalization of the practice of States'. *The North Atlantic Coast Fisheries* case (*Great Britain v United States of America*), Award, 7 September 1910, (1961) XI RIAA, 191.

Governments on drafts produced by the International Law Commission, state legislation, international and national judicial decisions, recitals in treaties and other international instruments, a pattern of treaties in the same form, the practice of international organs and resolutions relating to legal questions in the United Nations General Assembly'.[113] The actions and statements of de jure organs of State are influential in determination of custom. However, the influence of de facto organs cannot be ignored.

Custom is a 'clear and continuous habit of doing certain actions which has grown up under the aegis of the conviction that these actions are, according to international law, obligatory or right'.[114] The rule in question is either considered obligatory or treated as a matter of right. Regulatory freedom is an exercise that States consider to be a matter of right. Therefore, it is reflected in a negative form, i.e., absence of objection from other States, rather than a positive statement each time that State has a right. There are only few occasions where States have expressly mentioned the right and a physical action is not necessary every time to create customary law. Even abstract declarations by States, national laws and claims and other statements made by States in the context of specific disputes are capable of creating custom.[115]

For establishing custom two components are necessary: *opinio juris* and state practice. *Opinio juris* is the psychological element necessary for formation of custom.[116] It expresses the understanding of States that they consider certain actions to be obligatory rather than merely following them without any belief that those principles are binding legal principles.[117] *Opinion juris* is a belief of States that certain rule exists and statements by States adequately represent this belief.[118]

State practice is an equally important component for creation of custom along with *opinio juris*. ICJ has emphasized the concurrent presence of both by stating that

113. Above note 1 (Brownlie), 6–7.
114. Above note 46 (Oppenheim's International Law), 27.
115. Above note 52 (Akehurst), 2.
116. Above note 2 (Lotus case) (Dissenting Opinion of Judge Weiss), (1927) PCIJ Series A, No. 10, p. 4, 28; *North Sea Continental Shelf (Federal Republic of Germany/Netherlands)*, Judgment, 20 February 1969, (1969) ICJ Reports 3, 28, 32-41; *Continental Shelf (Libyan Arab Jamahiriyu/Malta)*, ICJ Reports *1985*, 29–30, para. 27; Above note 21 (Military & Paramilitary Activities against Nicaragua), para. 184; Above note 84 (Asylum case), paras 276–277; *North Sea Continental Shelf Cases (Federal Republic of Germany/Denmark Federal Republic of Germany/Netherlands)*, (1969) ICJ Reports 3, para. 77; Above note 108 (Legality of Use of Nuclear Weapons), paras 64–70.
117. Above note 1 (Brownlie), 6, 8; *ibid.*, (North Sea Continental Shelf Cases), 44; *ibid.*, (Asylum case), 277; Above note 47 (Right of Passage), 42–43; Above note 2 (Lotus case), 60 and 96–97; George Scelle, 'Règle Générales du Droit de la Paix' *Recueil des Cours* 46 (1933): 331, 434. Scelle stated that: 'le sentiment, ou tout au moins l'instinct, d'obéir à une nécessité sociale.'
118. Above note 52 (Akehurst), 36-7: 'a statement by a State about the content of customary law should be taken as *opinio juris* even if the State does not believe in the truth of the statement. It will often be impossible to prove that a state did not believe that its statement was true; however, even if such proof is forthcoming, it does not detract from the value of the statement. For instance, the Truman Proclamation of 1945 claimed that international law gave a coastal State exclusive rights over its continental shelf. It makes no difference whether the United States genuinely believed that international law gave such rights to costal States or not; the important thing is that the United States *said* that international law gave such rights to the costal State, and other States concurred.' At 37 (footnote omitted).

'the Court may not disregard the essential role played by general practice. Where two States agree to incorporate a particular rule in a treaty, their agreement suffices to make that rule a legal one, binding upon them; but in the field of customary international law, the shared view of the Parties as to the content of what they regard as the rule is not enough. The Court must satisfy itself that the existence of the rule in the *opinio juris* of States is confirmed by practice'.[119] State practice is the activity of State in conformity with the psychological belief that they consider a particular activity as binding. States regularly and continually exercise regulatory freedom. The practice of the organs of a State recognized by the domestic legal system is capable to result into state practice.[120] The actions of executive[121] are obviously important and so are the actions of judiciary.[122] Judicial decisions, legislations, the Constitution or basic laws are important evidence of practice.[123] Statements by Governments are an important source.[124] The generality of practice necessary to constitute custom need not be absolute and perfect. Any such expectation would make creation of a custom impossible. It is adequate to show generality in practice. The ICJ in the Military and Paramilitary Activities in *Nicaragua* case summarized this position as follows:

> It is not to be expected that in the practice of States the application of the rules in question should have been perfect, in the sense that States should have refrained, with complete consistency, from the use of force or from intervention in each other's internal affairs. The Court does not consider that, for a rule to be established as customary, the corresponding practice must be in absolutely rigorous conformity with the rule. In order to deduce the existence of customary rules, the Court deems it sufficient that the conduct of States should, in general, be consistent with such rules, and that instances of State conduct inconsistent with a given rule should generally have been treated as breaches of that rule, not as indications of the recognition of a new rule. If a State acts in a way prima facie incompatible with a recognized rule, but defends its conduct by appealing to exceptions or justifications contained within the rule itself, then whether or not the State's conduct is in fact justifiable on that basis, the significance of that attitude is to confirm rather than to weaken the rule.[125]

These occasions are adequate to establish regulatory freedom as a customary international law right. Additionally, States have continually exercised regulatory freedom. Investment treaty arbitration cases show that the subject under challenge is the regulation, which the State defends and the foreign investor objects. Therefore, there is ample evidence of practice by States. Additionally, there is evidence of *opinio juris* – whereby States have asserted regulatory freedom.

119. Above note 21 (Military & Paramilitary Activities against Nicaragua), para. 184.
120. Yoram Dinstein, 'The Interaction Between Customary International Law and Treaties' *Recueil des Cours* 322 (2006): 259, 269-271.
121. *Ibid.*, 272.
122. *Case Concerning the Arrest Warrant of 11 April 2000 (Congo v Belgium)* (2002) ICJ Reports 3, 24.
123. Above note 120 (Dinstein), 273 (footnote excluded).
124. *Ibid.*, 275-281.
125. Above note 21 (Military & Paramilitary Activities against Nicaragua), para. 186.

[A] Statements in Diplomatic Correspondences Between States

On similar lines, diplomatic correspondences have also referred to regulatory freedom. In 1975, the British Parliament passed Petroleum and Sub Pipelines Act of 1975. The Act introduced a wide range of ministerial powers which allowed introduction of approvals, control of price and modifications of terms of contract, including retrospective alteration. Oil companies raised objections that the Act was disturbing the contractual balance voluntarily entered into between parties. Rejecting the argument, the Secretary of Energy asserted that the power of the Parliament to make legislations in future could not be fettered through contractual clauses. The argument that any retrospective alteration to the contract has to be compensated, the Secretary of Energy said:

> 'the change in the legal framework that is available to governments and is regularly used by a whole host of environmental, health, tax and other measures, does not include the provision to compensation as a result.'[126]

In another communication, the Secretary of Energy stated that 'new taxation, exchange control, safety or other requirements also modify government profits but it is everywhere accepted that these measures do not necessitate the payment of compensation'. The Secretary of State was more candid in making the distinction between regulatory freedom and expropriation (discussed in detail in Chapter 2). He stated that the actions taken by the Government did not impact upon the basic property rights and therefore they did not amount to expropriation. Thus, the Government is not responsible to pay compensation.[127] The Canadian Government justified a similar measure.[128] States have also claimed permanent sovereignty over natural resources through resolutions in General Assembly[129] and the Charter of Economic Rights and Duties of States.[130]

There are two ways to test whether the approach adopted by these two states has achieved a generalized state practice status: general acceptability by other States or absence of objections, reflecting acquiescence on the part of other States. Claims that States are entitled to act in a particular way, whether they are made expressly or inferred from the conduct of States, must meet with acquiescence (i.e., lack of protest) from other States whose interests are affected, since international law governs the relations between States and not the position of a single State in isolation from other States.[131] In addition to the fact that these two States have clearly stated the position of law, their practice is of special relevance because they have traditionally been capital

126. Hansard, House of Commons Standing Committee D, 3 July, cols. 1146–1172.
127. *Ibid.*, 28 July 1975, cols. 1439–1440.
128. *See* E Mendes, 'The Canadian National Energy Programme: An Example of Assertion of Sovereignty or Creeping Expropriation in International Law' *Vanderbilt Journal of Transnational Law* 14 (1981): 475, 480.
129. Permanent Sovereignty over Natural Resources, G.A. res. 1803 (XVII), 17 U.N. GAOR Supp. (No.17) at 15, U.N. Doc. A/5217 (1962).
130. Charter of Economic Rights and Duties of States, G.A. res. 3281 (XXIX), 12 December 1974.
131. Above note 52 (Akehurst), 38.

exporting States and insisting on investor protection. They have sought liberal protection of investments. When it comes to the freedom of States regarding regulation, they take a position that it shall not be compromised and that States are not responsible to pay compensation for losses arising out or regulation. Additionally, these practices are specifically in the context of exercise of regulatory freedom. These two examples are specific in relation to the practice of claim of regulatory freedom. Specific practices always carry greater importance.[132]

[B] Restatement of the Law Third, the Foreign Relations Law of the United States

The Restatement of the Law Third, The Foreign Relations Law of the United States (Third American Restatement) is the most important and often quoted example of evidence of regulatory freedom as customary international law. This restatement is most pertinent since it specifically relates to 'injury to property and other economic interests of private persons who are foreign nationals'[133] in the context of treatment of aliens in international law and the rights and responsibilities of States. The Restatement excludes the responsibility of a State for losses arising out of a regulatory measure in the following words:

> A state is not responsible for loss of property or for other economic disadvantages resulting from bona fide general taxation, regulation, forfeiture for crime, or other action of the kind that is commonly accepted as within the police power of states, if it is not discriminatory.[134]

When phrases 'loss of property' and 'other economic disadvantages' are used, it is clear that they contemplate not only substantial but entire loss of property. They may result into destruction of property entirely – in other words 'effect' of the measure is an irrelevant consideration for an inquiry in cases of regulatory freedom. A mere loss is not sufficient to establish expropriation. There has to be a confiscatory action or an unreasonable interference for expropriation to exist. As per the American Restatement:

> A state is responsible as for an expropriation of property under Section (1) when it subjects alien property to taxation, regulation, or other action that is confiscatory or that prevents, unreasonably interferes with, or unduly delays, effective enjoyment of an alien's property or its removal from the state's territory.[135]

The formula used in recent American treaty practice is different from the American Restatement. The US Model BIT of 2012 adds the words 'except in rare cases', thereby limiting the availability of regulatory freedom only to rare cases.[136] A

132. *Ibid.*, 21.
133. Restatement of the Law Third, The Foreign Relations Law of the United States (American Law Institute, 1987), 197.
134. *Ibid.*, 201.
135. *Ibid.*, 200.
136. *See* Chapter 3 above.

question many then arise, whether such a change be said to have resulted into change of customary law?

The formula used by the US Model BIT of 2012 has incorporated the standard used by the American Supreme Court in the case of *Penn Central*[137] to distinguish between police powers (regulatory freedom) and takings (expropriation). This case was decided in the year 1978 and the American Restatement was published in the year 1987. The American Restatement does take account of the case but does not claim that the decision has resulted into change of the position of customary international law. The editorial note appended with the American Restatement acknowledges that in general terms, the position in international law is similar to that in United States jurisprudence for the purposes of the Fifth and Fourteenth Amendment and refers to *Penn Central* case, but does not state that the position of law in international law is exact as its position in municipal law.[138] Moreover, the intention of the drafters was clear that the position in international law on regulatory freedom was different from that under municipal law. This is clear from the sentence the American Restatement, whereby they note the position in municipal law and reject it as uncertain:

> As under United State constitutional law, the line between 'taking' and regulation is sometimes uncertain.[139]

The recent Model BIT may be an effort, as criticized by some commentators, to export its municipal jurisprudence on takings and regulation.[140] It is possible that this treaty practice, may in future, after receiving sufficient support could become a norm of customary international law. It would have to meet a high standard because if a practice is already settled, there is a need of great amount of evidence to establish that a change in that practice has occurred.[141]

Practice of one State, as such, is not important than that of other States.[142] If a State actively participates on an issue and generates state practice to which other States do not object, then that practice becomes custom.[143] The American Restatement represents the view of the United States regarding regulatory freedom. Other States have not objected to this rule. On the contrary they have used it to establish that the contents of the American Restatement represent customary international law. [144] It is often seen in practice that the process of formation of a custom involves assertion of a

137. *Penn Central Transportation Co. v New York City*, 438 U.S. 104 (1978).
138. Above note 145 (Third Foreign Relations Law), 211.
139. Above note 145 (Third Foreign Relations Law), 201.
140. *See* generally David Schneiderman, *Constitutionalizing Economic Globalization: Investment Rules and Democracies Promise* (Cambridge: Cambridge University Press, 2008); Santiago Montt, *State Liability in Investment Treaty Arbitration: Global Constitutional and Administrative Law in the BIT Generation*, (Oxford: Hart Publishing, 2009), 288–291.
141. Above note 52 (Akehurst), 19.
142. *Ibid.*, 48.
143. *Ibid.*, 22.
144. Pleadings of Mexico in *Marvin Feldman v Mexico*, Award, ICSID Case No. ARB (AF)/99/1, 16 December 2002, paras 105–106; *Saluka Investments BV (The Netherlands) v The Czech Republic*, Permanent Court of Arbitration, Partial Award, 17 March 2006, para. 260.

right by a State and passive acquiescence by others.[145] Regulatory freedom is a situation where the specific articulation of a customary norm has not met with objections from other States.

Certainly, the practice of few States - however influential they may be[146] - is insufficient to establish customary law. The evidence of custom reflected in the above cited incidents is from the US and Europe. There are other evidences of pleadings before the International Court, municipal laws and constitution that belong to other parts such as Asia, Africa and Latin America. These instances would show that the practice of asserting regulatory freedom is widespread and are discussed in the following sections.

[C] Pleadings of States Before International Courts and Tribunals

Pleadings by States before international court and tribunals are an important source for determination of *opinio juris* and state practice.[147] These statements are not a mere confirmation of custom but they create custom.[148] Also, in pleadings, if a certain principle is claimed to be custom and is not objected to by others, then it would be deemed to represent a customary norm.[149]

States have referred to the phrase 'police regulations' to express actions taken in furtherance of regulatory freedom[150] and have argued that regulatory freedom cannot be ignored simply because there are treaty obligations.[151] When States enter into obligations they are always mindful that the prerogative powers of the State are not prejudicially affected.[152] Even where States have objected to exercise of regulatory freedom in some cases, the challenge is not on the existence of right to regulate, but

145. Above note 97 (Hulsroj), 241-4, citing Friedman, 'Development of International Law' *AJIL* 57 (1963): 279, 288; I MacGibbon, 'Customary International Law and Acquiescence' *BYIL* 33 (1957): 115, 117–8, *see* footnote 67.
146. Above note 52 (Akehurst), 22-3.
147. Above note 1 (Brownlie), 10; A Roberts, 'Power and Persuasion in Investment Treaty Interpretation: The Dual Role of States' *AJIL* 104 (2010): 179, 218 footnote 183.
148. Above note 52 (Akehurst), 4-5. Akherst gives the example of *Mexican Railway Union Claim*, where the reply by the State was considered as the sole evidence of the rule in question. (1930 RIAA vol. 5), 115, 122-4.; *Eschauzier claim* (1931) RIAA 207, 210-2; *Mergé Claim* (1955) ILR 22 443, 449-50; *re Piracy Jure Gentium* [1934] AC 586, 599-600.
149. *Ibid.*, 5.
150. ELSI, Rejoinder of Italy, 'As to the later period, if it is admitted that management and control are protected by the Treaty in conformity with the applicable local laws and regulations, all the interference the public authorities may exercise under these laws and regulations musl be deemed to be compatible with the degree of protection afforded under the Treaty. Indeed such protection cannot be considered to be extended to the point that the United States shareholders are exonerated from the application of imperative measures, which are binding for all subjects; some of these measures may have an effect on the powers to manage and control an Italian company. In this regard it should be noted that the Italian legal provisions on the basis of which the requisition decree of 1 April 1968 was issued without doubt pursues public policy aims and could be characterized as police regulations.' (p. 460).
151. ELSI, Counter Memorial of Italy: 'In other words. The respect of these local laws and regulations is a limit that cannot be overstepped by virtue of a condition granted to foreigners protected by a Treaty of Friendship Commerce and Navigation.', 35. (sic).
152. ELSI, Annex to Memorial of United States, 396.

whether the actions of host State that have caused losses are in accordance with the laws of host State.[153]

The argument of regulatory freedom as customary law is evident from the arguments advanced by States before investment arbitration cases. In Chapter 3, cases were discussed where the State had raised the argument that regulatory freedom is customary law which was upheld. A comprehensive treatment of this argument can be found in the pleading of Canada in *Chemtura v Canada*. After relying on different sources to establish regulatory freedom is custom, Canada summarized its pleadings in the following words:

> Various authorities and tribunals have expressed concern that the police powers doctrine operate within certain limits so that it is not abused by governments who might enact police measures as a pretext to an expropriation. Factors considered in this context include whether the measure is arbitrary, discriminatory, excessive and whether it was adopted in good faith.[154]

The general right to regulate has been claimed across various other fields such as the right of costal State to regulate activities on the stream while a treaty regulating the use of watercourse exists. In the *Navigation Rights* case, both the parties to the dispute, Costa Rica and Nicaragua, agreed on one point: right to regulate. The disagreement was only in relation to the scope of activity covered under the regulations.[155] The pleadings of disputing parties in that case contain various statements made at different international conference which represent the commitment to recognize and protect regulatory freedom. In a Diplomatic Conference, the Foreign Minister of Nicaragua made a statement that Nicaragua was entitled to impose regulations in relation to transportation on the river during night hours, in the following words:

> In relation to the limitation on the navigation on the San Juan Kiver as regards the hours of the day, it should be noted that it is Nicaragua's right and obligation, as the sovereign State, to adopt the regulations necessary for guaranteeing the safety

153. ELSI, Pleadings of United States, 382-3.
154. *Chemtura Corporation v Government of Canada*, UNCITRAL (formerly Crompton Corporation v Government of Canada), Counter-Memorial, 20 October 2008, para. 594 (footnotes excluded), also *see* paras 565–593.
155. Memorial of Costa Rica, para. 4.03. 'It is apparently not disputed, either, that the exercise of Costa Rica's rights requires no prior authorization from Nicaragua. What Nicaragua challenges is the scope of those rights, arguing that most of the navigational uses relied on by Costa Rica are not covered by the Treaty of Limits and the Cleveland Award and that these are therefore–according to Nicaragua subject to its unilateral decision and regulation.' Citing: 'In his statement before the Permanent Council of the Organization of American States of 8 March 2000, Nicaraguan Minister of Foreign Affairs Eduardo Montcalegre declared: "Any navigation undertaken by Costa Rica in the waters of the San Juan River that does not correspond to the navigation expressly contemplated in the Jerez-Catas Treaty and the Cleveland Award in force in the part of the river established in the international instruments currently in effect should be expressly authorized by Nicaragua, as the country possessing full sovereignty over the waters of the said river and, as such, able to establish all manner of regulations that, by virtue of the said sovereignty, it deems necessary to establish" (Translation by Costa Rica) EA/Ser.G CP/ACTA 1224/00, 23: Annexes, Vol. 6, Annex 229. *See also* Acting Nicaraguan Foreign Minister, Carlos Gurdián, to Costa Rican. Foreign Minister, Roberto Rojas López, Note No, MRE/98/02638, 28 August 1998: Annexes, Vol. 3, Annex 51.'

> of the people and vessels travelling along the river and avoid all manner of criminal activities.[156]

The judicial proceedings in the WTO are replete with pleadings by States that regulatory freedom is a right of States emanating from sovereignty. The United States pleaded:

> The United States responds that Article XX (b) and (g) contain no jurisdictional limitations, not limitations on the location of the animals or natural resources to be protected and conserved and that, under general principles of international law relating to sovereignty, States have the right to regulate imports within their jurisdiction.[157]

In the same case, Australia argued that:

> Australia further stated that the Panel was not being asked to determine whether contracting parties had the right to enforce unilaterally-determined standards. In circumstances where unilateral standards were not enforced by trade or trade-related measures, there was obviously no role for the GATT. In most instances, it was possible to enforce such standards without risk to GATT obligations, including GATT rules of non-discrimination. In other instances, GATT exceptions provisions might be invoked in line with sovereignty principles. The text of the General Agreement clearly respected the sovereign right of contracting parties to maintain their own standards. However, sovereignty was a two-way street in the GATT. A contracting party which claimed the right to take trade restrictions based on unilaterally-determined standards must expect other contracting parties to claim the right to justify trade restrictions against that contracting party on the same grounds. The United States intermediary nation embargo effectively denied other contracting parties subject to the embargo the sovereignty to set their own standards for the like product.[158]

Regulatory freedom has been asserted by States in various WTO cases.[159] The Appellate Body accepted the argument that the regulatory freedom of States in not affected generally, except to the extent of specifically giving away.[160] In the *China-Audiovisuals* case, China asserted that despite the presence of General Agreement on Trade in Services, 'the sovereignty of WTO Members to decide upon the pace and the extent of liberalization of their services markets'.[161]

States have claimed right to impose regulations within their territory which they deem appropriate for public interest, unaffected by treaty obligations. This right to impose regulations within territory is seen as a sovereign prerogative of the State.

156. Nicaraguan Foreign Minister, Francisco Xavier Aguirrsl Sacasa, to Costa Rican Foreign Minister, Roberto ROJU Lopcz, Note No MREJDM-JU0818/UX/OI, Memorial of Costa Rica, 3 August 2001 Annexes, Vol. 3, Annex 72. Cited at para. 5.75, at 114.
157. *United States – Import Prohibition of Certain Shrimp and Shrimp Products*, (WT/DS58/R), Panel, para. 7.24.
158. *United States – Restrictions on Imports of Tuna*, Report of the Panel (DS29/R) para. 4.2.
159. *See* cases cited in above note 43, (US-Gambling, Report of Panel), para. 5.1.6.
160. *Ibid.*, para. 5.17.
161. *China – Measures Affecting Trading Rights and Distribution Services for Certain Publications and Audiovisual Entertainment Products*, Report of the Appellate Body, WT/DS363/AB/R, para. 46.

States have even argued that regulating activity within its borders is a duty of the State and the power to make regulations is an outcome of sovereign powers which grant them exclusive power over their territories.[162]

[D] Domestic Laws of States and Decisions of International and National Courts and Tribunals

It is normal for States to rely on laws of various countries to establish state practice.[163] ICJ too has relied on this methodology.[164] ILC considers national laws, regulations and judgments as 'primary evidence of state practice'.[165] Custom is reflected in not only the external behaviour of States, but even in internal matters.[166] Most of the national constitutions of States contain provisions which allow exercise of regulatory freedom. States are not responsible to pay compensation for losses occasioned by these regulatory exercises.[167] Article 25 (3) of the South African Constitution recognizes the distinction between losses arising out of expropriatory regulation and legitimate regulatory freedom. There is no responsibility to pay compensation in the later cases. Commonwealth constitutions also recognize regulations for which a State is not responsible to pay compensation.[168] There is a trend amongst newly created Constitutions to protect regulatory freedom with the objective of facilitating wide range of activities that a modern welfare State is required to undertake.[169]

The judicial decisions of international bodies are only subsidiary source of law, yet they are an important piece of evidence that a particular legal principle has attained customary status. Right to regulate has been so recognized by international tribunals.[170] Various tribunals have treated regulatory freedom as an exception from state

162. Memorial of Costa Rica, Pleadings, para. 5.89. Citing the Nicaraguan Foreign Minister, Norman Caldera Cardenal, to Costa Rican Foreign Minister, Roberto Tovar Faja, Note No MRWDM-3111284/11/05, 9 November 2005: Annexes, Vol. 3, Annex 82.
163. Above note 52 (Akehurst), 8-9, citing Lotus, arguments by Turkey, Cutting Incident. Arguments by Mexico, Foreign Relations of United States (1887), 859–867. US in response did not object to such reliance, but only that the number of laws are too few (754–755 and 718–817) and in turn relied on further laws (770–817).
164. *Nottebohm (Liechtenstein v Guatemala)*, Second Phase, Judgment of 6 April 1955, (1955) ICJ Reports 4,22; *Panevezys-Saldutiskis Railway*, Judgment of 28 February 1939, PCIJ Series A/B, No. 76, 923.
165. (1950) 2 Yearbook of ILC 370-1; Karol Wolfke, *Custom in Present International Law* (2nd ed., The Netherlands: Martinus Nijhoff, 1993)145–147.
166. Above note 46 (Oppenheim's International Law), 26. (footnotes omitted).
167. Andre van der Walt, *Constitutional Property Clauses: A Comparative Analysis* (The Hague: Kluwer Law International, 1999), 19.
168. For several other examples *see* Tom Allen, *The Right to Property in Commonwealth Constitutions* (Cambridge: Cambridge University Press, 2000), 162.
169. M Sornarajah, *Resistance and Change in the International Law on Foreign Investment*, (Cambridge: Cambridge University Press, 2015), 230.
170. *The Robert Wilson case* (1841), Moore, History and Digest of Arbitration, etc.(1898), vol. IV, p. 3373; and the *Louis Chazen International Arbitral case* (1930), United Nations, Reports of Awards, vol. IV, 564; *J Parsons* case (1925); *Nielsen American and British Claims Arbitrations, etc.* 1926, 587; *Fabar case (United States v Yugoslavia), Settlement of Claims by Foreign Claims Settlement Commission* (1955), 23; *Brewer, Moller & Co. case (Germany v Venezuela)* 10 RIAA

responsibility.[171] States enjoy discretion to regulate the entry and operation of foreigners in their jurisdiction. States are not responsible for losses caused to an alien due to regulations.[172] The 'countries differ in their methods and means by which these matters are accomplished, but the right is inherent in all sovereign powers and is one of the attributes of sovereignty, since it exercises it rightly only in a proper defense of the country from some danger anticipated or actual.'[173] Tribunals have recognized specific instances of regulatory freedom where a State, without being responsible, can resort to a regulation that causes losses for the investor. States can always adopt administrative measures which may cause losses to investors and are not responsible to pay compensation in these situations.[174] Specific instances of such internal freedom would be the general power of States to regulate their currency.[175] Since the losses suffered by foreign investors due to currency depreciation are indirect losses, international tribunals have held that States are not responsible for these losses.[176]

Decisions of municipal courts also play an important role in determining the customary nature of certain principles. Various decisions of municipal and regional judicial bodies have recognized the right of States to regulate the use of property. The regulations in such cases had affected the value of property, but the judicial bodies recognized that the States possess the necessary right to adopt legitimate regulations for public interest. States have been given wide discretion in their choice of public interest. Courts have recognized the difference between police powers and eminent domain.[177] For example, zoning regulations have been upheld;[178] statute limiting coal mining to avoid subsidence damage to surface buildings has been upheld.[179]

The Europe Court of Human Rights has recognized that various regulations could be adopted that may destruct the value of property, but they do not result into expropriation. Regulations in various forms have been recognized as legitimate

---

423 (1903); *Kugele v Polish State*, 6 Ann. Dig. 69 (1931-32). Also *see* F A Mann, 'State Contracts and State Responsibility' *AJIL* 54 (1960): 572.

171. *Allgemine Gold-und Silbersceideanstalt v Customs and Excise Commissioner*, (1980) 2 WLR 555; (1980) 51 BY 305; *AKU* case ILR 23 (1956), 21; *Assets of Hungarian Company in Germany* case ILR 32, 565; *Re Dohnert Muller, Schmidt & Company*, 570, cited in above note 1 (Brownlie) at footnotes 83–85, 536).
172. *Dickson Car Wheel Co.* case (1931) Op of Com 174, 192-3, cited in above note 1 (Brownlie), 536.
173. *Maal* case (1903) Ven Arb 914, 914-5; also *see Ben Tillet* case (1898) 92 BFSP 78. 105.
174. Bin Cheng, *General Principles of Law as Applied by International Courts and Tribunals* (London: Stevens and Sons, 1953), 52–53 (footnotes excluded).
175. In the *Serbian Loans case*, the Permanent Court declared that it was, of course, 'a generally accepted principle that a State is entitled to regulate its currency'. Publications of the Permanent Court of International Justice, Collection of Judgments, series A, Nos. 20–21, 44. As regards the scope of the State's rights in this respect, *see* F A Mann, 'Money in Public International Law' *BYIL* (1949), 259 et seq.
176. *Tabar Claim* (1953) 20 ILR 211; *Zuck Claim* (1958); Furst Claim; British Digest, vi. 350; Wortley, 107–109; Re Keim 44 ILR 120, cited in above note 1 (Brownlie) at footnote 63 at 532.
177. *Kelo v City of New London* 545 U.S. 469 (2005); 'Traditional uses of that regulatory power, such as the power to abate a nuisance, required no compensation whatsoever, in sharp contrast to the takings power, which has always required compensation. The question whether the State can take property using the power of eminent domain is therefore distinct from the question whether it can regulate property pursuant to the police power.'
178. *Agins v City of Tiburon* 447 U.S. 255 (1980), 261.
179. *Keystone Bituminous Coal Ass'n v DeBenedicti* 480 U.S. 470 (1987), 485, 493.

exceptions to right of property, such as regulations allowing long leasehold tenants to buy property at less than market value;[180] local planning regulations that affect the value of property;[181] regulations regarding calculation of rent;[182] or confiscation of property under taxing statutes.[183]

180. *James v The United Kingdom*, Judgment, EctHR, 21 February 1986, Application no. 8793/79, para. 54 The Court elucidated this power in the following words: 'Eliminating what are judged to be social injustices is an example of the functions of a democratic legislature. More especially, modern societies consider housing of the population to be a prime social need, the regulation of which cannot entirely be left to the play of market forces.', para. 47.
181. *Pine Valley Developments Ltd. v Ireland*, Judgment of 29 November 1991, Ser A No. 222 (1991), para. 57.
182. *Mellacher v Austria*, Judgment of 19 December 1989, PCIJ Ser A No. 169 (1989), paras 46–47.
183. *Gasus Dosier- ud Fördertechnik GmbH v The Netherlands*, Judgment, EctHR, 23 February 1995, Application no. 15375/89, paras 59–60.

CHAPTER 7

Regulatory Freedom (Customary Norm) and Indirect Expropriation (Treaty Norm): Interaction of Norms

This Chapter explores the relationship between regulatory freedom as a customary international law norm and indirect expropriation as a treaty norm. The aim is to look at the nuances of this relationship based on different principles on conflict of norms and the possibility and circumstances of their harmonious existence and the manner in which international courts and tribunals have addressed the role the regulatory freedom in light of treaty obligations purportedly dealing with a concerned subject matter exhaustively.

There is no discussion on the direct relationship between a little discussion on this relationship in the practice of investment tribunals. Whatever arbitral practice exists is inconsistent. Some tribunals acknowledged existence of custom but treated it to operate in the background, performing a subsidiary role or operating in a residual way. In *Phoenix v Czech Republic*, the Tribunal viewed that investment treaties cannot be interpreted in isolation from customary international law.[1] There is little clarity on the relationship.

§7.01 WHETHER INDIRECT EXPROPRIATION (AS A TREATY NORM) IS HIERARCHICALLY SUPERIOR TO REGULATORY FREEDOM (AS A CUSTOMARY NORMS)?

Prior to understanding the precise relationship between regulatory freedom as a customary norm and indirect expropriation as a treaty norm, it is necessary firstly to see whether indirect expropriation is normatively higher or hierarchically superior than

1. *Phoenix Action, Ltd. V The Czech Republic*, ICSID Case No. ARB/06/5, Award (15 April 2009), para. 78.

regulatory freedom because indirect expropriation is a treaty norm and regulatory freedom is a customary norm. If indirect expropriation is normatively higher because it is a treaty norm then there would be no scope for the operation of regulatory freedom. If not then, the nature of their relationship has to be explored, which is done in the following sections. There is a tendency to assume that indirect expropriation would have a higher value as compared to regulatory freedom because it is a treaty norm.

The relationship between regulatory freedom and indirect expropriation has to be seen in light of the relationship between treaties and customs. They both are sources of international law noted in Article 38 (1) of the Statute of ICJ, which reads as under:

> The Court, whose function is to decide in accordance with international law such disputes as are submitted to it, shall apply:
>
> a. international conventions, whether general or particular, establishing rules expressly recognized by the contesting states;
> b. international custom, as evidence of a general practice accepted as law.

The structure of Article 38 (1) may give the impression that there is some form of hierarchy between treaty and custom. The structure only represents practical convenience based on ease of identification. Normally, a treaty sets out the rights and obligations of States clearly, and it is easy to locate the contents and identify their purview. From a practical standpoint, it may be convenient to look into a treaty first and then into customary law.[2] This does not mean that a treaty is superior to customary law.

The drafters of Article 38 did not intend the order of presentation of treaty and custom to constitute a formal hierarchy. Article 38 (1) of the ICJ Statute is borrowed unaltered from the PCIJ Statute: the Statute creating the PCIJ (the predecessor of the ICJ).[3] Initially, words *en order successif* was added in the draft. However, during the deliberations of the Committee of Jurists - which was responsible for the drafting - those words were removed. Article 38 (1) represents the drafters intention of applying treaty and custom in sequence, rather than granting priority to treaty over custom. Thus, the presence of a treaty norm does not amount to the exclusion of customary law.[4]

The normative value of a customary norm is no less than a treaty norm. Their relationship is an 'equal relationship of interdependence and mutual support'.[5] As a source of law, treaty and custom are autonomous and independent. Dinstein conceptualizes the relationship as: 'the two strata are not to be imagined as vertically

2. Karol Wolfke, 'Treaties and Custom: Aspects of Interrelation' in Jan Klabbers and René Lefeber (eds) *Essays on the Law of Treaties: A Collection of Essays in Honour of Bert Vierdag*, (The Hague, Boston: M. Nijhoff Publishers, 1998), 37.
3. A J P Tammes, 'Inter-Action of the Sources of International Law' *Netherlands Journal of International Law* 10 (1963): 225, 227.
4. For a general discussion on 'norm' *see* Chapter 7.
5. L. Condorelli, 'Customary International Law: The Yesterday, Today, and Tomorrow of General International Law' in Antonio Cassese (ed.) *Realizing Utopia: The Future of International Law* (Oxford University Press, 2012), 149-50.

overlaying one another, but mostly as juxtaposed horizontally next to each other'.[6] They both are created by State consent - express or implied.[7] Therefore, they are equivalent with identical binding force.[8] There is no reason to assume that indirect expropriation, due to its treaty origin will supersede regulatory freedom, which is a originates in customary law.

The functioning of international law shows that custom plays a critical role, at times more frequently than treaties.[9] Custom is accorded importance in the practice of international law because it plays a central role in the life and of international relations. It facilitates a unitary framework of legal principles and rules, and ensures coherence in the system as a whole.[10] Treaties govern relationship between the parties, but custom has a wider application in the international community. Customary law is often and prominently applied in international adjudication. Although, the disputes before the International Court of Justice, arise mostly in relation to interpretation and application of treaties, custom often plays a decisive role. This role of custom, makes Lauterpacht to observe that custom has not only contributed to the development of international law, but has also resulted into broader reach and relevance of the Court's jurisprudence.[11] Fitzmaurice challenges whether treaties can even be treated as a source of law. Treaties merely constitute mutual contractual choices of States, understood appropriately as 'source of obligation' rather than a 'source of law'.[12] There are areas of international law where there are no treaties and the law is predominantly covered by customary law. [13] This is manifest in the area of law of treaties. A treaty is

6. Above note 55 (Dinstein), 260.
7. Georg Shwarzenberger, *International Law as applied by International Court and Tribunals* (London, Stevans and Sons Ltd. 1945); VD Degan, *Sources of International Law* (The Netherlands: Martinus Nijhoff Publishers, 1997), 181; D. Anzilotti, *Cours de droit international Public* (Paris: Libarairie de Recueil Sirey, 1929), 89-93; A Cavaligeri, *Corso di dirittointernazionale*, Tezaedizione, Napoli 1939, 63, K Struoo, 'Les regales generals du droit le la paix', RCV 1934 tom 47, 14. (other references in footnote 4).
8. Mark Villiger, *Customary International Law and Treaties: A Manual on the Theory and Practice of the Interrelation of Sources* (The Hague: Kluwer Law International, 1997), 58-59.
9. Oscar Schachter, 'Entangled Treaty and Custom' in Yoram Distein & Mala Tabory (eds) *International Law at a Time of Perplexity: Essays in Honour of Shabtai Rosenne* (Dordrecht, Boston, London: Martinus Nijhoff Publishers, 1989), 721. According to Schachter: 'Customary law, in contrast, tends to appeal to the conservative. Its case-by-case gradualism reflects particular needs in concrete situations. It avoids grand formulas and abstract ideas. The law that evolves is more malleable and more responsive to each State's individual interest. Not least in the minds of some of its supporters is that custom gives weight to effective power and responsibility whereas multilateral treaty-making unrealistically and unwisely, in their view, treats all States as equally capable.'
10. Luigi Condorelli, 'Customary International Law: The Yesterday, Today, and Tomorrow of General International Law' in Antonio Cassese (ed.), *Realizing Utopia: The Future of International Law* (Oxford: Oxford University Press, 2012), 150.
11. Hersch Lauterpacht, *The Development of International Law by the International Court* (Cambridge; Grotious Publications Ltd., 1982), 368-393.
12. Gerald Fitzmaurice, 'Some Problems Regarding the Formal Sources of International Law' in J.H.W. Vezjil (ed.) *'Symbolae Verzijl: présentées au professeur J.H.W. Verzijl à l'occasion de son LXXième anniversaire'* (The Hague: Martinus Nijhodd; 1958), 157-58. Also republished in Martti Koskenniemi, *Sources of International Law* (England: Ashgate, 2000).
13. Yoram Dinstein, 'The Interaction Between Customary International Law and Treaties' in *Recueil des Cours: Collected Courses of the Hague Academy of International Law (Vol. 322)*, Académie de Droit International de la Ha (The Hague: Springer, 2006) 259, 322-383.

binding due to the customary principle of *pacta sunt servanda.*[14] The exercise of treaty interpretation entirely depends on custom. Rules of interpretation specified in Articles 31 and 32 of VCLT are customary in nature. VCLT is a codificatory treaty, yet it does not exhaustively cover all principles of customary law governing the law of treaties. Even the VCLT acknowledges that customary law rules on the law of treaties continue to operate. [15] A custom can modify[16] or terminate (through the principle of destitute)[17] a treaty. If a customary norm reaches the status of *jus cogens* it will invalidate a treaty.[18] These observations do not belittle the role of treaties, but emphasize that customary law may play substantial role. Therefore, the status of regulatory freedom is same as indirect expropriation based upon their existence and operation as norms originating in custom and treaty respectively.

§7.02 THE RELATIONSHIP BETWEEN A CUSTOMARY NORM AND TREATY NORM IN INTERNATIONAL LAW

Having discussed that indirect expropriation is not normatively superior to regulatory freedom in the last section, this section would focus upon the precise relationship between them, based on the general relationship between customary and treaty norms. Regulatory freedom and indirect expropriation regulate the relationship between a host State and a foreign investor. This section develops the consequences of this fact and how far it affects the scope and operation of regulatory freedom in the presence of indirect expropriation.

[A] Systematic Integration

Investment treaties contain provisions that regulate the relationship between a host State and a foreign investor. There is a network of bilateral and multilateral investment

14. Antony D'Amato, 'Human Rights as Norms of Customary International Law' in Antony D'Amato (ed.) *International Law: Process and Prospect* (New York: Transnational Publishers, 1987) 125.
15. The preamble of the VCLT says: 'Affirming that the rules of customary international law will continue to govern questions not regulated by the provisions of the present Convention'; United National Convention on Jurisdictional Immunities of States and Their Properties, 2004 Preamble says: 'Affirming that the rules of customary international law continue to govern matters not regulated by the provisions of the present Convention'; Similar language is employed by Vienna Convention on Diplomatic Relations and Optional Protocols, 1961, Preamble; Vienna Convention on Consular Relations 1963, Preamble; Likewise, Art. 3.2 of the DSU: 'The Members recognize that it serves to preserve the rights and obligations of Members under the covered agreements, and to clarify the existing provisions of those agreements in accordance with customary rules of interpretation of public international law.'
16. Air Transport Services Agreement Arbitration (*United States of America v France*), Award, 22 December 1963, (1969) 38 ILR 182, 249.
17. Above note 13 (Dinstein), at 411-416.
18. *Jus cogens* norms are created through the process of creation of custom. They are understood as dense or intense custom. *See* Stefan Kadelbach, 'Jus Cogens, Obligations Erga Omnes and Other Rules – The Identification of Fundamental Norms' in Christian Tomuschat & Jean-Marc Thouvenin (eds) *The Fundamental Rules of the International Legal Order: Jus Cogens and Obligations Erga Omnes*, (Leiden; Boston: Martinus Nijhoff Publishers, 2006), 21-40.

protection treaties. This network is claimed to have created a 'self-contained' regime.[19] The notion of self-contained regimes is used in international law to represent a set of rules that treats a particular problem in a different manner than general international law.[20] Therefore, the network of investment treaties is said to have carved out a specialized regime out of general international law, where general rules of international law would have a limited relevance.

Although the notion of a specialized regime is used to represent a set of rules created through treaties regulating a specific area of international law, none of these exclude application of general international law.[21] A self-contained regime is not a 'closed legal circuit'.[22] No treaty can exist in isolation from general international law.[23] All treaty principles shall be 'applied and interpreted against the background of the general principles of international law'.[24] General international law is relevant to provide normative background or fulfil gaps let in the operation of such a regime. The application of substantive or procedural rules, such as treaty interpretation or state responsibility are not excluded simply because the regime is 'self-contained'.[25] The notion of a 'self-contained regime' is a misnomer because 'no regime is isolated from international law'. [26] Thus, the fact of a treaty obligations dealing specifically with a subject matter of international law cannot be given too much importance to discard the role of other principles.[27]

Assuming such loosely held regimes exist, they cannot contract out of the application of general international law. The modern-day understanding of international law is not strictly bilateral and involves upholding of community interests, which makes it necessary that even specialized treaty regimes operate in the broader context of general international law obligations. International community constitutes a society

19. The award discussed in Chapter 3 show that tribunals have disregarded the role of regulatory freedom, as a principle emanating from general international law. There is a subconscious understanding that investment treaties constitute a specialized regime, reflected in the reasoning of these awards. Schill argues that there is a specialized regime created by bilateral treaties and calls them to have caused multilateralization of international investment law. Stephan Schill, *Multilateralization of International Investment Law* (Cambridge: Cambridge University Press, 2009), 16-19.
20. Report of the Study Group of the International Law Commission, *Fragmentation of International Law: Difficulties Arising From the Diversification and Expansion of International Law* (A/CN.4/L.682, International Law Commission, 2006), para. 128.
21. *Ibid.*, para. 172.
22. *Ibid.*, para. 152 (3).
23. *See* Comments of Rosalyn Higgings, 'A Bavel of Judicial Voices? Ruminations from the Bench' *International and Comparative Law Quarterly* 55 (2006): 791; Patrick Daillier & Alain Pellet, *Droit International Public* (7th ed., Paris: Librairie générale de droit et de jurisprudence: 2002), 266. 'Un traité ne peut être considéré isolement. Non seulement il est encré dans les réalités sociales, mais encore ses dispositions doivent être confrontées avec d'autres normesjuridiques avec lesquelles elles peuvent entrer en concurrence.'
24. Arnold McNair, *The Law of Treaties* (Oxford: Clarendon Press, 1961) 466; Hersch Lauterpacht, 'Restrictive Interpretation and Effectiveness in the Interpretation of Treaties' *British Yearbook of International Law* 50 (1949):60, 76. Also, *See* Humphrey Waldock, Third Report on the Law of Treaties, (Yearbook of the ILC, 1964, Vol. II), 8.
25. *Ibid.*, para. 192.
26. *Ibid.*, para. 193.
27. Ian Brownlie, *Principles of Public International Law* (6th ed., Oxford: Oxford University Press, 2003), 529-530.

and is governed by *ubi societum ibi jus*. The purpose of international community is achievement of communitarian norms[28] which cannot be ignored. The balance between 'bilateral' and 'community'[29] interests is achieved through 'systematic integration of international law'.[30] Treaties are an outcome of mutual bargain. The task of treaty interpretation involves determination of intention of the parties.[31] The rules of interpretation enshrined in the Vienna Convention on the Law of Treaties (VCLT) make it necessary for the treaty interpreting body to keep the broader system of international law in mind. The objective is systematic integration is to ensure that the exercise of treaty interpretation is not merely a 'mechanical application of apparently random rules, decisions or behavioral patterns' but an operation of an entire system of international law in the background.[32] Article 31 (3) (c) of the VCLT imposes the responsibility of systematic integration on the interpreting body. Article 31 (3) (c) is a tool of treaty interpretation and not merely an aspiration to refer to other rules. It does not leave the discretion or choice with adjudicator, but expects it to take account of the 'normative environment' of international law.[33] Therefore, the principle of systematic interpretation is embedded in every adjudicative process. An investment tribunal will only be failing in its duty if it does not comply with this mandate.[34] Article 31 (3) (c) states that while interpreting the treaty in view of its object and purpose, 'any relevant rules of international law applicable in the relations between the parties' has to be taken into account.[35] The reference to 'rules of international law' includes rules emanating from all the sources including custom, general principles and treaty.[36] Custom plays an important role in the process since it achieves unification of the sectoral subsystems operating at times with autonomous institutional devices.[37] Custom operates in background for investment treaties as well.[38] Therefore, while

28. James Crawford, *State Responsibility: The General Part* (Cambridge: Cambridge University Press, 2014), 362-365.
29. For the relationship between 'bilateral' and 'community' interests *see* Bruno Simma, 'From Bilateralism to Community Interests in International Law' in Recueil des Cours: Collected Courses of the Hague Academy of International Law (Vol. 250), Académie de Droit International de la Ha (The Hague: Springer, 1994) (1994), 229-248.
30. *See* generally Campbell McLachlan, 'The Principle of Systematic Integration and Article 31 (3) I of the Vienna Convention' *International and Comparative Law Quarterly* 54 (2005): 279.
31. Richard Gardiner, *Treaty Interpretation* (Oxford: Oxford University Press, 2008), 6-7.
32. Above note 20 (ILC, Fragmentation Report), para. 34.
33. Above note 20 (ILC Fragmentation Report), para. 415. Citing the example of the arbitral award in *Franco-Belgian* case where while interpreting one treaty, another treaty provisions were taken into account. Différend concernant l'accord Tardieu-Jaspar *(Belgium v France)*, Award, (1 March 1937), UNRIAA, col. III, 1713.
34. The Appellate Body of the WTO considered this to be a duty when it said: 'our task here is to interpret the language of the chapeau, seeking additional interpretative guidance, as appropriate, from the general principles of international law' *United States – Import Prohibition of Certain Shrimp and Shrimp Products*, Appellate Body, WT/DS58/AB/R, 12 October 1998, para. 158.
35. Article 31(3)(c), Vienna Convention on the Law of Treaties (1969).
36. Above note 20, para. 426 (b).
37. Above note 10 (Condorelli), 150.
38. *See* above note 30 (Mclachlan), 361; TW Waelde, 'Interpreting Investment Treaties: Experience and Examples' in *International Investment Law for the [2]1st Century: Essays in Honour of Christoph Schreuer*, ed. Christina Binder, Ursula Kriebaum, August Reinisch & Stephan Wittich (Oxford: Oxford University Press, 2009); A Gourgourinis, 'Lex Specialis in WTO and Investment Protection Law' *German Yearbook of International Law* 53 (2010): 579; A Gourgourinis, 'The

interpreting any treaty, including investment treaty, the tribunal will also have to apply customary law and general principles, except and to the extent that the parties have excluded the custom by creating treaty provisions in the nature of *lex specialis*.[39] Regulatory freedom emanating from custom would have to be applied while interpreting an investment treaty as a matter of obligation on the adjudicating body. Unless, the operation of regulatory freedom is excluded in some manner.[40]

In addition to the overarching objective of unity of international law, another practical reason for systematic integration is that a treaty cannot exhaustively regulate the relationship between States. There are large numbers of rules that continue to operate outside treaties. There is always a tacit reference to application of general international law to resolve all questions that have not been specifically mentioned in a treaty.[41] Questions of attributability, nature of the breach and circumstances precluding wrongfulness, etc. can be determined only with reference to general international law.[42] There are various other principles that continue to operate irrespective of the treaty provisions. For example, criteria of statehood;[43] law of state responsibility;[44] economic counter-measures in the WTO; State immunity; the use of force; and the principle of good faith.[45] Thus, international law as a whole is applicable to investment treaties, [46] and the creation of a special regime for investor protection does not necessarily take away the application of customary law principles.[47] Contracting out in any case could be effected against specific rights or obligations from general international law, but there cannot be contracting out from the *system* of international law.[48] The principle that general principles of international law would not apply unless specifically referred to may have application in domestic law, but it does not have any

Distinction between Interpretation and Application of Norms in International Adjudication' *Journal of International Dispute Settlement* 2 (2011): 31; Alain Pellet, 'The Case Law of the ICJ in Investment Arbitration' *International Centre for Settlement of Investment Disputes Review* 28 (2013): 223.

39. Dispute Concerning Access to Information under Article 9 of the OSPAR Convention *(Ireland v United Kingdom of Great Britain and Northern Ireland)* Award, (2 July 2003), (2005) 126 ILR 364, para. 84.
40. *See* the discussion in the following sections of this Chapter.
41. *Georges Pinson* case *(France/United Mexican States)*, Award, of 13 April 1928, UNRIAA, Vol. V, 422. According to the Tribunal: 'Toute convention internationale doitêtre repute s'enréférertacitement au droit international commun, pour toutes les questions qu'elle ne résout pas elle-même en termesexprès et d'unefaçondifferente.'
42. Above note 30 (McLachlan), 373-4.
43. *See* James Crawford, 'The Criteria for Statehood in International Law' *British Yearbook of International Law* 48 (1976): 93.
44. *See* for example, *Loizidou v Turkey* (Preliminary Objections), Judgment (23 March 1995), ECHR Series A (1995) No. 310, paras 57–64. *See also* the reliance on the public international law rules of jurisdiction in *Bankovic v Belgium and others*, Decision of 12 December 2001, Admissibility, ECHR 2001-XII, 351–352, paras 59–60.
45. Joost Pauwelyn, *Conflict of Norms in Public International Law: How WTO Law Relates to Other Rules of International Law* (Cambridge: Cambridge University Press, 2003), 271.
46. *Ibid.*, 399.
47. Case Concerning Ahmadou Sadio Diallo (*Guinea v Congo)*, Preliminary Objections, Order of May 24 2007, 46 ILM 712 (2007), para. 90.
48. Above note 45 (Pauwelyn), 37.

application in international law.[49] They continue to operate in the background as 'fall-back' provisions.[50]

Two presumptions operate when States enter into a treaty and stipulate specific provisions regulating their relationship. The positive presumption is that the States have referred to general principles of international law for all questions that have not been resolved in express terms or in a different way in the treaty. The negative presumption is that by entering into a treaty the States intend to act consistently with the generally recognized principles of international law and previous treaty obligations undertaken towards third States.[51]

International courts and tribunals have been conscious towards the role of systematic integration and have insisted on the application of general rules of international law and in particular, on customary international law in the cases. The ICJ has emphasized that in any event general international law will always continue to apply.[52] Investment treaties cannot claim to cover the field of investor protection entirely, and many associated issues are left to be determined under international law. Emphasizing this relationship and impossibility of exclusion of general principles due to existence of a treaty, in the *Oil Platforms* case, the Court observed:

> Moreover, under the general rules of treaty interpretation, as reflected in the 1969 Vienna Convention on the Law of Treaties, interpretation must take into account 'any relevant rules of international law applicable in the relations between the parties' (Article 31, paragraph 3(c)). The Court cannot accept that Article XX, paragraph 1(d), of the 1955 Treaty was intended to operate wholly independently of the relevant rules of international law on the use of force, so as to be capable of being successfully invoked, even in the limited context of a claim for breach of the Treaty, in relation to an unlawful use of force. The application of the relevant rules of international law relating to this question thus forms an integral part of the task of interpretation entrusted to the Court by... the 1955 Treaty.[53]

The insistence of applying the general rules of international law while interpret ing a treaty and specifically a specialized treaty regime is evidenced from the jurisprudence of the Panels and the Appellate Body of the World Trade Organization (WTO). In the *US-Gasoline*, the Appellate Body, held that the WTO agreements are not to be read in 'clinical isolation from public international law'.[54] The regime created by the WTO operates in the background of international law and sovereignty is one such principle.[55] International law applies 'generally to the economic relations between

49. Above note 20 (ILC, Fragmentation Report), para. 177.
50. Pauwelyn calls these two mechanisms defending the continuous operation of general international law as 'fall-back' on other norms or international law. *See* above note 45 (Pauwelyn), 200-202.
51. Above note 20 (ILC, Fragmentation Report), para. 465 (footnote omitted).
52. Case Concerning Kasikili/Sedudu Islands *(Bostwana v Namibia)*, Judgment of 13 December 1999, [1999] ICJ Rep. 1045, para. 93.
53. *Oil Platforms* case *(Iran v United States of America)*, Merits, Judgment of 6 November 2003, [2003] ICJ Rep. 161, para. 41; also *see* (Separate opinion of Judge Simma), paras 5–16; (Separate opinion of Judge Higgins), paras 40–54.
54. United States-Standards of Reformulated and Conventional Gasoline, 20 May 1996, WT/DS2/AB/R, DSR 1996: I, 16.
55. *Ibid.*, 17.

WTO members', unless the Members have specifically 'contracted out' from it.[56] In the *Shrimp Turtle* case, the Panel interpreted the notion of 'exhaustible natural resources' in Article XX (g) of GATT to include only 'finite resources such as minerals, rather than biological or renewable resources'. The Appellate Body disagreed and said that the term 'natural resources' shall not be interpreted in a static way rather in an evolutionary manner. It then referred to other environment protection instruments.[57] States can contract out of a legal principle through an agreement to interpret the provisions in the WTO Agreement.[58] The Appellate Body has frequently resorted to 'additional interpretative guidance, as appropriate, from the general principles of international law'.[59] This jurisprudence is startling since Article 3.2[60] of the DSU in express words limits the use of customary international law for treaty interpretation. Upholding the general applicability of customary law beyond just treaty interpretation, the Panel in *Korea-Government Procurement* case took the following view:

> We take note that Article 3.2 of the DSU requires that we seek within the context of a particular dispute to clarify the existing provisions of the WTO agreements in accordance with customary rules of interpretation of public international law. However, the relationship of the WTO Agreements to customary international law is broader than this. Customary international law applies generally to the economic relations between the WTO Members. Such international law applies to the extent that the WTO treaty agreements do not 'contract out' from it. To put it another way, to the extent there is no conflict of inconsistency, or an expression in a covered WTO agreement that implies differently, we are of the view that the customary rules of international law apply at the WTO treaties and to the process of treaty formulation under the WTO.[61]

56. Korea-Measures Affecting Government Procurement, 19 January 2000, WT/DS163/R, para. 7.96.
57. United States-Import Prohibition of Certain Shrimp and Shrimp Products, 6 November 1998, WT/DS58/AB/R, DSR 1998:VII, Appellate Body, 2794-2797, paras 127–131. Also, it viewed their exhaustibility by reference to the fact that all seven sea turtles were listed in Appendix 1 of the CITES Convention, *see* paras 132–133.
58. *North Sea Continental Shelf Cases (Federal Republic of Germany/Denmark; Federal Republic of Germany/Netherlands)*, Judgment of 20 February [1969] I.C.J. Rep. 3 42. *See also* Case Concerning the Continental Shelf *(Tunisia/Libyan Arab Jamahiriya)* Judgment of 24 February 1982, [1982] ICJ Rep. 18, 38.
59. United States-Import Prohibition of Certain Shrimp and Shrimp Products, Appellate Body, 12 October 1998, WT/DS58/AB/R, 2755.
60. Article 3.2, Dispute Settlement Understanding (1994): 'The dispute settlement system of the WTO is a central element in providing security and predictability to the multilateral trading system. The Members recognize that it serves to preserve the rights and obligations of Members under the covered agreements, and to clarify the existing provisions of those agreements in accordance with customary rules of interpretation of public international law. Recommendations and rulings of the DSB cannot add to or diminish the rights and obligations provided in the covered agreements.'
61. Above note 56 (Korea- Government Procurement), para. 7.6; Canada-Terms of Patent Protection, Report of the Appellate Body, WT/DS170/AB/R, Sep. 18 2000, paras 71–74; *Brazil* - Export Financing Programme for Aircraft: Recourse to Arbitration by Brazil under Art. 22.6 of the DSU and Art. 4.11 of the SCM Agreement, Decision by the Arbitrators, WT/DS46/ARB, 28 August 2000, paras 3.6–3.10.

An investment tribunal cannot ignore the operation of general international law and specifically of regulatory freedom as a customary norm while interpreting treatment standards in investment treaties.

[B] No Implied Exclusion of a Customary Norm

The absence of specific reference to regulatory freedom in an investment treaty or a reference to a limited manner of exercise of regulatory freedom does not result into exclusion of regulatory freedom. There can be no implied exclusion of a customary norm, even when a treaty covers a certain area and does not refer to that norm. Regulatory freedom continues to operate the relationship between a foreign investor and a host State since it is an attribute of State sovereignty and exclusion of a customary norm has to be clearly excluded from a treaty.

Chapter 6 had set out that regulatory freedom is one of the attributes of State sovereignty. Therefore, regulatory freedom exists at the general level as an attribute of State sovereignty. It is an elementary principle of international law that entering into a treaty does not result into abandonment of sovereignty. In the *Wimbledon* case, the argument advanced was that by entering into the Treaty of Versailles, the sovereign right of Germany was extinguished. The Court rejected this argument. Elaborating on the effect of treaty making on sovereignty, it held that '[t]he Court declines to see in the conclusion of any Treaty by which a State undertakes to perform or refrain from performing a particular act an abandonment of its sovereignty'.[62] On the contrary, 'right of entering into international engagements is an attribute of State sovereignty'.[63]

An issue of whether regulatory freedom over fiscal powers was given away through an agreement arose in the *Austro-German Customs Union* case. Austria entered into a treaty with Germany to facilitate the creation and operation of customs union. It was contended that this action amounted to deprivation of economic sovereignty. The Court opined that the creation of a customs union does not transfer independence. The State continues to exercise freedom within its jurisdiction.[64] If it is claimed that the discretion of the State has been taken away or restricted, then there is a need to prove the existence of a principle of international law restricting that discretion,[65] which must be clear and specific.[66] To deprive certain rights naturally possessed by a State, a clear rule to the contrary must exist.[67] The limitation shall be

62. The Case of *The SS 'Wimbledon' (Britain v Germany)*, Decision of 17 August 1923, (1923) PCIJ Series A, No. 1, 15, 25.
63. *Ibid.*, Also *see* Exchange of Greek and Turkish Populations, (*Greece v Turkey*), Advisory Opinion of 21 February 1925, (!925) PCIJ Series B, No. 10, 6, 21.
64. Customs Régime Between Germany and Australia, Advisory Opinion of 5 September 1931, (1931) PCIJ Series A/B, No. 41, 37, 50-2.
65. Above note 79 (*Lotus case*), 21.
66. *Ibid.*, 21. The Court said: 'The Court therefore must, in any event, ascertain whether or not there exists a rule of international law limiting the freedom of States to extend the criminal jurisdiction of their courts to a situation uniting the circumstances of the present case.'
67. Above note 79 (*Lotus case*), 23.

specific and the Court would be loath to find specific limitations rather than assumed restrictions.[68]

Treaty is a process of carving out inherent rights encompassed by sovereignty. All the rights, except those taken away expressly or through direct implication through a treaty continue to operate. In other words, regulatory freedom, an attribute of State sovereignty, continues to operate until excluded or to the extent altered by treatment standards. Waldock elucidated this relationship in the following words:

> A presumption in favour of sovereignty implies that there is a certain burden of proof upon those who allege the existence of a restriction upon sovereignty. In treaty law, such a presumption is intelligible enough, since it involves no more than attributing an intention to the parties not to give up sovereign rights, unless contrary intention clearly appears in the treaty.[69]

Restrictions on sovereignty cannot be presumed.[70] This general principle - encapsulated in the phrase *exclusion unis est exclusion alterius* – is, what is not barred by a treaty is allowed.[71] Investment protection treaties do not contain limitations on exercise of regulatory freedom. For subjects unregulated by a treaty, i.e., where a treaty has not contracted out of the general international law norm or not modified it, the general international law issue regulating the subject continues to operate. There is no need to stipulate all customary law rights in the treaty; in other words, there is no need to incorporate a custom by reference or otherwise. Customary law is the backdrop from which if necessary, a treaty may deviate.[72] Any such deviation has to be clear and specific. There can be no tacit exclusion of customary law. The ICJ used strong language in *ELSI* to state this position in the following words:

> The Chamber has no doubt that the parties to a treaty can therein either agree that the local remedies rule shall not apply to claims based on alleged breaches of that treaty; or confirm that it shall apply. Yet the Chamber finds itself unable to accept that an important principle of customary international law should be held to have

68. *Ibid.*, 23: 'Again, the Court does not know of any cases in which governments have protested against the fact that the criminal law of some country contained a rule to this effect or that the courts of a country constituted their criminal law in this sense. Consequently, once it is admitted that the effects of the offence were produced on the Turkish vessel, it becomes impossible to hold that there is a rule of international law which prohibits Turkey from prosecuting Lieutenant Demons because the fact that the author of the offence was on board the French ship.'
69. Humphrey Waldock, 'General Course on Public International Law' in vol. 106 of Collected Courses of The Hague Academy of International Law - Recueil des cours, Académie de Droit International de la Ha (1962), 164.
70. *Ibid.*, 418; Free Zones of Upper Savoy and the District of Gex (*France v Switzerland*) (1932) PCIJ Series A/B, No. 46, 167: 'In this connection, the Court observes that no such limitation necessarily ensues from the old provisions relating to the free zones; that in case of doubt a limitation of sovereignty must be construed restrictively; and that while it is certain that France; cannot rely on her own legislation to limit the scope of her international obligations, it is equally certain that French fiscal legislation applies in the territory of the free zones as in any other part of French territory.'
71. Case Concerning Certain German Interests in Polish Upper Silesia (*Germany v Poland*), Judgment of 25 May 1926, (1925) PCIJ Series A-No.7, 21-22.
72. Above note 10 (Condorelli), 149.

been tacitly dispensed with, in the absence of any words making clear an intention to do so.[73]

In the *Chorzów Factory* case, the PCIJ referred to reparation – a customary principle – and observed that it 'is the indispensable complement of a failure to apply a convention, and there is no necessity for this to be stated in the convention itself.[74] In the Advisory Opinion in the *South West Africa* case, in the context of right of termination of a treaty in case of breach, the ICJ opined, 'The silence of a treaty as to the existence of such a right cannot be interpreted as implying the exclusion of a right which has its source outside of the treaty, in general international law.'[75] Absence of reference to regulatory freedom in investment treaties cannot form the basis of a presumption of its exclusion.

As a matter of international law, the right of States to regulate cannot be entirely alienated.[76] An investment treaty may derogate from custom, but it has to do so expressly.[77] Regulatory freedom of a State cannot be deemed to be abandoned unless there is an express undertaking given to the investor to that effect.[78] Exposing the inconceivable proposition that States would have to compensate for all losses arising from regulations, whether legitimate or not, Lowe retorts with a poignant question: 'How far do governments have to "buy back" from foreign investors the right to regulate their economies?'[79] Any exclusion of regulatory freedom has to be clear and specific in the treaty and cannot be presumed. It is not that investment treaties do not affect, regulatory freedom at all. They do and only legitimate regulatory exercises are protected.

The recent practice of specific incorporation of regulatory freedom in investment treaties is merely a reaffirmation of the right in customary law. After discussing several decisions of the ICJ, Thirlway concludes: 'What these cases do re-confirm is that the codification of the customary rule by its incorporation into a treaty does not lead to the abrogation or disappearance of the rule as part of customary international law, even in the relations between two states that are party to the relevant treaty.'[80]

[C] Concurrent Operation of Custom and Treaty

Norms originating in different sources and particularly in custom and treaty are to be interpreted as compatible obligations, whereby one norm could assist in interpretation

73. Elettronica Sicula S.P.A. (ELSI) (*United States of America v Italy*), Judgment of 20 July 1989, [1989] ICJ Rep. 15, 42.
74. Factory at Chorzów (*Germany v Poland*), Merits, Judgment of 13 September 19281928 PCIJ Series A No. 17, 22; Above note 71 (*German Interests in Polish Upper Silesia* case), 22.
75. Legal Consequences for States of the Continued Presence of South Africa in Namibia (South West Africa) notwithstanding Security Council Resolution 276 (1970), Advisory Opinion of 21 June 1971, [1971] ICJ Rep. 16, para. 96; Free Zones of Upper Savoy and the District of Gex [*France v Switzerland*] (1932) PCIJ Series A/B, No. 46, 167.
76. Vaughan Lowe, 'Regulation or Expropriation?' *Current Legal Problems* 55 (2002): 447, 451.
77. Above note 30 (McLachlan), 373.
78. Above note 76 (Lowe), 458.
79. *Ibid.*, 459.
80. Hugh Thirlway, *The Sources of International Law* (Oxford: Oxford University Press, 2014), 139.

of another.[81] The mere fact that they regulate the same subject matter does not result into a general conclusion that a treaty norm is superior to a customary norm or that a customary norm is subsumed by a treaty norm. In the *Jurisdiction of the Courts of Danzig* case, the PCIJ observed that despite a treaty dealing comprehensively with rights of individuals, other rules of customary law would continue to operate and the dispute was decided with reference to those provisions.[82] Lauterpacht elaborated this relationship through the example of the *Lotus* case. According to him, likewise, in the *Free Zones* case, the preoccupation of the PCIJ was with the interpretation of an article of Lausanne Treaty, but the Court went further to 'elaborate treatment of customary law on the question of jurisdiction over foreigners for crimes committed abroad, in a Judgment answering more general questions such as the basis of international law and the relative importance of its various sources'.[83] In the *La Grand* case, the Court held that customary rule of diplomatic protection continues to operate besides the Convention on Diplomatic Protection.[84] The most pertinent exposition is of the ICJ in the *Military and Paramilitary Activities in Nicaragua* case. The Court observed that even if the rules from different sources cover the same field and possess identical contents still it cannot be presumed that a set of rules from one source overtakes set of rules from another source. As per the Court, even if the content of treaty law and customary international law is same, it is not a reason to hold that 'the incorporation of the customary norm into treaty-law must deprive the customary norm of its applicability as distinct from that of the treaty norm'.[85] Furthermore, there are no grounds to establish that 'when customary international law is comprised of rules identical to those of treaty law, the latter "supervenes" the former, so that the customary international law has no further existence of its own.'[86] Even after codification of a customary norm in a treaty, it continues to operate, unless a contrary intention is established.

When a treaty norm and a customary norm cover the same field, firstly a treaty norm would be applied and thereafter customary norm would be applied. In the *Military and Paramilitary Activities in and against Nicaragua* case, the US had argued that Articles 2 (4) and 51 of the UN Charter exhaustively covered the law on 'self-defence' and there is nothing left within the sphere of custom.[87] This is a case

81. Above note 20 (ILC, Fragmentation Report), para. 4.
82. Jurisdiction of the Courts of Danzig (Pecuniary Claims of Danzig Railway Officials who have Passed into the Polish Service, against the Polish Railways Administration) Advisory Opinion of 3 March 1928, PCIJ Series B No. 15, 17.
83. Hersh Laterpacht, *Development of International Law* (London: Stevans and Sons Ltd. 1958), 28.
84. La Grand (*Germany v United States of America*), Judgment of 27 June 2001, [2001] ICJ Rep. 466, 483, 487-88.
85. Case Concerning Military and Paramilitary Activities in and Against Nicaragua (*Nicaragua v United States of America*), Merits, 27 Jun. 1986, [1986] ICJ Rep. 14, para. 177.
86. *Ibid.*, paras 177, 179.
87. The Court noted the argument of the United States in the following words: 'The United States contends that the only general and customary international law on which Nicaragua can base its claims is that of the Charter: in particular, the Court could not, it is said, consider the lawfulness of an alleged use of armed force without referring to the "principal source of the relevant international law", namely, Article 2, paragraph 4, of the United Nations Charter. In brief, in a more general sense "the provisions of the United Nations Charter relevant here subsume and supervene related principles of customary and general international law"....it further prevents it

where the treaty and custom, both covered the same subject. The Court rejected this argument and took the view that there are various components of the law of self-defence such as proportionality, etc. that belong to customary international law and are not subsumed by the treaty. In the words of the Court, the relationship is as under:

> The Court therefore finds that Article 51 of the Charter is only meaningful on the basis that there is a 'natural' or 'inherent' right of self-defense, and it is hard to see how this can be other than of a customary nature, even if its present content has been confirmed and influenced by the Charter. Moreover the Charter, having itself recognized the existence of this right, does not go on to regulate directly all aspects of its content. For example, it does not contain any specific rule whereby self-defense would warrant only measures which are proportional to the armed attack and necessary to respond to it, a rule well established in customary international law. Moreover, a definition of the 'armed attack' which, if found to exist, authorizes the exercise of the 'inherent right' of self-defense, is not provided in the Charter, and is not part of treaty law. It cannot therefore be held that Article 51 is a provision which 'subsumes and supervenes' customary international law. It rather demonstrates that in the field in question, the importance of which for the present dispute need hardly be stressed. Customary international law continues to exist alongside treaty law. The areas governed by the two sources of law thus do not overlap exactly, and the rules do not have the same content. This could also be demonstrated for other subjects, in particular for the principle of non-intervention.[88]

This paragraph shows that customary law is not affected even if there is a multilateral treaty that covers the field.

The ICJ has recognized the relevance and influence of principles of international law in addition to the treaty to a given dispute.[89] According to the Court, exclusion of custom has to be clear. One has to be circumspect while concluding that a conflict exists and interpret conflict narrowly, otherwise rigours of another rule, which is also a manifestation of State consent will be made redundant. Two norms appearing identical but originating in different sources have to be retained since the manner of their interpretation and application would depend on their source.[90] Conflict has to be construed narrowly. Treaty and custom may not be 'competing'[91] each time, but they could be 'complementing'. The Court reflected on the interrelationship and effect of a treaty and custom on each other in the following words:

---

from applying in its decision any rule of customary international law the content of which is also the subject of a provision in those multilateral treaties.' Above note 85 (*Nicaragua* Case), para. 173.

88. *Ibid.*, para. 176.
89. Gabčíkovo-Nagymaros Project (*Hungary v Slovakia*), Judgment of 25 September 1997, [1997] ICJ Rep. 7, para. 140; Questions of Interpretation and Application of the 1971 Montreal Convention arising from the Aerial Incident at Lockerbie (*Libyan Arab Jamahiriya v United States of America*), Judgment of 27 February 1998, [1998] ICJ Rep. 115, para. 42.
90. Above note 85 (*Nicaragua* Case), para. 178.
91. The word 'competing' is borrowed from the observations of Schachter. In his view supporters of liberal view argue that treaty shall be given precedence over custom, whereas as per conservatives, customs should prevail over treaties. Oscar Schachter, 'Entangled Treaty and Custom' in *International Law at a Time of Perplexity: Essays in Honour of Shabtai Rosenne*, ed. Yoram Distein & Mala Tabory, (Dordrecht, Boston, London: Martinus Nijhoff Publishers, 1989), 720-721.

> On a number of points, the areas governed by the two sources of law do not exactly overlap, and the substantive rules in which they are framed are not identical in content. But in addition, even if a treaty norm and a customary norm relevant to the present dispute were to have exactly the same content, this would not be a reason for the Court to take the view that the operation of the treaty process must necessarily deprive the customary norm of its separate applicability. Nor can the multilateral treaty reservation be interpreted as meaning that, once applicable to a given dispute, it would exclude the application of any rule of customary international law the content of which was the same as, or analogous to, that of the treaty-law rule which had caused the reservation to become effective.[92]

In the context of investment treaty arbitration, the relationship between treaty and custom is symbiotic. There may be identical obligations owed by a State under custom and an investment treaty, but one cannot be seen as inhibiting the provisions of custom.[93] In the field of investment treaty arbitration, this relationship is discussed in relation to the defence of 'necessity'.[94] The Annulment Committee in *CMS v Argentina*, took the view that the treaty provision on necessity is *lex specialis* in relation to the customary law principle of necessity, prescribed under Article 25 of ILC Articles on State Responsibility.[95] However, customary principle would still continue to operate and if the provision under the treaty is not satisfied, then the customary standard can be invoked.[96] Likewise in *Sempra v Argentina*, the Tribunal relied on customary rules on necessity because 'the treaty itself did not deal with the legal elements necessary for the legitimate invocation of a state of necessity'.[97]

The interaction between treaty and custom is further elucidated by the relationship between treaty obligations and circumstances precluding wrongfulness (customary law) in cases of breach of treaty obligations, which are now codified as the ILC Draft Articles on State Responsibility.[98] In the *Military and Paramilitary Activities in and against Nicaragua* case, the Court referred to the coextensive application of rules arising from custom and treaty, but it did not comment on the extent of role left for a custom where a treaty exists. This question came up instead in the *Rainbow Warrior* case. New Zealand argued that violations of obligations occurred under a treaty, therefore the VCLT would exhaustively deal with all the issues. Reference to customary law could be made only '1) to clarify some ambiguity in the treaty, 2) to fill an evident gap, or 3) to invalidate a treaty provision by reference to a rule of *jus cogens* in customary international law'. Otherwise, there is 'no basis upon which a clear treaty

92. Above note 85 (*Nicaragua* Case), para. 175.
93. Above note 30 (McLachlan), 364.
94. Above note 30 (McLachlan), 385-91; Antonie Martin, 'Investment Disputes after Argentina's Economic Crisis: Interpreting BIT Non-precluded Measures and the Doctrine of Necessity under Customary International Law', *Journal of International Arbitration* 29 (2012): 49.
95. *CMS Gas Transmission Co. v Argentina*, ICSID Case No. ARB/01/8, Decision on Annulment, (25 September 2007), para. 133.
96. *Ibid.*, para. 134.
97. *Sempra Energy International v The Argentine Republic*, Award, ICSID Case No. ARB/02/16, 28 September 2007, paras 375–378.
98. Case Concerning the Difference Between New Zealand and France Concerning the Interpretation or Application of Two Agreements, Concluded on 9 July 1986 Between the Two States and Which Related to the Problem Arising From the Rainbow Warrior Affair (*New Zealand v France*), Award, 30 April 1990, Vol. XX RIAA 215, para. 72.

obligation can be altered by reference to customary international law'.[99] The response of the Tribunal to this argument was that treaty and custom, both were applicable and the Tribunal, held:

> 'The reason is that the general principles of International Law concerning State responsibility are equally applicable in the case of breach of treaty obligation, since in the international law field there is no distinction between contractual and tortuous responsibility, so that any violation by a State of any obligation, of whatever origin, gives rise to State responsibility and consequently, to the duty of reparation.
>
> ...
>
> The conclusion to be reached on this issue is that, without prejudice to the terms of the agreement which the Parties signed and the applicability of certain important provisions of the Vienna Convention on the Law of Treaties, the existence in this case of circumstances excluding wrongfulness as well as the question of appropriate remedies, should be answered in the context and in the light of the customary Law of State Responsibility.'[100]

This was a case where the defence to the breach of a treaty was decided exclusively with reference to customary law. Applying this principle to regulatory freedom and indirect expropriation, the question of validity of regulation exclusively depends on customary law. The effect on foreign investor is of no consequence. A substantial deprivation of property cannot *ipso facto* result into breach of a treaty – neither in form nor in substance. The exercises of State would be permissible and covered under the customary right to regulate.

Application of regulatory freedom as a customary principle despite standards of treatment is possible because there are no treaty provisions covering questions of regulation. The investment treaties are silent on regulatory freedom. In such a case the customary law on regulatory freedom would continue to operate. Even where regulatory freedom has been specified in the treaty, regulatory freedom in customary law would remain applicable. A customary norm could be excluded through a treaty if there is a clear statement to that effect or an unavoidable direct incompatibility.

§7.03 WHETHER THERE IS A CONFLICT BETWEEN REGULATORY FREEDOM AND INDIRECT EXPROPRIATION?

After having shown the concurrent application of regulatory freedom and indirect expropriation, this section explores the question of whether there is a conflict between them in any manner. If there is any, which are the ways of addressing this conflict.

99. *Ibid.*, para. 73.
100. *Ibid.*, para. 75. The Tribunal extensively relied on these principles to see if the treaty breaches by France were justified within these principles, paras 76–79.

[A] What is a Conflict?

There is a presumption against conflict unless the new norm is created to replace the pre-existing norm.[101] Classical writers such as Grotius[102] and Vattel[103] have supported this position. The rationale for the presumption is that States are aware of obligations that they have entered into in past and would not want to contradict them through subsequent commitments.[104] If they had an intention to alter their past obligations, they would state it clearly in the new set of obligations.[105] Whenever the interpretation of a treaty is doubtful, the presumption is against conflict.[106]

Conflict arises when two norms are in a rule-exception or an either-or relationship.[107] What one norm directs to be obligatory is incompatible with what the other norm directs as obligatory. Whereby, observance of one norm 'necessarily' or 'possibly' involves violation of the other norm,[108] thus, making simultaneous compliance with the two norms impossible.[109] Conflict conveys 'two forces operating in different directions on the same point'.[110]

The choice of one norm over the other arises only when harmonization is impossible. For such a situation to arise in practical terms, there are two requirements: the subject matter of the two norms has to be identical and one norm exhaustively covers the area of activity of another norm. It is not sufficient that both norms relate to the same subject matter and that they must overlap in their functioning. The conflict has to be covering *ratione materiae*. [111] The mere existence of a treaty in a field does not result into exclusion of custom. There has to be an explicit 'contracting-out'.[112] There is no possibility of implicit exclusions.[113]

Conflict has to be distinguished from divergence. Divergence is a situation where two norms deal with the same subject matter in a different manner, whilst not in

101. Above note 45 (Pauwelyn), 242.
102. Hugo Grotius, 'De Jure Belli ac Pacis Libri Tres' in James Brown Scott (ed.) *The Classics of International Law* Book II (Oxford: Clarendon Press, 1925), 428; *See also* Samuel Pufendorf, Book V, *Le Droit de la Nature et des Gens ou Systéme Général des Principes les Plus Importants de la Morale, de la Jurisprudence, et de la Politique*, trans. J. Barbeyrac) (Basle: Thourneisen, 1732), 138-140.
103. Emmerich de Vattel, *Le droit des gens ou principes de la Loi Naturelle, appliqués à la conduite et aux affaires des nations et des Souverains* (Londres, 1758), Vol. I, Book II, cap. 17, para. 293.
104. Hersh Lauterpact, vol. 1 of *Oppenheim's International Law* (7th ed., 1948), 858-859.
105. Wilferd Jenks, 'Conflict of Law Making Treaties', *British Yearbook of International Law* 30 (1953): 401, 428.
106. *Ibid.*, 451.
107. Above note 30 (Pauwelyn) 185. For various instances of conflict *see* 175-188.
108. Hans Kelsen, *General Theory of Norms*, Michael Hartney trans., (Oxford: Clarendon Press, 1991), 123. Also *see* examples explaining these conflicts in detail at 123-124.
109. Above note 105 (Jenks), at 451.
110. Above note 108 (Kelsen), at 124-125.
111. Above note 45 (Pauwelyn), at 164-165.
112. *Ibid.*, at 212-217.
113. *Ibid.*, compare at 217-218 with 240. Pauwelyn does initially propose that there could be implicit exclusions, but he appears to tend in favour of explicit exclusions only. Even assuming there is an implicit exclusion, then the exclusion would have be so manifest that compliance with one norm must in all situations result into violation of the other norm.

conflict.[114] For a conflict to exist, it is insufficient that the two norms deal with the same subject matter, there must be a 'direct incompatibility' to the extent that a party 'cannot simultaneously comply with its obligations under both treaties.'[115] The role of a customary norm would be diminished in comparison to a treaty if the treaty is codificatory – i.e., it codifies the customary norm exhaustively.[116] Investment treaties are not codificatory in any manner but an outcome of a quid pro quo bargain between States. They mostly introduce new treatment standards, except for crystallizing few customary law rules such as the international minimum standard. The treatment standards and in particular, indirect expropriation does not in any manner seek to codify regulatory freedom.

A conflict between regulatory freedom and indirect expropriation would arise only if indirect expropriation is determined based upon the sole effects doctrine. Since effect is the sole determinative criterion, the purpose for adoption of regulation would not matter. All actions would amount to indirect expropriation – whether legitimate regulations or not – as long as a certain threshold of loss is met. The so-called conflict between regulatory freedom and indirect expropriation, based on the sole effects doctrine is not a 'conflict of norm' scenario, rather a 'hierarchy of norms' scenario because pedigree of regulatory freedom and the sole effects doctrine is different: regulatory freedom is a customary norm and the sole effects doctrine is a creation of academic writings and judicial decisions – a subsidiary source of international law. The distinction between regulatory freedom and the sole effects doctrine is between a rule and a principle. Regulatory freedom is a rule, whereas the sole effects doctrine is at best a principle. Principles are only a persuasive mechanism for finding solutions but they do not replace or supervene the rules.[117] Principles are relied upon by judicial bodies only in cases where rules are absent.[118]

In investment treaty arbitration, choice between regulatory freedom and the sole effects doctrine is seen as an interpretative choice. In *Patrick Michel v Congo*, the ad hoc Annulment Committee took the view that:

> In any event, regardless of the various positions adopted in legal doctrine and case law on the question of determining whether the effect should be the sole and unique criterion to be used in assessing an indirect expropriation or a measure tantamount to expropriation, or whether the purpose sought by the State is also to be taken into account, it cannot but be found in the case at hand that the Arbitral

114. Above note 105 (Jenks), 425.
115. *Ibid.*, 426.
116. Above note 58 (*North Sea Continental Shelf* cases), para. 63.
117. George Schwarzenberger, *The Inductive Approach to International Law* (London: Stevens and Sons Ltd, 1965), 50; Bruno Simma, Daniel-Erasmus Khan, Georg Nolte, and Andreas Paulus, *The Charter of the United Nations: A commentary* (2nd ed., Oxford: Oxford University Press, 1994), 63.
118. Neil MacCormick, *Legal Reasoning and Legal Theory* (Oxford: Clarendon Press, 1994), 152; Andrew Mitchell, *Legal Principles in WTO Disputes* (Cambridge: Cambridge University Press, 2011), 8-9.

Tribunal, in apparently opting for the 'sole effect' doctrine, was merely exercising its freedom of judgment.[119]

The Annulment Committee assumed there is a conflict between two customary principles, by elevating the sole effects doctrine to the status of custom. There was no effort made whatsoever to defend this position, and as argued above, the sole effects doctrine is fundamentally a construct of academic writings without any support whatsoever in state practice. Thus, the conflict in this case would be between norms at two levels[120] - custom versus subsidiary sources (academic writings). Academic writing, stipulated as a subsidiary source in Article 38 (1) (d) of the ICJ statute, judicial decisions and opinion of experts has a lower hierarchical value than treaties, custom and general principles of law.[121] It will thus have to give way to the norm having customary nature.

The characterization of the sole effects doctrine, as a legal principle, differs amongst investment tribunals. In *Techmed v Mexico*, the Tribunal took an outwardly puzzling, but implicitly radical position *observing* that it must apply customary international law to decide the question of indirect expropriation. Customary law arises from Article 38 of the Statute of the International Court of Justice and is not fixed in time, but evolving. Having said that, the Tribunal then relied on the sole effects doctrine, as set out by the Iran-US Claims Tribunal, giving the impression that it treats the sole effects doctrine as customary international law.[122]

The police powers doctrine is a classical doctrine established in international law, whereas the sole effects doctrine is a relatively recent phenomenon, an outcome of the jurisprudence of the Iran-US Claims Tribunal.[123] No other tribunal has gone to the extent of claiming that the sole effects doctrine has become customary international law. Even scholars, who have traditionally been sympathetic towards the sole effects doctrine have restrained from going to the extent of claiming that the doctrine has attained the status of customary international law.[124] The claim of creation of customary international law based on the decisions of a tribunal constituted under a specific treaty is farfetched.

119. *Mr Patrick Mitchell v Democratic Republic of the Congo*, Decision on the Application for Annulment of the Award, ICSID Case No. ARB/99/7, 1 November 2006, para. 54.
120. Kelsen uses the example of legal and moral norms. Evidently, moral norms would lose their prowess in case of a conflict with a legal norm since legal norm is of a higher order. Above note 108 (Kelsen), 125-6.
121. Michael Akehurst, 'The Hierarchy of the Sources of International Law' *British Yearbook of International Law* 47 (1975): 274, 280.
122. *Medioambientales Techmed S.A. v The United Mexican States*, Award, ICSID Case No. ARB (AF)/00/2, (29 May 2003), para. 116.
123. Veijo Heiskanen, 'The Doctrine of Indirect Expropriation in Light of the Practice of the Iran-United States Claims Tribunal', Journal of World Investment and Trade 8 (2007): 215, 218.
124. Dolzer states sole effects doctrine to be 'dominant thinking' in arbitral awards, but adds a caveat that there is a line of awards which emphasizes on the context and purpose of the measure in question. Rudolph Dolzer, 'Indirect Expropriations: New Developments?', *New York University Environmental Law Journal* 11 (2002): 64, 90-92.

[B] The Role of Conflict of Norms in Resolving a Conflict Between Regulatory Freedom and Indirect Expropriation

This section addresses the situation where, assuming, there is a conflict between regulatory freedom and indirect expropriation, what is the role played by the two prominent rules on resolving a conflict of norms: *lex spcialis derogat lege generali* and *lex posterior derogat lega priori*. The third rule, *lex superior derogat legi inferori* is not discussed here since it was already discussed in the preceding sections that indirect expropriation is not superior to regulatory freedom because it originates in treaty law. The origin of both the rules is of equal importance.

According to the *lex specialis derogat generali* rule, if there is a special and a general rule covering the same subject matter, then the special rule will supersede the general rule.[125] The application of the *lex specialis* rule can be understood in two contexts. First, a 'self-contained' regime would exclude operation of general principles. Second, from the norms in conflict, one norm is special in relation to another.

In the first situation, if investment arbitration is treated as a 'self-contained regime' then it would automatically exclude the operation of general international law and therefore of regulatory freedom. Some investment tribunals have treated the regime of investment arbitration as *lex specialis* (special law) and declared other principles originating in custom to be of a *lex generalis* (general law) status.[126] The rule of *lex specialis* does not operate in legal vacuum. It is always tied to the context and informed by different legal principles. Principles such as sovereignty always form an inseparable context for interpretation, especially while taking a decision based on *lex specialis*.[127] The *lex specialis* rule is a 'rule of interpretation': a presumption that 'the authority laying down a general rule intended to leave room for the application of more specific rules which already exist which might be created in the future.'[128] Therefore, rules may belong to different branches but they possess an intrinsic relationship and have to be so interpreted.[129] This point was also elucidated at the general level of systematic integration above.

125. Above note 45 (Pauwelyn), 387; Above note 20 (ILC, Fragmentation Report), para. 56.

126. *Archer Daniels Midland Company and Tate & Lyle Ingredients Americas, Inc. v United Mexican States*, ICSID Case No. ARB(AF)/04/5, Award, 21 November 2007, para. 119; *Corn Products International Inc. v United Mexican States*, Decision on Responsibility, ICSID Case No. ARB(AF)/04/1, (15 January 2008), para. 76; Tarcisio Gazzini, 'The Role of Customary International Law in the Field of Foreign Investment', *Journal of World Trade and Investment* 8 (2007): 691, 697-98; Above note 94 (Martin), 54-55, 67-70.

127. Above note 20 (ILC, Fragmentation Report), paras 119–120. The Study Group elaborated the position in the following words: 'If a legal subject invokes a right based on "special law", then the validity of that claim can only be decided by reference to the whole background of a legal system that tells how "special laws" are enacted, what is "special" about them, how they are implemented, modified and terminated. It is impossible to make legal claims only in a limited sense, to opt for a part of the law, while leaving the rest out. For legal reason works in a closed and circular system in which every recognition or non-recognition of a legal claim can only be decided by recognizing the correctness of other legal claims', para. 122.

128. Above note 121 (Akehurst), 273, 273.

129. Above note 3 (ILC, Fragmentation Report), para. 118. Giving the example of Legality of the Threat or Use of Nuclear Weapons case, it is stated that the Court did not brush aside human

The nomenclature of 'self-contained regime' is a misnomer. They are 'informal labels' to describe a set of instruments from the perspective of different interests or different policy objectives.[130] For a regime to be self-contained, it will have to exhaustively deal with all concerned rules on that subject. In the *Tehran Hostage Crises* case, the ICJ held that the regime established by the Vienna Convention on Diplomatic Relations was a self-contained regime *vis-á-vis* customary international law on state responsibility. According to the Court:

> The rules of diplomatic law, in short, constitute a self-contained régime which, on the one hand, lays down the receiving State's obligations regarding the facilities, privileges and immunities to be accorded to diplomatic missions and, on the other, foresees their possible abuse by members of the mission and specifies the means at the disposal of the receiving State to counter any such abuse.[131]

To become a specialized regime, the regime ought to cover all norms within the branch of law the regime claims to apply. In reality, the reference to specialized regime in contemporary international law is a reference to no more than a loosely held system that does not exclude operation of rules originating in other streams.[132] The sphere of application and subject matter of those rules ought to be the appropriate criterion. A proper approach would be to look at the competing norms and see which is special in comparison to another.

Investment treaties do not exhaustively cover regulatory freedom. Most of them do not make a mention of it. Treaties concluded recently make a reference to regulatory freedom, but they cannot be said to deal with the subject exhaustively. The interrelationship between investor protection and regulation was aptly summarized in *Saluka v Czech Republic* in the following words:

> This is a more subtle and balanced statement of the Treaty's aims than is sometimes appreciated. The protection of foreign investments is not the sole aim of the Treaty, but rather a necessary element alongside the overall aim of encouraging foreign investment and extending and intensifying the parties' economic relations. That in turn calls for a balanced approach to the interpretation of the Treaty's substantive provisions for the protection of investments, since an interpretation which exaggerates the protection to be accorded to foreign investments may serve to dissuade host States from admitting foreign investments and so undermine the overall aim of extending and intensifying the parties' mutual economic relations.[133]

The choice between regulatory freedom and indirect expropriation would depend upon which rule specifically covers the subject matter to which rules are to be applied.

rights law or other branches of the law, such as environmental law, humanitarian law or the law on the use of force. They all were simultaneously applied since they all were *lex specialis* in some regard.

130. *Ibid.*, para. 21.
131. United States Diplomatic and Consular Staff in Tehran (*United States of America v Iran*), Judgment of 24 May 1980, [1980] ICJ Rep. 3, para. 86.
132. Bruno Simma and Dirk Pulkowski, 'Of Planets and Universe: Self-contained Regimes in International Law', *European Journal of International Law* 17 (2006): 483, 492-493.
133. *Saluka Investments B.V. v Czech Republic*, Partial Award, UNCITRAL, (17 March 2006) para. 300.

A conflict between a special and a general provision can occur only if they deal with the same subject matter.[134] The term 'same subject-matter' should be construed strictly.[135] There 'must be some inconsistency between them, or else a discernible intention that one provision is to exclude the other'.[136]

Lex specialis cannot operate simply at the regime level. It has to function in relation to each of the norms which are claimed to be incompatible. They have to be firstly dealing with the same subject matter and then it is to be seen, how far is one norm special in comparison to another. [137] The decision of which rule is special depends on the context in which the rule is applied.[138] The ICJ in the *Gabčíkovo-Nagymaros* case expounded this principle - in relation to the application or rules of state responsibility and rules of treaty interpretation. It treated the rules on state responsibility to be *lex specialis* in comparison to rules of treaty interpretation because when it came to determining responsibility they would be superior.[139]

Keeping this discussion in mind, the scope of application of regulatory freedom and indirect expropriation can be delineated. Regulatory freedom and indirect expropriation operate in different fields. The nature of a regulatory measure and expropriatory measure is different. The distinction was discussed above in Chapter 2. The principles for determining regulatory measure and expropriatory measure are applied to the same set of measures, but the outcome of the analysis decides whether a measure is regulatory or expropriatory. The outcome is an 'either-or consequence'. The impugned measure would either be a legitimate regulation or an indirect expropriation. Therefore, a measure cannot be regulatory as well as expropriatory at the same time. The distinguishing factor in the precise aspect of the relationship that is regulated by the rule in question.

If it is a specific rule on the subject then weight is attached to the precision of the rule.[140] A norm that directly and precisely governs a specific aspect of the relationship would supersede a norm governing another aspect of that relationship.[141] Regulatory freedom is a more direct and precise rule that governs regulatory freedom. The object of inquiry in cases of regulatory freedom is the regulation. Thus, the specific rule on regulation i.e., customary law on legitimate regulatory exercises would be *lex specialis*. The subject of regulatory freedom is comprehensively and precisely covered by customary principles of regulatory freedom and it is the only source.

134. Gerald Fitzmaurice, 'The Law and Procedure of the International Court of Justice 1951-5: Treaty Interpretation and Other Treaty Points', *British Yearbook of International Law* 33 (1957): 237.
135. United Nations, vol. 2 of *United Nations Conference on the Law of Treaties: Official Records* (New York, United Nations, 1970), 222.
136. ILC, Draft articles on Responsibility of States for Internationally Wrongful Acts, with Commentaries (2001) Yearbook of the International Law Commission, vol. II, Part Two, 140.
137. Above note 132 (Simma and Pulkowski), 487-9.
138. *Ibid.*, 385.
139. Above note 89 (*Gabčíkovo-Nagymaros* case), para. 132.
140. Akehurst seems to look at the distinction as 'particular' and 'general', giving the impression that he does not imply the field of operation, rather specificity of the rule in question. Above note 121 (Akehurst), 273, 273.
141. Above note 45 (Pauwelyn), 389.

Another potent argument to claim superiority of indirect expropriation over regulatory freedom as a norm emanates from *lex posterior derogat legi priori rule*. Treaty norms are subsequent in time than regulatory freedom. Unlike the *lex specialis* rule, this rule is codified in Article 30 of the VCLT. It provides for rules regarding successive treaties applicable to the same subject matter. Article 30 (2) provides, 'When a treaty specifies that it is subject to, or that it is not to be considered as incompatible with, an earlier or later treaty, the provisions of that other treaty prevail.' The reason for this rule is to grant preference to latest legislative intent of the State parties that have entered into two treaties consecutively.[142] This rule, however, is applicable in case of 'treaties' rather than 'norms'. The overlap necessary to constitute conflict could arise if it has the same 'subject matter of relevant rules' and 'legal subjects bound by it'.[143] Priority of one norm over another cannot be based merely on chronological criterion. It would be improper to fix regulatory freedom in a certain time frame since it is ever-evolving although its constituent ingredients remain same.

[C] Co-existence of Regulatory Freedom and Indirect Expropriation

As far as possible co-extensive rules of international law, despite whether they originate in custom or treaty should co-exist and an interpretation that results into conflict should be avoided. The principle of 'effective treaty interpretation' engenders the idea of allowing distinct rule to function simultaneously.[144] The principle of effective treaty interpretation- *ut res magis valeat quam pereat*, expects that every term in a treaty is given its full meaning. But that does not authorize extensive or liberal interpretation that 'goes beyond what is expressly or necessarily to be implied in the terms of the treaty'.[145] The principle of effective treaty interpretation is normally limited to the words of the treaty. There is no reason to exclude its understanding as an acknowledgement of application of general principles with full force until excluded.[146]

In case there is a conflict, the divergence between the two norms could be in the nature of 'abrogation' or 'derogation'. In the case of abrogation, the original norm is entirely substituted by the subsequent norm and there is total incompatibility. In case of derogation, divergence is partial. After derogation the remaining part of the original norm continues to operate.[147] Obligations from two sources may not be strictly in conflict, but the divergence may be to such a degree that compliance with one would blunt the rigour of another. The reduction in scope of absolute sovereign power through treaty making can be appropriately understood as derogation. This phenomenon is aptly described in the *Wimbledon* case as: 'No doubt any convention creating an obligation of this kind places a restriction upon the exercise of the sovereign rights

142. *Ibid.*, 375-376.
143. Above note 20 (ILC, Fragmentation Report), para. 21.
144. *See* Alexander Orakhelashvili, *The Interpretation of Acts and Rules in Public International Law* (Oxford University Press, 2008), 393-440.
145. *Ibid.*, 248.
146. *Ibid.*, 410-411.
147. Above note 108 (Kelsen), 111-112.

of the State, in the sense that it requires them to be exercised in a certain way.'[148] Treaties cannot abrogate sovereign rights entirely. Although two norms diverge, it is possible to apply them simultaneously with some adjustments. It is necessary to 'achieve a resolution that integrates the conflicting obligations in some optimal way in the general context of international law'.[149]

In light of existence of a treaty, an absolute regulatory freedom cannot be claimed. Regulatory freedom as a customary norm is recognized only as long as it is a legitimate regulatory measure. A measure, if expropriatory, will not fall under a legitimate regulatory measure. The elements of a legitimate regulatory measure are identified in the jurisprudence of international courts and tribunals.

§7.04 THE SCOPE OF REGULATORY FREEDOM IN LIGHT OF TREATY PROVISIONS IN THE JURISPRUDENCE OF INTERNATIONAL COURTS AND TRIBUNALS

International courts and tribunals have been posed with the question of harmonizing regulatory freedom of States in view of treaty obligations. They have acknowledged that regulatory freedom is unhindered, as long as it satisfies the conditions laid down in customary international law. In the *North Atlantic Fisheries* case and the *Nicaragua Navigation Rights* case, presence and operation of regulatory freedom was recognized. In both the cases, a treaty comprehensive covered the subject matter of the dispute.

In the *North Atlantic Fisheries* case, the question was whether Great Britain had retained regulatory freedom regarding fishing after granting exclusive and perpetual fishing rights to the United States. The Great Britain argued that it could adopt reasonable regulations, that were necessary for the preservation and protection of fisheries on the grounds of public order and morals.[150] The argument emphasizes the indispensable autonomy of regulation that is necessary. Grant of certain treaty rights does not deprive a State of its residual power of regulation. Any measure for conservation of fisheries would amount to a restriction on the right of fishing of the Americans. The American argument in response was that the exercise of liberty of fishing is not subject to limitations or restraints from Great Britain. It is further claimed that the regulations would be appropriate, necessary, reasonable and fair only if both States specifically agreed to the exercise of regulatory freedom through a common accord. Thus, concurrence of the United States was indispensable before any regulation was adopted by Great Britain.[151] The Tribunal was posed with two questions: a) whether there was a right to regulate after the rights of the parties were comprehensively stated in relation to a subject matter in a treaty; and b) if there is such a right, whether there is a need to take concurrence of the other State before the regulation is applied. As is the case with investment treaties, the treaty under which rights were

148. Above note 79 (*Wimbledon* case), 25.
149. Above note 20 (ILC, Fragmentation Report), para. 43.
150. *The North Atlantic Coast Fisheries* case (*Great Britain v United States of America*), Award, 7 September 1910, (1961) XI RIAA 167, 174.
151. *Ibid.*, 174-175.

claimed by Great Britain did not contain any explicit reference to the right to regulate. The right to regulate was neither reserved expressly nor was it referred in any other manner.[152]

Even in the absence of any specific reference - positive or negative - the Great Britain argued that the right was an 'attribute of sovereignty' and it must be held to 'reside in the territorial sovereign, unless the contrary is provided'. The right to regulate is one of the 'essential elements of sovereignty... to be exercised within territorial limits' and 'failing proof to the contrary, the territory is co-terminus with the Sovereignty, it follows that the burden of the assertion involved in the contention of the United States (viz. that the right to regulate does not reside independently in Great Britain, the territorial Sovereign) must fall on the United States'.[153]

The Tribunal rejected the arguments of the United States and commented on the relationship between regulatory freedom and treaty obligations in the following words:

> 'The Tribunal is unable to agree with this contention:
> Because there is no necessary connection between the duration of a grant and its essential status in its relation to local regulation; a right granted in perpetuity may yet be subject to regulation, or, granted temporarily, may yet be exempted therefrom; or being reciprocal may yet be unregulated, or being unilateral may yet be regulated: as is evidenced by the claim of the United States that the liberties of fishery accorded by the Reciprocity Treaty of 1854 and the Treaty of 1871 were exempt from regulation, though they were neither permanent nor unilateral.'[154]

The position of United States was much stronger than treatment standards in investment treaties. The right of fishing was a right granted in perpetuity. Based on the perpetual grant, US argued that the treaty created servitude over the right of another State, a form of derogation of sovereignty.[155] The Tribunal rejected the argument of creation of servitude, since the right to fish was not a sovereign right but 'a purely economic right, to the inhabitants of another State'.[156]

The Tribunal acknowledged that the regulatory freedom is bound to be limited by treaty rights in some way. However, this is not a sufficient basis to deny regulatory freedom altogether. Regulatory freedom cannot be denied as long as the restrictions imposed on the rights granted under a treaty are reasonable.[157] Furthermore, even if the regulatory freedom has not been exercised in past, this does not mean it cannot be exercised in future. The fact that the right remained dormant and utilized in past is no ground to reject its application.[158] The principle of *expression unius exclusio alterius*

152. *Ibid.*, 180.
153. *Ibid.*, 180.
154. *Ibid.*, 181.
155. 'That the liberties of fishery granted to the United States constitute an International servitude in their favour over the territory of Great Britain, thereby involving a derogation from the sovereignty of Great Britain, the servient State, and that therefore Great Britain is deprived, by reason of the grant, of its independent right to regulate the fishery.' *Ibid.*, 181.
156. *Ibid.*, 181.
157. *Ibid.*, 182.
158. *Ibid.*, 183.

does not apply to sovereign right.[159] Meaning thereby, non-mention of a right to regulate does not exclude the operation of that right. Problems arise if the regulations are selective and targeted towards the beneficiaries under a treaty. In this case, the regulations were equally applicable to all concerned – American and British, the regulation would be saved, as a right of the territorial sovereign.[160]

On the second issue of the need of concurrence of United States for any regulation that Great Britain intended to impose, the Tribunal held that recognition of a concurrent right of consent of the United States would affect the independence of the Great Britain. It would make Great Britain dependent on the consent of another State to exercise the sovereign right of regulation, a situation which is not recognized in the constitutions of either of the States.[161] Regulatory freedom is implicit in each treaty provision, unless excluded by the treaty. Any limitation on the right to regulate cannot be presumed.[162] The State possessed the right to legislate that would result into restrictions on the right of fishing. The 'right of legislation is limited by the obligation to execute the Treaty in good faith'.[163] Good faith, i.e. bona fide emerges as an important element of a legitimate regulatory freedom.

The approach of investment tribunals on regulation is dictated by the quest of drawing a dividing line between a regulation and indirect expropriation. Tribunals have often observed that it is not possible to draw a 'bright line' distinguishing the two.[164] The need of drawing such a line does not arise. It is not a balancing exercise.

---

159. *Ibid.*, 185.
160. *Ibid.*, 185.
161. *Ibid.*, 186. In recent arbitral practice, some States incorporate a provision of prudential measures which requires determination of appropriateness by the home State for the measure the host state has imposed. *See* discussion in Chapter 6 on treaty practice chapter. These provisions are incorporated as a part of express agreement between the parties. If implied, they would violate the principle of sovereign equality of States.
162. *Ibid.*, 186: 'But no reason has been shown why this Treaty, in this respect, should be considered as different from every other Treaty under which the right of a State to regulate the action of foreigners admitted by it on its territory is recognized;

  (b) Because the exercise of such a right of consent by the United States would predicate an abandonment of its independence in this respect by Great Britain, and the recognition by the latter of a concurrent right of regulation in the United States. But the Treaty conveys only a liberty to take fish in common, and neither directly nor indirectly conveys a joint right of regulation.'
163. *Ibid.*, 187: 'In any event, Great Britain, as the local sovereign, has the duty of preserving and protecting the fisheries. In so far as it is necessary for that purpose, Great Britain is not only entitled, but obliged, to provide for the protection and preservation of the fisheries; always remembering that the exercise of this right of legislation is limited by the obligation to execute the Treaty in good faith.'
164. Above note 133 (*Saluka v Czech Republic* case). The Tribunal said that: 'That being said, international law has yet to identify in a comprehensive and definitive fashion precisely what regulations are considered "permissible" and "commonly accepted" as falling within the police or regulatory power of States and, thus, non-compensable. In other words, it has yet to draw a bright and easily distinguishable line between non-compensable regulations on the one hand and, on the other, measures that have the effect of depriving foreign investors of their investment and are thus unlawful and compensable in international law.', para. 263; Andrew Newcomb, 'The Boundaries of Regulatory Expropriation in International Law' *International Centre for Settlement of Investment Disputes Review – Foreign Investment Law Journal* 20 (2005): 1, 3.

Regulatory freedom is not an exception but a positive rule emanating from sovereignty.[165] It is a norm of customary law that operates distinctly and autonomously from treaty or contract law.[166] What ought to be seen is whether the requirements of a legitimate regulation are satisfied. The argument of 'bright line' was raised by United States: 'yet there is somewhere a line, beyond which it is not competent for Great Britain to go, or beyond which she cannot rightfully go, because to go beyond it would be an invasion of the right granted to the United States in 1818. That the legal effect of the grant of 1818 was not to leave the determination as to where that line is to be drawn to the uncontrolled judgment of the grantor, either upon the grantor's consideration as to what would be a reasonable exercise of its sovereignty over the British Empire, or upon the grantor's consideration of what would be a reasonable exercise thereof towards the grantee.'[167] The Tribunal rejected this contention in totality because the right to regulate is a right independent of the treaty and cannot be circumscribed based on the provisions of a treaty. It said so clearly in the following words:

> 'But this contention is founded on assumptions, which this Tribunal cannot accept for the following reasons in addition to those already set forth:
>
> (a) Because the line by which the respective rights of both Parties accruing out of the Treaty are to be circumscribed, can refer only to the right granted by the Treaty; that is to say to the liberty of taking, drying and curing fish by American inhabitants in certain British waters in common with British subjects, and not to the exercise of rights of legislation by Great Britain not referred to in the Treaty;
> (b) Because a line which would limit the exercise of sovereignty of a State within the limits of its own territory can be drawn only on the ground of express stipulation, and not by implication from stipulations concerning a different subject-matter;
> (c) Because the line in question is drawn according to the principle of international law that treaty obligations are to be executed in perfect good faith, therefore excluding the right to legislate *at will* concerning the subject-matter of the Treaty, and limiting the exercise of sovereignty of the States bound by a treaty with respect to that subject-matter to such acts as are consistent with the treaty;
> (d) Because on a true construction of the Treaty the question does not arise whether the United States agreed that Great Britain should retain the right to legislate with regard to the fisheries in her own territory; but whether the Treaty contains an abdication by Great Britain of the right which Great Britain, as the sovereign power, undoubtedly possessed when the Treaty was made, to regulate those fisheries;
> (e) Because the right to make reasonable regulations, not inconsistent with the obligations of the Treaty, which is all that is claimed by Great Britain, for a fishery which both Parties admit requires regulation for its preservation, is not a restriction of or an invasion of the liberty granted to the inhabitants of the United States. This grant does not contain words to justify the assumption that

165. Jorge E. Viñuales, 'Sovereignty in Foreign Investment Law' in Zachary Douglas, Joost Pauwelyn & Jorge E. Viñuales (eds) *The Foundations of International Investment Law: Bringing Theory into Practice* (Oxford: Oxford University Press, 2014), 343.
166. *Ibid.*, 344.
167. Above note 150 (*North Atlantic Fisheries* Case), 187.

the sovereignty of Great Britain upon its own territory was in any way affected; nor can words be found in the Treaty transferring any part of that sovereignty to the United States. Great Britain assumed only duties with regard to the exercise of its sovereignty. The sovereignty of Great Britain over the coastal waters and territory of Newfoundland remains after the Treaty as un- impaired as it was before. But from the Treaty results an obligatory relation whereby the right of Great Britain to exercise its right of sovereignty by making regulations is limited to such regulations as are made in good faith, and are not in violation of the Treaty;

(f) Finally to hold that the United States, the grantee of the fishing right, has a voice in the preparation of fishery legislation involves the recognition of a right in that country to participate in the internal legislation of Great Britain and her Colonies, and to that extent would reduce these countries to a state of dependence.'[168]

The Tribunal upheld the right of Great Britain to regulate and summarized its conclusions as under:

'Now therefore this Tribunal decides and awards as follows:

The right of Great Britain to make regulations without the consent of the United States, as to the exercise of the liberty to lake fish referred to in Article I of the Treaty of 20th October 1818, in the form of municipal laws, ordinances or rules of Great Britain, Canada or Newfoundland is inherent to the sovereignty of Great Britain.

The exercise of that right by Great Britain is, however, limited by the said Treaty in respect of the said liberties therein granted to the inhabitants of the United States in that such regulations must be made bona fide and must not be in violation of the said Treaty.

Regulations which are (1) appropriate or necessary for the protection and preservation of such fisheries, or (2) desirable or necessary on grounds of public order and morals without unnecessarily interfering with the fishery itself, and in both cases equitable and fair as between local and American fishermen, and not so framed as to give unfairly an advantage to the former over the latter class, are not inconsistent with the obligation to execute the Treaty in good faith, and are there- fore reasonable and not in violation of the Treaty.'[169]

Commenting on this case McNair observed: 'the right of a State to regulate the enjoyment by another State of rights derived from a treaty or from customary international law must be exercised reasonably and in good faith and not in such a way as to destroy the effective enjoyment of those rights.'[170] These observations encapsulate the elements of regulatory freedom as set out in the decision.

The ICJ had the occasion to comment upon the relationship between regulatory freedom and a treaty provision in the *Navigation Rights* case. The case related to the extent of regulation that could be applied on the navigation on the San Juan river. The contested portions of the San Juan river belonged to Nicaragua and right of free navigation over that portion was granted in favour of Costa Rica under the treaty of

168. *Ibid.*, 187-188.
169. *Ibid.*, 188-9.
170. *See* above note 24 (McNair), 764.

1958.[171] The right created under the treaty of 1858 was a general and open-ended navigational right for commercial purposes – '*libre navegación…con objetos de comercio*'.[172] The 1858 treaty 'completely defines the rules applicable to the section of the San Juan River that is in dispute in respect of navigation'.[173] This provision granted right of free navigation and commerce in favour of Costa Rica on the San Juan river.[174] Despite existence of a treaty, Nicaragua argued that it had extensive rights to regulate operations on the San Juan River. The general stand adopted by the Court on treaty interpretation was that it is not necessary that a treaty imposing restrictions on sovereignty of a State need not be interpreted narrowly, but at the same time 'limitations of the sovereignty of a State over its territory are not to be presumed'.[175] As on one side a treaty provision limiting sovereignty is not to be restrictively interpreted, likewise a provision need not be liberally interpreted in favour of a party claiming benefit under that treaty.[176]

Initially the parties substantially diverged on the issue whether in view of existence of a treaty, the state retained the power to regulate. As the case proceeded to the merits stage, the parties were in agreement that the power did exist, but the only dispute was about the extent of this power.[177] The Court noted the agreed position of the parties on regulatory freedom in the following words:

> It states that the 'regulations must be lawful, public, reasonable, non-arbitrary and non-discriminatory, and adopted to fulfill a legitimate public purpose. Nicaragua accepts Costa Rica's statement of principle.'[178] The ICJ noted the following characteristics of a legitimate regulation in the *Navigation Rights* case: legitimate purpose, non-discriminatory and reasonable.[179]

Commenting on the interrelationship between a perpetual right of free navigation and freedom to regulate, the Court held that a perpetual right guaranteed under a treaty cannot 'prejudice the key prerogative of territorial sovereignty'.[180] The scope of regulatory freedom, which is otherwise broad, is conscribed by operation of a treaty. The exercise of sovereign rights shall not prejudice the substance of Costa Rica's rights.[181] According to the ICJ, 'the power to regulate…is not unlimited, being tempered by the rights and obligations of the Parties'.[182] In situation of exercise of

171. Dispute regarding Navigational and Related Rights (*Costa Rica v Nicaragua*), Judgment of 13 July 2009, (2009) ICJ Rep. 213, paras 30–31.
172. *Ibid.*, para. 19.
173. *Ibid.*, para. 36.
174. *Ibid.*, para. 32.
175. *Ibid.*, para. 48.
176. *Ibid.*, para. 48.
177. *Ibid.*, para. 86.
178. *Ibid.*, para. 86.
179. Above note 171 (*Costa Rica v Nicaragua* case), para. 87.
180. *Ibid.*, para. 48.
181. *Ibid.*, para. 48.
182. *Ibid.*, para. 87.

regulatory measures, the extent of inconvenience caused is not a relevant factor to challenge the legitimacy of a measure.[183]

According to the ICJ, regulatory freedom had to be interpreted in an evolutionary manner to address the challenges of the time.[184] International law is to be seen in the context of contemporary concerns of the international community.[185] In the *Gabčíkovo-Nagymaros Project* case, the ICJ held that the developments in the field of environmental law have to be kept in mind while interpreting the treaty between States.[186] The obligations in the treaty cannot be fixed in time. States would be undertaking different regulations from time to time to achieve its legitimate sovereign objectives. In recognition of evolutionary approach to regulatory freedom, in the context of environmental protection, the ICJ said:

> The Court considers that, over the course of the century and a half since the 1858 Treaty was concluded, the interests which are to be protected through regulation in public interest may well have changed in ways that could never have been anticipated by the Parties at the time: protecting the environment is a notable example. ... Nicaragua, in adopting certain measure which have been challenged, in the Court's opinion, is pursuing the legitimate purpose of protecting the environment.[187]

After discussing the position of regulatory freedom as a customary principle and manner of its interpretation in view of treaty obligations under investment treaties, the next Chapter elaborates the contents of regulatory freedom and the standard of review investment tribunals ought to apply.

With some degree of variance, the three elements: bona fide (or good faith), non-discriminatory and public interest emerge from State practice and the jurisprudence of international courts and tribunals and investment tribunals.[188] Furthermore, these elements are adequate to ensure that a State does not resort to disguised regulations to confiscate or deprive foreign investor of its property. In *Saluka v Czech Republic*, the Tribunal recognized independent existence of a regulatory measure and identified its elements as follows:

183. *Ibid.*, para. 109. In this case clearance certificates were required to be obtained while navigating from the San Juan river. Costa Rica challenged these measures are a significant impediment to its right of free navigation specifically protected under the treaty. The Court held that these requirements do not amount to significant impediments to its rights. Likewise in relation to the argument that imposition of a timetable for journey on the river also impeded the navigational right, the Court rejected the argument on the basis that: 'the exercise of a power to regulate may legitimately include placing limits on the activity in question.' *See* para. 126.
184. The Court in *Navigation Rights* case dealt with evolutionary interpretation in two contexts. In first it was in relation to evolutionary interpretation of treaty provisions (paras 63–71). It separately dealt with the need to interpret regulatory freedom in an evolutionary fashion considering practical realities. For evolutionary principle *see* above note 75 (*South West Africa* case), para. 96.
185. Above note 34 (*US-Shrimp Turtle* case), paras 128–132.
186. Above note 89 (*Gabčíkovo-Nagymaros* case), para. 140; followed in The Indus Waters Kishenganga Arbitration (*Pakistan v India*), Final Award, 20 December 2013, PCA Case No. 2011-01, para. 85.
187. Above note 171 (*Costa Rica v Nicaragua* case), para. 89.
188. Above note 171 (*Costa Rica v Nicaragua* case), para. 87.

> It is now established in international law that States are not liable to pay compensation to a foreign investor when, in the normal exercise of their regulatory powers, they adopt in a non-discriminatory manner bona fide regulations that are aimed at the general welfare.[189]

189. Above note 133 (*Saluka v Czech Republic* case), para. 255.

CHAPTER 8

Elements of Regulatory Freedom and Standard of Review

The last Chapter argued that regulatory freedom continues to operate alongside treatment standards, and it is not superseded by indirect expropriation. While regulatory freedom is not absolute, it has to be exercised in a legitimate manner, its elements were identified in the last Chapter. This Chapter develops the elements of regulatory freedom, namely, bona fide, non-discriminatory and public interest. The later section of this Chapter elaborates on the standard of review that should be applied in cases where the relationship between regulatory freedom and indirect expropriation is in question.

§8.01 BONA FIDE

Bona fide is also known as good faith.[1] Good faith is 'one of the basic principles governing the creation and performance of legal obligations'[2] and the foundation of all laws and convention.[3] States have stated the requirement of performing treaty obligations in the text of treaties.[4] The UN General Assembly resolution, entitled Declaration

---

1. Bryan Garner, *Black's Law Dictionary* (10th ed., United States of America: Thomson Reuters; 2014), 210.
2. Nuclear Tests, (*Australia/ New Zealand v France*), 20 December 1974, (1974) ICJ Reports 268, para. 49.
3. *The Megalidis* case (*A.A. Megalidis v Turkey*) (1927-8) 4 Annual Digest of International Law Cases 395 (Turkish-Greek Mixed Arb. Trib. 1928); According to Lauterpacht: 'Unquestionably, the obligation to act in accordance with good faith, being a general principle of law, is also part of international law.' *Certain Norwegian Loans (France v Norway)* (Judgment of 6 July 1957) (Separate Opinion of Judge Lauterpacht) (1957) ICJ Reports, 9, 53.
4. Article 13 of the Draft Declaration on Rights and Duties of States, General Assembly Resolution 375 (IV), 4th Session, 6 December 1949 states that: 'Every State has the duty to carry out in good faith its obligations arising from treaties and other sources of international law,...'; The Helsinki Accord notes is a good example of commitment of states to conduct sovereign exercises of adoption of regulations in good faith, in the following words:

of Friendly Relations and Cooperation Among States declares that: '[e]very State has the duty to fulfill in good faith its obligations under the generally recognized principles and rules of international law.'[5] Even where treaties do not provide for good faith, it is extant. It constitutes a part of customary law principle of *pacta sunt servanda;*[6] and codified in Article 26 of the Vienna Convention on the Law of Treaties as: 'Every treaty in force is binding upon the parties to it and must be performed by them in good faith.' The duty of the interpreting authority to interpret a treaty in good faith is a corollary of this obligation.[7] Article 31 (1) of the VCLT states this clearly in the following words: '[a] treaty shall be interpreted in good faith.'

Good faith is 'freedom from intent to deceive'.[8] It means acting sincerely or genuinely,[9] and requires parties to act fairly in relation to each other.[10] It is a general principle of law.[11] Its importance has been sought to be discredited due to lack of precise contents.[12] However, it would be improper to reject good faith merely because it has a subjective element to it. Defending the relevance of good faith for adjudication despite its subjective nature, Fitzmaurice rightly points out that:

> It would be paradoxical indeed if the very absence of any certain method of asserting a right to action in good faith by other States were to be regarded as negativating the existence of the right itself.[13]

Despite the subjective character of good faith, concrete elements of good faith can be identified.[14]

> 'X. Fulfillment in good faith of obligations under international law
>
> The participating States will fulfil in good faith their obligations under international law, both those obligations arising from the generally recognized principles and rules of international law and those obligations arising from treaties or other agreements, in conformity with international law, to which they are parties.
>
> In exercising their sovereign rights, including the right to determine their laws and regulations, they will conform with their legal obligations under international law; they will furthermore pay due regard to and implement the provisions in the Final Act of the Conference on Security and Cooperation in Europe.'

5. United Nations Declaration on Principles of International Law concerning Friendly Relations and Co-operation among States in accordance with the Charter of the United Nations, Resolution adopted by the General Assembly on 24 October 1970, UN Doc. A/RES/25/2625.
6. *The North Atlantic Coast Fisheries* case (*Great Britain v United States of America*), Award of the Tribunal, Permanent Court of Arbitration, 7 September 1910, (1961) XI RIAA 167, 187 para. 169; *Dispute Concerning Filleting within the Gulf of St Laurence*, Award, 17 July 1986 82 ILR 590, para. 27; *See* Andrew Mitchell, 'Good Faith in WTO Dispute Settlement' *Melbourne Journal of International Law* 7 (2006): 339, 346-7.
7. *Ibid.*, (Mitchell), 347-9.
8. John Simpson & Edmund Weiner (eds.), *The Oxford English Dictionary* 2nd ed., vol. II (Oxford: Oxford University Press, 1989), 379.
9. Lesley Brown (ed), *The New Shorter Oxford English Dictionary: On Historical Principles*, vol. I (Oxford: Clarendon Press, 1993), 257.
10. Antony D'Amato, 'Good Faith' *Encyclopedia of Public International Law* (1992): 599.
11. Andrew Mitchell, *Legal Principles in WTO Disputes* (Cambridge: Cambridge University Press, 2008), 108-110. Mitchell even argues that good faith is customary law, 110-2.
12. Shabtai Rosenne, *Developments in the Law of Treaties, 1945-1986* (Cambridge: Cambridge University Press, 1989), 135.
13. Gerald Fitzmaurice, *The Law and Procedure of the International Court of Justice*, vol. II (Cambridge: Grotious Publications Limited, 1986), 614.
14. *Ibid.*, 610-11.

The discussion here on good faith is not in relation to good faith as a general principle of international law, rather as an element of customary international law requirement of regulatory freedom. The effort is to firstly establish its relevance as an element of regulatory freedom, and thereafter identify its contents that could be applied by investment tribunals.

Schreuer has argued that the distinction between regulatory freedom and expropriation is superficial because the elements of expropriation flowing from the treaty text are similar to the provisions of regulatory freedom.[15] In addition to the conceptual difference between regulatory measure and expropriatory measure, the constitutive elements of regulatory freedom are different from expropriation in treaties. The distinguishing factor is bona fide. A close look at the criteria of expropriation in the investment treaties shows that requirement of bona fide is absent. The reason for this exclusion from the definition of expropriation is because the question of nature of measure is irrelevant in cases of direct expropriation, since the measure is admittedly expropriatory.[16] This inquiry of presence of good faith becomes indispensable in cases of indirect expropriation, which also includes equivalent and tantamount to expropriation. Amador noted in his Report to the ILC that the basis of delineation between regulation and expropriation is the intention for adoption of the measure in the following words:

> In distinguishing between expropriation *stricto sensu* and the other forms in which the State's right to 'affect' the property of private individuals may be exercised, it was shown that the 'destination' which the expropriated property is given, in other words, the motives and purposes of the action taken by the State, is one of the essential component elements of expropriation.[17]

The 'intention' behind the measure determines whether the damage caused to the property is an outcome of regulation and thus justified or expropriation, which would result into breach of treaty obligations. Even generally, intention plays a crucial role, particularly in situations where a treaty provision operates alongside other obligations. If a State acts with bad faith (absent good faith), it will result into violation

15. After reproducing the provisions of the ECT on expropriation, Schreuer says that: 'It follows from provisions such as this one that the fact that a measure is in the public interest and non-discriminatory cannot be the answer to the question whether an expropriation has occurred. An expropriation may take place under perfectly legitimate circumstances. Arbitrariness, bad faith, lack of proportionality and other improprieties are not constitutive elements of expropriation. Their absence does not mean that an expropriation could not have taken place.' Christoph Schreuer, 'The Concept of Expropriation under the ECT and other Investment Protection Treaties' in *Investment Arbitration and the Energy Charter Treaty*, ed. Clarisse Ribeiro (Juris Publishing, 2006), 110-1; also *see* Prabhash Ranjan &Pushkar Anand, 'Determination of Indirect Expropriation and Doctrine of Police Power in International Investment Law: A Critical Appraisal' in ed. Leila Choukroune *Judging the State in International Trade and Investment Law* (Springer, 2016).
16. Chapter 2 has elaborated on the distinction between a regulatory and expropriatory measure.
17. International Law Commission, International Responsibility, Fourth Report by F.V. García Amador, Special Rapporteur: Responsibility of the State for Injuries Caused in its Territory to the Person or Property of Aliens – Measures Affecting Acquired Rights Document A/CN.4/119 (26 February 1959), (1959) II Yearbook of the International Law Commission 1, para. 57.

of treaty obligations, i.e., an unlawful act.[18] It thus becomes necessary to investigate whether the regulatory measure is adopted in good faith.[19] Judge Spender summarized the position in the *Guardianship of Infants* case in the following words:

> If in a particular case it could be shown that a law comparable to the relevant provisions of the Swedish law had been used by a contracting State not *bona fide* to carry out that law but for a purpose *aliunde*, for example to interfere with and restrict a guardian in the exercise of his right of custody and control as such, other and quite different considerations would arise. But that is not the instant case. The Netherlands has very properly conceded that Sweden acted in complete good faith under the provisions of its law.[20]

A reasonable and bona fide exercise of a right is necessary for the furtherance of rights protected under the treaty.[21] If a treaty does not bar a specific activity, a State is free to undertake such an activity and enjoys wide discretion. The restriction of performing legislative functions in a bona fide manner arises only once there is a treaty obligation.[22] Whenever there are treaty obligations existing simultaneously, the sovereign power has to be exercised reasonably. Then the exercise is considered compatible with treaty obligations.[23] Once a treaty obligation is undertaken by a State, this discretion is tapered by the requirement of good faith.[24]

Good faith ensures that the rights of State are reasonably exercised. It acts as a balance between the conflicting interest of State to exercise its power and the obligations undertaken under a treaty.[25] Commenting on the balancing function performed by good faith, the Permanent Court of Arbitration in the *North Atlantic Coast Fisheries* case stated:

> 'The exercise of that right by Great Britain is, however, limited by the said Treaty in respect of the said liberties therein granted to the inhabitants of the United States in that such regulations must be made bona fide and must not be in violation of the said Treaty.
>
> Regulations which are (1) appropriate or necessary for the protection and preservation of such fisheries, or (2) desirable or necessary on grounds of public order and morals without unnecessarily interfering with the fishery itself, and in both

18. Bin Cheng, *General Principles of Law as Applied by International Courts and Tribunals* (London: Stevens and Sons, 1953), 128.
19. *The North Atlantic Coast Fisheries* case *(Great Britain v United States of America)*, Award of the Tribunal, Permanent Court of Arbitration, 7 September 1910, (1961) XI RIAA 167, 187: 'In so far as it is necessary for that purpose, Great Britain is not only entitled, but obliged, to provide for the protection and preservation of the fisheries; always remembering that the exercise of this right of legislation is limited by the obligation to execute the Treaty in good faith. This has been admitted by counsel and recognized by Great Britain in limiting the right of regulation to that of reasonable regulation.'
20. *Application of the Convention of 1902 Governing the Guardianship of Infants (Netherlands v Sweden)* (Judgment of 28 November 1958) (Separate Opinion of Sir Percy Spender) (1958) ICJ Reports 55, 120.
21. Above note 18 (Cheng), 125.
22. *Ibid.*, 124.
23. *Ibid.*, 125.
24. Conditions of Admission of a State to Membership in the United Nations (Art. 4 of the Charter), Advisory Opinion of 28 May 1948, Individual Opinion by M. Alvarez, (1948) ICJ Reports 57, 71.
25. Above note 18 (Cheng), 132.

> cases equitable and fair as between local and American fishermen, and not so framed as to give unfairly an advantage to the former over the latter class, are not inconsistent with the obligation to execute the Treaty in good faith, and are therefore reasonable and not in violation of the Treaty.'[26]

The 'substance of the principle of good faith is the negation of unintended and literal interpretations of words that might result in one of the parties gaining an unfair or unjust advantage over another party'.[27] In the *Certain German Interests in Polish Upper Silesia* case, the PCIJ held that regulatory actions could not be deemed to violate treaty obligations if adopted in good faith.[28] The Court held that a State would not attract responsibility unless there is misuse of the right - i.e., alienation intended to defeat treaty obligations.[29] If restriction of good faith is not imposed, the discretion would be exercised abusively to defeat a treaty. Discretion of States, including that of administration, shall be exercised in good faith.[30] Good faith is the linkage of interdependence between the rights of State to regulate and the obligations undertaken under a treaty.

Good faith requires that the rights are not exercised in a manner incompatible with international law.[31] The reasonable and bona fide exercise of power implies an exercise genuinely in 'pursuit of those interests which the right is destined to protect and which is not calculated to cause any unfair prejudice to the legitimate interest of another State, whether these interests be secured by treaty or general international law'.[32] A regulatory exercise would not be bona fide if the right is exercised in such a manner as to prejudice the interests of other party[33] - in the case of investment treaties, the beneficiaries of the treaties, i.e. foreign investors. In other words, if the 'exercise of the right in such a manner as to prejudice the interests of the other contracting party arising out of the treaty is unreasonable and is considered as inconsistent with the bona fide execution of the treaty obligation, and a breach of the treaty'.[34] Thus, bona fide establishes interdependence between rights of a State and its obligations.[35] This relationship was emphasized in the *US-Shrimp Turtle* case by the Appellate Body of the WTO in the following words:

> The chapeau of Article XX is, in fact, but one expression of the principle of good faith. This principle, at once a general principle of law and a general principle of international law, controls the exercise of rights by states. One application of this

26. Above note 6 (*The North Atlantic Fisheries* case), para. 189.
27. Above note 10 (D'Amato), 599.
28. Certain German interests in Polish Upper Silesia, *Germany v Poland*, Merits, Judgment, (1926) PCIJ Series A no. 7, ICGJ 241 (PCIJ 1926), 25 May 1926, League of Nations (historical); PCIJ, 30.
29. *Ibid.*, 30.
30. Legal Consequences for States of the Continued Presence of South Africa in Namibia (South West Africa) notwithstanding Security Council Resolution 276 (1970), Advisory Opinion of 21 June 1971, (1971) ICJ Reports 16, para. 90.
31. Preferential Treatment of Claims of Blockading Powers Against Venezuela, *Germany and ors v Venezuela*, Award, (1959) IX RIAA 99, ICGJ 408 (PCA 1904), 22 February 1904, Permanent Court of Arbitration at 107, 110.
32. Above note 18 (Cheng), 131-2.
33. Above note 18 (Cheng), 125.
34. *Ibid.*
35. *Ibid.*

> general principle, the application widely known as the doctrine of *abus de droit*, prohibits the abusive exercise of a state's rights and enjoins that whenever the assertion of a right 'impinges on the field covered by [a] treaty obligation, it must be exercised bona fide, that is to say, reasonably'. An abusive exercise by a member of its own treaty right results in a breach of the treaty rights of the other members and, as well, a violation of the treaty obligation of the Member so acting.[36]

Good faith is not a self-judging criterion and *post hoc* characterization of State action is immaterial.[37] The determination of intention is a question of fact. Intention of a State can be found in a similar manner as it is found in municipal law to find the intention of individuals. The exercise of determination of intention gives the impression that it is some form of psychological inquiry – peeping in the mind of an actor. A third party cannot view thoughts of individuals. The situation is further complex for a State, which cannot even possess a unified mind. All this does not mean that, in law, intention of an individual and a State cannot be found out. Intention can be deduced from the decision-making process of the individual.[38] Similarly in the case of States, intention proved through circumstantial evidence based on words and actions of the agents of the State.[39]

It is 'neither impossible to retrieve nor judicially unmanageable' to present evidence and find out State's subjective intent.[40] There is a great deal of convergence in the manner of determination of good faith amongst various international tribunals.[41] The ICJ has ascertained the subjective intention of the State from circumstances to decide if the measure was resorted to in good faith.[42] For example, protectionist regulation is a necessary ingredient for determining breach of national treatment in trade law.[43]

Bad faith cannot be presumed. It has to be established through positive evidence.[44] Investment tribunals have ascertained bona fides from the material used by

36. *United States-Import Prohibition of Certain Shrimp and Shrimp Products* Case, Appellate Body, WT/DS58/AB/R, 12 October 1998, para. 158.
37. Andrei Mamolea, 'Good Faith Review' in *Deference in International Courts and Tribunals: Standard of Review and Margin of Appreciation*, eds. Lukasz Gruszczynski & Wouter Wermer (Oxford: Oxford University Press, 2014), 76.
38. *Ibid.*, 85.
39. *Ibid.*, 76 (footnote excluded).
40. *Ibid.*, 75-6.
41. *Ibid.*, 76.
42. Certain Questions of Mutual Assistance in Criminal Matters (*Djibouti v France*), Judgment of 4 June 2008, para. 140, 150-2. The Court said: 'The Court must review the circumstances under which the French judicial authorities took the decision to refuse to execute the international letter rogatory and the way in which the decision was notified to Djibouti.' Para. 140; Military and Paramilitary Activities in and against Nicaragua (*Nicaragua v United States of America*), Judgment of 27 June 1986, 1986 ICJ Reports 14, para. 200, 234-6; Armed Activities on the Territory of the Congo (*Democratic Republic of the Congo v Uganda*), Judgment of 19 December 2005, paras 119, 143.
43. *See* Chile – Taxes on Alcoholic Beverages WT/DS110/AB/R, Report of Appellate Body, 13 December 1999, para. 71.
44. Free Zones of Upper Savoy and the District of Gex (*France v Switzerland*), Judgment of 6 December 1930, 1930 PCIJ Series A/B, No. 24, 12.

the State to support the measure. In *S. D. Myres v Canada*, the Tribunal determined the intention of the State in adopting a regulation. The Tribunal stated that:

> The intent of government is a complex and multifaceted matter. Government decisions are shaped by different politicians and officials with differing philosophies and perspectives. Each of the many persons involved in framing government policy may approach a problem from a variety of different policy objectives and may sometimes take into account partisan political factors or career concerns. The Tribunal can only characterize Canada's motivation or intent fairly by examining the record of the evidence as a whole.[45]

After analysing the decision-making process at various levels: starting from formulation of policy, bureaucratic process and debates in the Parliament, the Tribunal found that the regulations were passed with the intention to protect Canadian industry. It was established that the regulations were adopted to defeat the rights of foreign investors in a discriminatory fashion.[46]

The Panels and Appellate Body of the WTO have also used this methodology to determine subjective intent for adoption of regulation and whether it satisfies the good faith test.[47] Likewise States can also present evidence to establish lack of subjective intention. In *Methanex v United States*, the Respondent used scientific evidence to justify its regulation banning sale and use of gasoline additive MTBE.[48]

Efforts have been made to identify contents of 'good faith'.[49] There are some specific points that emerge from the application of good faith that can be applied by an adjudicator to see if the challenged measure is in good faith or not. These constituting indices flow from the concept of good faith. Abuse of rights is an important application of principle of good faith.[50] It provides a threshold at which good faith is deemed to be absent.[51] The objective of good faith is to ensure that while a State is performing its treaty obligations, it does not evade them in a surreptitious manner. An unreasonable exercise of sovereign freedom is abuse of rights, and inconsistent with the responsibility to carry out the treaty obligations in good faith. Abuse of rights was introduced in interstate relations for the first time during the discussion of the Committee of Jurists

45. *S.D. Myres, Inc. v Government of Canada*, Partial Award, 13 November 2000, para. 285; *Pope & Talbot Inc v The Government of Canada*, Interim Award, 26 June 2000, para. 161.
46. *Ibid.*, (*S.D. Myers* case) para. 285; *ibid.*, (*Pope & Talbot Inc.* Case) paras 162, 195, 263.
47. Japan – Taxes on Alcoholic Beverages, Appellate Body, WT/DS8/AB/R, WT/DS10/AB/R, WT/DS11/AB/R, 1 November 1996, paras 27–28; Canada – Certain Measures Concerning Periodicals, Appellate Body WT/DS31/AB/R, 30 July 1997, paras 30, 74; Mexico- Tax Measures on Soft Drinks and Other Beverages, Panel Report, WT/DS308/R, 24 March 2006, paras 8.91–8.95; United States – Certain Country of Origin Labeling (COOL) Requirements, Appellate Body, WT/DS384/AB/R, 23 July 2012, para. 420; Nicolas Diebold, *Non-Discrimination in International Trade in Services* (Cambridge: Cambridge University Press, 2010), 84.
48. *Methanex Corporation v United States of America*, UNCITRAL, Award, 3 August 2005, Part III, Chapter A; Also *see Parkerings-Compagniet AS v Republic of Lithuania*, ICSID Case No. ARB/05/8, Award, 11 September 2007, para. 368; Rumeli Telekom A.S. and Telsim Mobil Telekomunikasyon Hizmetleri A.S. v Republic of Kazakhstan, Award, 29 July 2008, para. 715.
49. Above note 11(Mitchell), at 144-121; Steven Reinhold, 'Good Faith in International Law' *University College of London Journal of Law and Jurisprudence* 2 (2013): 40, 47-57.
50. Above note 18 (Cheng), 121.
51. Michael Byers, 'Abuse of Rights: An Old Principle, A New Age' *McGill Law Journal* 47 (2002): 389, 411.

that drafted the Statute of the PCIJ. Abuse of rights was noted as one of the instances of general principles recognized in different jurisdictions.[52] States have used this principle not only as an argument to prohibit other States from abusing rights, but also a duty on concerned State not to exercise its powers abusively. The evidence of this state practice can be found in written pleadings and oral arguments before international tribunals.[53] A good faith performance consists of a sincere and honest effort evidenced by a genuine effort to fulfil the substance of mutual agreement.[54]

Lauterpacht identified the methodology for determining good faith in the following words:

> Any attempt to embark upon the examination of the question whether a Government has acted in bad faith in determining that a matter is essentially within its domestic jurisdiction may involve an exacting enquiry into the merits of the dispute-an enquiry so exacting that it could claim to determine, with full assurance, that the juridical view advanced by a Government is so demonstrably and palpably wrong and so arbitrary as to amount to an assertion made in bad faith. Only an enquiry into the merits can determine that although an assertion made by the defendant Government is not legally well-founded it is nevertheless reasonable; or that although it is not reasonable, it is not wholly arbitrary. The Court has no power to make such determination.[55]

The determination of whether actions are taken in good faith is done on the basis of abuse of rights. It is a corollary of good faith and states that a party shall refrain from abusing the rights conferred by a treaty.[56] Abuse of rights cannot be presumed and the party alleging it has to establish.[57] International courts and tribunals have reviewed the actions of States to test whether they constitute abuse of rights.[58]

Following specific principles emerge from the application of good faith. An investment tribunal can apply them to check if a regulation is bona fide:

52. A Ricci-Busatti in Permanent Court of Justice: Advisory Committee of Jurists (ed) *Procès Verbaux of the Proceedings of the Committee* (The Hague:Van Langenhuysen Brothers, 1920), 314-5.
53. *The Oscar Chinn* case (*Belgium v United Kingdom*), 12 December 1934, (1934) PCIJ Series A/B 63; *Case Concerning* The Barcelona Traction, Light and Power Company, Limited (*Belgium v Spain*), Second Phase, Judgment, 5 February 1970, (1970) ICJ Reports 3, 17.
54. Above note 18 (Cheng), 117-8 (footnotes omitted).
55. Above note 3 (*Norwegian Loan* case) at 54.
56. *Sartori v Peru* (Mixed Commission of Peru and the United States of America), 24 November 1863 (1863) XXIX RIAA 91, 94.
57. Free Zones of Upper Savoy and the District of Gex (*France v Switzerland*), Judgment of 6 December 1930, 1930 PCIJ Series A/B, No. 24, 12.
58. Case concerning Rights of Nationals of the United States of America in Morocco (*France v United States of America*) at 212; (*United States Nationals in Morocco* case) in the practice of the ICJ as well as to arbitral awards in the Trail Smelter Arbitration (*US v Canada*) (1941) ('Trail Smelter Arbitration'), the Delagoa Bay Arbitration, the *El Triunfo* case (*United States v El Salvador*) and to some of the Venezuelan arbitrations (9 RIAA 111–553, 10 RIAA; *The Venezuelan Preferential* case 9 RIAA 99–110).

[A] Intention to Injure

A State is said to have abused its rights if it exercises the right for the sole purpose of causing injury.[59] Cheng describes abusive actions as follows:

> The exercise of right – or supposed right, since the right no longer exists – for the sole purpose of causing injury to another is thus prohibited. Every right is the legal protection of a legitimate interest. An alleged exercise of a right not in furtherance of such interest, but with the malicious purpose of injuring others can no longer claim the protection of the law. *Malitiis non est indulgendum*.[60]

Applying this principle to investment cases, if it is found that the regulation was made for the sole purpose of injuring the foreign investor, the regulation will lack the essential element of good faith and will amount to indirect expropriation.

[B] Fictitious Exercise Aimed at Defeating Treaty Provisions

Abuse of rights exists whenever the alleged exercise of right is a 'fictitious exercise' aimed at evasion of treaty obligations.[61] In the *Free Zones* case, France was under an obligation to keep the certain frontier zones with Switzerland, free from customs barriers. The PCIJ recognized the sovereign right of France to impose regulations of fiscal nature, but it was inappropriate for France to impose police cordon at the political frontier, on the customs barrier, and control of traffic, and impose taxes other than the customs duties. The Court held that:

> A reservation must be made as regards the case of abuse of a right ['les cas d'abus de droit'], since it is certain that France must not evade the obligation to maintain the zones by erecting a customs barrier under the guise of a control cordon.[62]

Regulations adopted by a State for the purported objective of public interest, but in reality achieving the objective of protection of national investors in competition with foreign investors would be an example of fictitious exercise aimed at defeating the interests of investors.

[C] Colourable Exercise

Abuse of rights happens when a State intentionally exercises the power for an end different from that for which it was created with the aim of causing injury. This is the concept of *détournement de pouvoir* – well known in administrative practice within States.[63] For example, a State has purportedly adopted a regulation for limiting monopolistic practices. In fact, the regulation is benefitting a competing public

59. Above note 10 (D'Amato), 600.
60. Above note 18 (Cheng), 122.
61. *Ibid.*, 123.
62. Above note 57 (*Free Zones of Upper Savoy* case), 12.
63. Alexandre Kiss, 'Abuse of Rights' in *Max Planck Encyclopedia of Public International Law* ed. Rüdiger Wolfrum (New York: Oxford University Press, 2008), para. 5.

corporation at the expense of a foreign investor. In this case, the actual motive will be different from the alleged objective. This will be a case of oblique exercise of regulatory freedom amounting to abuse of rights.

[D] Regulations Adopted Solely for a Malicious Purpose

Regulations adopted solely for a malicious purpose are in violation of obligation to behave in good faith.[64] If there is malice driving the regulation, then there is absence of bad faith. Malice could be arising from the factual circumstances. If a part of the establishment is unhappy with the foreign investor due to personal animosity, and a regulation is made simply to harass the investor, then it will be an example of malicious exercise. *Biloune v Ghana Investments* discussed in Chapter 2 would be a good example of such actions.

[E] Arbitrary or Unreasonable Actions

Arbitrary and unreasonable actions amount to abuse of rights.[65] The notion of arbitrary action is very closely linked to the doctrine of abuse of rights and in practice, they are largely coterminous.[66] Arbitrariness of State action is decided based upon various criteria. The first relates to the motives and purposes of the State's action. These are issues not exclusively within the municipal sphere, and an international tribunal will have to decide the motive and purpose that justifies the State action. Unreasonableness is the method and procedure followed by the State authorities. This criterion too is within the domain of international law. If a measure fails on these tests, it is not a measure with genuine public interest in mind and it would be evident that it is arbitrary in nature.[67] Arbitrary and unreasonable not only form substantive grounds, but they also constitute the standard of review. They are therefore discussed in detail in the following section on the standard of review: role of proportionality analysis.

§8.02 NON-DISCRIMINATION

The second element of regulatory freedom is that the measure should be non-discriminatory. Non-discrimination is a general principle of international law and plays an important role in human rights and trade law.[68] Obligation of non-discrimination is

64. Above note 18 (Cheng), 122.
65. Gerald Fitzmaurice, 'The Law and Procedure of the International Court of Justice' *British Yearbook of International Law* 30 (1953): 1, 53.
66. International Law Commission, International Responsibility, Fourth Report by F V García Amador, Special Rapporteur: Responsibility of the State for Injuries Caused in its Territory to the Person or Property of Aliens – Measures Affecting Acquired Rights Document A/CN.4/119 (26 February 1959), (1959) II Yearbook of the International Law Commission 1, para. 28.
67. *Ibid.*, para. 26.
68. A.F.M. Manuruzzaman, 'Expropriation of Alien Property and the Principle of Non-Discrimination in International Law of Foreign Investment: An Overview', *Journal of Transnational Law and Policy* 8 (1998-9): 57, 57-8.

rooted in the requirement of equal treatment. Equality is considered as a part of public policy in municipal law and is also a part of international law.[69]

Discrimination may take a number of forms, such as discrimination based on race, religion, political affiliation, disability, etc. In investment arbitration, mostly discrimination would be based on nationality. But, there are several cases of discrimination based upon race, religion, etc.

Non-discrimination does not mean absolute equality. Similarity of situations of nationals and foreign investors is an indispensable requirement. On certain occasions, discrimination based on public policy grounds becomes necessary to achieve equality.[70] On public policy grounds, a State may justify differential treatment in similar cases.[71] It is therefore possible that an unequal treatment is justified.[72] In such a case, the justification has to be based upon bona fide and legitimate public interest goals.[73] A regulation could lead to some discriminatory effect on foreign investors, since they are very small in numbers. Measures that are exclusively aimed at the foreign investor and intended to single out the alien property for unfavourable treatment are discriminatory.[74] Certain discriminations, such as racial discrimination are *ex faci* bad since they cannot be defended on public policy grounds.[75]

States may discriminate based on public policy ground because there are no obligations in international law to treat aliens at par with nationals or treat two aliens at par, unless such obligations are undertaken under a treaty. In the context of trade and commerce, the Friendship Commerce and Navigation Treaties sought to achieve equality.[76] In the present context, investment treaties achieve this through Most Favoured Nation (MFN) and National Treatment (NT) standard. Nationality as a ground for discrimination is inapplicable unless there is a specific provision for MFN or NT present in a treaty.[77] States are under no obligation to receive all aliens and they

69. Warwick McKean, *Equality and Discrimination under Intentional Law* (Oxford: Clarendon Press, 1983), 11.
70. Above note 68 (Manuruzzaman), 58-62 (*see* footnotes therein); Muthucumaraswamy Sornarajah, *The Pursuit of Nationalized Property* (Dordrecht; Boston: Martinus Nijhoff, 1986), 185-7.
71. United Nations Conference on Trade and Development, *Most-Favoured-Nation Treatment: UNCTAD Series on Issues in International Investment Agreements* (New York and Geneva: United Nations, 2010), 27-28; *See Parkerings-Compegnite AS v Republic of Lithuania*, Award, ICSID Case No. ARB/05/8, 11 September 2007.
72. Isi Foighel, *Nationalization: A Study in the Protection of Alien Property in International Law* (London: Stevens & Sons Limited, 1957), 47.
73. Above note 68 (Manuruzzaman), 63-9.
74. Gillian White, *Nationalization of Foreign Property* (London: Stevens & Sons Limited, 1961), 44.
75. Muthucumaraswamy Sornarajah, *International Law on Foreign Investment* 3rd ed. (Cambridge: Cambridge University Press, 2010), 409-10.
76. Rudolf Dolzer & Margarete Stevens, *Bilateral Investment Treaties* (Hague: Martinus Nijhoff Publishers, 1995), 9-10.
77. Ian Brownlie, *Principles of Public International Law* (7th ed., Oxford: Oxford University Press, 2008), 524, 536-543. According to Brownlie: 'Before examining the validity of the principle of national treatment, it must be observed that it is agreed on all hands that certain sources of inequality are admissible. Thus it is not contended that the alien should have political rights in the host state as of right. Moreover, the alien must take the local law as he finds it in regard to regulation of the economy and restriction on employment of aliens in particular type of employment. Access to the courts may be maintained, but with modified rules in ancillary matters: thus an alien may not have access to legal aid and may have to give security for costs.

have a right to make their entry and stay conditional.[78] In *Methanex v USA*, the Tribunal held that:

> As to the question of whether a rule of customary international law prohibits a State, in the absence of a treaty obligation, from differentiating in its treatment of nationals and aliens, international law is clear. In the absence of a contrary rule of international law binding on the States parties, whether of conventional or customary origin, a State may differentiate in its treatment of nationals and aliens. As the previous discussion shows, no conventional rule binding on the NAFTA Parties is to the contrary with respect to the issues raised in this case. Indeed, the text of NAFTA indicates that the States parties explicitly excluded a rule of non-discrimination from Article 1105.[79]

In the absence of a NT clause, and depending on the language of the clause, States enjoy the discretion to decide the manner of treatment.[80] MFN too is only a treaty based standard and does not constitute a customary law.[81] Thus, in the absence of MFN/NT, a host State can discriminate between national and foreign investors as long as the treatment does not fall under the international minimum standard.[82] The scope and nature of the obligation of not to discriminate on the basis of nationality would depend on the specific language of MFN and NT. Even in situations where MFN/NT exists, public policy exception is available.[83] A regulation enacted for public interest can be discriminatory and be a valid justification against violation of an MFN clause.[84] But such regulations would have to be defended on rational grounds.[85] Public policy considerations act as an exception to the MFN clause, substantially narrowing the scope of the clause and leaving wide range of activities to be undertaken as a part of regulatory freedom.[86] Some investment tribunals have recognized such exceptions.[87] They have recognized a wide variety of activities as amounting to public policy exception.[88] These public policy grounds may relate to protection of human rights and

---

More general variations may of course be created by treaty.' (p. 524). An ideal example would be exclusion of foreign entities from manufacturing or trading in defence industry.

78. Robert Jennings & Arthur Watts (eds), *Oppenheim's International Law*, 9th ed. Vol. 1. (Harlow, Essex, England: Longman, 1992), 897-900; Above note 77 (Brownlie), 520.
79. Above note 48 (*Methanex Corporation v United States of America*), para. 25.
80. Above note 78 (Oppenheim's International Law), 904-911; Above note 77 (Brownlie), 520.
81. Above note 71 (UNCTAD), xiii; Rudolf Dolzer &Christopher Schreuer, *Principles of International Investment Law* (Oxford: Oxford University Press, 2012), 206.
82. Above note 77 (Brownlie), 525-528.
83. Article 3, German Model Bilateral Investment Treaty, 2008; Art. 4 &Annexure B, Norway Draft Model Bilateral Investment Treaty, 2007.
84. Above note 45 (*S.D. Myres* case), para. 250.
85. Above note 81 (Dolzer and Schreuer), 181.
86. *Emilio Agustín Maffezini v The Kingdom of Spain*, Jurisdiction, ICSID Case No. ARB/97/7, 25 January 2000, para. 62; *See* Egypt-German Bilateral Investment Treaty, 2005.
87. Fredrico Ortino 'Non-discriminatory Treatment in Investment Disputes' in *Human Rights in International Investment Law and Arbitration*, Pierre-Marie Dupuy, Ernst-Ulrich Petersmann & Francesci Franiconi (eds) (Oxford: Oxford University Press, 2010), 361. *See* above note 45 (*S.D. Myres* Case).
88. Tribunals have held that following actions would not attract responsibility although they were discriminatory: regulations adopted to comply with the standards stipulated in the Basel Convention. Above note 45 (*S.D. Myres* Case), para. 255; regulations aimed at allowing new entrants in the lumber industry [Above note 45 (Talbot Inc v The Government of Canada), para.

vulnerable persons. Several resolutions have been adopted by the General Assembly of the United Nations, allowing discriminatory treatment for: a) protective measures to promote welfare of particular indigenous groups; b) the measures must be wanted by these groups; c) based on the needs of particular groups and not race or colour or classification; and d) not be continued for longer than strictly necessary.[89] These examples show that there are a wide variety of public interests, which would have to be achieved, and they cannot be limited in a fixed list.

§8.03 PUBLIC INTEREST

The importance of public interest is reflected in the phrase *salas populi suprema lex esto*: public interest is supreme. Public interest is considered to be a general principle of law covered by Article 38 (1) (c) and 'permits the welfare and security of the nation as a whole to override the rights and interests of individuals, nationals or aliens…'.[90] The maxim represents a fundamental law of every civilized country, of which an international tribunal shall take judicial notice.[91] International tribunals have recognized this principle.[92] State has the discretion to decide which actions are necessary in public interest, unless it can be shown that the actions are clearly arbitrary and violate rights of jurisdiction.[93] A State has to show that 'a case for the exercise of this discretion' existed.[94] The priorities of a society that would fall within the purview of public purpose shall be decided 'by reference to the society's current standard of reasonably acceptable behavior.'[95] Measure for the protection of environment and labour standards are definitely within the category of legitimate public interests to pursue.[96]

As a compromise between indirect expropriation, and the need for conservation of regulatory freedom, it has been suggested that in limited, such as, protection of public order and morality, protection of human health and environment and taxation

72]; regulations undertaken for control of tax revenues, discouraging smuggling, protection of intellectual property rights and prohibition of gray market sales (*Marvin Feldman v Mexico*, Award, ICSID Case No. ARB (AF)/99/1, 16 December 2002, para. 170); regulations to ensure that sugar industry remains only in the hands of solvent enterprise (*Gami Investments, Inc. v The Government of the United Mexican States*, Final Award, UNCITRAL, 15 November 2004, para. 114.

89. Above note 69 (McKean), 91.
90. Above note 18 (Cheng), 30-31.
91. *Ibid.*, 30.
92. *Great Venezuelan Railroad* case, (1903) X RIAA 468, 472-473.
93. *Lozar Rokash* case, American Turkish Claims Settlement (1937) Nielson's Opinion and Reports 503, 509; Hochbaum Case, *Upper Silesian Arbitral Tribunal* (1934) 5 Collection of Decisions 140, 162.
94. *Faber* case, Ven. Arb.(1903), 600, 626, 630.
95. Thomas Waelde & Abba Kolo, 'Environmental Regulation, Investment Protection and 'Regulatory Taking' in International Law' *International and Comparative Law Quarterly* 50 (2001): 811, 827.
96. Allan Weiner, 'Indirect Expropriations: The Need for a Taxonomy of "Legitimate" Regulatory Purposes' *International Law Forum* 5 (2003): 166, 174-175.

(word omitted?).[97] Any effort to limit regulatory freedom and public interest to some limited specific situations, obviates the very essence of flexibility involved in the term 'public interest'. An illustrative definition of regulatory freedom or public interest introduces rigidity. Therefore, it is best left to the States to determine if appropriate situations exist, which could be then reviewed by the investment tribunal to see if there is a reasonable nexus between the measure and the objective aimed to be achieved. The choice of public interest to be achieved is defended based upon on positive law as well as principles of morality.[98]

The choice of its contents differs from one country to another.[99] This is natural since there would be cultural sensitivities, and societal objectives that would differ from one country to another. As Judge Spender pointed out that 'it cannot be determined within a formula. It is a conception'.[100] It is not that there are no criteria. There are criteria that domestic systems have evolved, but they are open ended.[101] The ICJ has consistently followed a deferential approach to determinations of domestic courts, declaring them to be 'sensitive issues' because these are matters of 'public policy', on which only the domestic courts are competent and aptly equipped to comment.[102] States enjoy a 'wide regulatory "space" for regulations' on issues of public policy – 'reflecting national views on public morals' and the states are free to change their regulatory framework for achievement of these public policy objectives.[103] A state can override the rights of aliens if there are genuine public interest concerns.[104] 'Public policy considerations' act as an important exception to treatment standards. For example, the scope of the MFN clause is substantially limited in the context of public policy and regulatory exercise in furtherance of public policy would not attract liability for breach of the MFN treatment standard.[105]

In the context of ECT, Schreuer argues that public purpose is one of the criteria for legal expropriation, and also one of the criteria for a valid regulatory measure. Thus, the distinction between a regulation and expropriation is irrelevant. State must pay compensation in all situations.[106] Public interest, as a criterion for regulation is different from 'public purpose' criteria for legal expropriation. Public purpose or public

97. Andrew Newcomb, 'The Boundaries of Regulatory Expropriation in International Law', *International Centre for Settlement of Investment Disputes Review – Foreign Investment Law Journal* 20 (2005): 1, 3.
98. Levi, The International Ordre Public Revue de Droit International 57 (1994): 66-67; *Kuwait Airways Corporation v Iraqi Airways Company and the Republic of Iraq*, 116 ILR 571.
99. Alexander Orakheashvili, *Peremptory Norms in International Law* (Oxford: Oxford University Press, 2006), 14.
100. Above note 20 (*Guardianship and Infants* case), 122.
101. Above note 99 (Orakheashvili), 15.
102. *Payment of Various Serbian Loans Issued by France (France v Kingdom of Serbs, Crovates and Slovanes)*, 1929 PCIJ (Series A) No. 20, 46.
103. *International Thunderbird Gaming Corporation v Mexico*, Award, UNCITRAL, IIC 136 (2006), 26 January 2006, Ad Hoc Tribunal.
104. Above note 18 (Cheng), 31.
105. Above note 86 (*Maffezini v Spain*), para. 62; *See* Agreement Between Arab Republic of Egypt and the Federal Republic of German concerning Encouragement and Reciprocal Protection of Investments, 2005.
106. Above note 15 (Schreuer), 144; Aikaterini Titi, *The Right to Regulate in International Investment Law* (Germany: Nomos Verlagsgesellschaft, Baden-Baden, 2014), 148-50.

utility is much narrower, and limited to expropriation cases. For a valid expropriation, the property ought to be taken and then applied for a public utility. But for a regulation, there is no question of public utility. The other problem with the argument is that it stakes far too much weight on the only criterion of public purpose. It ignores the role of a bona fide action. It is not a criterion for valid expropriation. It is an important criterion originating in customary international law for determining the legitimacy of the regulation. This determination is crucial. If it is found that the regulation is not adopted in good faith, it would amount to expropriation; otherwise it would be protected as a regulation.

While identifying specific instances of public interest introduced undesired inflexibility, some of the umbrellas under which exercise of regulation for protection of public interest may be identified. These areas are also termed as areas of public policy, since these policies are aimed at protecting public interest. Thus, public interest and public policy could be safely used interchangeably.

Public policy exists in private as well as public international law. In public international law, it represents common interests of the international community – expressed through *jus cogens* and *erga omnes* obligations. *Jus cogens* norms are supreme and non-derogable norms of international law, also referred as peremptory norm. A peremptory norm is 'a norm accepted and recognized by the international community of States as a whole as a norm from which no derogation is permitted and which can be modified only by a subsequent norm of general international law having the same character'.[107] A treaty that is contrary to these peremptory norms is illegal and invalid.[108] Needless to say, these norms are applicable to investment treaties.[109] The peremptory norms are not only negative in nature, imposing restrictions on exercise of their power, but they are also positive and enabling in nature. Peremptory norms can be enforced in a national system through the doctrine of incorporation.[110] States are under an obligation to undertake regulations that give effect to these norms. Any such legislation, in spite of contravening treatment standards would be justified. In view of the supremacy of the peremptory norms, any other treaty obligation conflicting with this obligation disappears.[111] Although these norms are limited to vital interests, such as, torture and slavery, the treatment standards have to yield to regulatory exercise undertaken to perform these obligations because 'peremptory norms operate as a public order protecting the legal system from incompatible laws, acts and transactions'.[112] Additionally, States may have to legislate to protect *erga omnes* norms:

107. Article 53, Vienna Convention on the Law of Treaties, 1969.
108. *Ibid.*
109. Above note 75 (Sornarajah), 469-473; See Moshe Hirsch, 'Conflicting Obligations in International Investment Law: Investment Tribunal's Perspective' in *The Shifting Allocation of Authority in International Law: Considering Sovereignty, Supremacy and Subsidiary*, Yuval Shany and Tomer Broude (eds) (Hart Publishing, 2008), 323-343; *See Desert Lines Project LLC v The Republic of Yemen*, Award, ICSID Case No. ARB/05/17, 6 February 2008.
110. Above note 99 (Orakheashvili), 541-542. This discussion is limited to court actions, but there can be regulations passed for implementation of *jus cogens* norms.
111. Below note 165, para. 35, this discussion is in the context of norms conflicting with *jus cogens*.
112. Above note 99 (Orakheashvili), 10.

responsibility owed by the State towards the international community.[113] Maintaining and respecting cultural diversity is the responsibility of international law.[114] These responsibilities of the State fall under the category of international public policy.[115]

States have obligation to legislate and to implement obligations under international law. These may be stipulated in treaties, where treaties provide for the minimum standard and leave the manner of its implementation with the State, for example, labour standards.[116] States have the freedom to decide the manner to give effect to international obligations at the municipal level. This could happen through the process of 'transformation' where the international obligation is incorporated in domestic legal system as a national statute.[117] Once this process takes place, the international obligation is transformed in municipal system and then interpreted in accordance with municipal law.[118] There are various other situations such as, economic, cultural, and social development, covered under the right of self-determination, where regulations are made for achievement of these purposes which would satisfy the requirement of public interest.[119]

There are other norms of international law that may have to be protected through regulations, although they are not strictly binding in nature. States may have to enact legislations for protection of community interests, such as environment,[120] peace and security, cultural rights,[121] development,[122] human rights,[123] public health,[124] etc. Some norms possess enormous significance in the international community and in the psyche of the States. Example of such a norm would be eradication of corruption. There are various aspects of corruption that are yet not covered by traditional international law, but condemned by the international society. Bribery is unanimously condemned by societies around the world, including major religious and moral schools of thought

113. *See* Case Concerning East Timor (*Portugal v Australia*), Judgment, (1995) ICJ Report 90.
114. International Covenant on Economic, Social and Cultural Rights; Art. 2 & Art. 15(4) United Nations Educational, Scientific and Cultural Organisation Convention.
115. Juliane Kokott & Frank Hoffmeister, 'International Public Order', in *The Max Planck Encyclopedia of Public International Law*, Rüdiger Wolfrum (ed.) (Oxford University Press, 2008) www.mpepil.com, 28 April 2013. Investment tribunals have recognised the role and importance of international public policy. *See World Duty Free Company Ltd v The Republic of Kenya*, ICSID Case No. ARB/00/7, Award, 4 October 2006, paras 138–157; *Inceysa Vallisoletana S.L. v Republic of El Salvador*, Award, 2 August 2006, paras 245–252; *Phoenix Action, Ltd. v The Czech Republic*, ICSID Case No. ARB/06/5, Award, 15 April 2009, paras 111–113.
116. Pierre-Marie Dupuy, 'International Law and Domestic (Municipal) Law' in *Max Planck Encyclopedia of Public International Law*, Rüdiger Wolfrum (ed.) (New York: Oxford University Press, 2008), para. 45.
117. *Ibid.*, paras 46, 48.
118. *Ibid.*, para. 52.
119. Article 1(2), The Charter of United Nations, 1945.
120. Jorge Viñuales, *Foreign Investment and the Environment in International Law* (Cambridge: Cambridge University Press, 2012).
121. Valentina Vadi, *Cultural Heritage in International Investment Law and Arbitration* (Cambridge: Cambridge University Press, 2014).
122. Muthucumaraswamy Sornarajah, *Resistance and Change in the International Law of Foreign Investment* (Cambridge: Cambridge University Press, 2015).
123. Pierre-Marie *Dupuy*, Ernst-Ulrich *Petersmann*, and Francesco *Francioni* eds., *Human Rights in International Investment Law and Arbitration* (Oxford; New York: Oxford University Press, 2009).
124. Above note 121(Vadi).

due to the immense consequences on the society at large, especially in developing countries.[125] The field of international treaty making in this field lacks precision, but no one can doubt the evil effects of corruption.[126] There are other examples as well. The Principles for Responsible Investment were issued under the auspice of the United National Environment Programme,[127] the Basel Convention on the Control of Transboundary Movements of Hazardous Wastes and their Disposal,[128] Basel Committee on Banking Supervision,[129] etc. These norms are imposed on the actors in the market to protect public interest and assist the market economy.[130] Through international public policy, States can legislate and take regulatory measures to enforce those international conventions, although the host State is not formally a party to them.[131] States may even undertake regulations to ensure that corporate behaviour confirms with international human rights standards.[132] Regulation to give effect to international public policy is necessary for human dignity and fundamental principles because international commercial and economic activity cannot exist in isolation of the interests of the society at large.[133]

In private international law, public policy is called *ordre public*. *Ordre public* is a private international law concept that is originally from municipal law.[134] It is understood in two forms: *ordre public interne* (domestic public policy) and *ordre public international* (international public policy). In both the forms, the freedom of determining the scope of these concepts rests with the States.[135] Public order and policy are interchangeable terms.[136]

---

125. *See* Phillip M Nicholos, 'Outlawing Transnational Bribery Throught the World Trade Organization', *Law and Policy International Business* 28 (1997): 305, 318-21.
126. It is shocking and intimidating to note that an author, under the garb of 'global public interest' tried to undermine the seriousness of corrupt activities. The claim is other interests also need to be considered while repudiating investments tainted by fraud. There can be no relaxation on any technicalities to accommodate any activity of corruption. Goal of investor protection cannot claim precedence over behaviour out rightly immoral and unacceptable. *See* Andreas Kulick, *Global Public Interest in International Investment Law* (Cambridge: Cambridge University Press, 2012), 186.
127. United Nations Principle for Responsible Investment, available at http://www.unpri.org.
128. The Basel Convention the Control of Transboundary Movements of Hazardous Wastes and their Disposal, 1989, available at http://www.basel.int/TheConvention/Overview/TextoftheConvention/tabId/1275/Default.aspx.
129. Working under the Bank for International Settlements, available at http://www.bis.org/bcbs/index.htm.
130. Catherina Kessedjian, 'Transnational Public Policy' in *International Arbitration 2006: Back to Basics*, ed. Albert Jan van den Berg (Kluwer Law International, 2007), 859.
131. Conventions that have come into force but to which State has not become a party yet are an important ingredient of transnational public policy. *Ibid.*, 866.
132. *See* UNHRC, 'Guiding Principles on Business and Human Rights' (United Nations, 2011), available at: http://www.ohchr.org/Documents/Publications/GuidingPrinciplesBusinessHR_EN.pdf.
133. *Ibid.*, 869.
134. Martin Gebauer 'Ordre Public (Public Policy)' in *The Max Planck Encyclopedia of Public International Law*, ed. R Wolfrum Oxford University Press, 2008-, para, 1 www.mpepil.com, 10 October 2015.
135. Above note 99 (Orakheashvili), 17-20.
136. *Ibid.*, 11-21.

Domestic public policy or *ordre public* is an outcome of domestic law. It originates in private international law and is employed to protect basic values. It is used as a device to avoid unacceptable outcomes that violate those basic values of a State.[137] Domestic public policy emanates from mandatory national laws that are of utmost importance to the society and citizens of the State from which they cannot derogate.[138] These principles are fundamental principles of law and morality, which the State wishes to protect, and would normally be engendered in the constitution or parts of civil laws.[139] States are frequently required to make regulations to achieve social, economic and political goals of the society. They are based on the premise that the responsibility of States towards its citizens cannot be obviated. *Ordre public internationale* is different from international public order in international law, which is concerned with community interests of the international community as a whole.[140]

Public policy plays an important role in treaty interpretation. Judge Lauterpacht has aptly stated its importance: 'it is seldom, if ever, suggested that it is not an indispensable instrument of the interpretation, application and development of the law.'[141] A treaty obligation cannot be presumed to operate in contravention of public policy and legislations passed towards domestic policy are to be upheld.[142] According to Judge Lauterpacht, there are certain principles of law that are implicit and they continue to operate irrespective of the presence of a treaty. These are considerations of public policy and reflect regulatory freedom. He said:

> It can be found only in the fact that that particular object is expressly permitted by the treaty or implicitly authorized by it by virtue of some principle of public or private international law-a principle such as stems from public policy or from a cognate, although more limited, principle, which is often no more than another formulation of public policy, namely, that certain categories of laws, such as criminal laws, police laws, fiscal laws, administrative laws, and so on, are binding upon all the inhabitants of the territory notwithstanding any general applicability of foreign law.[143]

Explaining the relationship of *ordre public* to the sources of international law, Judge Quintana stated that:

> *Ordre public* is indissolubly bound up with the general principles of law recognized by civilized nations which, under Article 38, paragraph I (c) of the Statute, the Court is required to apply as a main source of law in discharging its function of deciding in accordance with international law such disputes as are submitted to it. This means that the application of these principles is the subject of an international

137. Above note 134 (Gebauer).
138. Above note 130 (Kessedjian), 859.
139. Herbert Kronke Patricia Nacimientom Dirk Otto & Nicola Christine Port, *Recognition and Enforcement of Foreign Arbitral Awards: A Global Commentary on the New York Convention.* (Wolters Kluwer Law & Business, 2010), 367.
140. Above note 134 (Gebauer), para. 2.
141. Above note 20 (*Guardianship of Infants* case), 95.
142. *Ibid.*, 72-3. In that case, the Swedish law on guardianship of minors was upheld on the ground of public policy, irrespective of the provisions of Convention on the Guardianship of Infants 1902.
143. *Ibid.*, (Separate Opinion of Judge Lauterpacht), 81.

> undertaking by all Members of the United Nations and by those States which have adhered to the Statute of the Court.[144]

Judge Quintana expressed the view that *ordre public* of a national order would override international treaty obligations.[145] Fitzmaurice rightly criticized this an extreme view.[146] A balanced approach would be the one adopted by Judge Lauterpacht, where he considers that a domestic legislation would continue to operate if it is reasonable and adopted in good faith.[147]

Thus, public interest or public policy may take a variety of forms, for which, regulations may be adopted by States.

The discussion of the three criteria of regulatory freedom is done under distinct sub-headings. They all are interconnected and each one is a constitutive element of others. As shown above, non-discrimination depends upon whether the measure is justified on the grounds of public policy and the public policy has to be in turn bona fide. The determination of subjective intent, i.e., bona fide is determined based on three factors: discriminatory; outside the scope of authority; and arbitration or unreasonable.[148] The practical application of these principles is reflected in the standard of review to be applied by investment tribunals. The standard of review and the recent emergence of the proportionality principle are discussed in the following part.

§8.04 STANDARD OF REVIEW

The pertinent and complicated task, after setting out the contents of regulatory freedom is the standard of review a tribunal should apply to decide if the impugned measure satisfies the conditions of regulatory freedom. It is argued that the appropriate standard of review is 'reasonableness' or 'good faith review'.

[A] Meaning of Standard of Review

Standard of review is the extent of scrutiny an international tribunal would exercise to determine if the State has complied with its obligations.[149] Standard of review has been a matter of extensive discussion in domestic law. It has received attention in international law only recently and is an outcome of proliferation of international courts and tribunals. The notion of standard of review represents the degree of deference a judicial

144. *Ibid.*, (Separate Opinion of Moreno Quitana), 107.
145. *Ibid.*
146. Above note 13 (Fitzmaurice), 624-7.
147. Above note 20 (*Guardianship of Infants* Case, Separate Opinion of Judge Lauterpacht), 99-101.
148. Above note 37 (Mamolea), 75-6.
149. Jan Bohanes &Nicholas Lockhart, 'Standard of Review in WTO Law' in Daniel Bethleham, Donald McRae, Rodnet Neufekdm & Isabelle Damme (eds) *The Oxford Handbook of International Trade Law* (Oxford: Oxford University Press, 2009), 378-9; Lukasz Gruszczynski, Wouter Werner, 'Introduction' in Lukasz Gruszczynski and Wouter Werner (eds) *Deference in International Courts and Tribunals: Standard of Review and Margin of Appreciation* (Oxford: Oxford University Press, 2014), 3-4.

body would grant to institutions exercising discretion.[150] The degree of deference represents the extent of discretion that a State enjoys in adopting appropriate regulations. In municipal law, the standard of review may flow from the constitution or a statue. But in most of the cases, the choice of standard is judicially determined. It is based on the constitutional system, in particular, the system of separation of powers a State adopts, and the extent to which the judicial wing intends to grant freedom and discretion to the decision-making body. In international law, since the jurisdiction of international tribunals is founded upon State consent, the standard of review depends on the treaty, based upon which jurisdiction is exercised by the adjudicating body. In the absence of any standard of review stipulated in a treaty that forms the basis of jurisdiction, the standard of reasonableness or good faith review shall be applied, as is done by the ICJ. While the standard of review applied by investment tribunals was inconsistent in the past,[151] the present discourse in investment treaty arbitration leans in favour of proportionality analysis and the necessity test.[152] Prior to discussing the appropriateness of reasonableness, the relevance of proportionality analysis and the necessity test needs to be investigated.

[B] Proportionality Analysis and Necessity Test

Proportionality analysis has been developed by the European Court of Human Rights (ECHR) and the European Court of Justice (ECJ) in cases of right to property under Protocol 1 of the European Convention of Human Rights (ECHR) and measures affecting free movement rights respectively. The GATT Panels, predecessor of the Panel and the Appellate Body of the WTO used to apply the 'necessity test'. However, the Panel and the Appellate Body now apply proportionality analysis.

150. Chiara Ragni, 'Standard of Review and the Margin of Appreciation before the International Court of Justice' in Lukasz Gruszczynski and Wouter Werner (eds) *Deference in International Courts and Tribunals: Standard of Review and Margin of Appreciation* (Oxford: Oxford University Press, 2014), 320.
151. Caroline Henckels, 'The Role of the Standard of Review and the Importance of Deference in Investor-State Arbitration', *Deference in International Courts and Tribunals: Standard of Review and Margin of Appreciation*, eds. Lukasz Gruszczynski and Wouter Wermer (eds.) (Oxford: Oxford University Press, 2014), 117-20.
152. *Te cnicas Medioambientales Tecmed S.A. v The United Mexican States*, ICSID Case No. ARB(AF)/00/2, Award, 29 May 2003, paras 117–119, 121–22; *LG&E Energy Corp., LG&E Capital Corp., LG&E International Inc v Argentine Republic*, ICSID Case No. ARB/02/1, Decision on Liability, 3 October 2006, paras 177, 189–95; *Azurix Corporation v* The Argentine Republic, ICSID Case No. ARB/01/12, Award, 14 July 2006, at paras 310–312; *Suez, Sociedad General de* Aguas de Barcelona S.A., and *InterAgua Servicios Integrales del Agua S.A. v Argentne Republic*, ICSID Case No. ARB/03/17, Decision on Liability, 30 July 2010, paras 215–217; *Glamis Gold Ltd. v United States of America*, UNCITRAL (NAFTA), Award, 8 June 2009, at paras 624–625, 726, 761–71, 779, 803–05; *Deutsche Bank AG v Democratic Socialist Republic of Sri Lanka*, ICSID Case No. ARB/09/2, Award, 31 October 2012, para. 522; Above note 91(Occidental Petroleum Award), paras 402–403.

Although not uniformly applied, the proportionality analysis is understood as a three-prong test. The three stages are: suitability, necessity and proportionality principle *sensu strictio*.[153]

The first stage is 'suitability'. It involves determination of whether the measure is actually suitable to protect the interest sought to be protected. There must be a 'causal relationship between the measure and its object'.[154] There are two aspects of the 'suitability test'. First, the measure shall be for pursuing a legitimate governmental purpose and second, the measure should be generally suitable for achieving that purpose.[155] If a measure is adopted in good faith, then it satisfies these conditions.[156] This test is akin to the standard of reasonableness.

The second stage is of 'necessity'. At this stage, it is investigated whether another alternative measure was available to achieve the objective in a least restrictive manner.[157] Defending State must establish that there was no other alternative available.[158] The requirement of necessity is not satisfied if another less restrictive measure available and that less restrictive measure is equally effective and reasonably feasible.[159] This standard is applied where defences under Article 25 of the ILC Articles on State Responsibility are raised, and was applied by GATT Panels in past. It is discussed in detail below.

The third stage is 'proportionality principle *sensu stricto*'. This is where element of proportionality is applied to determine whether the measure is disproportionate to the restrictions caused.[160] This is the pivotal component of the proportionality test. It involves weighing and evaluation of the interests involved and consideration of other relevant factors.[161] This stage involves complex balancing of interests, including assessment of losses suffered due to the measure and the public interest ultimately achieved.[162]

The second stage of necessity is also available as an independent standard of review in situations of Article 25 of the ILC Articles on state responsibility and Article XX (General Exceptions) GATT. It is an exclusive standard of review for the defence of necessity under Article 25 of the ILC Draft Article's on State Responsibility. If a State has acted contrary to its obligations under a treaty, a State can defend the measure on the ground that the gravity and imminence of the peril was such that the measure

153. Jan Jans, 'Proportionality Revisited' *Legal Issues of Economic Integration* (3)27 (2000): 239, 240-1.
154. *Ibid.*, 239, 240.
155. Above note 126 (Kulick), 186.
156. *Ibid.*, 186-7.
157. Above note 153 (Jans), 239, 240.
158. Panel Report, Canada – Wheat Exports and Grain Imports, para. 6.226; Panel Report, EC – Trademarks and Geographical Indications (US), paras 7.458–7.460; Appellate Body Report, Dominican Republic – Import and Sale of Cigarettes, para. 70.
159. Benedict Kingsbury & Stephan Schill, 'Investor-State Arbitration as Governance: Fair and Equitable Treatment, Proportionality and the Emerging Global Administrative Law', IILJ Working Paper 2009/6 (Global Administrative Law Series) Finalized 08/19/2009, http://www.iilj.org/publications/documents/2009-6.KingsburySchill.pdf; last visited 10 October 2015.
160. Above note 153 (Jans), 239, 241.
161. Above note 126 (Kulick), 188.
162. For various relevant factors *see ibid.*, 198-202.

adopted was the only available safeguard.[163] It must be established that there was no other alternative available.[164] As per the principle of necessity under GATT Article XX, a contracting party cannot resort to a measure contrary to GATT obligations, if an alternative measure is available and could be reasonably expected to be applied, which is not inconsistent with other GATT provisions.[165] The requirement of necessity is satisfied, depending upon 'the extent to which the measure contributes to the realization of the end pursued' and the determination of necessity of the measure 'involves in every case a process of weighing and balancing a series of factors which prominently include the contribution made by the compliance measure to the enforcement of the law or regulation at issue, the importance of the common interests or values protected by the law or regulation, and the accompanying impact of the law or regulation...'.[166] Therefore, the stage of necessity and necessity test as an independent standard requires a party to establish that there was no effective and comparable alternative. Some have argued that this test is appropriate for investment arbitration.[167] There is no justification to import the standard from WTO, which is applied due to specific treaty text. The proportionality and necessity test do not find a justification in investment treaties, except where expressly mentioned, which is not frequent. Both the tests are far more onerous in comparison to the reasonableness test.

During GATT, the test was limited to necessity. However, now the test is similar to proportionality analysis of the ECtHR.[168] The necessity test is subdivided into three parts: first, whether the measure is designed to protect or further an objective permissible under the relevant treaty;[169] second, whether the measure is necessary which in turn requires the assessment of whether the measure contributes to the realization of the ends and is least restrictive for international trade;[170] and third, a comparison between the challenged measure and the available alternatives.[171]

The ICJ has applied proportionality in cases where either the text of customary international law so directed, or the text of the treaty so directed. The ICJ never set out

163. International Law Commission, 'Draft articles on Responsibility of States for Internationally Wrongful Acts, with commentaries 2001' (2001) II Yearbook of the International Law Commission, 31, 83-4.
164. Advisory Opinion Concerning Legal consequences of Palestinian Wall in the Occupied Palestinian Territory, (9 July 2004) ICJ reports, para. 140.
165. Thailand – Restrictions on Importation of and Internal Taxes on Cigarettes, GATT Panel Report, GATT BISD (DS10/R – 37S/200), 7 November 1990, 223; United States- Section 337 of the Tariff Act of 1930, GATT Panel Report, GATT BISD (L/6439-36S/345 36th Sup.), 7 November 1989, 345; US – Gasoline, Panel Report, paras 6.26, 6.28; Brazil – Retreaded Tyres, Appellate Body Report, para. 172; Above note 165 (Canada), para. 6.226.
166. Korea – Measures Affecting Imports of Fresh, Chilled and Frozen Beef, Appellate Body Report, 11 December 2000, WT/DS161/AB/R, para. 164.
167. Valentina Vadi & Lukazs Gruszczynski, 'Standard of Review in International Investment Law and Arbitration: Multilevel Governance and the Commonweal' *Journal of International Economic Law* (2013): 613, 628-31; Above note 151 (Henckels), 117-8.
168. According to Kulick, the reason for adoption of proportionality analysis into WTO jurisprudence is the presence of European members on the Panel and Appellate Body who had served in different capacities in the European Commission. Above note 126 (Kulick), 182.
169. United States – Measures Affecting the Cross-Border Supply of Gambling and Betting Services, Appellate Body Report, WT/DS285/AB/R, 7 April 2005, para. 294.
170. *Ibid.*, para. 306.
171. *Ibid.*, para. 307.

or followed the necessity and proportionality test as applied by the ECHR or the WTO. The references to proportionality and necessity in international law are in relation to actions of States, rather than adjudication. Proportionality as 'the effect of a countermeasure must be commensurate with the injury suffered, taking into account the rights in question'.[172] Instances where the ICJ has applied these tests is where the law specifically demands their application and not as generally applicable standard of review. For example, in the law of countermeasures, the actions taken in response to actions of another State have to be necessary and proportionate in response.[173] The determination of whether a response to armed attack is lawful depends on 'the necessity and the proportionality of the measures taken in self-defense.'[174] The extent of action that may be taken in self-defence has to be proportional to the armed attack.[175] In humanitarian law, the attack has to be proportional to the objectives intended to be achieved by attacking a military target.[176]

In the overall process of proportionality analysis, there are other factors that play a role, such as 'margin of appreciation'. Margin of appreciation means the extent of discretion a State enjoys in making choices, and the restraint in the exercise of review that the judicial authority would exercise.[177] It has developed in the context of ECHR and represents 'the breadth of deference' European Court of Human Rights will grant to the decisions of national legislative, executive and judicial decision makers.[178] Margin of appreciation is intertwined into proportionality, and at the last stage of balancing, it is expected to perform a greater role for determining if the impugned regulation is appropriate.[179] Some view that margin of appreciation is adequate to protect regulatory freedom.[180]

The premise for application of proportionality analysis and margin of appreciation is that a State is in breach of international obligations. The ECHR and DSB have applied necessity test for exceptions rather than substantive rights. The premise of this argument is that regulatory freedom is a prohibited action or in the nature of exception.[181] The discussion in Chapters 6 and 7 has shown that regulatory freedom is a separate and distinct right and it does not breach provisions of investment treaties. Regulatory freedom and indirect expropriation are not in an 'either or' relationship. A

---

172. Gabčíkovo-Nagymaros Project (Hungary/Slovakia), Judgment of 25 September 1997, (1997) ICJ Reports 7, para. 85.
173. *See* E Cannizzaro, 'The Role of Proportionality in the Law of International Countermeasures' *European Journal of International Law*, 12 (2001): 889, 898; Above note 42 (Case Concerning Military and Paramilitary Activities), paras 237, 249.
174. *Ibid.*, (*Military and Paramilitary Activities* case), para. 194.
175. *Ibid.*, para. 249; Above note 42 (Armed Activities on the Territory of the Congo), para. 147.
176. Michael Newton and Larry May (eds.), *Proportionality in International Law* (Oxford; New York: Oxford University Press, 2014).
177. Above note 126 (Kulick), 189-192.
178. William Burke-White & Andreas von Staden, 'Private Litigation in a Public Law Sphere: The Standard of Review in Investor- State Arbitration' *Yale Journal of International Law* 35 (2010): 283, 304-305.
179. *Ibid.*, 306-308.
180. *Ibid.*, 342-344.
181. Caroline Henckels, 'Indirect Expropriation and the Right to Regulate: Revisiting Proportionality Analysis and the Standard of Review in Investor-State Arbitration' *Journal of International Economic Law* 15(1) (2012): 223, 226-7 (footnotes excluded).

norm is violated when the behaviour contradicts the norm.[182] Since regulatory freedom is a free-standing right and not in violation of a treaty norm, margin of appreciation is inappropriate.

If a State has breached its obligations, then there is no need to show deference. But at the same time, a State shall not be held responsible if it has not breached any obligation. For international responsibility to arise, the action in question should be 'wrongful'.[183] An action is wrongful if it causes injury to an alien 'without sufficient justification' and the injury is intended or facilitated.[184] A sufficient cause includes laws enacted for 'maintaining public order, health, or morality'.[185] Losses arising out of a legitimate regulatory measure do not amount to indirect expropriation.[186] Passing of regulation by a State on a topic covered by a treaty does not by itself constitute violation of the treaty. The answer normally depends on circumstances and there can be no fixed rule.[187] Enacting of legislation would not result into violation of treaty provisions per se.[188]

Proportionality test can be applied only when it has a basis in the treaty text.[189] The ECtHR has applied it in relation to expropriation because Article 1, Protocol 1 of the ECHR, specifically protects right to property.[190] Investment treaties do not protect right to property, instead they only direct that the investments be subject to certain treatment standards. Protection of property is a higher standard as compared to the treatment standards in investment treaties.[191] In other cases where proportionality has been applied by the ECHR, its concern has been to ensure 'least restrictive negative effects for market integration' in the European Union.[192]

Various arguments are advanced to proffer the relevance of proportionality analysis for investment arbitration, especially indirect expropriation cases.[193] Burke-White and Von Staden have supported the use of proportionality analysis on two grounds. First, since investment arbitration involves review of regulatory actions of States, it is better understood as public law adjudication. Second, in situations where treaty text allows.[194] The first reasoning is purely based on analogy of subject matter of adjudication or review. Similarity of subject matter of adjudication cannot be the basis of transplant where the text does not support. Similarity of subject matter can help in

182. Hans Kelsen, *Principles of International Law* (New York: Rinehart, 1952),133.
183. Article 1, Draft Convention on the International Responsibility of States for Injuries to Aliens, (hereinafter 'Harvard Draft for Injuries to Aliens'), *American Journal of International Law* 55 (1961): 545, 548.
184. Article 3.1 a), Harvard Draft for Injuries to Aliens.
185. *Ibid.*, Art. 4.2.
186. *Ibid.*, Art. 5.
187. Applicability of the Obligation to Arbitrate under Section 21 of the United Nations Headquarters Agreement of 26 June 1947 (footnote [71] 83 above), at 30, para. 42.
188. (2001) vol. II part II Yearbook of the International Law Commission 31, 57, citing ICJ held in LaGrand, Judgment at 497, paras 90–91.
189. Above note 153 (Jans), 239, 242-3.
190. *See* Christoph Grabenwarter, *European Convention on Human Rights: Commentary* (Germany: C.H. Beck, Hart, Nomos, Helbing Lichtenhahn Verlag, 2014), 367-88.
191. Above note 75 (Sornarajah), 374-375.
192. Above note 153 (Jans), 239, 240-241.
193. Above note 151 (Henckels), 228-237.
194. Above note 178 (Burke-White & Staden), 288-295.

understanding the conceptual framework but cannot form the basis for importing substantive provisions from another system. Proportionality is not a secondary norm, it is a primary norm emanating from the treaty text. This critique goes to the root of the second argument as well, which claims to rely on the text. In present investment treaties, there is no justification to rely on proportionality except in limited situations, where defence of necessity, or other circumstances precluding wrongfulness have been expressly mentioned. Again, the standard in cases of necessity defence under Article 25 is different from proportionality analysis. There is no basis in investment treaties to apply proportionality analysis.[195] Application of proportionality analysis obfuscates the clear language of expropriation clauses which do not warrant application of any such principle.[196] Application of proportionality analysis defeats the well-recognized customary principle of powers for which a State does not attract responsibility.[197] Likewise, relevance of proportionality on the ground that arbitrators and State have an agent-principal relationship[198] does not provide any doctrinal support for invocation of proportionality analysis in investment arbitration cases.

The three stage proportionality analysis grants wide discretion to the adjudicator, especially at the stage of deciding whether other reasonable alternatives were available. The adjudicator is free to be imaginative, without realizing the financial, social and other constrains that a State would have to operate with.[199] The extent of this discretion may be justifiable in domestic set-up, where judges are fully aware of the local situations or within an integrated treaty framework, like the EU. Proportionality has been applied in the European context due to the presence of a community, and the need to uphold specifically agreed community interests stipulated in the treaty. The ECtHR has held that European Union constitutes a distinct community with distinct goals, very different from the international community.[200] Even in the case of WTO, there is a community of interest which the Panels and Appellate Body are to protect and promote.[201] Investment treaties do not create such a distinguishable community with its own objectives and priorities.[202] Investment treaty arbitration lacks 'key characteristics of domestic legal system such as institutional safeguards and constitutional features like "independence of the judiciary", "appellate review", "separation of powers", and a written constitution that gives judges the right to decide which compelling interest should prevail…'.[203] Investment treaty arbitration is a unique

195. Above note 75 (Sornarajah), 365-366.
196. Prabhash Ranjan, 'Using the Public Law Concepts of Proportionality to Balance Investment Protection with Regulation in International Investment Law: A Critical Appraisal' *Cambridge Journal of International and Comparative Law* 3 (2014): 853, 864-867.
197. *Ibid.*, 853, 870.
198. Alex Stone Sweet, 'Investor State Arbitration: Proportionality's New Frontier', *Law and Ethics of Human Rights* 4(1) (2010): 69.
199. For a multilayered criticism of the proportionality analysis *see* above note 126 (Kulick), 172-3.
200. *Al-Jedda v The United Kingdom*, European Court of Human Rights, Grand Chamber, Application no. 27021/08, Judgment, Strasbourg, 7 July 2011, para. 102.
201. *See* Deborah Cass, *The Constitutionalization of the World Trade Organization: Legitimacy, Democracy and Community in the International Trading System* (Oxford: Oxford University Press, 2005).
202. Above note 151 (Henckels), 129-130.
203. Above note 196 (Ranjan), 853, 862.

system, with ad hoc tribunals composed of party appointed arbitrators. They are unaware of the overall legal, social and political context of the dispute and not in a position to 'weigh and balance complex value-laden regulatory objectives'.[204] Also, an investment tribunal is unfit for applying margin of appreciation. For conducting such an exercise, the judicial body shall be enforcing uniform principles of governance in the background of 'relatively homogenous cultural and religious background'.[205] In a diverse system of investment arbitration, application of proportionality analysis raises issues of legitimacy and transparency in the adjudicative process.

The application of proportionality analysis in municipal law has shown that it inevitably involves the exercise of replacing the decisions made of the decision-making body by the adjudicating body.[206] Leading municipal jurisdictions are skeptical about proportionality analysis. In the United States, proportionality test is not applied as it would be inconsistent with the doctrine of separation of powers.[207] The UK Courts have been skeptical about the proportionality analysis. They have applied it only in four situations: a) cases involving an element of European Community Law,[208] b) determination of appropriateness of penalty by administrative authority,[209] c) violation of fundamental rights[210] and d) violations of UK Human Rights Act.[211] The last two situations have arisen in the context of detentions in relation to terrorist activities. The role of proportionality in balancing individual rights versus community interests has arisen in cases of terrorism, where the balancing involves liberties of an individual on one hand and security of the community on the other; a situation hardly comparable to investor protection.[212] If proportionality is not applicable in contexts, either specifically or implicitly, UK courts stick to reasonableness.[213] None of the four circumstances can be equated with investor protection. If investors wish to claim fundamental rights, then they would have to go to municipal courts which are the only and appropriate forum to agitate it. Regarding human rights, as stated in Chapter 5, it is doubtful if investors can claim human rights, unless they have been violated independently. Furthermore, in *Biloune v Ghana Investments*, the Tribunal declined to decide human rights violations, since they fell outside the jurisdiction of the tribunal.[214] In view of the disagreement in major municipal jurisdictions, it can hardly be called a general principle.[215]

204. *Ibid.*, 853, 862.
205. Above note 75 (Sornarajah), 368-9.
206. Paul Craig, 'Unreasonableness and Proportionality in UK Law' in Eyelyn Ellis (ed.) *The Principle of Proportionality in the Laws of Europe* (Oxford: Hart Publishing, 1999), 87-89.
207. Above note 75 (Sornarajah), 373.
208. Above note 206 (Craig), 89-90.
209. *Ibid.*, 91.
210. *Ibid.*, 92-3.
211. *Ibid.*, 93-4.
212. Above note 75 (Sornarajah), 367-8.
213. Above note 206 (Craig), 90-1.
214. *Antoine Biloune, Marine Drive Complex Ltd. v Ghana Investments Centre, the Government of Ghana, Awards*, 27 October 1989, (1994) XIX Yearbook Commercial Arbitration 11, 15.
215. Above note 75 (Sornarajah), 380-1.

[C] Reasonableness or Good Faith Review

If investment treaties do not contain proportionality or any other standard of review, then what is the appropriate standard of review? It is assumed that due to silence of investment treaties, standard of review may be borrowed from other fields.[216] The standard of review for determining whether regulatory freedom is legitimate, and if it satisfies all the elements is 'reasonableness' or 'good faith review'. The ICJ has used this standard in two situations: in the absence of any other standard flowing from the treaty, and specifically in cases where regulatory freedom has been challenged by treaty provisions. The ICJ has laid down the principle that if the treaty or customary norm does not stipulate a higher standard of review, then the standard of good faith review has to be applied, whereby a State is not responsible as long as it is acting in good faith.[217] Also, since investment treaties are silent on the standard and cases which involves a confrontation between regulatory freedom and treaty standards, reasonableness is the appropriate standard.

In the cases of exercise of discretion, power must be exercised reasonably and in good faith.[218] Good faith review requires that the exercise shall be reasonable.[219] Good faith obligation would be violated where the actions are manifestly unreasonable.[220] Good faith, non-arbitrariness and reasonableness, are all interconnected, and reference to one, encompasses others.

Reasonableness is an important ingredient for establishing that the regulatory measure is a disguised measure. Any such measure would be an exercise constituting abuse of rights and thus, fail to be bona fide. On the extent of inquiry that an international court can conduct in situations of alleged reasonableness, the ICJ viewed that a State enjoyed large degree of discretion since 'the primary responsibility for assessing the need for regulation and for choosing, on the basis of its knowledge of the situation, the measure that it deems most appropriate to meet that need. It will not be enough in a challenge to a regulation simply to assert in a general way that it is unreasonable. Concrete and specific facts will be required to persuade a court to come to that conclusion'.[221]

In the *Navigation Rights* case, the ICJ pointed out that reasonableness is a part of bona fide. A measure is unreasonable if it does not have any relationship with the

216. Above note 167 (Vadi and Gruszczynski), 613, 616.
217. Above note 41 (Certain Questions of Mutual Assistance), para. 145; Barcelona Traction, para. 9; Above note 181 (Nagyamaros), para. 142; Case Concerning Territorial Dispute (Libya Arab Jamahiriya/Chad), Judgment, para. 51; ICJ Jurisdictional Immunities of the State (*Germany v Italy*) para. 137; For practice of ICJ *see* John F O'Connor, Good Faith in International Law (Aldershot, Dartmouth Publishing, 1991), 81.
218. Rights of Nationals of the United States of America in Morocco (*France v United States of America*), Judgment of 27 August 1952, (1952) ICJ Reports 176, 212.
219. Oliver Corten, 'Reasonableness in International Law' in *Max Planck Encyclopedia of Public International Law*, ed. Rüdiger Wolfrum (New York: Oxford University Press, 2008), paras 2, 7.
220. *Fisheries* case (*United Kingdom v Norway*), Judgment of 18 December 1951 (1951) ICJ Reports 116, 141-2.
221. *Ibid.*, para. 101, at 253.

objective it seeks to achieve.[222] The allegation of unreasonableness of a measure has to be substantiated with evidence that the measure does not achieve the objective for which the measure was adopted. In the words of the ICJ:

> It will not be enough in a challenge to a regulation simply to assert in a general way that it is unreasonable. Concrete and specific facts will be required to persuade a court to come to that conclusion.[223]

Similarly, in the *Whaling in the Antarctic* case, the ICJ applied reasonableness as a standard of review. The Court did not discuss the standard independently, but legal principles can be deducted from its application. The reasonableness standard of review depends on 'whether a State's decision is objectively reasonable, or "supported by coherent reasoning and respectable scientific evidence and ..., in this sense, objectively justifiable."'[224] The test is whether the measures are reasonable for achieving the objectives for which the measure is adopted.[225]

Overall, two factors emerge from the standard of reasonableness or good faith review: whether there are reasons for adopting of regulations, and if/whether those reasons are sufficient to achieve the objective for which regulations are adopted.[226] If this relationship fails, then it would not be a bona fide measure. The scale of reasonableness employed by the tribunals to show nexus between measure and policy is widely inconsistent between international tribunals.[227] An appropriate approach is the one adopted by the ICJ in the *Whaling in the Antarctic* case, wherein the ICJ declined to impose any precise threshold, in excess of which an action would be unreasonable.[228] The Court has to see 'design and implementation are reasonable in relation to achieving its stated objectives. This standard of review is an objective one'.[229] The decision of reasonableness will depend on facts and circumstances, and all these factors have to be considered cumulatively.[230]

An international tribunal posed with the question of determining whether the actions of a State are undertaken in good faith, it 'must examine whether the exercise of the right was in pursuit of legitimate interests protected' and 'whether, in light of the obligations assumed by the State, the exercise of the right was calculated to prejudice

222. Dispute Regarding Navigational and Related Rights (*Costa Rica v Nicaragua*) (2009) ICJ Reports 213, para. 87 (a).
223. *Ibid.*, para. 101, also *see* para. 106.
224. Whaling in the Antarctic (*Australia v Japan: New Zealand intervening*), Judgment of 31 March 2014, para. 66.
225. *Ibid.*
226. Elettronica Sicula S.p.A. (ELSI) (*United States of America v Italy*) (Judgment of 20 July 1989) (1989) ICJ Reports 15, para. 129, at 76.
227. Above note 89 (Ortino), 362. In some cases plausible connection is considered to be adequate; Above note 90 (UNCITRAL, Final Award), para. 144; a slightly rigid approach was adopted in Pope & Talbot, where the policy had to be reasonably related to the rational policy, *See* above note 44 (Pope & Talbot), paras 78, 81; In *S.D. Myres* strict necessity test was applied, Above note 45 (*S.D. Myres* Case), para. 255.
228. Above note 42 (*Military and Paramilitary Activities* Case), 419-20.
229. Above note 238 (*Whaling in the Antarctic* Case), para. 67.
230. The 'Camouco' Case (*Panama v France*), Application for Prompt Release, Judgment, 7 February 2000, ITLOS, List of Cases No. 5, paras 65–70.

the rights and legitimate interests of the other party under the Treaty'.[231] Thus, the principle of good faith, sometimes called the theory of abuse of rights, governs the exercise of rights. While protecting the legitimate interests of the owner of the right, it imposes limitations that would render its exercise compatible with other party's legitimate interests. It keeps a 'fair balance... between the respective interests of the parties and a line is drawn delimiting their respective rights.' Any overstepping is abuse of rights and absence of good faith would attract responsibility.[232]

The nature of norm subject to review also has an impact on the standard of review. Norms are aimed at achieving certain end, and States are left with greater discretion for achievement of these end-oriented measures.[233] Regulatory measures adopted for legitimate public interest are such end-oriented measures and shall not be subject to a standard of review higher than that emanating from investment treaties.

231. Above note 18 (Cheng), 128-129.
232. *Ibid.*, 129.
233. Jean-Pierre Cot, 'Margin of Appreciation' in Rüdiger Wolfrum (ed.) *Max Planck Encyclopedia of Public International Law*, (New York: Oxford University Press, 2012), para. 13.

CHAPTER 9
Conclusions

Regulatory freedom is not subsumed or destroyed by indirect expropriation. It exists independently as a customary international law right. It is controlled to the extent that it must satisfy the conditions of bona fide, non-discriminatory and public interest. Once a regulation satisfies these conditions, then a State is not responsible for losses caused due to regulatory freedom.

In the first part, composed of a set of introductory Chapters (1, 2 and 3), the aim was to introduce two concepts: regulatory freedom and indirect expropriation, interaction of which has been discussed in this thesis. After introducing the objective and methodology of the thesis in Chapter 1, the second Chapter was dedicated to the meaning of regulatory freedom (police powers) in international law. The Chapter was aimed at dispelling the impression that regulatory freedom or police powers is exclusively a municipal law concept originating in the decision of American courts. In reality, regulatory freedom has independently belonged to international law and has been referred to in the writings of classical writers of international law. The concept of regulatory freedom may have been absolute in relation to internal administration of State, but in international law, it was always limited. The precise limitations have developed over time and now recognized in decisions of different international adjudication bodies. Another fundamental point is that there is a difference between a regulatory measure and an expropriatory measure. In the first case, a State is not responsible for payment of compensation, whereas in the second, it is. An expropriatory measure may take various forms such as indirect, creeping or tantamount to, but the underlying character of the measure remains the same, i.e., expropriatory. An expropriatory measure is juridically different from a regulatory measure, and their conceptual difference was explored in Chapter 2. Chapter 3 analytically scrutinized the approach of investment tribunals towards regulatory freedom. It was noticed that although negligible in number, some tribunals have out rightly rejected the presence of regulatory freedom after States have entered into investment treaties. The second group has recognized regulatory freedom, but subjected it to the sole effects doctrine. As per the sole effects doctrine, only the effect on the investments is to be seen and the reasons for the adoption of the measure, i.e. the nature of the measure is irrelevant. The consequence of this approach is that in all cases, State has to pay compensation once the extent of loss crosses a certain threshold. This second group, even after recognizing regulatory freedom, makes it practically ineffective by subjecting regulatory freedom to sole effects doctrine. The third group has fully recognized regulatory freedom and emphasized the need to analyse the nature of the measure to decide if the measure is expropriatory or regulatory. However, possibly due to judicial economy, they have not dwelt in detail into these issues. The following parts elaborated on regulatory freedom and its relationship with indirect expropriation.

The second part was concerned with the choice between two conflicting concepts: nature of the measure versus the sole effects doctrine to decide whether the standard of indirect expropriation was breached. The problems with the sole effects doctrine, emanating from its origin and its application were established in Chapter 4 and towards the end of that Chapter, it was noted that international tribunals have preferred the nature of the measure rather than the effect. They have looked at the nature of the measure to decide whether a measure is regulatory or expropriatory rather than the effect of the measure. Chapter 5 explored theoretical arguments advanced to understand regulatory freedom. It was found that some scholars and tribunals have professed case-by-case analysis. According to this principle, the arbitrator shall be left with complete discretion to decide how to delineate between regulatory freedom and indirect expropriation because no 'bright line' between the two can be drawn. This excessive discretion with arbitrators will only enhance the legitimacy crises in investment treaty arbitration, and an international tribunal cannot claim, the extent of discretion the supporters of the case-by-case method make. There are serious theoretical flaws with the sole effects doctrine as well. Therefore, the sole effects doctrine is not a suitable basis for distinguishing regulatory freedom from indirect expropriation. Regulatory freedom has been sought to be discredited through the emergence of Global Administrative Law (GAL). As originally conceived, GAL was meant to be a comment on the emergence of international institutions and their influence. This concept was applied to investment tribunals to claim that they are controlling States through the review of their actions. By relying on awards, where the tribunals have given capacious interpretations to treaty provisions and limited regulatory freedom of States, GAL is seeking to grant legitimacy to the interpretation extravagance of investment tribunals. There are deeper challenges about doctrinal basis for raising the GAL argument, which the proponents themselves are conscious about.

After discrediting the sole effects doctrine and establishing the role of nature of the measure, the next step was analysing the character of regulatory freedom, which was done in the third set of chapters (Chapters 6–8). It was established in Chapter 6 that regulatory freedom is a customary international law norm which emanates from sovereignty. Sovereignty is a multifaceted legal concept and regulating freedom is a part of it. Regulatory freedom also satisfies the requirements of *opinio juris* and state practice to qualify as a custom. Once it is established that regulatory freedom is a custom, the next stage is of interaction of regulatory freedom as a customary norm and indirect expropriation as a treaty norm. It was found that customary norms are not subsumed or destroyed by treaty norms, rather they continue to operate until they are expressly excluded or are directly incompatible. Furthermore, the area of application of regulatory freedom is distinct from indirect expropriation. There is no conflict between the two norms as long as regulatory freedom satisfies the constitute elements set out in customary law: which are bona fide, non-discriminatory and public interest. These three elements of regulatory freedom, and the appropriate standard of review were discussed in Chapter 8. It was found that the appropriate standard of review in cases of regulatory freedom is of good faith review or reasonableness. There is no basis to invoke the proportionality analysis or the necessity test.

In the quest for finding the 'bright line' dividing regulatory freedom and indirect expropriation, the investment tribunals and academic scholarship have trailed a wrong path. The bright line, already exists. The concern is then a harmonious application of the two norms, originating in two different sources: custom and treaty. The creation of conflict is hypothetical and unsustainable. Accordingly, the exercise of balance of the two rights through interpretative mechanisms such as proportionality, which does not have any basis in the treaty text, is ill founded. The exercise commences on the wrong premise. It first disregards the role of regulatory freedom in totality, and then tries to do a favour to States by declaring that proportionality may be used, as alms to protect regulatory freedom, which is otherwise non-existent. The discussion above has shown that regulatory freedom is of a same stature as indirect expropriation (a treaty standard) and they are not in conflict with one another.

General conclusions relating to the relationship between regulatory freedom and indirect expropriation:

(a) Regulatory freedom is an inalienable part of State sovereignty and satisfies the requirements of a custom. It is also referred to as 'police powers' and includes wide range of functions from protection of health, security, environment, morals, economic health, etc. The tasks falling under regulatory freedom are constantly changing and evolving, depending on the need of the times and cannot be rigidly defined.

(b) The losses caused by a regulation are an indirect consequence of a regulatory measure, whereas expropriatory measure - direct or indirect, has an element of direct losses - either intended for taking the property away or destroying the property with malafide intentions.

(c) The conventional understanding in present scholarship and arbitral tribunals is that indirect expropriation exists if there is interference with property rights. This impression is incorrect and is created due to the prevalence of the sole effects doctrine in the jurisprudence of investment tribunals. However, the scholarships as well as the tribunals have failed to notice that the sole effects doctrine has a doubtful origin. The appropriate approach is to look at the nature of the regulatory measure and decide whether it is a legitimate regulatory exercise. A regulation is a legitimate exercise if it satisfies the condition of bona fide, non-discriminatory and public interest.

(d) There is no conflict between regulations and expropriation clauses. The customary law, 'right to regulate' is not taken away by the treaty clause of indirect expropriation. The effect of the treaty clause is to taper or modify the regulatory freedom. These restrictions are comprehensively covered in the bona fide/good faith requirement.

(e) Regulatory freedom being a custom, always operates despite the presence of treaty provisions. There is no need of specific reference in a treaty. Its scope is not affected unless specifically so altered in the treaty.

(f) A 'bright line' between regulatory freedom and indirect expropriation already exists. A State is not responsible for losses caused to the foreign investor due to legitimate regulations. A regulation fails to be legitimate if it fails one of the tests of bona fide, non-discriminatory and public interest. All these requirements have to exist, and they are customary international law.

(g) Regulatory freedom cannot be fixed into specific examples, such as taxation measures or measures undertaken for protection of health and environment. The subjects of regulatory freedom are ever-evolving. They all would be protected, provided they satisfy the constitutive elements of regulatory freedom.

(h) Thus, regulatory freedom operates as an exception to the responsibility to pay compensation for losses suffered to the foreign investors, as a result of regulations, that satisfy the conditions of regulatory freedom.

The next stage of this research could be to explore the inter-relationship between regulatory freedom and other treatment standards, especially the fair and equitable treatment standard. Additionally, since the elements of regulatory freedom are developed on the basis of general international law, the operation of regulatory freedom of States in other branches of international law such as WTO law and the law of the sea, could be explored.

Bibliography

Books

Bruce Ackerman, *Economic Foundations of Property* (Boston: Little Brown, 1975).

George Aldrich, *The Jurisprudence of the Iran-United States Claims Tribunal* (New York: Clarendon Press Oxford, 1996).

Tom Allen, *The Right to Property in Commonwealth Constitutions* (Cambridge: Cambridge University Press, 2000).

C Amerasinghe, *Evidence in International Litigation* (The Hague: Martinus Nijhoff, 2005).

R P Anand, *Sovereign Equality of States in International Law* (Delhi: Hope India Publications, 2008).

Hannah Ardent, *On Violence* (San Diego, California: Harcourt, Brace & Co., 1970).

Albert Badia, *Piercing the Veil of State Enterprises in International Arbitration* (Alphen aan den Rijn: Kluwer Law International, 2014).

R Doak Bishop, James Crawford and W Michael Reisman, *Foreign Investment Disputes: Cases, Materials and Commentary* (The Hague: Kluwer Law International, 2005).

Eirik Bjørge, *The Evolutionary Interpretation of Treaties* (Oxford: Oxford University Press, 2014).

Nigel Blackaby, Constantine Partasides, Alan Redfern and Martin Hunter, *Redfern and Hunter on International Arbitration* (Oxford: Oxford University Press, 2009).

J Brierly, *The Law of Nations* (Oxford: Oxford University Press, 1955).

Ian Brownlie, *Principles of Public International Law* (7th ed.; Oxford: Oxford University Press, 2008).

Lesley Brown (ed.), *The New Shorter Oxford English Dictionary: On Historical Principles* (vol. I, Oxford: Clarendon Press, 1993).

Charles N Brower and Jason D Brueschke, *The Iran-United States Claims Tribunal* (The Hague: Martinus Nijhoff Publishers, 1998).

Deborah Cass, *The Constitutionalization of the World Trade Organization: Legitimacy, Democracy and Community in the International Trading System* (Oxford: Oxford University Press, 2005).

Bin Cheng, *General Principles of Law as Applied by International Courts and Tribunals* (London: Stevens and Sons, 1953).

Richard Collings and Nigel White, *International Organizations and the Idea of Autonomy: Institutional Independence in the International Legal Order* (Abingdon, Oxon: Routledge, 2011).

James Crawford, *State Responsibility: The General Part* (Cambridge: Cambridge University Press 2013).

James Crawford, *The Creation of States in International Law* (2nd ed.; Oxford: Oxford University Press, 2006).

Patrick Daillier and Alain Pellet, *Droit International Public* (7th ed.; Paris: Librairie générale de droit et de jurisprudence, 2002).

Anthony D'Amato, *The Concept of Custom in International Law*, (Ithaca, New York: Cornell University Press, 1971).

V D Degan, *Sources of International Law* (The Netherlands: Martinus Nijhoff Publishers, 1997).

Nicolas Diebold, *Non-Discrimination in International Trade in Services* (Cambridge: Cambridge University Press, 2010).

Rudolf Dolzer and Christoph Schreuer, *Principles of International Investment Law* (2nd ed.; Oxford: Oxford University Press, 2012).

Rudolf Dolzer and Margarete Stevens, *Bilateral Investment Treaties* (Hague: Martinus Nijhoff Publishers, 1995).

Pierre-Marie Dupuy, F Francioni and E U Petersmann (eds), *Human Rights in International Investment Law and Arbitration* (Oxford: Oxford University Press, 2009).

Pierre-Marie Dupuy, 'International Law and Domestic (Municipal) Law' in Rüdiger Wolfrum (ed.), *Max Planck Encyclopedia of Public International Law* (New York: Oxford University Press, 2008).

Sebastian Escarcena, *Indirect Expropriation in International Law* (Cheltenham, UK: Edward Elgar Publishing, 2014).

Sidney Fine, *Laissez Faire and the General-Welfare State: A Study of Conflict in American Thought, 1865–1901* (USA: University of Michigan, 1956).

Gerald Fitzmaurice, *The Law and Procedure of the International Court of Justice* (vol. II, Cambridge: Grotius Publications Ltd, 1986).

Isi Foighel, *Nationalization: A Study in the Protection of Alien Property in International Law* (London: Stevens and Sons Ltd, 1957).

S Friedman, *Expropriation in International Law* (London: Stevens and Sons Ltd, 1953).

Bryan Garner, *Black's Law Dictionary* (10th ed.; USA: Thomson Reuters, 2014).

Richard Gardiner, *Treaty Interpretation* (Oxford: Oxford University Press, 2008).

Christoph Grabenwarter, *European Convention on Human Rights: Commentary* (Germany: C.H. Beck, Hart, Nomos, Helbing Lichtenhahn Verlag, 2014).

Christine Gray, *Judicial Remedies in International Law* (Oxford: Oxford University Press, 1987).

Hugo Grotius, 'De Jure Belli ac Pacis Libri Tres' in James Brown Scott (ed.), *The Classics of International Law* (Oxford: Clarendon Press, 1925).

Gus Van Hartern, *Investment Treaty Arbitration and Public Law* (New York: Oxford University Press, 2007).

Grigorio Ivanovich Tunkin, Kunihiro Jjima, Theodor Dams and Rüdiger Wolfrum, *International Law and Municipal Law: Proceedings of the German Soviet Colloquy on International Law* (Berlin: Dunker & Humblot, 1968).

John H Jackson, *The World Trading System: Law and Policy of International Economic Relations* (2nd ed.; Cambridge: MIT Press, 1989).

Robert Jennings and Arthur Watts (eds), *Oppenheim's International Law* (vol. 1, 9th ed.; Harlow, Essex: Longman Group UK, 1992).

Konstantin Katzarov, *The Theory of Nationalisation* (The Hague: Martinus Nijhoff, 1964).

James Kent, *Commentaries on American Law* (15th ed.; New York: O Halsted, 2002).

Hans Kelsen, *Principles of International Law* (New York: Rinehart, 1952).

Hans Kelsen, *General Theory of Norms* (translated by Michael Hartney) (Oxford: Clarendon Press, 1991).

Hege Elisabeth Kjos, *Applicable Law in Investor-State Arbitration: The Interplay Between National and International Law* (Oxford: Oxford University Press, 2013).

Bladine Kriegel, *The State and the Rule of Law* (translated by Marc A LePain and Jeffry C Cohen) (Princeton: Princeton University Press, 1995).

Herbert Kronke and Others, *Recognition and Enforcement of Foreign Arbitral Awards: A Global Commentary on the New York Convention* (The Netherlands: Wolters Kluwer Law & Business, 2010).

Andreas Kulick, *Global Public Interest in International Investment Law* (Cambridge: Cambridge University Press, 2012).

Hersch Lauterpact, *Oppenheim's International Law* (7th ed.; vol. 1, London: Longman Group UK, 1948).

Hersch Lauterpacht, *The Development of International Law by the International Court* (Cambridge: Grotius Publications Ltd., 1982).

Martin Loughlin, *The Idea of Public Law*, (Oxford: Oxford University Press, 2004).

Neil MacCormick, *Legal Reasoning and Legal Theory* (Oxford: Clarendon Press, 1994).

Warwick McKean, *Equality and Discrimination under Intentional Law* (Oxford: Clarendon Press, 1983).

Campbell McLachlan, Laurence Shore and Matthew Weiniger, *International Investment Arbitration: Substantive Principles* (Oxford: Oxford University Press, 2007).

Arnold McNair, *The Law of Treaties* (2nd ed.; Oxford: Clarendon Press, 1961).

Andrew Mitchell, *Legal Principles in WTO Disputes* (Cambridge: Cambridge University Press, 2008).

Mohsen Mohebi, *The International Law Character of the Iran-United States Claims Tribunal* (The Netherlands: Kluwer Law International, 1999).

Montesquieu, *The Spirit of the Laws* [1978] (translated by Anne M Cohler, Basia Carolyn Miller, and Harold Samuel Stone (eds)) (Cambridge: Cambridge University Press, 1989).

Santiago Montt, *State Liability in Investment Treaty Arbitration: Global Constitutional and Administrative Law in the BIT Generation* (Oxford: Hart Publishing, 2009).

Allahyar Mouri, *The International Law of Expropriation as Reflected in the Work of the Iran-U.S. Claims Tribunal* (The Netherlands: Martinus Nijhoff Publishers, 1994).

Stephan W Schill, *Multilateralization of International Investment Law* (Cambridge: Cambridge University Press, 2009).

Michael Newton and Larry May (eds), *Proportionality in International Law* (Oxford; New York: Oxford University Press, 2014).

Andrew Newcombe and Lluis Paradell, *Law and Practice of Investment Treaties: Standards of Treatment* (The Netherlands: Kluwer Law International, 2009).

John F O'Connor, *Good Faith in International Law* (Aldershot: Dartmouth Publishing, 1991).

Alexander Orakhelashvili, *Peremptory Norms in International Law* (Oxford: Oxford University Press, 2006).

D Osborne and T Gaebler, *Reinventing Government: How the Entrepreneurial Spirit is Transforming the Public Sector* (USA: Addison Wesley, 1992).

Martins Paparinskis, *The International Minimum Standard and Fair and Equitable Treatment* (Oxford: Oxford University Press, 2013).

Joost Pauwelyn, *Conflict of Norms in Public International Law: How WTO Law Relates to Other Rules of International Law* (Cambridge: Cambridge University Press, 2003).

B Charles Proctor, *Mann on the Legal Aspect of Money* (6th ed., Oxford: Oxford University Press, 2005).

J Rabkin, *Why Sovereignty Matters* (Washington DC: American Enterprise Institute, 1998).

Andres Rigo Sureda, *Investment Treaty Arbitration: Judging under Uncertainty* (Cambridge, New York: Cambridge University Press, 2012).

Shabtai Rosenne, *Developments in the Law of Treaties, 1945-1986* (Cambridge: Cambridge University Press, 1989).

Jeswald W Salacuse, *The Law of Investment Treaties* (New York: Oxford University Press, 2010).

Dan Sarooshi, *International Organizations and Their Exercise of Sovereign Powers* (Oxford: Oxford University Press, 2005).

Stephan W Schill, *The Multilateralisation of International Investment Law*, (Cambridge: Cambridge University Press, 2009).

Stephan W Schill (ed.), *Investment Treaty Arbitration and Comparative Public Law* (Oxford: Oxford University Press, 2010).

David Schneiderman, *Constitutionalizing Economic Globalization: Investment Rules and Democracies Promise* (USA: Cambridge University Press, 2008).

Georg Schwarzenberger, *The Inductive Approach to International Law* (London: Stevens and Sons Ltd, 1965).

Georg Schwarzenberger, *International Law: As Applied by International Courts and Tribunals*, (3rd ed.; vol. I, London: Stevens and Sons Ltd, 1957).

George Sharswood (ed.) Sir William Blackstone, *Commentaries on the Laws of England in Four Books* (vol. 1 [1753], Philadelphia: J.B. Lippincott Company, 1893).

Bruno Simma, Daniel-Erasmus Khan, Georg Nolte and Andreas Paulus (eds), *The Charter of the United Nations* (2nd ed.; Oxford: Oxford University Press, 1994).

John Simpson and Edmund Weiner (eds), *The Oxford English Dictionary* (2nd ed.; vol. II, Oxford: Clarendon Press, 1989).

Walter Skeat, *Etymological Dictionary of the English Language* (new revised edition and enlarged 1935) (Oxford: Clarendon Press, 1935).

Adam Smith, *Lectures on Jurisprudence*, R. L. Meek and Others (eds) (Oxford: Clarendon Press, 1978).

M. Sornarajah, *The Pursuit of Nationalized Property* (Dordrecht, Boston: Martinus Nijhoff, 1986).

M. Sornarajah, *Resistance and Change in the International Law on Foreign Investment* (Cambridge: Cambridge University Press, 2015).

M. Sornarajah, *The International Law on Foreign Investment* (3rd ed.; Cambridge: Cambridge University Press, 2010).

John Sprankling, *The International Law of Property* (Oxford: Oxford University Press, 2014).

Hugh Thirlway, *The Sources of International Law* (Foundations of Public International Law, Oxford: Oxford University Press, 2014).

Daniel Thürer, *International Humanitarian Law: Theory, Practice, Context* (The Netherlands: Martinus Nijhoff, 2011).

Aikaterini Titi, *The Right to Regulate in International Investment Law* (Germany: Nomos Verlagsgesellschaft, Baden-Baden, 2014).

Valentina Vadi, *Cultural Heritage in International Investment Law and Arbitration* (Cambridge: Cambridge University Press, 2014).

Kenneth Vandevelde, *Bilateral Investment Treaties: History, Policy and Interpretation* (New York: Oxford University Press, 2010).

Emer de Vattel, *The Law of Nations: Or, Principles of the Law of Nature, Applied to the Conduct and Affairs of Nations and Sovereigns, with Three Early Essays on the Origin and nature of Natural Law and on Luxury*, Edited and with an Introduction by Béla Kapossy and Richard Whatmore (USA: Liberty Fund, 2008).

Emer de Vattel, Le droit de gens, ou principles de la loi naturelle (Neuchâtel, 1774).

Jorge Viñuales, *Foreign Investment and the Environment in International Law* (Cambridge: Cambridge University Press, 2012).

Michael Waibel, *Sovereign Defaults Before International Courts and Tribunals* (Cambridge: Cambridge University Press, 2011).

Michael Waibel and Others, *The Backlash Against Investment Arbitration: Perceptions and Reality* (The Netherlands: Wolters Kluwer Law & Business, 2010.

A. J. van der Walt, *Constitutional Property Clauses: A Comparative Analysis* (Cambridge, Massachusetts: Kluwer Law International, 1999).

Gillian White, *Nationalization of Foreign Property* (London: Stevens and Sons Ltd, 1961).

Marjorie M. Whiteman, *Damages in International Law* (Washington: U.S. Govt. Print Office, 1937).

Karol Wolfake, *Custom in Present International Law* (2nd ed.; The Netherlands: Martinus Nijhoff, 1993).

Joseph Worcester, *Worcester's Academic Dictionary: A New Etymological Dictionary of the English Language* (Philadelphia: J.B. Lippincott Company, 1910).

B.A. Wortley, *Expropriation in International Law* (Cambridge: Cambridge University Press, 1959).

M. Moran, *The British Regulatory State: High Modernism and Hyper Innovation* (Oxford: Oxford University Press, 2003).

Robert Baldwin, Martin Cave and Martin Lodge (eds), *The Oxford Handbook of Regulation* (Oxford; New York: Oxford University Press, 2010).

Books Chapters and Articles

Michael Akehurst, 'The Hierarchy of the Sources of International Law' (1975) 47 British Yearbook of International Law 273.

George Aldrich, 'What Constitutes Compensable Taking of Property? The Decisions of the Iran-United States Claims Tribunal' (1994) 88(4) American Journal of International Law 585.

Gudmundur Alfredsson 'Article 17' in Asbjørn Eide and Others (eds), *The Universal Declaration of Human Rights: A Commentary* (Scandinavian University Press: Norway, 1992).

José Alvarez, 'State Sovereignty is Not Withering Away: A Few Lessons for the Future' in Antonio Cassese (ed.), *Realizing Utopia: The Future of International Law* (Oxford: Oxford University Press, 2012).

Wolfgang Alschner, 'Americanization of the BIT Universe: The Influence of Friendship, Commerce and Navigation (FCN) Treaties on Modern Investment Treaty Law' (2013) 5 Goetting Journal of International Law 455.

José Alvarez, 'The Once and Future Foreign Investment Regime' in Mahnoush Arsanjani (ed.), *Looking to the Future: Essays on International Law in Honour of W Michael Reisman*, (Boston: Martinus Nijhoff Publishers, 2011).

José Alvarez, 'The Return of the State' (2011) 20 Minnesota Journal of International Law 223.

José Alvarez, 'Why are We "Re-calibrating" our Investment Treaties?' (2010) 4 World Arbitration and Mediation Review 143.

R P Anand, 'The Role of Individual and Dissenting Opinions in International Adjudication' (1965) 14 International and Comparative Law Quarterly 788.

Freya Baetens, 'Enforcement of Arbitral Awards: "To ICSID or Not to ICSID is Not the Question" in Todd Weiler, Ian Laird (eds), *The Future of ICSID* (The Netherlands: Juris Arbitration Series, Martinus Nijhoff Publishers, 2013).

Robert Baldwin, Martin Cave and Martin Lodge, 'Introduction: Regulation – The Field and the Developing Agenda' in Robert Baldwin, Martin Cave and Martin Lodge (eds), *The Oxford Handbook of Regulation* (Oxford; New York: Oxford University Press, 2010).

Robert Baldwin, Martin Cave and Martin Lodge 'The Future of Regulation' in Robert Baldwin, Martin Cave and Martin Lodge (eds), *The Oxford Handbook of Regulation* (Oxford; New York: Oxford University Press, 2010).

Yas Banifatemi, 'The Law Applicable in Investment Treaty Arbitration' in Katia Yannaca-Small (ed.), *Arbitration under International Investment Agreements: A Guide to the Key Issues* (New York: Oxford University Press, 2010).

Vicki Been and Joel C. Beauvais, 'The Global Fifth Amendment? NAFTA's Investment Protections and the Misguided Quest for an International "Regulatory Takings" Doctrine' (2003) 78(1) NYU Law Review 30.

Albert Jan van den Berg, 'Dissenting Opinions by Party-Appointed Arbitrators in Investment Arbitration' in Mahnoush Arsanjani et al. (eds), *Looking to the Future: Essays on International Law in Honor of W. Michael Reisman* (The Netherlands: Martinus Nijhof Publishers, 2011).

Samantha Besson, 'Sovereignty' in Rüdiger Wolfrum (ed.), *Max Planck Encyclopedia of Public International Law* (New York: Oxford University Press, 2008).

Jan Bohanes and Nicholas Lockhart, 'Standard of Review in WTO Law' in Daniel Bethlehem and Others (eds), *The Oxford Handbook of International Trade Law* (Oxford: Oxford University Press, 2009).

J Braithwaite, 'The New Regulatory State and the Transformation of Criminology' (2007) 40 British Journal of Criminology 222.

Ian Brownlie, 'The Reality and Efficacy of International Law' (1981) 52 British Yearbook of International Law 1.

Maurizio Brunetti, 'The Iran-United States Claims Tribunal, NAFTA Chapter 11, and the Doctrine of Indirect Expropriation' (2001) 2 Chicago Journal of International Law 203.

Michael Byers, 'Abuse of Rights: An Old Principle, A New Age' (2002) 47 McGill Law Journal 389.

Giacintodella Cananea, 'Minimum Standards of Procedural Justice in Administrative Adjudication' in Stephan Schill (ed.), *International Investment Law and Comparative Public Law,* (Oxford: Oxford University Press, 2010), p. 35.

E Cannizzaro, 'The Role of Proportionality in the Law of International Countermeasures' (2001) 12 European Journal of International Law 889.

G C Christie, 'What Constitutes A Taking of Property under International Law' (1962) 38 British Yearbook of International Law 307.

Luigi Condorelli and Antonio Cassese, 'Is Leviathan Still Holding Sway over International Dealings?' in Antonio Cassese (ed.), *Realizing Utopia: The Future of International Law* (Oxford: Oxford University Press, 2012).

Luigi Condorelli, 'Customary International Law: The Yesterday, Today, and Tomorrow of General International Law' in Antonio Cassese (ed.), *Realizing Utopia: The Future of International Law* (Oxford: Oxford University Press, 2012).

Olivier Corten, 'Reasonableness in International Law' in Rüdiger Wolfrum (ed.), *Max Planck Encyclopedia of Public International Law* (New York: Oxford University Press, 2008).

Jean-Pierre Cot, 'Margin of Appreciation' in Rüdiger Wolfrum (ed.), *Max Planck Encyclopedia of Public International Law* (New York: Oxford University Press, 2012), para. 13.

Paul Craig, 'Unreasonableness and Proportionality in UK Law' in Eyelyn Ellis (ed.), *The Principle of Proportionality in the Laws of Europe* (Oxford: Hart, 1999).

James Crawford, 'The Criteria for Statehood in International Law' (1976) 48 British Yearbook of International Law 93.

John R Crook, 'Decision of the Iran-United States Claims Tribunal' (1984) 78 American Society of International Law Proceedings 221.

Antony D'Amato, 'Human Rights as Norms of Customary International Law' in Antony D'Amato (ed.), *International Law: Process and Prospect* (New York: Transnational Publishers, 1987).

Antony D'Amato, 'Good Faith' (1992) Encyclopedia of Public International Law vol. 2, 599.

Antony D'Amato, 'Domestic Jurisdiction' (1992) Encyclopedia of International Law vol. 2, 1090.

Nicolas DiMascio and Joost Pauwelyn, 'Non-discrimination in Trade and Investment Treaties: Worlds Apart or Two Sides of the Same Coin?' (2008) 102 American Journal of International Law 48.

Yoram Dinstein, 'The Interaction Between Customary International Law and Treaties' (2006) 322 Recueil des Cours 259.

Rudolph Dolzer, 'Indirect Expropriation of Alien Property' (1988) 1 ICSID Review-FILJ 41.

Martin Domle, 'Foreign Nationalizations: Some Aspects of Contemporary International Law', (1961) 55 American Journal of International Law 585.

Edward Dumbauld, 'Dissenting Opinions in International Adjudication' (1942) 90 University of Pennsylvania Law Review 929.

Dunham, 'A Legal and Economic Basis for City Planning' (1958) 58 Columbia Law Review 650.

T Epps and C Flood, 'Have We Traded Away the Opportunity of Innovative Health Care Reform? The Implications of the NAFTA for Medicare' (2002) 47 McGill Law Journal 747.

Antonios Estache and Liam Wren-Lewis, 'On the Theory and Evidence on Regulation of Network Industries in Developing Countries' in Robert Baldwin, Martin Cave and Martin Lodge (eds), *The Oxford Handbook of Regulation* (New York: Oxford University Press, 2010).

Alexander P Fachiri, 'The Oscar Chinn Case' (1935) 16 British Yearbook of International Law 189.

Mike Feintuck, 'Regulatory Rationales Beyond the Economic: In Search of the Public Interest' in Robert Baldwin, Martin Cave and Martin Lodge (eds), *The Oxford Handbook of Regulation* (New York: Oxford University Press, 2010).

Gerald Fitzmaurice, 'Some Problems Regarding the Formal Sources of International Law' in J. H. W. Verzijl (ed.) '*Symbolae Verzijl: présentées au professeur J.H.W. Verzijl à l'occasion de son LXXiéme anniversaire*' (The Hague: Martinus Nijhodd, 1958).

Gerald Fitzmaurice, 'The Law and Procedure of the International Court of Justice 1951-5: Treaty Interpretation and Other Treaty Points' (1957) 33 British Yearbook of International Law 237.

Christopher Ford, 'Judicial Discretion in International Jurisprudence: Article 38(1)(c) and "General Principles of Law"' (1994–1995) 5 Duke Journal of Comparative and International Law 35, 53–56.

L Yves Fortier and Stephen Drymer, 'Indirect Expropriation in the Law of International Investment: I Know It When I See It, or *Caveat Investor*' (2004) 19 ICSID Review-FILJ 293.

Susan Franck, 'Legitimacy Crisis in Investment Treaty Arbitration: Privatizing Public International Law Through Inconsistent Decisions' (2005) 73 Fordham Law Review 1521.

James W Garner, 'An Arbitration Case Between Norway and the United States' (1923–1924) 4 British Yearbook of International Law 159, 160.

Tarcisio Gazzini, 'The Role of Customary International Law in the Field of Foreign Investment' (2007) 8 Journal of World Trade and Investment 691.

Christopher Gibson and Christopher Drahozal, 'Iran-United States Claims Tribunal Precedent in Investor-State Arbitration' (2006) 23(6) Journal of International Arbitration 521.

Martin Gebauer 'Ordre Public (Public Policy)' in R Wolfrum (ed.), *The Max Planck Encyclopedia of Public International Law* (Oxford: Oxford University Press, 2008).

E Gillman, 'The End of ISA in Ecuador? An Analysis of Article 422 of the Constitution of 2008', (2008) 19 American Review of International Arbitration 269.

E Gillman, 'The End of ISA in Ecuador? An Analysis of Article 422 of the Constitution of 2008', (2008) 19 American Review of International Arbitration 269.

A Gourgourinis, 'The Distinction Between Interpretation and Application of Norms in International Adjudication' (2011) 2 Journal of International Dispute Settlement 31.

A Gourgourinis, 'Lex Specialis in WTO and Investment Protection Law' (2010) 53 German Yearbook of International Law 579.

Lukasz Gruszczynski, Wouter Werner, 'Introduction' in Lukasz Gruszczynski and Wouter Werner (eds), *Deference in International Courts and Tribunals: Standard of Review and Margin of Appreciation* (Oxford: Oxford University Press, 2014).

Carol Harlow, 'Global Administrative Law: The Quest for Principles and Values' (2006) 17 European Journal of International Law 187.

G Van Harten and M Loughlin, 'Investment Treaty Arbitration as Species of Global Administrative Law' (2006) 17 European Journal of International Law 121.

V Heiskanen, 'The Doctrine of Indirect Expropriation in Light of the Practice of the Iran-United States Claims Tribunal' (2007) 8 Journal of World Investment and Trade 215.

Caroline Henckels, 'The Role of the Standard of Review and the Importance of Deference in Investor-State Arbitration' in Lukasz Gruszczynski and Wouter Wermer (eds), *Deference in International Courts and Tribunals: Standard of Review and Margin of Appreciation* (Oxford: Oxford University Press, 2014).

Caroline Henckels, 'Indirect Expropriation and the Right to Regulate: Revisiting Proportionality Analysis and the Standard of Review in Investor-State Arbitration' (2012) 15(1) Journal of International Economic Law 223.

John Herz, 'Expropriation of Foreign Property' (1941) 35 American Journal of International Law 243.

Rosalyn Higgings, 'The Taking of Property by the State: Recent Developments in International Law' (1982) 176 Recueil des Cours 267.

Rosalyn Higgings, 'A Bavel of Judicial Voices? Ruminations from the Bench' (2006) 55 International Comparative Law Quarterly 791.

Rosalyn Higgins, '"Fundamentals of International Law" in "Legal Precondition of Foreign Investment"' in Rosalyn Higgins (ed.) *Themes and Theories* (Oxford: Oxford University Press, 2009).

M. Hirsch, 'Conflicting Obligations in International Investment Law: Investment Tribunal's Perspective' in Y. Shany and T. Broude (eds), *The Shifting Allocation of Authority in International Law: Considering Sovereignty, Supremacy and Subsidiarity* (Oxford and Portland, Oregon: Hart Publishing, 2008).

Anne K. Hoffmann, 'Indirect Expropriation' in August Reinisch (ed.), *Standards of Investment Protection* (Oxford: Oxford University Press, 2008).

Rainer Hofmann and Tilmann Laubner (eds), 'Article 57' in Andreas Zimmerman, Christian Tomuschat and Karin Oellers-Frahm (eds), *The Statute of the International Court of Justice: A Commentary* (New York: Oxford University Press, 2006).

Seidl-Hohenveldren, 'The Social Functions of Property and Property Protection in Present-day International Law' in Frits Kalshoven et al. (eds), *Essays on the Development of the International Leal Order: In Memory of Haro F Van Panhuys* (USA: Sijthoff & Noordhoff, 1980).

Robert Howse, 'Sovereignty, Lost and Found' in Wenhua Shan, Penelope Simons and Dalvinder Singh (eds), *Redefining Sovereignty in International Economic Law* (USA: Hart Publishing, 2008).

Peter Hulsroj, 'Three Sources – No River, A Hard Look at the Sources of Public International Law with Particular Emphasis on Custom and "General Principles of Law"', (1999) 54 Zeitschrift für öffentliches Recht 219.

John Jackson, 'Sovereignty: Outdated Concept or New Approaches' in Wenhua Shan, Penelope Simons and Dalvinder Singh (eds), *Redefining Sovereignty in International Economic Law* (USA: Hart Publishing, 2008).

Jan H Jans, 'Proportionality Revisited' (2000) 27 Legal Issues of Economic Integration 239.

Robert Jennings, 'What is International Law and How Do We Tell It When We See It?' in *Schweitzerisches Jahrbuchfür Internationales Recht* Martti Koskenniemi (ed.), *Sources of International Law* (England: Ashgate, 2000).

Robert Jennings, 'Sovereignty and International Law' in Gerard Kreijen and Others (eds), *State Sovereignty and International Governance* (Oxford: Oxford University Press, 2002).

Wilferd Jenks, 'Conflict of Law Making Treaties' (1953) 30 British Yearbook of International Law 401.

Daniel Kalderimis, 'Investment Treaty Arbitration as Global Administrative Law: What this Might Mean in Practice?' in Chester Brown and Katie Miles (eds), *Evolution in Investment Treaty Law and Arbitration* (Cambridge: Cambridge University Press, 2012).

Stefan Kadelbach, 'Jus Cogens, Obligations Erga Omnes and Other Rules - The Identification of Fundamental Norms' in Christian Tomuschat and Jean-Marc Thouvenin (eds), *The Fundamental Rules of the International Legal Order: Jus Cogens and Obligations Erga Omnes* (Leiden, Boston: Martinus Nijhoff Publishers, 2006).

Hans Kelsen, 'Sovereignty and International Law' (1960) 48 Georgetown Law Journal 627.

Catherina Kessedjian, 'Transnational Public Policy' in Albert Jan van den Berg (ed.), *International Arbitration 2006: Back to Basics* (The Hague: Kluwer Law International, 2007).

B Kingsbury and S Schill, 'Public Law Concepts to Balance Investor's Rights with State Regulatory Actions in the Public Interest - The Concept of Proportionality' in Stephan W. Schill (ed.), *International Investment Law and Comparative Public Law* (Oxford: Oxford University Press, 2010).

Benedict Kingsbury, Nico Krisch and Richard Stewart, 'The Emergence of Global Administrative Law' (2004–2005) 68 Law and Contemporary Problems 15.

Benedict Kingsbury and Others, 'Global Governance as Administration - National and Transnational Approaches to Global Administrative Law' (2004–2005) 68 Law and Contemporary Problems 1.

Benedict Kingsbury and Stephan W Schill, 'Public Law Concepts to Balance Investor's Rights with State Regulatory Actions in the Public Interest - The Concept of Proportionality' in Stephan W Schill (ed.), *International Investment Law and Comparative Public Law* (Oxford: Oxford University Press, 2010), p. 76.

Alexandre Kiss, 'Abuse of Rights' in Rüdiger Wolfrum (ed.), *Max Planck Encyclopedia of Public International Law* (New York: Oxford University Press, 2008).

E N Van Kleffens, 'Sovereignty in International Law' (1953) 82 Recueil Des Cours 5.

Gabrielle Kauffman-Kohler, 'Arbitral Precedent: Dream, Necessity or Excuse?: The 2006 Freshfields Lecture' (2007) 23(3) Arbitration International 357.

Marek Korowicz, 'Some Present Aspects of Sovereignty in International Law' (1961) 102 Recueil des Cours 5.

Martti Koskenniemi, 'General Principles. Reflections on Constructivist Thinking in International Law' in Martti Koskenniemi (ed.), *Sources of International Law*, (England. Ashgate, 2000) pp. 359–399.

Ursula Kriebaum and Christoph Schreuer, 'The Concept of Property in Human Rights Law and International Investment Law' in Stephan Breitenmoser ua (eds), *Liber Amicorum Luzius Wildhaber, Human Rights Democracy and the Rule of Law* (Germany: Nomos Verlagsgesellschaft, Baden-Baden, 2007).

Ursula Kriebaum, 'Partial Expropriation' (2007) 8 Journal of World Trade & Investment 69.

Nico Krisch and Benedict Kingsbury, 'Introduction: Global Governance and Global Administrative Law in the International Legal Order' (2006) 17 European Journal of International Law 1.

Jurgen Kurtz, 'The Merits and Limits of Comparativism: National Treatment in International Investment Law and the WTO' in Stephan Schill (ed.), *International*

Investment Law and Comparative Public Law (Oxford: Gus Van Harten ord, Oxford University Press, 2010), p. 250.
H L, 'The Chinn Case' (1935) 16 British Yearbook of International Law 162.
Hersch Lauterpacht, 'Restrictive Interpretation and Effectiveness in the Interpretation of Treaties' (1949) 50(1) British Yearbook of International Law 60.
Santiago Legarre, 'The Historical Background of the Police Power' (2007) 9(3) Journal of Constitutional Law 745.
W Levi, 'The International Ordre Public' (1994) 57 Revue de Droit International 57.
M Loughlin and C Scott, 'The Regulatory State' in P. Dunleavy, A Gamble, I Holliday and G Peele (eds), *Developments in British Politics* (Basingstoke: Macmillan Press, 1997).
Vaughan Lowe, 'Regulation or Expropriation?' (2002) 55 Current Legal Problems 447.
I. MacGibbon 'Customary International Law and Acquiescence' (1957) 33 British Yearbook of International Law 115.
G D Majone, 'The Rise of the Regulatory State in Europe' (1994) 17 West European Politics 77.
G D Majone, 'From the Positive to the Regulatory State: Causes and Consequences of Changes in the Modern Governance' (1997) 17(2) Journal of Public Policy 139.
Andrei Mamolea, 'Good Faith Review' in Lukasz Gruszczynski and Wouter Wermer (eds), *Deference in International Courts and Tribunals: Standard of Review and Margin of Appreciation* (Oxford: Oxford University Press, 2014).
A F M Manuruzzaman, 'Expropriation of Alien Property and the Principle of Non-Discrimination in International Law of Foreign Investment: An Overview' (1998–1999) 8 Journal of Transnational Law and Policy 57.
Antonie Martin, 'Investment Disputes after Argentina's Economic Crisis: Interpreting BIT Non-precluded Measures and the Doctrine of Necessity under Customary International Law' (2012) 29 Journal of International Arbitration 49.
Campbell McLachlan, 'Investment Treaties and General International Law' (2008) 57 International Comparative Law Quarterly 361.
F. Mendes, 'The Canadian National Energy Programme: An Example of Assertion of Sovereignty or Creeping Expropriation in International Law' (1981) 14 Vanderbilt Journal of Transnational Law 475.
Frank Michelman, 'Property, Utility, and Fairness: Comments on the Ethical Foundations of the "Just Compensation" Law' (1967) 80 Harvard Law Review 1165.
Andrew Mitchell, 'Good Faith in WTO Dispute Settlement' (2006) 7 Melbourne Journal of International Law 339.
M Moran, 'Understanding the Regulatory State' (2002) 32(2) British Journal of Political Science 391.
Ben Mostafa, 'The Sole Effects Doctrine, Police Powers and Indirect Expropriation under International Law' (2008) 15 Australian International Law Journal 267.
Andrew Newcomb, 'The Boundaries of Regulatory Expropriation in International Law' (2005) 20 ICSID Review – FILJ 1.
Phillip M Nicholos, 'Outlawing Transnational Bribery Throught the World Trade Organization' (1997) 28 Law and Policy International Business 305.

Vincent Nmehielle, 'Enforcing Arbitration Awards under the International Convention for the Settlement of Investment Disputes (ICSID Convention)' (2001) 7 Annual Survey of International and Comparative Law 19.

Michael Oakeshott, 'On the Character of a Modern European State' in *Michael Oakeshott on Human Conduct* (Oxford: Clarendon Press, 1975).

Fredrico Ortino 'Non-discriminatory Treatment in Investment Disputes' in Pierre-Marie Dupuy, Ernst-Ulrich Petersmann and Francesci Franiconi (eds), *Human Rights in International Investment Law and Arbitration* (Oxford: Oxford University Press, 2010).

William W Park, 'Arbitration and the Fisc: NAFTA's "Tax Veto"' (2001) 2 Chinese Journal International Law 231.

William W Park, *Arbitration of International Business Disputes* (New York, Oxford: Oxford University Press, 2012), pp. 319–321.

Cynthia Galvez, '"Necessity," Investor Rights, and State Sovereignty for NAFTA Investment Arbitration' (2013) 46 Cornell International Law Journal 143.

A Parra, 'ICSID and Bilateral Investment' (2000) 17(1) ICSID News 7.

Jan Paulsson and Zachary Douglas, 'Indirect Expropriation in Investment Treaty Arbitration' in Norbert Horn and Stephan Kroll (eds), *Arbitrating Foreign Investment Disputes: Procedural and Substantive Legal Aspects* (The Hague: Kluwer Law International, 2004).

Alain Pellet, 'The Case Law of the ICJ in Investment Arbitration' (2013) 28 ICSID Review-FILJ 223.

James Penner, 'The "Bundle of Rights" Picture of Property' (1966) 43 UCLA Law Review 711.

Asif Qureshi, 'Sovereignty Issues in the WTO Dispute Settlement – A "Development Sovereignty" Perspective' in Wenhua Shan, Penelope Simons and Dalvinder Singh (eds), *Redefining Sovereignty in International Economic Law* (USA: Hart Publishing, 2008).

Aniruddha Rajput, 'Definition of Investment – A Developmental Perspective' (2013) 2 Indian Journal of Arbitration Law 12.

Prabhash Ranjan, 'Using the Public Law Concepts of Proportionality to Balance Investment Protection with Regulation in International Investment Law: A Critical Appraisal' (2014) 3 Cambridge Journal of International and Comparative Law 853.

Chiara Ragni, 'Standard of Review and the Margin of Appreciation before the International Court of Justice' in Lukasz Gruszczynski and Wouter Werner (eds), *Deference in International Courts and Tribunals: Standard of Review and Margin of Appreciation* (Oxford: Oxford University Press, 2014).

Kal Raustiala, 'Rethinking the Sovereignty Debate in International Economic Law' (2003) 6 Journal of International Economic Law 841.

August Reinisch, 'Expropriation' in Peter Muchlinski, Frederico Ortino and Christoph Schreuer (eds), *The Oxford Handbook of International Investment Law* (Oxford: Oxford University Press, 2008).

Steven Reinhold, 'Good Faith in International Law' (2013) 2 UCL Journal of Law and Jurisprudence 40.

W Michael Reisman, 'Has the International Court Exceeded Its Jurisdiction?' (1986) 80 American Journal of International Law 128.

W Michael Reisman and Robert D Sloane, 'Indirect Expropriation and Its Valuation in the BIT Generation' (2003) 74 British Yearbook of International Law 115.

W Michael Reisman, '"Case Specific Mandates" versus "Systematic Implications": How Should Investment Tribunals Decide?: The Freshfields Arbitration Lecture' (2013) 29 Arbitration International 131.

Anthea Roberts, 'The Present – Investment Arbitration as a Governance Tool for Economic International Relations?' in Albery Jan van den Berg (ed.), *Arbitration: The Next Fifty Years, ICCA Congress Series*, Vol. 16 (The Netherlands: Kluwer Law International, 2012).

Susan Rose-Ackerman and Peter Lindseth, 'Comparative Administrative Law: Outlining a Field of Study' (2010) 28(2) Windsor Yearbook of Access to Justice 435.

Alfred Rubin, 'The International Legal Effects of Unilateral Declarations' (1977) 1 American Journal of International Law 1.

G Sacerdoti, 'Bilateral Treaties and Multilateral Instruments on Investment Protection' (1997) 269 Recueil des Cours 261.

Dan Sarooshi, 'The Essentially Contested Nature of The Concept of Sovereignty: Implications for the Exercise by International Organizations of Delegated Powers of Government' (2003–2004) 25 Michigan Journal of International Law 1107.

Gary H Sampliner, 'Arbitration of Expropriation Cases under US Investment Treaties – A Threat to Democracy or the Dog that Didn't Bark?' (2003) 18 ICSID Review-FILJ 1.

Joseph Sax, 'Takings and the Police Power' (1964) 74 Yale Law Journal 36.

George Scelle, 'Règle Générales du Droit de la Paix' (1933) 46 Recueil des Cours 331.

Oscar Schachter, 'International Law in Theory and Practice: General Course in Public International Law' (1982) 178 Recueil des Cours 21.

Oscar Schachter, 'Entangled Treaty and Custom' in Yoram Dinstein and Mala Tabory (eds), *International Law at a Time of Perplexity: Essays in Honour of Shabtai Rosenne* (Dordrecht, Boston, London: Martinus Nijhoff Publishers, 1989).

James Brown Scott, 'United States-Norway Arbitration Award' (1923) 17 American Journal of International Law 287.

Christoph Schreuer, 'The Concept of Expropriation under the ECT and Other Investment Protection Treaties' in Clarisse Ribeiro (ed.), *Investment Arbitration and the Energy Charter Treaty* (Huntington, New York: Juris Publishing, 2006).

Christoph Schreuer, 'Protection against Arbitrary or Discriminatory Measures' in Catherine Rogers and Roger Alford (eds), *The Future of Investment Arbitration* (Oxford; New York: Oxford University Press, 2009).

Christoph Schreuer, 'The Waning of the Sovereign State: Towards a New Paradigm for International Law?' (1993) 4 European Journal of International Law 447.

Christoph Schreuer, 'Rapport: The Concept of Expropriation under the ECT and Other Investment Protection Treaties' in Clarisse Ribeiro (ed.), *Investment Arbitration and the Energy Charter Treaty* (Huntington, New York: Jurisnet, 2006).

Hassan Sedigh, 'What Level of Host State Interference Amounts to a Taking under Contemporary International Law?' (2001) 2 Journal of World Investment 631.

Yuval Shany, 'Towards a General Margin of Appreciation Doctrine in International Law' (2006) 16(5) European Journal of International Law 907.

Bruno Simma and Andreas Paulus, 'The Responsibility of Individuals for Human Rights Abuses in International Conflicts: A Positivist View' (1999) 93 American Journal of International Law 302.

Bruno Simma and Dirk Pulkowski, 'Of Planets and Universe: Self-contained Regimes in International Law' (2006) 17 European Journal of International Law 483.

Bruno Simma, 'From Bilateralism to Community Interests in International Law' (1994) 250 Recueil des Cours 217.

M Sornarajah, 'A Coming Crisis: Expansionary Trends in Investment Treaty Arbitration' in Karl P Sauvant (ed.), *Appeals Mechanism in International Investment Disputes* (New York: Oxford University Press, 2008).

M Sornarajah, 'India, China and Foreign Investment' in M Sornarajah and Jiangyu Wang (eds), *China, India and the International Economic Order* (Cambridge: Cambridge University Press, 2010).

M Sornarajah, 'The Case Against a Regime on International Investment Law' in Trakman and Rainieri (eds), *International Investment Law* (Oxford: Oxford University Press, 2012).

M Sornarajah, 'Sovereign Wealth Funds and International Investment Law' (2011) 1 Asian Journal of International Law 267.

Alex Stone Sweet, 'Investor State Arbitration: Proportionalities New Frontier' (2010) Faculty Scholarship Series 69.

A J P Tammes, 'Inter-Action of the Sources of International Law' (1963) 10 Netherlands Journal of International Law 225.

Leon E Trakman, 'Investor State Arbitration or Local Courts: Will Australia Set a New Trend?' (2012) 46(1) Journal of World Trade 83.

David Turns, 'The Law of Armed Conflict (International Humanitarian Law)' in Malcolm Evans (ed.), *International Law* (4th ed.; Oxford: Oxford University Press, 2014).

Valentina Vadi, 'Cultural Diversity Disputes and the Judicial Function in International Investment Law' (2011) 39 Syracuse Journal of International Law and Commerce 89.

Valentina Vadi and Lukasz Gruszczynski, 'Standard of Review in International Investment Law and Arbitration: Multilevel Governance and the Commonweal' (2013) 16(3) Journal of International Economic Law 613.

Kenneth Vandevelde 'A Brief History of International Investment Agreements' (2005) 12 UC – Davis Journal of International Law & Policy 157.

Cento Veljanovski, 'Economic Approaches to Regulation' in Robert Baldwin, Martin Cave and Martin Lodge (eds), *The Oxford Handbook of Regulation*, (New York: Oxford University Press 2010).

Francisco Vicñia, 'Carlos Calvo: Honorary NAFTA Citizen' (2002–2003) 11 NYU Environmental Law Journal 19.

Mark Villiger, *Customary International Law and Treaties: A Manual on the Theory and Practice of the Interrelation of Sources* (The Hague: Kluwer Law International, 1997).

Jorge E Viñuales, 'Sovereignty in Foreign Investment Law' in Zachary Douglas, Joost Pauwelyn and Jorge E Viñuales (eds), *The Foundations of International Investment Law: Bringing Theory into Practice* (Oxford: Oxford University Press, 2014).

Thomas Waelde and Abba Kolo, 'Environmental Regulation, Investment Protection and "Regulatory Taking" in International Law' (2001) 50 International Comparative Law Quarterly 811.

T W Waelde, 'Interpreting Investment Treaties: Experience and Examples' in C Binder and Others (eds), *International Investment Law for the 21st Century: Essays in Honour of Christoph Schreuer* (Oxford: Oxford University Press, 2009).

Humphrey Waldock, 'General Course on Public International Law' (1962) 106 Recueil des Cours 1.

Romesh Weeramantry, 'The Law of Indirect Expropriation and the Iran-United States Claims Tribunal's Role in Its Development' in Leon E Trakman and Nicola W Raneri (eds), *Regionalism in International Investment Law* (Oxford: Oxford University Press, 2013).

Todd Weiler, 'Saving Oscar Chin: Non-Discrimination in International Investment Law' in N Horn and S Kroll (eds), *Arbitrating Foreign Investment Disputes: Procedural and Substantive Legal Aspects* (The Hague: Kluwer Law International 2004).

Allan Weiner, 'Indirect Expropriations: The Need for a Taxonomy of "Legitimate" Regulatory Purposes' (2003) 5 International Law Forum 166.

Burns H Weston, '"Constructive Takings" under International Law: A Modest Foray into the Problem of "Creeping Expropriation"' (1975) 16 Virginia Journal of International Law 103.

Luzius Wildhaber, 'Sovereignty and International Law' in R St J Macdonald and Douglas M Johnston (eds), *The Structure and Process of International Law: Essays in Legal Philosophy, Doctrine, and Theory* (The Hague: Kluwer Boston, 1983).

William W Burke-White and Andreas von Staden, 'Private Litigation in a Public Law Sphere: The Standard of Review in Investor State Arbitrations' (2010) 35 Yale Journal of International Law 283.

Luzius Wildhaber, 'Sovereignty and International Law' in R St J Macdonald and Douglas M Johnston (eds), *The Structure and Process of International Law: Essays in Legal Philosophy, Doctrine, and Theory* (The Hague: Kluwer Boston, 1983).

John Fischer Williams, 'Justiciable and Other Disputes' (1932) 26 American Journal of International Law 31.

Karol Wolfke, 'Treaties and Custom: Aspects of Interrelation' in Jan Klabbers and René Lefeber (eds), *Essays on the Law of Treaties: A Collection of Essays in Honour of Bert Vierdag* (The Hague, Boston: M. Nijhoff Publishers, 1998).

William Burke-White and Andreas von Staden, 'Private Litigation in a Public Law Sphere: The Standard of Review in Investor- State Arbitration' (2010) 35 Yale Journal of International Law 283.

Karen Yeung, 'Regulatory State' in Robert Baldwin, Martin Cave and Martin Lodge (eds), *The Oxford Handbook of Regulation* (Oxford, New York: Oxford University Press, 2010).

Reports

Fragmentation of International Law: Difficulties Arising From the Diversification and Expansion of International Law (A/CN.4/L.682, International Law Commission, 2006), para. 128.

Humphrey Waldock, 'Third Report on the Law of Treaties' (1964) II Yearbook of International Law Commission 8.

International Law Commission, 'Draft Articles on Responsibility of States for Internationally Wrongful Acts, with Commentaries, 2001' (2001) II Yearbook of International Law Commission 31.

International Law Commission, International Responsibility, Fourth Report by F V García Amador, Special Rapporteur: Responsibility of the State for Injuries Caused in its Territory to the Person or Property of Aliens – Measures Affecting Acquired Rights Document A/CN.4/119 (26 February 1959), (1959) II Yearbook of the International Law Commission 1, para. 43.

Permanent Court of International Justice *Procès Verbaux of the Proceedings of the Committee* (The Hague: Van Langenhuysen Brothers, 1920).

Permanent Sovereignty over Natural Resources, G.A. res. 1803 (XVII), 17 U.N. GAOR Supp. (No.17) at 15, U.N. Doc. A/5217 (1962).

United Nations, United Nations Conference on the Law of Treaties: Official Records (vol. 2, New York, United Nations, 1970).

Websites/Online Resources

www.italaw.com.

Juliane Kokott and Frank Hoffmeister, 'International Public Order' in R Wolfrum (ed.), *The Max Planck Encyclopedia of Public International Law, Oxford University Press* (2008), online edition, www.mpepil.com.

Scott Appleton, Latin American Arbitration the Story Behind the Headlines, International Bar Association available at http://www.ibanet.org/Article/Detail.aspx?ArticleUid=78296258-3B37-4608-A5EE-3C92D5D0B979.

Benedict Kingsbury and Stephan Schill, 'Investor-State Arbitration as Governance: Fair and Equitable Treatment, Proportionality and the Emerging Global Administrative Law', IILJ Working Paper 2009/6 (Global Administrative Law Series) Finalized 08/19/2009, available at: http://www.iilj.org/publications/documents/2009-6.KingsburySchill.pdf.

Investment Treaty News, 'NGOs Claim the Philippine-Japan Free Trade Agreement is Unconstitutional', 5 June 2009, available http://www.iisd.org/itn/2009/06/05/ngos-claim-the-philippine-japan-free-trade-agreement-is-unconstitutional/.

Investment Treaty News, 'Norway Shelves its Draft Model Bilateral Investment Treaty', (8June 2009) available at http://www.iisd.org/itn/2009/06/08/norway-shelves-its-proposed-model-bilateral-investment-treaty/.

Gillard Government Trade Policy Statement: Trading Our Way to More Jobs and Prosperity, (Australian Government, Department of Foreign Affairs and Trade, April 2011), available at http://www.dfat.gov.au/publications/trade/trading-our-way-to-more-jobs-and-prosperity.pdf.

Article 4, Public Statement on the International Investment Regime 31 August 2010, available at http://www.osgoode.yorku.ca/public_statement.

http://www.unpri.org.

http://www.basel.int/TheConvention/Overview/TextoftheConvention/tabid/1275/Default.aspx.

Working under the Bank for International Settlements, available at http://www.bis.org/bcbs/index.htm.

http://www.iilj.org/publications/documents/2009-6.KingsburySchill.pdf.

https://www.iisd.org/itn/2012/04/13/venezuelas-withdrawal-from-icsid-what-it-does-and-does-not-achieve/.

http://www.un-documents.net/a25r2625.htm.

http://www.worldtradelaw.net/nafta/chap-11.pdf.

http://www.pcacases.com/web/view/5.

International Law Commission on Unilateral Actions: http://legal.un.org/ilc/summaries/9_9.htm#_ftn27.

Article I, Conference on Security and Co-operation in Europe, Final Act, Helsinki, 1975; 1 August 1975; available at: https://www.osce.org/mc/39501?download = true.

http://legal.un.org/ilc/documentation/english/a_cn4_569.pdf.

Convention on the High Seas, 1958, available at: http://www.gc.noaa.gov/documents/8_1_1958_high_seas.pdf.

Article 2(1), UN Charter, available at http://www.un.org/en/documents/charter/chapter1.shtml.

Remarks by David Kennedy, 'How Should Sovereignty be Defended?' available at http://www.law.harvard.edu/faculty/dkennedy/publications/DKennedy_SovereigntyDefended.pdf.

Remarks by Michael Doyle, 'How Should Sovereignty be Defended?' available at http://www.law.harvard.edu/faculty/dkennedy/publications/DKennedy_SovereigntyDefended.pdf.

Article 57, Statute of the International Court of Justice. Available at http://www.icj-cij.org/documents/?p1 = 4&p2 = 2.

Resolution of the Permanent Court of International Justice dated 17 February 1928, reproduced in the Fourth Report PCIJ, p. 291 available at http://www.icj-cij.org/pcij/serie_E/English/E_04_en.pdf.

Article 34 (1), Tribunal Rules of Procedure, 3 May 1983, available at http://www.iusct.net/General%20Documents/5-TRIBUNAL%20RULES%20OF%20PROCEDURE.pdf.

Article 1110: No Party may directly or indirectly nationalize or expropriate an investment of an investor of another Party in its territory or take a measure tantamount to nationalization or expropriation of such an investment, NAFTA, available at http://www.worldtradelaw.net/nafta/chap-11.pdf.

Jan Paulsson, 'Indirect Expropriation: Is the Right to Regulate at Risk?' Paper presented on 12 December 2005 in Paris at a symposium on 'Making the Most of International Investment Agreements' organized by ICSID, OECD and UNCTAD, available at http://www.oecd.org/investment/internationalinvestmentagreements/36055332.pdf.

Article 38 (2) of the ICJ Statute provides that: 'This provision shall not prejudice the power of the Court to decide a case ex aequo et bono, if the parties agree thereto.' Available at http://legal.un.org/avl/pdf/ha/sicj/icj_statute_e.pdf.

Article 42 (3) ICSID Convention. It says: 'The provisions of paragraphs (1) and (2) shall not prejudice the power of the Tribunal to decide a dispute ex aequo et bono if the parties so agree.' Available at https://icsid.worldbank.org/ICSID/StaticFiles/basicdoc/partA.htm.

Antonio Parra, 'Applicable Law in Investor-State Arbitration' in Arthur Rovine (ed.), Contemporary Issues in International Arbitration and Mediation: The Fordham Papers 2007 (The Netherlands: Martinus Nijhoff, 2013) available at http://www.arbitration-icca.org/articles.html?author=Antonio_Parra&sort=author.

Atlantic Charter, 14 August 1941; 2625 (XXV). Declaration on Principles of International Law concerning Friendly Relations and Co-operation among States in accordance with the Charter of the United Nations, 24 October 1970, available at http://www.un-documents.net/a25r2625.htm.

Declaration on the Inadmissibility of Intervention and Interference in the Domestic Affairs of States (UNGA resolution 2131 (XX) 1965), available at http://www.un.org/documents/ga/res/36/a36r103.htm.

Available at http://www.ohchr.org/en/professionalinterest/pages/ccpr.aspx.

Universal Declaration of Human Rights, available at http://www.ohchr.org/en/udhr/documents/udhr_translations/eng.pdf.

American Convention on Human Rights, available at: http://www.oas.org/dil/treaties_B-32_American_Convention_on_Human_Rights.htm.

Convention on the Elimination of All Forms of Discrimination Against Women, available at http://www.un.org/womenwatch/daw/cedaw/text/econvention.htm.

Elimination of All Forms of Racial Discrimination, available at http://www.ohchr.org/EN/ProfessionalInterest/Pages/CERD.aspx.

Writings and activities in this area are regularly updated on the website of the Global Administrative Law Project, available at http://www.iilj.org/gal/.

Kenneth Vandevelde, 'Model Bilateral Investment Treaties: The Way Forward' available at: http://www.swlaw.edu/pdfs/lawjournal/18_1vandevelde.pdf.

Table of Cases

Permanent Court of International Justice and International Court of Justice

Accordance with International Law of the Unilateral Declaration of Independence in Respect of Kosovo (Advisory Opinion) (22 July 2010) (2010) ICJ Reports 403, 479, 117

Application of the Convention of 1902 Governing the Guardianship of Infants (Netherlands v Sweden) (Judgment of 28 November 1958) (Separate Opinion of Sir Percy Spender) (1958) ICJ Reports 55, 168

Armed Activities on the Territory of the Congo (Democratic Republic of the Congo v Uganda),Judgment of 19 December 2005, ICJ. Reports 2005, 168, 106

Asylum Case (*Columbia v Peru*) Judgment of 20 November 1950, (1950) ICJ Reports 266, 117

Case Concerning AhmadouSadio Diallo (Guinea v Congo), Preliminary Objections, 24 May 2007, (2007) ICJ Reports 582, 139

Case Concerning Certain German Interests in Polish Upper Silesia (Germany v Poland) (1926) PCIJ Series A-No. 6, 52

Case Concerning Certain German Interests in Polish Upper Silesia (Germany v Poland) (1926) PCIJ Series A-No. 7, 143

Case Concerning East Timor (Portugal v Australia), Judgment, (1995) ICJ Reports 90, 180

Case Concerning Kasikili/Sedudu Islands (Bostwana v Namibia) (1999) ICJ Reports 1045, 140

Case concerning Pulp Mills on the River Uruguay (Argentina v Uruguay), Judgment of 20 April 2010, (2010) ICJ Reports 14, 120

Case concerning the Application of the Convention on the Prevention and Punishment of the Crime of Genocide (Bosnia and Herzegovina v Serbia and Montenegro), Judgment of 11 July 1996,(2007) ICJ Reports 43, at para. 204, 120

Case Concerning the Arrest Warrant of 11 April 2000 (Congo v Belgium) (2002) ICJ Reports 3, 123

Case Concerning The Barcelona Traction, Light and Power Company, Limited (Belgium v Spain), Second Phase, Judgment, 5 February 1970, (1970) ICJ Reports 3, 118, 172

Certain Questions of Mutual Assistance in Criminal Matters (Djibouti v France), Judgment of 4 June 2008, (2008) ICJ Reports 177, 170

Conditions of Admission of a State to Membership in the United Nations (Article 4 of the Charter), Advisory Opinion of 28 May 1948, (1948) ICJ Reports 57, 168

Continental Shelf (Libyan Arab Jarnahiriyu/Malta), 3 June 1985, (1985) ICJ Reports 13, 76, 122

Continental Shelf (Tunisia v Libya), Merits, Judgment of 24 February 1982, ICJ Rep 18, 76

Corfu Channel Case (merits) (1949) ICJ Reports 15, 120, 121

Customs Regime Between Germany and Austria (Advisory Opinion) 5 September 1931, Individual Opinion by Judge M Anzilotti, (1931) PCIJ Series A/B, No. 41, 57, 110, 142

Customs Régime Between Germany and Australia, Advisory Opinion, 5 September 1931, (1931) PCIJ Series A/B, No. 41, 142

Delimitation of the Maritime Boundary in the Gulf of Maine Area (Canada/United States of America), Judgment of 12 October 1984, (1984) ICJ Reports 246, 76

Dispute Regarding Navigational and Related Rights (Costa Rica v Nicaragua) (2009) ICJ Reports 213, 161, 192

Electricity Company of Sofia and Bulgaria, Preliminary Objection, 4 April 1939, (1939) PCIJ Series A/B, No. 77, 111

ElettronicaSicula S.p.A. (ELSI) (United States of America v Italy) (Judgment of 20 July 1989) (1989) ICJ Reports 15, 144, 192

Exchange of Greek and Turkish Populations (Advisory Opinion of 21 February 1925) (1925) PCIJ Series B, No. 10, 142

Factory at Chorzów(Germany v Poland)), Merits, Judgment of 13 September 19281928 PCIJ Series A No. 17, 144

Fisheries (United Kingdom v Norway), Judgment of 18 December 1951, (1951) ICJ Reports 116, 191

Free Zones of Upper Savoy and the District of Gex (*France v Switzerland*), Judgment of 6 December 1930, (1930) PCIJ Series A/B, No. 24, 170, 172

GabchikovoNagyamaros (Hungury/Slovakia),Judgment of 25 September1997, (1997) ICJ 7, 187

Interpretation of Peace Treaties with Bulgaria, Hungary and Romania (Second Phase), Advisory Opinion, 18 July 1950, (1950) ICJ Reports 221, 85

Jurisdiction of the Courts of Danzig, Advisory Opinion, 3 March 1928, PCIJ Series B No. 15, 145

LaGrand (Germany v United States of America), Judgment of 27 June 2001, (2001) ICJ Reports 466, 145

Legal Consequences for States of the Continued Presence of South Africa in Namibia (South West Africa) notwithstanding Security Council Resolution 276 (1970), Advisory Opinion, 21 June 1971,(1971) ICJ Reports 16, 169

Legal Consequences of Construction of Wall Opinion, Advisory Opinion,9 July 2004, (2004) ICJ Reports 136, 186

Legal Status of Eastern Greenland (5 April 1933), (1933) PCIJ Series No. 53, 109

Legality of the Threat or Use of Nuclear Weapons, Advisory Opinion, (1996) ICJ Reports 226, 121

Mellacher v Austria, Judgment of 19 December 1989, PCIJ Ser A No. 169, 132

Military and Paramilitary Activities in and against Nicaragua (Nicaragua v United States of America), 27 June 1986, (1986) ICJ Reports 14, 106, 145, 170

Minquiers and Ecrehos (France/United Kingdom) Judgment of 17 November 1953, (1953) ICJ Rep 47, 76

Nationality Decrees Issued in Tunis and Morocco, Advisory Opinion of 7 February 1923, PCIJ Series B, Nos 4, 12, 109, 117

North Sea Continental Shelf Cases (Germany v Denmark; Germany v Netherlands), Merits, Judgment of 20 February 1969, ICJ Rep 3, 76, 122, 141, 150

Norwegian Loans (France v Norway) (Judgment of 6 July 1957) (1957) ICJ Reports 9, 165, 172

Nottebohm (Liechtenstein v Guatemala), Second Phase, Judgment of 6 April 1955,(1955) ICJ Rep 4, 130

NuclearTests (Australia/ New Zeeland v France) (20 December 1974) (1974) I.C.J.Reports 268, 165

Oil Platforms Case (Iran v United States of America), Merits, Judgment of 6 November 2003, (2003) ICJ Reports 161, para. 41, 140

Panevezys-Saldutiskis Railway, Judgment of 28 February 1939, PCIJ Series A/B, No. 76, p. 923, 97

Payment of Various Serbian Loans Issued by France (France v Kingdom of Serbs, Crovates and Slovanes), 1929 PCIJ (Series A) No. 20, 178

Questions of Interpretation and Application of the 1971 Montreal Convention arising from the Aerial Incident at Lockerbie (*Libyan Arab Jamahiriya v United States of America*), Judgment of 27 February 1998, (1998) ICJ Reports 115, 146

Right of Passage Case (Portugal v India), (1957) ICJ Reports 125, 111

Rights of Nationals of the United States of America in Morocco (France v United States of America) (Judgment of 27 August 1952) (1952) ICJ Reports 176, 191

The Case of the S.S. 'Lotus' (France v Turkey), 7 September 1927 (Dissenting Opinion of Judge Weiss), (1927) PCIJ Series A, No. 10, 104

The Case of The SS 'Wimbledon' (Britain v Germany), Decision, 17 August 1923, (1923) PCIJ Series A, No. 1, 142

The Losinger& C. Case, Preliminary Objections, 27 June 1936, (1936) PCIJ Series A/B No. 67, 111

The Oscar Chinn Case (Belgium v United Kingdom), 12 December 1934, (1934) PCIJ Series A/B No. 63, 172

United States Diplomatic and Consular Staff in Tehran (United States of America v Iran), Judgment of 24 May 1980, (1980) ICJ Reports 3, 153

Whaling in the Antarctic (Australia v Japan: New Zealand intervening), Judgment of 31 March 2014 para. 66, 192

Investment and Other Arbitral Tribunals

Air Transport Services Agreement Arbitration (United States of America v France), Award, 22 December 1963, (1969) 38 ILR 182, 136

Antoine Biloune, Marine Drive Complex Ltd. v Ghana Investments Centre, the Government of Ghana, Awards, 27 October 1989, (1994) XIX Yearbook Commercial Arbitration 11, 12, 35, 190

Archer Daniels Midland Company and Tate & Lyle Ingredients Americas, Inc. v United Mexican States, ICSID Case No. ARB(AF)/04/5, Award, 21 November 2007, 152

Atlantic Triton Company Limited v People's Revolutionary Republic of Guinea, ICSID Case No. ARB/84/1, Award, 21 April 1986, 77

AutopistaConcesionada de Venezuela C.A. (Aucoven) v Bolivarian Republic of Venezuela, Award, ICSID Case No. ARB/00/5, 23 September 2003, 77

Azurix Corporation v The Argentine Republic (Azurix v Argentina), ICSID Case No. ARB/01/12, Award, 14 July 2006, 184

BG Group Plc. v The Republic of Argentina, Final Award, UNCITRAL Arbitration Rules, 24 December 2007, 61

Case Concerning the Difference Between New Zealand and France Concerning the Interpretation or Application of Two Agreements, Concluded on 9 July 1986 Between the Two States and Which Related to the Problem Arising From the Rainbow Warrior Affair (*New Zealand v France*), Award, 30 April 1990, Vol. XX RIAA 215, 147

Chemtura Corporation v Government of Canada, Award, UNCITRAL Rules, 2 August 2010, paras 259–265, 43

CME Czech Republic B.V. v The Czech Republic, UNCITRAL, Partial Award, 13 September 2001, 77

CMS Gas Transmission Co. v Argentina (ICSID Case No.ARB/01/8) Decision on Annulment, 25 September 2007, 147

Compañiá de Aguas del Aconquija S.A. and Vivendi Universal S.A. v Argentine Republic, Award, ICSID Case No. ARB/97/3, para. 7.5.1, 33, 61

Compañía del Desarrollo de Santa Elena, S.A. v The Republic of Costa Rica, ICSID Case No. ARB/96/1, Award, 17 February 2000, 33

Corn Products International Inc. v United Mexican States, ICSID Case No. ARB(AF)/04/1, Decision on Responsibility, 15 January 2008, 152

Desert Lines Project LLC v The Republic of Yemen, ICSID Case No. ARB/05/17, Award, 6 February 2008, 179

Deutsche Bank AG v Democratic Socialist Republic of Sri Lanka, ICSID Case No. ARB/09/2, Award, 31 October 2012, 184

Différendconcernanyl'accord Tardieu-Jaspar (Belgium v France) Award, 1 March 1937, UNRIAA Vol. III 1713, 138

Dispute Concerning Access to Information under Article 9 of the OSPAR Convention (Ireland v United Kingdom of Great Britain and Northern Ireland) Final Award, 2 July 2003, Permanent Court of Arbitration, (2005) 126 ILR 364, 139

Dispute Concerning Filleting within the Gulf of St Laurence, Award, 17 July 1986 82 ILR 590, para. 27, 166

Duke Energy International Peru Investments No. 1, Ltd. v Peru, ICSID Case No. ARB/03/28; Award, 18 August 2008, 87

El Paso Energy International Company v The Argentine Republic, Award, ICSID Case No. ARB/03/15, 31 October 2011, 37, 81, 87

Emilio AgustínMaffezini v The Kingdom of Spain, ICSID Case No.ARB/97/7, Award, 13 November 2000, 87

EnCana Corporation v Republic of Ecuador, Award, UNCITRAL Rules, 3 February 2006, 41, 87

Enron Corporation and Ponderosa Assets, L.P. v Argentine Republic, ICSID Case No. ARB/01/3, Award, 22 May 2007, 77

Eudoro Armando Olguínvv Republic of Paraguay, Award, ICSID Case No. ARB/98/5, 26 January 2001, 11

Eureko B.V. v Republic of Poland, Partial Award, 19 August 2005, 87

Faber Case (1903) Ven Arb 600, 177

Fireman's Fund Insurance Company v United Mexican States, ICSID Case No. ARB(AF)/02/01, Award, 17 July 2006, 30

Gami Investments, Inc. v The Government of the United Mexican States, UNCITRAL, Final Award, 15 November 2004, para. 114, 177

Generation Ukraine Incorporation v Ukraine, ICSID Case No. ARB/00/9, Award, 16 September 2003, 74, 76

Georges Pinson Case (France/United Mexican States) Award of 13 April 1928, UNRIAA, Vol. V, p. 422, 139

Glaims Gold Ltd. v United States of America, Award, NAFTA Chapter 11 Tribunal (UNCITRAL), 8 June 2009, 85

Great Venezuelan Railroad Case (1903) X RIAA 468, 472–473, 177

InceysaVallisoletana S.L. v Republic of El Salvador, Award, 2 August 2006, 180

International Thunderbird Gaming Corporation v Mexico, Award, UNCITRAL, IIC 136 (2006), 26 January 2006, Ad Hoc Tribunal, 178

Kuwait Airways Corporation v Iraqi Airways Company and the Republic of Iraq, 116 ILR 571, 178

LG & E Energy Corp., LG & E Capital Corp., LG & E International Inc. v The Argentine Republic, ICSID Case No. ARB/02/1, Decision on Liability, 3 October 2006, 44

Link-Trading Joint Stock Company v Department for Customs Control of Moldova, Final Award, 18 April 2002, para. 3, 40

LozarRokash Case, American Turkish Claims Settlement (1937) Nielson's Opinion and Reports 503, 177

Maal Case (1903) Ven Arb 914, 131

Marvin Feldman v Mexico, Award, ICSID Case No. ARB (AF)/99/1, 16 December 2002, 27, 39, 76, 85, 86, 87, 126, 177

MedioambientalesTechmed S.A. v The United Mexican States, Award, ICSID Case No. ARB (AF)/00/2, 29 May 2003, 24, 86, 151

Metaclad Corporation v The United Mexican States, Award, ICSID Case No. ARB(AF)/97/1, 30 August 2000, 35

Methanex Corporation v United States of America, Final Award of the Tribunal on Jurisdiction and Merits, 3 August 2005, 41, 86, 171, 176

Mr Patrick Mitchell v Democratic Republic of the Congo, Decision on the Application for Annulment of the Award, ICSID Case No. ARB/99/7, 1 November 2006, 151

Mutual Assistance in Criminal Matters (Djibouti v France), Judgment of 4 June 2008, 170

Norwegian Shipowner's Claims (Norway v United States of America), Permanent Court of Arbitration, Award, 13 October 1922, (1922) I RIAA 307, 48–51

NykombSynergetics Technology Holding AB, Stockholm v The Republic of Latvia, The Arbitration Institute of Stockholm Chamber of Commerce, Award, 16 December 2003, 34

Occidental Exploration and Production Company v The Republic of Ecuador, UNCITRAL Arbitration Rules (London Court of International Arbitration Administered Case No. UN 3467), Final Award, 1 July 2004, 44

Parkerings-Compagniet AS v Republic of Lithuania, ICSID Case No. ARB/05/8, Award, 11 September 2007, 171

Petrobart Limited v The Kyrgyz Republic, Arbitration Institute of the Stockholm Chamber of Commerce, Award, 29 March 2005, p. 77, 27

Phoenix Action, Ltd. v The Czech Republic, ICSID Case No. ARB/06/5, Award, 15 April 2009, 133, 180

Pope & Talbot Inc v The Government of Canada, Interim Award, 26 June 2000, 27, 66, 171

Preferential Treatment of Claims of Blockading Powers Against Venezuela, *Germany and ors v Venezuela, Award*, (1959) IX RIAA 99, ICGJ 408 (PCA 1904), 22 February 1904, Permanent Court of Arbitration at 107, 110., 169

Robert Azinian, Kenneth Davitian, & Ellen Baca v The United Mexican States, Award, ICSID Case No. ARB (AF)/97/2, 1 November 1999, 87

Ronald S. Lauder v The Czech Republic, UNCITRAL, Final Award, 3 September 2001, 77

Rumeli Telekom A.S. and Telsim Mobil TelekomunikasyonHizmetleri A.S. v Republic of Kazakhstan, Award, 29 July 2008, 171

S.D. Myers, Inc. v Government of Canada, UNCITRAL/NAFTA, First Partial Award, 13 November 2000, 28, 63

SaliniCostruttoriSpA et ItalstradeSpA v Morocco, Decision on Jurisdiction, 23 July 2001, 97

Saluka v Czech Republic, UNICTRAL, Partial Award, 17 March 2006, 74

Sempra Energy International v The Argentine Republic, Award, 28 September 2007, 38, 81, 147

SGS SociétéGénérale de Surveillance S.A. v Islamic Republic of Pakistan, ICSID Case No. ARB/01/13, Decision of the Tribunal on Objections to Jurisdiction, 6 August 2003, 3

Suez, Sociedad General de Aguas de Barcelona, S.A.and Vivendi Universal, S.A. v Argentine Republic, ICSID Case No. ARB/03/19, Decision on Liability, 30 June 2010, 8

Telenor v Hungary, Award, ICSID Case No. ARB/04/15, 13 September 2006, 27, 61

The 'Camouco'Case (Panama v France), Application for Prompt Release, Judgment, 7 February 2000, ITLOS, List of Cases No. 5, paras 65–70, 192

The Indus Waters Kishenganga Arbitration (Pakistan v India), Permanent Court of Arbitration, Final Award, 20 December 2013, 162

The Megalidis Case (A.A. Megalidis v Turkey) (1927–1928) 4 Annual Digest of International Law Cases 395 (Turkish-Greek Mixed Arb. Trib. 1928), 165

The North Atlantic Coast Fisheries Case (Great Britain v United States of America), Award, Permanent Court of Arbitration, 7 September 1910, (1961) XI RIAA 167, 121, 156, 166, 168

Waste Management Inc. v United Mexican States, ICSID Case No. ARB(AF)/00/3, Award, 30 April 2004, 26, 87

World Duty Free Company Ltd v The Republic of Kenya, ICSID Case No. ARB/00/7, Award, 4 October 2006, 180

WTO Cases

Brazil –Retreaded Tyres, Appellate Body Report,WT/DS332/AB/R, 3 December 2007, 186

Brazil – Export Financing Programme for Aircraft: Recourse to Arbitration by Brazil under Article 22.6 of the DSU and Article 4.11 of the SCM Agreement, Decision by the Arbitrators, WT/DS46/ARB, 28 August 2000, 141

Canada –Wheat Exports and Grain Imports, Panel Report, WT/DS276/R, 6 April 2004, 185

Canada – Certain Measures Concerning Periodicals, Appellate Body, WT/DS31/AB/R, 30 July 1997, 171

Canada-Terms of Patent Protection, Report of the Appellate Body, WT/DS170/AB/R, 18 September 2000, 141

Chile – Taxes on Alcoholic Beverages,Report of Appellate Body, WT/DS110/AB/R, 13 December 1999, 170

China–Measures Affecting Trading Rights and Distribution Services for Certain Publications and Audiovisual Entertainment Products, Report of the Appellate Body, WT/DS363/AB/R, 129

Dominican Republic –Import and Sale of Cigarettes, Appellate Body Report,WT/DS302/AB/R, 25 April 2005, 185

EC –Trademarks and Geographical Indications (US), Panel Report, WT/DS174/R, 15 March 2005, 185

Japan – Taxes on Alcoholic Beverages, Appellate Body, WT/DS8/AB/R, WT/DS10/AB/R, WT/DS11/AB/R, 1 November 1996, 171

Korea – Measures Affecting Imports of Fresh, Chilled and Frozen Beef, Appellate Body Report, 11 December 2000, WT/DS161/AB/R, 186

Korea-Measures Affecting Government Procurement (19 January 2000) WT/DS163/R, 141

Mexico – Tax Measures on Soft Drinks and Other Beverages, Panel Report, WT/DS308/R, 24 March 2006, 171

Thailand – Restrictions on Importation of and Internal Taxes on Cigarettes, GATT Panel Report, GATT BISD (DS10/R–37S/200), 7 November 1990, 186

United States–Import Prohibition of Certain Shrimp and Shrimp Products (6 November 1998) WT/DS58/AB/R, DSR 1998:VII, pp. 2794–2797, 141

United States –Import Prohibition of Certain Shrimp and Shrimp Products, WT/DS58/R, Panel, 129

United States – Certain Country of Origin Labeling (COOL) Requirements, Appellate Body, WT/DS384/AB/R, 23 July 2012, para. 420, 171

United States – Measures Affecting the Cross-Border Supply of Gambling and Betting Services, Appellate Body Report, WT/DS285/AB/R, 7 April 2005, 186

United States – Restrictions on Imports of Tuna, Report of the Panel (DS29/R), 129

United States – Section 337 of the Tariff Act of 1930, GATT Panel Report, GATT BISD (L/6439-36S/345 36th Sup.), 7 November 1989, 345, 186

United States – Tax Treatment For 'Foreign Sales Corporations' Panel Report, WT/DS108/R,para. 7.1222 and Appellate Body Report,WT/DS108AB/R, 109

United States–Gasoline, Panel Report, WT/DS2/9, 20 May 1996, 140

Decisions of the Iran-US Claims Tribunal

Alfred L W Short v The Islamic Republic of Iran, Award No. 312-11135-3, 14 July 1987, (1987) 16 Iran-U.S. CTR 76, 64

Amco International Finance Corporation v Islamic Republic of Iran, Partial Award No. 310-56-3, 14 July 1987, (1987)15 Iran-U.S. CTR 189, 59

American International Group Inc. v The Islamic Republic of Iran, Award No. 93-2-3, 19 December 1983, (1983) 4 Iran-U.S. CTR 96, 62

Arthur Young & Company Short v The Islamic Republic of Iran, Award No. 338-484-1, 1 December 1987, (1987) 17 Iran-U.S. CTR 245, 64

AtaollahGolpira v Islamic Republic of Iran, Award No. 32-211-2, 29 March 1983, (1983) 2 Iran-U.S. CTR 171, 58

Constantine A. Gianoplus v Islamic Republic of Iran, Award No. 237-314-1, 20 June 1986, (1986) 11 Iran-U.S. CTR 217, 222, 59

Dames and Moore v The Islamic Republic of Iran, Award No. 97-53-1, (1983) 4 Iran-U.S. CTR 212, 221–222, 68

Eastman Kodak Company v The Government of Iran, Award No. 329-227/12384-3, 11 November 1987, (Concurring and Dissenting Opinion of Judge Brower) 1987 (17) Iran-U.S. Claims Tribunal 153, 173–174, 64

Emanuel Too v Greater Modesto Insurance Associates, Award No. 460-880-2, 29 December 1989, (1989) 23 Iran-U.S. CTR 378, 378–379, 66

Foremost Tehran Inc v Islamic Republic of Iran, Award No. 220-37/231-1, 11 April 1968, (1987) 10 Iran-U.S. CTR 228, 244, 58

Harza Engineering Co. v Islamic Republic of Iran, Award No. 19-98-2, 30 December 1982, (1982-3) 2 Iran-U.S. CTR 499, 504, 58, 59

International Technical Products Corporation v Islamic Republic of Iran, Final Award No. 196-302-3, 28 October 1985, (1985) 9 Iran-U.S. CTR 206, 238–239, 58

ITT Industries Inc. v The Islamic Republic of Iran, Award No. 47-156-2, 26 May 1983, (1983) 2 Iran-U.S. CTR 348, 351–352 (Separate Opinion of Judge Aldrich), 58

Phelps Dodge Corpn. v Islamic Republic of Iran, Award No. 217-99-2, 19 March 1986, (1987) 10 Iran-U.S. CTR 121, 130, 58

Sea-Land Service Inc. v The Islamic Republic of Iran, Award No. 135-33-1, 20 June 1984, (1986) 6 Iran-U.S. CTR 149, 164–165, 67

Sedco Inc. v National Iranian Oil Company, Award No. ITL 55-129-3, 24 October 1985, (1985) 9 Iran-U.S. CTR 248, 275, 64, 68

Starrett Housing Corp. v Government of Islamic Republic of Iran, 19 December 1982, (1983) 4 Iran-U.S. CTR 122, 162, 58

Decisions of Regional and Municipal Courts

Agins v City of Tiburon 447 U.S. 255 (1980), 261, 131
Al-Jedda v The United Kingdom, European Court of Human Rights, Grand Chamber, Application No. 27021/08, Judgment, Strasbourg, 7 July 2011, para. 102, 189
Allen v McClellan, 75N.M. 400, 405 P.2d405 (1965), 90
Allgemine Gold-und Silbersceideanstalt v Customs and Excise Commissioner, (1980) 2 WLR 555, 131
Aronson v Town of Sharon, 346 Mass. 598, 195 N.E.2d 341 (1964), 89
Assets of Hungarian Company in Germany Case ILR 32, 565, 131
Ayres v City of Los Angeles, 34 Cal. 2d 31, 207 P.2d 1 (1949), 89
Banković v Belgium and others, Decision of 12 December 2001, Admissibility, ECHR 2001-XII, pp. 351–352, paras 59–60, 139
Barnes v Glen Theatre 501 U.S. 560, 569 (1991), 16
Batten v United States, 306 F.2d 58o (10th Cir. 1962), 91
Brewer, Moller &Co.Case (Germany v Venezuela) 10 RIAA 423 (1903), 130
Brown v Maryland 25 US (12 Wheat) 419, 442–443 (1827), 16
Cantos v Argentina Series C No. 85 (IACtHR, 7 September 2001), 96
Case of Sporrong and Lönnroth v Sweden, Application No. 7151/75; 7152/75, Judgment, 23 September 1982, 97
ChaparroÁlvarez and Lapoíñiguez v Ecuador (Judgment) Inter-American Court of Human Rights Series C No. 170 (21 November 2007) [183]–[218], 97
City of Jacksonville v Schumann, 167 So. 2d 95 (Fla. 1964), 91
City of Los Angeles v Allen, i Cal. 2d 572, 36 P.2d 61 (1934), 91
Dickson Car Wheel Co. Case (1931) Op of Com 174, 192–193, 131
First Nat'l Stores, Inc. v Town Plan & Zoning Comm'n, 26 Conn. Supp. 302, 222 A.2d 228 (C.P. 1966), 91
Gardner v Michingan, 199 U.S. 325, 330 (1905), 89
GasusDosier- udFördertechnik GmbH v The Netherlands, Judgment, ECtHR, 23 February 1995, Application No. 15375/89, 132
Griggs v Allegheny County, 369 U.S. 84 (1962), 91
Hadacheck v Sebastian, 239 U.S. 394 (1915), 91
Handyside v United Kingdom, ECtHR, paras 62–63. (App No. 5493/72) (1975) Series B No. 22, 97
Island of Palmas Case (Netherlands v USA), 4 April 1928, (1928) 2 RIAA 829, 838, 106
Ivcher-Bronstein v Peru (Judgment) Inter-American Court of Human Rights Series C No. 74 (6 February 2001) [119]–[131], 97
James v The United Kingdom, European Court of Human Rights, Judgment, 21 February 1986, Application No. 8793/79,para. 54, 132
Kenneth P. Yeager v The Islamic Republic of Iran, Award No. 324-10199-1, 2 November 1987, (1987) 17 Iran-U.S. CTR 92, 99, 62
Keystone Bituminous Coal Ass'n v DeBenedicti 480 U.S. 470 (1987), 485, 493, 131
Leavell v United States, 234 F. Supp. 734 (E.D.S.C. 1964), 91
Loizidou v Turkey (Preliminary Objections) Judgment of 23 March 1995, ECHR Series A (1995) No. 310, paras 57–64, 139

Morris County Land Improvement Co. v Township of Parsippany-Troy Hills, 40 N.J. 539,555–556,193 A.2d 232, 241–242 (1963), 89

Motorola Inc. v Iranian National Airlines Corporation, Award No. 374-481-3, Dissenting Opinion of Judge Brower, (1988) 19 Iran-US CTR 73, 95–96, 63

MouvementIvoirien de Droits de l'Homme v Cote d'Ivorie, Comm No. 262/02 (ACmHPR, May 22, 2008), 96

Mugler v Kansas 123 U.S. 623 (1887), p. 668, 15

Nashville, C. & St. L. Ry. v Walters, 294 U.S. 405 (I935), 89

National Land &Inv.Co. v Easttown Town- ship Bd. of Adjustment, 419 Pa. 504, 529, 215 A.2d 597,61o-ii (1966), 89

Penn Central Transportation Co. v New York City, 438 U.S. 104 (1978), 125

Pennsylvania Coal Co. v Mahon, 260 U.S. 393 (1922), 89, 91

Perozo v Venezuela, Inter-American Court of Human Rights Series C No. 195, 28 February 2009, 96

Phillips Petroleum Co. Iran v Islamic Republic of Iran, Award No. 425-39-2 (29June 1989), reprinted in (1989) 21 Iran-U.S. C.T.R. 79, 115, 58

Pine Valley Developments Ltd. v Ireland, Judgment of 29 November 1991, Series A No. 222 (1991), 132

R v Sussex Justices, Ex parte McCarthy [1923] All ER Rep 233, 77

Roark v City of Caldwell, 87 Idaho 557, 394 P.2d 641 (1964), 89

Salvador Chiriboga v Ecuador (Judgment) Inter-American Court of Human Rights Series C No. 179 (6 May 2008) [60]–[118], 97

Sartori v Peru (Mixed Commission of Peru and the United States of America), 24 November 1863 (1863) XXIX RIAA 91, 94, 172

Sylvania Technical Systems Inc. v The Islamic Republic of Iran, Award No. 180-64-1, 27 June 1985, (1985) 8 Iran-U.S. CTR 298, 308, 56

The United Mexican States v Metaclad Corporation, The Supreme Court of British Columbia, (2001) BCSC 664, para. 99, 27, 65

Thornburg v Port of Portland, 233 Ore. 178, 376 P.2nd 100 (1962), 91

Tippets, Abbett McCarthy, Stratton v TAMS-AFFA Consulting Engineers of Iran, Award No. 141-7-2, 22 June 1984, (1984) 6 Iran-U.S. CTR 219, 225–226, 58

United States v Causby, 328 U.S. 256 (1946), 91

United States v Cress, 243 U.S. 316 (I917), 91

United States v Lopez 514 U.S. 549, 566–568 (1995), 16

United States v Willow River Power Co., 324 U.S. 499, 502 (1945), 90, 91

Table of Treaties

Argentina-United Kingdom BIT, 1990, 25
ASEAN Human Rights Declaration, 18 November 2012, (2012) 32 Human Rights LJ 219, 95
Australia-Egypt BIT, 2002, 29
Australia-Vietnam BIT, 1991, 29
Bolivia-United States BIT, 1988, 27, 30
Canada Model BIT, 2004, 22, 30, 31
Canada-Costa Rica BIT, 1998, 29
Canada-Ecuador BIT, 1996, 25
Canada-Peru FTA, 2008, 31
Canada-Slovakia BIT, 2010, 25, 32, 65
Czech Republic-Moldova BIT, 1999, 30
Declaration of the Government of the Democratic and Popular Republic of Algeria (General Declaration), 19 January 1981, (1981–1982), 56
Declaration of the Government of the Democratic and Popular Republic of Algeria Concerning the Settlement of Claims by the Government of the United States of America and the Government of the Islamic Republic of Iran (Claims Settlement Declaration), 19 January 1981, (1981–1982), 56
Egypt-Germany BIT, 2005, 56
Energy Charter Treaty, 1994, 25
European Convention on Human Rights, 1950, 95
French Model BIT, 2006, 8
France-Mexico BIT, 1998, 24, 30
German Model BIT, 2008, 8, 176
Germany-Jamaica BIT, 1992, 28
Inter-American Convention on Human Rights 1959, 94, 95
Japan-Lao People's Democratic Republic BIT, 2008, 25, 65
Mexico-UK BIT, 2006, 25, 65
Netherlands-Bosnia and Herzegovina BIT, 1998, 30
Netherlands-Oman BIT, 2009, 25, 65
North America Free Trade Agreement between Canada, Mexico and the United States, 1 January 1994, 22
Singapore-Mongolia BIT, 1994, 29
Singapore-Vietnam BIT, 1992, 29–30

Treaty of Friendship Commerce and Navigation between Italy and the United States, 2 February 1948, 4
UK-Sierra Leone BIT, 2000, 25, 29
United States of America, Model BIT, 2004, 22, 31, 125
United States of America, Model BIT, 2012, 22, 31
United States-Jordan BIT, 1997, 28, 30
US-Australia FTA, 2004, 31, 79
US-Chile FTA, 2003, 31
US-Singapore FTA, 2003, 31
US-Uruguay Bilateral Investment Treaty, 2005, 25, 79
US- Egypt BIT, 1986, 24
US-Jordan, 1997, 24
US-Honduras BIT, 1995, 25
US-Sri Lanka, 1991, 21
US-Ukraine BIT, 1994, 22, 24
US-Turkey BIT, 1985, 25
Russia-Egypt BIT, 1997, 25
Egypt-Japan BIT, 1977, 25
Japan-Cambodia BIT, 2007, 25
Japan Turkey BIT, 1992, 25
Japan-Vietnam BIT, 2003, 25
Treaty for Peace, Friendship, Commerce and Navigation between Bolivia and the USA, 1958, 84
Treaty of Friendship, Commerce and Navigation between Paraguay and the USA, 1959, 84
Canada Model Foreign Protection and Promotion Agreement, 2004, 8
Treaty of Friendship Commerce and Navigation between the United States and Germany, 1923, 4
Treaty for the Promotion and Protection of Investments, with Protocol and Exchange Notes (Germany-Pakistan), 1959, 23
China-Germany BIT, 2003, 24
Germany-Libya BIT, 2004, 24
UK-Chile BIT, 1996, 22
UK-Kenya BIT, 1999, 22
Canada-China BIT, 2012, 22
Canada-Argentina BIT, 1991, 22
India- Qatar BIT, 1999, 24

Index

A

Abrogation, 144, 155
  Ad hoc Annulment Committee, 150–151
  African Commission on Human and People's Rights, 95
  Algiers Accord, 56
  Arbitral jurisprudence, 32–44

B

Bona fide, 165–172
    arbitrary or unreasonable actions, 174
    bad faith; intention to injure, 173
    colourable exercise, 173–174
    fictitious exercise, 173
    intention behind the measure, 167–168
    malicious purpose, 174

C

Case-by-case method, 73–79
  Certain German Interests in Polish Upper Silesia, 47, 52, 54, 60, 71, 169
  Competition, 68, 88, 89, 91, 92, 119, 173
  Concurrent operation of custom and treaty, 144–148
  Creeping expropriation, 24–28
  Customary international law
    no implied exclusion, 142–144
    opinio juris, 118, 120, 122, 123, 127, 196
    state practice, 6, 18, 38, 51, 52, 75, 121–124, 126, 127, 130, 151, 162, 172, 196

D

Declaration of the United Nations General Assembly on Friendly Relations, 106
  Deprivation of property, 25, 28, 64, 66, 67, 148
  Derogation, 112, 114, 155, 157
  Destruction of property, 44, 66, 125
  Diplomatic protection, 84, 145
  Direct expropriation, 22–23
  Dispute Settlement Body (DSB), 85, 187
  Domain réservé, 110–111

E

Eminent domain, 4, 7, 8, 12, 15, 16, 51, 80, 81, 131
  Energy Charter Treaty, 29, 178
  Equivalent to expropriation, 24–28, 32, 65
  European Convention on Human Rights, 95
  European Court of Human Rights, 6, 35, 36, 184, 187
  Evolutionary interpretation, 141, 162
  Expropriation, 22–28, 133–163
  Expropriatory measure, 7–45

F

Friendship, Commerce and Navigation Treaties (FCN), 4, 82, 84

G

GATT Article XX, 6, 32, 186
Global Administrative Law (GAL), 98–101, 196
Good faith, 191–193

H

Helsinki Declaration, 165
Human rights, 93, 95–97, 107, 108, 174, 176, 180, 181, 190

I

ICJ Statute, 35, 60, 121, 134, 151
ICSID, 77, 101
ICSID Convention, 3, 77, 101
Indirect Expropriation, 23–24, 133–163
Inter-American Court of Human Rights, 97
International Convention on Civil and Political Rights (ICCPR), 93–94
International Convention on Economic, Social and Cultural Rights, 93–94
International Law Commission, 121
International public policy, 180, 181
Iran US Claims Tribunal, 5, 47, 55–66, 81, 86, 151

J

Jus cogens, 105, 136, 147, 179

L

Legitimacy, 85, 86, 100, 101, 106, 162, 179, 190, 196
Lex posterior derogatlega priori, 152
Lex spcialis, 152
Lex superior derogatlegiinferori, 152
Lotus principle, 114, 115, 117–120

M

Margin of appreciation, 187, 188, 190
Measure, 7–72
Most Favoured Nation (MFN), 175, 176, 178

N

Nationalization, 21–23, 25, 28–30, 39, 57, 62, 80
Nature of the measure, 66–72
Necessity, 11, 56, 70, 84, 144, 147, 184–190, 197
Necessity test, 184–190, 197
Neutralization, 18, 37, 38, 42, 43, 81, 88
Non-discriminatory, 5, 6, 18, 21, 31–33, 37, 39–41, 43, 161–163, 165, 195, 197, 198
North America Free Trade Agreement (NAFTA), 8, 21, 22, 26–29, 33, 65, 176
Norwegian Shipowners Case, 48, 49, 53, 54, 71
NT, 175, 176

O

'Other measures affecting property rights', 61–66, 81
Oscar Chinn Case, 68, 71, 114

P

Partial expropriation, 87
Penn Central, 15, 126
Police powers doctrine, 7, 9–11, 15, 35, 36, 39, 88, 128, 151
Problems with the sole effects doctrine, 86–92
Proportionality analysis, 184–190

Public interest, 177-183
Public policy (*ordre public*), 82, 175, 176, 178-183
Public purpose, 21, 32, 33, 37, 39, 41, 42, 109, 161, 177-179

R

Reasonableness or good faith review, 191-193
Regulation and indirect expropriation
'bright line', 158, 159, 196-198
diving line, 74, 158
Regulatory chill, 87
Regulatory measure, 9-11, 13-16
Relationship between customary norm and treaty norm
conflict, 149-151
conflict of norms, 152-155
hierarchically superior, 133-136
Restatement of the Law Third, The Foreign Relations Law of the United States, 125-127
Right to property, 92-97, 184, 188

S

Self-contained regime, 137, 152, 153
Sole effects doctrine, 34-38, 47-66, 79-92
Sovereignty
attributes of, 6, 106, 107, 111, 131, 142
evolutionary concept, 105
sovereign rights, 106, 110, 129, 142, 143, 155-158, 161, 173
Stabilization clause, 80, 87
Standard of review, 183-193

T

Takings, 12, 26, 62, 64, 78, 125, 126
Tantamount to expropriation, 24-29, 41, 61, 65, 84, 150, 167
Transparency, 69, 77, 82, 85, 99, 107, 190
Treaty interpretation
expression uniusexclusioalterius, 157-158
systematic integration, 136-142
textual interpretation, 28-30
ut res magisvaleat quam pereat, 155

U

Universal Declaration of Human Rights (UDHR), 94, 95
Unjust enrichment, 12, 13, 15, 18, 67, 92
US Model BIT, 31, 125

W

Wealth deprivation, 63, 64, 66, 80, 81
Wimbledon case, 107, 119, 142, 155
World Trade Organization (WTO), 6, 85, 98, 101, 129, 139, 140, 141, 169, 171, 184, 186, 187, 189, 198